The Methodist Defense of Women in Ministry

The Methodist Defense of Women in Ministry

A Documentary History

PAUL W. CHILCOTE

CASCADE *Books* · Eugene, Oregon

THE METHODIST DEFENSE OF WOMEN IN MINISTRY
A Documentary History

Cascade Books
An Imprint of Wipf and Stock Publishers
199 W. 8th Ave., Suite 3
Eugene, OR 97401

www.wipfandstock.com

PAPERBACK ISBN: 978-1-4982-8332-8
HARDCOVER ISBN: 978-1-4982-8334-2
EBOOK ISBN: 978-1-4982-8333-5

Cataloguing-in-Publication data:

Names: Chilcote, Paul Wesley, 1954–, author.
Title: The Methodist defense of women in ministry : a documentary history / Paul W. Chilcote.
Description: Eugene, OR : Cascade Books, 2017 | Includes bibliographical references.
Identifiers: ISBN 978-1-4982-8332-8 (paperback) | ISBN 978-1-4982-8334-2 (hardcover) | ISBN 978-1-4982-8333-5 (ebook)
Subjects: LCSH: Women clergy—England—History—18th century. | Women clergy—United States—History—18th century. | Women clergy—England—History—19th century. | Women clergy—United States—History—19th century. | Women clergy—England—History—20th century | Women clergy—United States—History—20th century. | Methodist Church—England—History—18th century. | Methodist Church—United States—History—18th century. | Methodist Church—England—History—19th century. | Methodist Church—United States—History—19th century. | Methodist Church—England—History—20th century. | Methodist Church—United States—History—20th century. | Ordination of women. | Women in church work. | Holiness movement.
Classification: BX8345.7 .C47 2017 (print) | BX8345.7 .C47 (ebook)

Manufactured in the U.S.A.   NOVEMBER 8, 2017

For all those women and men who have supported
Christians for Biblical Equality International
and have championed its cause

Contents

Foreword

Cicero said: "Who knows only their own generation remains always a child."[1] We gain extraordinary vitality from the stories of Christian women and men who came before us. In fact, our advocacy for women in ministry leans heavily on their stories. Few are better suited to bring this history to life than Dr. Paul Chilcote, author of more than twenty books and publications on the subject. For thirty-five years, he has amplified the history of women's leadership in the church with his work. Like the author of Hebrews, Chilcote calls us to "remember your leaders who spoke the word of God to you. Consider the outcome of their lives and imitate their faith" (13:7).

Chilcote's newest book is dedicated to "those women and men who have supported CBE International and have championed its cause." We are deeply honored! Truth be told, CBE International (CBE) stands on the shoulders of early Methodist women: scholars like Lee Anna Starr and Katharine Bushnell whose biblical tradition roused *every* believer to develop their gifts "as a sacred trust from God."[2] Methodism itself was a theological "self-defense and a subversive challenge"[3] to gender and racial prejudice. It forged gospel partnership across gender and racial lines. Those working toward similar goals find traveling companions, mentors, and friends in times of need among the early Methodist women on these pages.

---

1. Carved over the entrance of Norlin Library at the University of Colorado, Boulder, the original quote was a translation by George Norlin (1871–1942) and reads: "Who Knows Only His Generation Remains Always a Child." A professor of Greek, Dr. Norlin became acting president of the University in 1917. The quote from Cicero was original phrasing by Norlin and comes from: *Nescire autem quid ante quam natus sis acciderit, id est semper esse puerum.* Translated it reads: "To be ignorant of what occurred before you were born is to remain always a child." Leading the institution through the great depression, challenging the Ku Klux Klan and anti-Semitism, Norlin believed that the study of history was essential in providing education that supported moral action. https://www.colorado.edu/libraries/about/history/george-norlin

2. See below, 6.

3. Ibid., 13.

Why were women nurtured by Wesley's theology and how did it help women's leadership flourish globally? The stories of known and lesser-known women like Sarah Crosby, Mary Bonsanquet and Amanda Berry Smith contain the answer. I know of no other book in which the original documents defending Methodist women in ministry are so carefully assembled and analyzed.

The strongest defense of women's leadership comes from women themselves, especially women of color. Jarena Lee's *Life and Religious Experience* illustrates the hardships of women itinerant preachers. Lee traveled more than 2,000 miles without support. With holy boldness, she challenged gender and racial bias and pioneered a path others would follow. Consider the courageous resistance of Zilpha Elaw, another Methodist woman of color. When an American man challenged her ministry, Elaw retorted that she had no will but God's and "durst not confer with flesh and blood."[4] Each account is a front row seat to turning points in history.

Consider Amanda Berry Smith, world-renowned leader and author of *The Story of the Lord's Dealings with Mrs. Amanda Smith, the Colored Evangelist*. She made clear that God's power and call transcends race and gender:

> Somehow I always had a fear of white people—that is, I was not afraid of them in the sense of doing me harm or anything of that kind—but a kind of fear because they were white, and were there, and I was black and was here! But that morning on Green Street, as I stood on my feet trembling, I hear these words distinctly. . . . "There is neither Jew nor Greek, there is neither bond nor free there is neither male nor female for you are all one in Christ Jesus" (Gal 3:28). . . . And as I looked at white people that I had always seemed to be afraid of, now they looked so small. The great mountain had become a mole hill. "Therefore, if the Son shall make you free, then are you free, indeed." All praise to my victorious Christ![5]

As racial and gender barriers continue to plague the church today, Chilcote brings wisdom from Methodist women and their allies like B. T. Roberts. Roberts was the first to align abolition with "freedom of women in Christ."[6] He believed that "racism and barring women from ordination were the two glaring contradictions of the gospel."[7]

4. Ibid., 97.

5. Ibid., 104

6. Ibid., 157.

7. Benjamin Wayman, *B. T. Roberts Ordaining Women: New Edition with Introduction and Notes* (Eugene, OR: Wipf & Stock, 2015) xv.

Finally, Chilcote shows how Methodist women, for centuries, challenged flawed bible interpretations that obstruct women's dignity and agency while fueling abuse. According to Phoebe Palmer, women were excluded from leadership in the church due to "faulty interpretation of the Bible and a distorted and unchristian view most men had of women."[8] Catherine Booth, co-founder of the Salvation Army, exposed flawed biblical interpretations in her book, *Female Ministry or Women's Right to Preach the Gospel.* Katharine Bushnell showed how the church has oppressed women through "mistranslated, misinterpreted, and misapplied scriptural texts."[9] Georgia Harkness observed that Scripture has "done more than any other agency for the emancipation of women, yet the church itself is the most impregnable stronghold of male dominance."[10] Frances Willard, president of the Women's Christian Temperance Union, believed that men's refusal to share power with women, "especially sacred power,"[11] compels women to ordain themselves and start their own denominations.[12]

Booth, Bushnell, Willard and others not only opposed patriarchy's twisting of Scripture but also its consequences. They were on the forefront of ending sex trafficking while exposing the link between theological patriarchy and the abuse of girls and women globally. They called on women themselves to use their abilities for better biblical scholarship, more accurate translations of Scripture and service to the abused.

These Methodist women rooted their renewing work in a high view of Calvary, an unshakable trust that God speaks through the ancient texts, and a commitment to "fan into flames" God's power in every believer. They built diverse and strategic alliances that advanced the gospel harmoniously across race and gender lines. Through the power of story, beaming on its pages, *The Methodist Defense of Women in Ministry* compels us to consider these courageous women's lives and to imitate their faith.

—Mimi Haddad, PhD, President of CBE International
(www.cbeinternational.org)

---

8. See below, 110.

9. See below, 241.

10. Ibid., 268–69.

11. Ibid., 200

12. Ibid.

Preface

This documentary history began with my earlier studies of women in Methodism. Having prepared two anthologies of primary documents related to early Wesleyan women—*Her Own Story* and *Early Methodist Spirituality*—it did not take long for me to realize that a large body of literature existed related to the defense of these women. I knew that these resources were extremely relevant for the life of the church today, but they were little known. Some of the most significant names in the history of Methodism—Mary Fletcher, Catherine Booth, Jarena Lee, Phoebe Palmer, Anna Howard Shaw, Mary Lee Cagle, and Georgia Harkness—contributed to this apologetic library. I listened to that still, small voice within that simply said, "Do something about this." So I began to collect defenses of women in ministry, and as the shelf began to swell with these books, pamphlets, and articles my passion to publish these materials grew as well. This volume, then, contains some of the most notable and instructive primary sources that document the Methodist defense of women in ministry.

A project of this nature presents a number of challenges. The issue of what gets included and what must be excluded looms large. Space considerations were paramount. I have included those readings I considered primary; I have had to leave out others. I determined to give equal weight to each chapter. But while the fact that all are roughly the same length provides balance for the volume as a whole, this proportionality also misshapes the reader's sense of the importance attached to the documents. Not all are equal—how could they be?—so I deal with the issue of relative influence in the introductory material. I attempted to avoid repetitiousness in the documents, but this consideration created other problems that called for resolution. As one would imagine, in the defense of any issue over a lengthy period of time, many of the same arguments get repeated in subsequent works. In some instances, later apologists even included major sections from previous defenses in the development of their own arguments. So eliding material, while attempting to maintain the integrity of an argument, can be precarious. In instances like these, with regard to the excerpted material, my governing principle has been to include and focus upon the authors' fresh insights, new forms of argument, or salient themes. I also provide the necessary guidance to readers in introductory material to help them apprehend the ambiance of the whole document in context. Very few of these documents have been presented in their entirety, but wherever they are I have noted this where the source is identified.

With regard to the chapter introductions, my primary goal has been to provide the necessary background information for a proper reading of the documents in their social settings. I have written them in such a way, introducing the primary actors, so that those with little familiarity with Methodist history can comprehend the developments swiftly without having to constantly check other sources. The introductions also function to prepare the reader for a critical reading of the texts and to provide a fresh landscape for the surveying of the larger field of study. The persistent challenge was not to deviate from a sharp focus on the defenses themselves in order to discuss the fascinating lives of the women and men involved. They are just so interesting! But there are ample references to lead the reader to other resources to pursue those trails, which I heartily encourage. So, the most critical issue in a volume of this nature is to strike the right balances; I hope I have navigated those difficult waters in helpful ways.

All these texts reflect the contexts in which they were written. Some of them, published in the eighteenth or nineteenth centuries, contain archaic conventions that have long disappeared from contemporary English expression. They have been "modernized," therefore, particularly in terms of sentence structure, syntax, and punctuation, in order to make the documents more suitable to the contemporary reader. Errors in the originals have been silently corrected, spelling regularized, and quotations conformed in the documents to modern usage. Every effort has been made to retain the original meaning of the texts in the voices of the authors.

I offer this documentary history in the hope that it may contribute, in however limited a fashion, to the realization of the full equality of women in the life of the church. I trust that it will stimulate its readers to explore this quest more fully. Certainly, the ideal of biblical equality deserves the attention of every committed follower of Christ. While this story "has a happy ending," so to speak, most of us realize that this quest is far from complete. Like most things in the Christian pilgrimage, it has an "already, but not yet" character that stirs the believer to delight and hope simultaneously. I seek to work toward and look forward to that day when the words "in Christ there is neither male nor female" are real in every way. In this spirit I dedicate this volume to all those women and men who have supported Christians for

Biblical Equality International since its inception nearly thirty years ago. A truly inspirational organization, CBE International believes "that the Bible, properly interpreted, teaches the fundamental equality of men and women of all ethnic groups, all economic classes, and all age groups, based on the teachings of Scriptures such as Galatians 3:28." Mimi Haddad, the current CBE president, exemplifies the spirit of all those brave souls who have advocated biblical equality whether it was convenient or not. I offer a personal word of thanks to her for her willingness to prepare a foreword for this volume. I am thankful for all this organization does, and I hope this volume contributes in some small way to the goals of CBE.

Paul W. Chilcote
Women's Equality Day, August 26, 2016

Acknowledgments

I have incurred a substantial debt of gratitude to many who have assisted me in the preparation of this volume over some years now, and I want to acknowledge the contributions of those institutions and individuals who have supported the project. The task of gathering these materials has taken me to many different libraries and research centers in the United States and the United Kingdom. The staff of the following institutions have been extremely helpful, guiding me in the right directions and providing access to some treasures long hid: Ashland Theological Seminary, Roger Darling Memorial Library; Athenaeum of Ohio, Eugene H. Maly Memorial Library; Case Western Reserve University, Kelvin Smith Library; College of Wooster, Andrews Library; Drew University, United Methodist Archives & History Center; Duke Divinity School Library; John Carroll University, Grasselli Library; Garrett-Evangelical Theological Seminary, The United Library; Kenyon College Library; Methodist Archives and Research Centre, John Rylands University Library of Manchester; Methodist Theological School in Ohio, J. W. Dickhaut Library; Mount Vernon Nazarene University, Thorne Library/Learning Resource Center; the Ohio State University Libraries; Oxford Brookes University, Oxford Centre for Methodism and Church History; Trinity Lutheran Theological Seminary, Hamma Library; University of Cincinnati, Langsam Library; University of Dayton, Roesch Library; and Wright State University, Paul L. Dunbar Library. Frances Lyons-Bristol, Chris Anderson, and Dale Patterson at the United Methodist Archives & History Center were always unbelievably accommodating, answered virtually every question I ever raised and provided every document I requested at lightning speed. Special thanks to my colleagues in the Darling Library at Ashland Theological Seminary, Sylvia Locher and Sarah Thomas, for their assistance in obtaining many publications vital to my research. I appreciate all these institutions and colleagues who made this volume possible.

Prior to publication various sections of this work were kindly read by colleagues and friends, most of whom have particular expertise in Methodist and women's studies. Some are experts on the particular men and women featured in this volume, so their insights were particularly helpful. My sincere appreciation, therefore, to Collin Dews, Dennis Dickerson, Kristin Du Mez, Robert Glen, Dorothy Graham, Roger Green, Elaine Heath, Stan Ingersol, Kendra Irons, Rebecca Laird, John Lenton, Priscilla Pope-Levison, Russ Richey, Ken Rowe, and Laceye Warner. Their comments, questions, and insights have shaped this documentary history in significant ways. I found myself on many occasions wanting to send drafts of these chapters to my dear friend Rosemary Keller; alas, she resides with the saints in glory and parties, no doubt, with the women whose ministry was defended in these texts. My wife, Janet, always supports my work in more ways than she knows.

My daughter, Rebekah Chilcote, read the entire manuscript and assisted with copy editing the text, a huge labor for which I am deeply grateful. Methodist historian and colleague Ulrike Schuler reviewed all the introductory material in the volume. I am thankful to her for her meticulous evaluation of the narrative and her suggested improvements to the text, particularly for those whose native language is not English. Donna Johnson undertook the painstaking task of translating many of the original documents—sometimes nearly illegible photocopies—into user-friendly typed Word documents. I appreciate that labor of love more than I can say. Without her assistance there is little chance this project would have come to fruition on schedule. I offer my sincere appreciation to my editor at Wipf and Stock, Charlie Collier, and the entire production team for the guidance they provided throughout the process leading to publication.

I am thankful to the Ashland Seminary advisory committee and the president at the time, John Shultz, for approving a special leave for me during the fall semester of 2015, affording me the opportunity to make significant progress on this project. A Women in United Methodist History Research Grant for 2016 from the General Commission on Archives and History of the United Methodist Church provided support for my work on this volume as well. I am extremely grateful to Dr. Alfred ("Fred") Day, the general secretary, and the selection committee for this honor. It has always been a great joy to collaborate with these denominational stewards of the church's ministry of memory who take their mandate seriously, as should the church, in order to help us learn from our past and anticipate our future.

Introduction

The purpose of this volume is to bring together the essential documents related to the defense of women in ministry in the Methodist tradition. The various denominations that trace their spiritual roots back to John and Charles Wesley often continued the legacy of their founders by positioning themselves on the crest of the wave of renewal in the life of the church. Their innovative practices, which frequently included the affirmation of women and their gifts, often distinguished them dramatically from other Christian traditions and society in general. The quest for women's equality within Methodism, however, was hardly an effortless or painless story of progressive advance. On the contrary, each stage and each respective tradition reflects the tensions and acrimony that the "woman question" fomented. Standing in a heritage that places high value on the biblical witness, Methodists struggled with texts; the story of their apologetics related to women is necessarily a study in biblical hermeneutics and the desire to understand Scripture well. But this history also reflects the inescapable interface of religion and culture. Social trends and movements in the various cultural contexts in which Methodist women and men sought to be faithful shaped the trajectories of their apologetic strategies. Ultimately, the Methodist defense of women in ministry reveals the centrality of liberation—spiritual, cultural, and communal—one of the central themes of the gospel vision recaptured by the Wesleys.

A secondary purpose of this volume relates to contemporary dynamics within the life of the church. To put it bluntly, women continue to struggle to find affirmation both within the Wesleyan heritage and in the larger Christian community. Many denominations—ranging from Roman Catholicism and the Orthodox traditions on one end of the spectrum to evangelical and fundamentalist churches on the other—still prohibit women from exercising what they know to be a call to the ministry of the church. And while most Methodist churches have ordained women for several generations, many still suffer as the victims of injustice with regard to their status and role in the church. To have some understanding of the defense of women in this particular tradition—Methodism—may shed light on the struggle of Christian women everywhere. The complexities of the issue demand study because they affect the majority of Christian disciples across the globe. And, indeed, the issues are complex. While it might seem that women's apologetics must have been somewhat straightforward, the evidence points to the opposite conclusion. The defenses marshaled by Methodist apologists varied greatly depending on context. In fact, the way in which these defenses evolved reflects the challenge even to define terms and establish the parameters for this study. Three terms leap out just from the title of this volume and beg for definition: Methodist, defense, ministry.

Who are the "Methodists"? With regard to the issue of the defense of women in ministry, this was a particularly perplexing question. Should the vast multitude of Pentecostal traditions that consider themselves the spiritual descendants of the Wesleys be included? What about some of the holiness denominations, like the Church of God (Anderson) or the Brethren in Christ Church, that claim Wesleyan origins? With regard to this issue, including in this study those churches with membership in the World Methodist Council seemed to have integrity. Members of these particular churches, as well, produced most of the apologetic literature related to the defense of women: the African Methodist Episcopal Church, the African Methodist Episcopal Zion Church, the Church of the Nazarene, the Free Methodist Church, the Methodist Church of Great Britain, the United Methodist Church, and the Wesleyan Church, and all the antecedent bodies of these denominations (e.g., Primitive Methodists and Bible Christian in the United Kingdom and the Protestant Methodist Church in the United States). While the Salvation Army is not a member of the Council, because of its unique ecclesial status, its close affiliation and partnership in dialogue with the Council merited its inclusion. While this approach could be debated, it has demarcated the volume in helpful ways and provides a breadth of primary source materials.

The term "defense" presents difficulties of its own. Defenses can be formal or informal, overt or covert. Most of the apologetic documents in this volume are, in fact, formal, published defenses, the titles of which imply this orientation (e.g., "A Discourse in Vindication of the Gospel Being Published by Females" and *The Right of Women to Preach the Gospel*). Others are sermons, such as that of Luther Lee, preached on the occasion of the first female ordination in the United States and entitled *Woman's Right to Preach the Gospel*. One of the most interesting genres of defense is the autobiography. *Autobiography: The Story of the Lord's Dealings with Mrs. Amanda Smith the Colored Evangelist* obviously falls into this category. But women and men also embedded their defenses in correspondence, official church documents, petitions to conferences, magazine articles, and Bible studies. This volume includes all these kinds of apologetic material.

What "ministry" did these apologists defend? It is easy to determine what aspects of Christian ministry did not concern these Methodist apologists. They did not focus their energy on the full range of women's activities in the life of the church. The ministry they sought to defend did not include Sunday school teaching, for example, or participating in or even leading small groups related to discipleship or mission. Their defenses addressed something much more complex. They revolved primarily around those male-dominated activities in the life of the church from which women were excluded; the apologies reflect concerns about power used and abused in the Christian community. Women's ministry, as understood here, defies precise definition because "it" was being pushed forward perennially into new frontiers. The documents reveal how women's ministry can be understood legitimately as a "flying goal." Whatever the church prohibited defined the ministry begging for defense, and this focus changed over time.

Initially, ministry referred to practices that had been traditionally restricted to men, namely, evangelistic work and public preaching in particular, to which women felt called. Having defended the right of women to engage in these practices—regardless of whether they were viewed as extraordinary or regular—a new apologetic emerged that sought to ameliorate the issue of women's ordination. Proponents eventually secured the ordination of women, but often without dismantling non-biblical structures of power in the church. Because ordination did not necessarily challenge male dominance in questions of authority, a final step in the evolution of this apologetic trajectory, therefore, entailed a full defense of "women's equal rights" in the life and ministry of the church. The history of the defense of women in ministry, in other words, reflects a kind of hierarchical development with each stage moving women closer to full equality with men. Apologetics related to women's preaching morphed into the defense of women's ordination, which evolved into the argument for women's equal rights in the church. Moreover, changes in society, and even historical events—like the Civil War in America and the two World Wars that dramatically impacted women's lives—shaped these developments as well. This documentary history demonstrates how this process unfolded by studying the apologists and the writings that reflect this development over two and a half centuries.

Scholars have collected a few of the documents presented here in previous anthologies. In terms of these earlier collections, several stand out. In the 1980s, Garland Publishing undertook the production of a thirty-six volume facsimile reprint collection demonstrating the breadth and diversity of roles played by women in American religion. In this series Donald Dayton introduces the writings of Luther Lee, B. T. Roberts, Catherine Booth, and Fannie Hunter in a volume dedicated to holiness tracts.[1] Carolyn Gifford's volume on the defense of women's rights to ordination in the Methodist Episcopal Church included publications by Frances Willard and William Warren.[2] Andrew Williams published autobiographical materials on three black women evangelists—Jarena Lee, Zilpha Elaw, and Julia Foote—in a volume entitled *Sisters of the Spirit*.[3] Several other documentary histories, such as the multivolume *Women & Religion in America*, by Rosemary Keller and Rosemary Ruether,[4] and Priscilla Pope-Levison's *Turn the Pulpit Loose*[5] include excerpts from a few of the writings presented here. The same can be said of *The Methodist Experience in America: A Sourcebook*, edited by Richey, Rowe, and Schmidt.[6] But the full range of documents included in this volume has never appeared together previously as a coherent unit.

The remainder of this introduction falls into three brief sections. The first contains a general overview of the Wesleyan legacy and the place of women within the Methodist heritage. The second identifies the primary arguments for the ministry of women that were utilized by Methodists. The last section affords a brief but panoramic overview of the fifty-five documents included in this volume, with more detailed and contextual analysis provided in the introductions of the individual chapters.

The Wesleyan Legacy and Place of Women in Methodism

Women played a major role in the origins of the Methodist movement.[7] The fact of female preponderance in the Methodist network of societies under the direction of John and Charles Wesley only serves to illustrate a much larger reality.[8] Evidence concerning the formative influence of women abounds in journals, diaries, and letters, and has been preserved in local

1. Dayton, *Higher Christian Life*.
2. Gifford, *Defense of Women's Rights*.
3. Andrews, *Sisters of the Spirit*.
4. Ruether and Keller, *Women and Religion in America*, 1:212–14, 217–18; 2:237–40, 251–56, 258–59, 378–79.
5. Pope-Levison, *Turn the Pulpit Loose*, 27–29, 33–34, 66–68, 89–90, 93,
6. Richey, Rowe, and Schmidt, *Methodist Experience in America*, 391–400, 502–3.
7. See Chilcote, *Wesley and Women Preachers*, and Chilcote, *She Offered Them Christ*.
8. For a full discussion of the evidence related to female initiative in the formation and establishment of Methodist societies, see Chilcote, *Wesley and Women Preachers*, 49–54.

history. Women ventured into arenas that were traditionally confined to men. They functioned as some of Methodism's most indefatigable pioneers and even preached in the network of Methodist societies that stretched the length and breadth of Britain. A wealth of factors combined both in the founder and the movement to create a climate conducive to the acceptance and empowerment of women. Three factors, in particular, stand out.[9]

First, the elevated status of women in Methodism cannot be understood apart from the person of John Wesley. Much of his appreciation for the place of women in the life of the church can be traced to his formative years in the Epworth rectory. Largely due to the influence of his mother, Susanna, Wesley seldom wavered from this fundamental principle: no one, including a woman, ought to be prohibited from doing God's work in obedience to the inner calling of her conscience. This conviction would later lead him not only to sanction but to encourage the controversial practice of women's preaching.

Second, the Methodist societies, which functioned as catalysts of renewal inside the established church, provided a liberating environment for women.[10] One of the unique features of early Methodism was its capacity to create its own leadership from within small groups. The early pioneers who were responsible for the initiation of new societies naturally assumed positions of leadership. The large extent to which women functioned in this sphere was a major factor contributing to the inclusiveness and vitality of the movement. By allowing women to assume important positions of leadership within the structure of the societies, Wesley gave concrete expression to the freedom he proclaimed in his preaching.

Third, while the Wesley brothers and their followers never used the language of "biblical equality," nor would they have felt compelled to do so, their theology and understanding of the New Testament bore witness to a new vision of life in Christ for all of God's children. Wesley's emphases on the value of the individual soul, the possibility of direct communion with God, the present activity of the Holy Spirit in the life of the believer, the rights of conscience, and the doctrine of the priesthood of all believers coalesced to create a theological environment conducive to the empowerment of women.

Wesley's goal was personal, religious experience and its power to transform both individuals and society. His dynamic view of salvation and

9. These three themes were first identified by Chilcote in "Empowerment of Women."

10. For a full account of the rise and development of the Methodist societies, see Wesley, *Works*, 9:1–29; cf. Heitzenrater, *Wesley and Methodists*, and Hempton, *Methodism and Politics*.

the Christian life, evoked by a gift of grace, tended to transcend gender and social boundaries. His stress on charismatic leadership fostered a leveling sentiment among the Methodists. The unity and equality of all believers in Christ became an inherent aspect of the evangelical preaching of Wesleyan itinerants. Not only was faith to be expressed in the works of all, but also individual talents were to be developed as a sacred trust from God. These attitudes undercut prevailing stereotypes about the status and role of women in society. And so, the phenomenon of female leadership was a natural progression, a logical extension of the Wesleyan theology of religious experience. While the argument can be made that this inertia related to the liberation of women pervades the various forms of Methodism throughout its history, forces both inside and outside the church militated against this legacy as well. So the history of women in Methodism feels much more like a roller coaster than a persistent and progressive movement toward deeper levels of empowerment for women. Those who sought to defend the ministry of women, therefore, found it necessary to nuance or even dramatically change their arguments in the successive phases of British and American history.

Almost within a decade of John Wesley's death a strong misogynistic movement swept through the nascent church he had founded. In a new era characterized by respectability and institutional consolidation under strong male leadership—what Elisabeth Schüssler Fiorenza described classically as the "patriarchalization of the church"[11]—many viewed the ministry of women as an embarrassment incompatible with their vision of a privileged future. The repression of women in a burgeoning, male-dominated sect-become-church led to a cycle repeated many times over in the history of Methodism. New movements spun out of the parent Methodist body to reclaim what in their view was the primitive vision of their founder. In nearly all these groups in Britain during the opening decades of the nineteenth century—such as the Bible Christians and Primitive Methodists—the ministry of women figured prominently both in terms of theology and practice. But, as in the parent body, increasingly dominant male leaders pushed women to the fringe. This same pattern of repression-secession-liberation-patriarchalization can be seen in American Methodism with the rise of the holiness movement in the nineteenth century. Whether the influence of feminism during the twentieth century in the mainline bodies—and the successful battle for women's equal rights in these churches—broke this cycle remains to be seen. History seems to demonstrate that those communities in which freedom and equality flourish find it difficult to maintain

---

11. Schüssler Fiorenza, *In Memory of Her*, 53, 80–84, 230–33.

a biblical egalitarian vision. Regardless, given the kind of resistance women almost always encountered as they sought to exercise their gifts for ministry, Methodist women and men developed arguments that were responsive to the concerns of their specific contexts in an effort to justify their actions.

Arguments for the Ministry of Women

Georgia Harkness provided one of the most succinct categorizations of the variety of arguments for the ministry of women, describing them tersely as biblical, practical, and spiritual.[12] Indeed, almost all the strategies of the Methodist apologists can be classified under these three categories. But the arguments of these Methodists over two and a half centuries reflect a complexity shaped by at least three major factors.

The study of Scripture changed radically over the course of the period covered in this volume, and the arguments follow the contours of these hermeneutical transitions. The arguments also reflect multiple layers of engagement with different biblical texts—some defenses more reactive and revisionary in nature (e.g., questioning traditional interpretations of critical passages), others more proactive (e.g., simply highlighting the biblical material that affirms and illustrates the ministry of women in both Testaments). Sometimes an author's approach clearly or even explicitly revolves around a singular text, like Galatians 3:28 or Acts 2:17–18. Almost all the arguments, whether explicitly biblical or not, reflect fundamental biblical concerns; virtually all the Methodist arguments are biblical at root because the Bible functions as such a critical norm within this family of churches.

While practical issues pervade the documents, they dominate the more recent material. Biblical arguments never disappear but, particularly in the twentieth century, the issues surrounding purportedly prohibitive texts like those in 1 Corinthians 14 and 1 Timothy 2 had become passé. Protagonists of the women had so thoroughly dismantled the literalistic interpretive framework, at least in their view, that it seemed superfluous to rehash contextual and more sophisticated exegetical arguments. Practical arguments ranged from the urgent need for preachers in Methodism (for a multitude of reasons) and the documented success of women to the warrant required for ministry already being practiced by women in the churches.

The spiritual arguments, perhaps obviously, are somewhat difficult to differentiate from those built upon biblical foundations. Certainly, they overlap. The apologists who use these arguments tend to root them in the concept of a divine call. These arguments are spiritual in the sense that the

---

12. See Harkness, "Women Ministers."

Holy Spirit, directly apprehended by the women, both calls and empowers them for ministry. The statement, "If God calls, who are men to refuse them," illustrates the potency of this argument. What greater authority was there to which they could appeal? Some of these arguments also emphasize the "gender-transcendent" nature of ministry in the Spirit. Especially in autobiographical apologetics the Holy Spirit enabled women to transcend traditional gender roles, implying a kind of spiritual instrumentalism; the Spirit was more critical than the instrument.

Historians and sociologists, in particular, have identified a number of the arguments for women in ministry across the spectrum of Christian traditions—but often highly dependent upon the Methodists—that fall into these kinds of categories. Beverly Zink-Sawyer, for example, employs essentially the same categories laid out by Harkness.[13] She claims that the spiritual argument dominates the defense of women's preaching. In her view, Phoebe Palmer exemplified this approach best. These arguments necessarily presumed a biblical argument that revolved around texts featuring women in significant roles of leadership in Scripture. What she describes as "pragmatic" arguments emphasize the success of women and the urgency of pressing needs within the church met by women. In similar fashion Barbara Brown Zikmund maintains that woman's right to preach was: "(1) grounded in the work of the Holy Spirit, (2) justified by practical considerations, (3) already happening on the mission field, (4) acceptable because of new enlightened interpretations of scripture."[14] In her discussion of "Basic Arguments about Women's Preaching and Ordination," Susan Lindley notes that for Protestants the Bible was the central battleground with regard to the argumentation. Advocates of the women cited a sense of divine call superseding all earthly authorities, argued pragmatically from women's success (particularly in mission contexts) and the church's need for effective evangelism, and insisted that woman's nature made her a more suitable and effective minister than a man.[15] Mark Chaves takes special note of the critical shift in the defenses of women in the late nineteenth century. "Although advocates of female clergy found biblical support for their position from early on," he argues, "it became more and more common in the closing decades of the nineteenth century to express that support in terms of a principle of gender equality."[16] There is a somewhat natural progression

13. Zink-Sawyer, *From Preachers to Suffragists*, 84–86; cf. Brekus, *Strangers & Pilgrims*, 216–21.

14. Zikmund, "Protestant Women's Ordination Movement," 205.

15. Lindley, *You Have Stept Out*, 126.

16. Chaves, *Ordaining Women*, 73. He identifies four categories of evidence linking the defense of women's ministry and the emerging "women's movement" (75–80).

from a biblical to a spiritual to a practical emphasis in the argumentation, with later apologists building upon the foundations established by previous generations.

Methodists employed all these arguments and they conformed, essentially, to this basic pattern. An attempt to categorize the biblical, spiritual, and practical arguments in this tradition reveals something of their complexity. Seldom did any of the fifteen arguments defined here stand alone; the apologists wove them together in ways they felt appropriate and persuasive for their particular context.

Biblical Arguments

Questioned Prohibitionism. This argument was primarily reactive, calling into question the traditional interpretation and countering the purportedly prohibitive statements of St. Paul in 1 Corinthians 14 and 1 Timothy 2, in particular. A contextual reading of these texts that was descriptive of a peculiar situation and not prescriptive for all time dominated this approach.

Pauline Egalitarianism. Galatians 3:28 provided a proactive argument for the equality of men and women who participate "in Christ" in the life of the church. For many of those who defended women's ministry, this was the primary source of a theological argument for equality. Some intentionally linked the liberation of both slaves and women explicit in the text.

Apostolic Practice. Many found a dynamic illustration of St. Paul's egalitarianism in Romans 16, which provided an amazing snapshot of women in the ministry of the earliest church. Here Paul described many women as coworkers with him in the ministry of the gospel. New Testament texts that feature women leaders in the apostolic age also figure prominently in this argument.

Messianic Witness. Evidence was also drawn from the ministry and teachings of Jesus to defend women's ministry. Two passages, in particular, among many others, reveal the Messiah's attitude toward women and his affirmation of their ministry: the woman of Samaria (John 4) who proclaims the Messiah and Mary Magdalene, first to proclaim the resurrection of Jesus (Matt 28).

Biblical Exceptionalism. Not arguing equality as much as exceptionalism, some apologists drew on the biblical witness to exceptional women leaders, particularly in the Old Testament, who were elevated by God. At particular times, so it was argued, God raises up exceptional women who are authorized to step out of the normal roles prescribed for women.

Prophetic Fulfillment. The prophecy of Joel 2:28–29—the promise of the Father—figures prominently in the biblical arguments. Joel, it was argued, foresaw a time in which men and women would function as equals in God's realm and this ancient prophecy was fulfilled on the Day of Pentecost when God poured the Spirit out on all people (Acts 2:17–18).

Prophetic Millennarianism. Closely related to the prophetic fulfillment argument, some interpreted the coming of the Spirit at Pentecost as the birth of a new dispensation. Radical egalitarianism in this age of the Spirit anticipated the second coming of Christ and God's fulfillment of all things in him. This interpretation of events not only affirmed women, it mandated their ministry.

Revisionist Narrative. Another biblical argument focused not so much on individual texts or contextual dynamics within Scripture, but on the whole of Scripture and the need to develop a completely new narrative about women. This project of the early twentieth century placed the ministry of women in a new story of God's action that affirmed and empowered women from beginning to end.

Spiritual Arguments

Spiritual Vocation. Closely aligned with biblical exceptionalism, apologists argue that God calls extraordinary women to ministry who then step out of their proper gender roles temporarily for an exceptional mission. This was the earliest argument put forward by Methodist women preachers and it is distinguished by its simple emphasis on the "call of God."

Gender Transcendence. In her examination of women preachers' autobiographies, Susie Stanley maintains that their appeal to the calling of the Holy Spirit enabled them to transcend traditional gender roles.[17] Through the instrumentality of the Spirit—almost reminiscent of the *sursum corda* (lift up your hearts) of the eucharistic liturgy—women are elevated above the prescriptions of gender. Rather than an exceptionalist argument, this approach generally emphasized the normalcy of women in ministry.

Practical Arguments

Historical Attestation. Leaders of the early church and others throughout Christian history have attested to the ministry of women, particularly those within the Methodist movement. The apologists include the testimony of

17. Stanley, *Holy Boldness*, 195.

figures of authority—like John Wesley or Adam Clarke—in their defense of the women. Church history attests to women's ministry.

Uncontested Fruit. Opponents found it difficult to contest the documented success of women preachers, particularly with regard to the issue of conversion. As women swelled the ranks of women-sponsored mission societies in the nineteenth century, the reports they filed related to their success in mission—engaging in work alongside their male counterparts—provided a compelling argument for their recognition.

Conspicuous Need. In certain contexts in which there were not enough male preachers to meet the needs of the burgeoning church, to exclude women from ministry seemed self-defeating. This argument can be seen, in particular, in those periods immediately following the Civil War of the nineteenth century and the two World Wars of the twentieth century.

Authorized Warrant. Sometimes Methodist women engaged in ministries without formal recognition or authorization. In such circumstances, many argued that it was ridiculous not to authorize what they were already doing—to warrant their activities. Many aligned this argument with missionary contexts in which women necessarily engaged in traditional pastoral practices.

Gender Equality. Arguments based on gender equality do not surface until the twentieth century, although the groundwork for them was well laid during the closing decades of the previous century as women began to subvert the "cult of true womanhood" and the "separate spheres" ideology of that previous era.[18] The argument for the equality of women, based both on biblical and philosophical grounds and strongly aligned with the "women's movement," proved a potent tool leading to both ordination and full rights for women in the life of the church.

Catherine Brekus provides a heuristic model to understand the unfolding of this multiplicity of defenses related to women in ministry in the American Protestant context that is instructive with regard to the Methodists.[19] The way in which she categorizes the arguments traces their development in an essentially chronological fashion. First, women defended their preaching on the basis of "an immediate revelation." This spiritual argument dominated the apologetic writings of the eighteenth century. Second, a prophetic emphasis that employed the images of women as "sisters in Christ" and "mothers of Israel" informed many of the nineteenth-century arguments. Comparing themselves to biblical heroines provided a platform less susceptible to attack. Also, as Brekus observes, "By describing themselves

18. See Laird, *Ordained Women*, 24–25.
19. Brekus, "Protestant Female Preaching," 965–73.

in traditionally feminine terms as mothers, sisters, and daughters, female preachers tried to assure the American public that they had no intention of usurping male authority."[20] After the 1848 women's rights convention, however, some took the language of motherhood in revolutionary directions by claiming their unique maternal qualifications for ministry. Third, most of the arguments of the twentieth century revolved around the "quest for equal rights," both in church and society. Brekus notes that "the 1910s and 1920s marked a watershed in women's history: Growing numbers of 'working girls' became nurses, teachers, and secretaries; outspoken female reformers founded settlement houses and other charitable organizations; and most revolutionary, in 1920 the Nineteenth Amendment gave women the right to vote."[21] The Methodist defenses follow this pattern, moving from exceptionalism through domestication to equality.

The Apologists and Their Writings: An Overview

A quick overview of the material collected in this documentary history reveals this shift from apologetics related to women's preaching, through the quest for ordination, to the defense of equal rights in the life of the church. It provides a panoramic view of the apologists and the most critical documents. The first three chapters address the defense of women in ministry in Great Britain from the formative period of the Methodist movement under John and Charles Wesley to the early nineteenth century. Mary Bosanquet, the author of the first defense of women in ministry (chapter 1), argued for the legitimacy of her activities on the basis of "an extraordinary call." Other documents from this period underscore this perspective on women's ministry. Zechariah Taft and Disney Alexander (chapter 2) represent the second-generation protagonists who continued the defense of women in the face of growing opposition within Wesleyan Methodism. In their efforts to consolidate the gains of the previous century, Methodist leaders during the opening decades of the nineteenth century pushed women to the periphery of the movement. Reacting vehemently against these developments, Taft anchored his arguments in the egalitarian prophecy of Joel 2:28–29. His *Thoughts on Female Preaching* was the earliest published Methodist apology for the ministry of women. Hugh Bourne and William O'Bryan, founders of the Primitive Methodists and the Bible Christians—secessionist groups that left Wesleyan Methodism—promoted the exceptionalism of Taft (chapter 3). O'Bryan was the first to link his arguments with millennialist themes

20. Ibid., 969.
21. Ibid., 970.

that pressed the urgency of women's ministry in the new dispensation of the Holy Spirit. John Stamp's *Female Advocate* argued for the scriptural, historical, and practical justification of women's ministry in the Primitive Methodist Church.

Chapter 4 presents a segue from the British to the American context and links the calling of women with the experience of sanctification. Four autobiographical apologies, all by African-American evangelistic preachers of the African Methodist Episcopal and the African Methodist Episcopal Zion Churches—Jarena Lee, Zilpha Elaw, Julia A. J. Foote, and Amanda Berry Smith—illustrate how each autobiography functioned as a self-defense and a subversive challenge to male domination. The apologetic strategies revolved around three primary themes: the irresistible call of God, the considerable success of women preachers, and the biblical precedence for their ministry rooted in the quest for holiness. While all these women accepted the natural subordination of women, they explored new frontiers by virtue of their spiritual aptitude.

The next four chapters trace the development of the defense of women in the holiness movement within Methodism in nineteenth-century America. Chapter 5 introduces the theme of holiness in relation to women's ministry through the ordination sermon of Luther Lee, "Woman's Right to Preach the Gospel," delivered on the occasion of the first female ordination in a major denomination in the United States—that of Antoinette Brown Blackwell in 1853. Phoebe Palmer stands out, not only as "the mother of the holiness movement," but as one of the greatest female apologists in the history of Methodism. Her *The Promise of the Father* (1859) is the largest and most fully developed argument for women's ministry in any tradition. Its formative influence cannot be overestimated. In fact, it shaped the thinking of three major figures in the chapters that follow. Catherine Booth's *Female Ministry; or, Woman's Right to Preach the Gospel* (1870) not only helped to establish the egalitarian ethos of the Salvation Army, which she cofounded with her husband, it established a template for later defenses (chapter 6).

B. T. Roberts, the founder of another holiness denomination, the Free Methodist Church, published *Ordaining Women* in 1891 (chapter 7). Not only did he intimate the possibility of equal rights for women in the church, but he was one of the first to describe the repression of women as an injustice parallel with racism. His colleague in ministry, W. A. Sellew, issued his own "plea for the ordination of those women whom God has called to preach the gospel," entitled *Why Not?* in 1894. The other holiness tradition reviewed in this volume is the Church of the Nazarene (chapter 8). This Nazarene material consists of a diverse collection of materials ranging from autobiographies to sermons. Most noteworthy among them are the composite document of Fannie McDowell Hunter—which summarized the standard arguments for the ministry of women, but also included a collection of women's call narratives—and the stock sermon "Woman's Right to Preach," by Mary Lee Cagle. Most of the holiness apologists justified women's ministry without challenging the authority of men or undermining the cultural values associated with womanhood. The holiness traditions reflect the principle articulated by Mark Chaves: "the greater the social and cultural distance from the larger women's movement, the less likely it is that women's ordination will be understood in gender equality terms."[22]

Chapters 9 and 10 examine Methodist arguments in the late nineteenth century and reflect the shift to a quest for equal rights. In the 1870s and 1880s Anna Oliver and Anna Howard Shaw personified this pursuit (chapter 9). Oliver's "Test Case," a terse apology distributed to the delegates of the 1880 General Conference of the Methodist Episcopal Church, sounded a clarion call for the rights of women. The failure of these efforts provided the impetus for Frances Willard's *Woman in the Pulpit* of 1889. This apologetic volume heralded a new biblical exegesis, advocated the ordination of women, rejected the subordination of women in the home, and promoted a "mother model" of women in ministry that quietly subverted the oppression of women in the church. Chapter 10 presents the defenses of three male counterparts in the late nineteenth century who sought common cause with these giants. While the work of the eccentric W. B. Godbey represented something of a regression in women's apologetics—more conservative and rooted in the cultural South—the arguments of both Luther Townsend and William Warren reflected the progressive elements of the Boston tradition that emphasized the dignity of every human person. Frances Willard commissioned Townsend's response to a misogynistic tract that she published in her apologetic volume. Warren's "Dual Human Unit" attempted to defend the ministry of women on the basis of a sophisticated philosophical argument advocating the equality of the sexes.

Two women of the early twentieth century—Katharine Bushnell and Lee Ann Starr—pioneered new terrain in biblical exegesis (chapter 11) in an effort to advance the cause of biblical equality. The most significant contribution of their respective works—*God's Word to Women* (1916) and *The Bible Status of Women* (1926)—was their effort to construct a completely new biblical narrative concerning women by means of a detailed examination of the entirety of the biblical witness. Bushnell's volume has been described as "the most extensive biblical treatment of gender ever published."[23]

22. Chaves, *Ordaining Women*, 81.
23. Haddad, "Irrepressible Legacy," 10.

Similarly, two women of the mid-twentieth century discussed in chapter 12—Madeline Southard and Georgia Harkness—emerged as the indefatigable champions of full clergy rights in the Methodist Church. Southard, founder of the International Association for Women Ministers, rooted her arguments in Jesus' attitude toward women. Harkness, the apologist whose advocacy led to 1956 General Conference action that affirmed full clergy rights for women, presented her mature views on women's ministry in *Women in Church and Society*, published in 1972.

The defense of women in ministry contributed greatly to the enlarged role that women now play in the various Methodist churches reviewed in this study. As a consequence of the transformational witness of so many in the life of these institutions, women no longer have to validate their ministry through roles marginal and subversive to the church.[24] This volume documents the history of this struggle for acceptance, validation, and equal rights.

24. Ruether and McLaughlin, *Women of Spirit*, 28.

1

The Early Methodist Defense of Women in Ministry

Introduction

John Wesley (1703–91) affirmed the gifts of every person and his advocacy led to the ministry of women in spheres traditionally reserved for men. In his 1786 sermon "On Visiting the Sick" he articulated the emancipatory implications of the egalitarian vision that led many women to join his movement (Document 1). Wesley came to affirm female preachers over time, and not without some personal struggle, but once he was convinced that God was working through a whole host of women called to preach, he embraced their work on behalf of his movement wholeheartedly. While he never endorsed a fully egalitarian perspective—always viewing their ministries as "extraordinary"—his defense of exceptional women encouraged and empowered many who would have otherwise languished on the margins of society.

A number of these women emerged as key actors in the drama of female emancipation and promotion that typified many aspects of the movement. Primary among them are Sarah Crosby (1729–1804), the first authorized woman preacher; Margaret Davidson (fl. c. 1776), blind evangelist and first woman preacher in Ireland; Mary Bosanquet (1739–1815);[1] Hannah Harrison (1734–1801); Elizabeth Hurrell (1740–98); Sarah Mallet (1764–?); Dorothy Ripley (1767–1831); Mary Stokes (1750–1823); and

---

1. Also known by her married name, Mary Fletcher.

Mary Barritt (1772–1851),[2] one of the most significant female evangelists of the nineteenth century, among others. According to Cindy Wesley, John Wesley "justified the public role of women on the basis of four points."[3] Firstly, he argued that St. Paul himself admitted to exceptions to his general prohibition of women speaking, and he highly praised several women for this very thing. Secondly, Wesley believed that some women had an "extraordinary call" to be instruments of God in a public ministry. Thirdly, he accepted the ministry of women if it was the consequence of their transparent devotion to God. Fourthly, the marked success of female ministry, like the ministry of all Wesley's itinerant preachers, proved the validity of their calling and labor. Defended by Wesley on the basis of these arguments, early Methodist women functioned as coworkers, pastors, and partners in God's renewal of the church.

Opponents of Methodism and these women, in particular, marshaled St. Paul's purported prohibitions—1 Corinthians 14:34 and 1 Timothy 2:12, in particular—in their arguments against the first women preachers.[4] The Methodist defense of women in ministry arose in response to this polemical dynamic, but also reflected ambiguities, or even tensions, within the movement itself and among the women themselves that begged for resolution with regard to this issue. The women found great precedent for their own arguments in the pioneering work of a self-reliant woman who had blazed this trail in the previous century. In 1666 Margaret Fell (1614–1702), cofounder of the Religious Society of Friends, published the first extant defense of women in ministry in the English language. In *Womens Speaking Justified* she addressed the statements of St. Paul that led many to oppose the public ministry and preaching of women.

Concern about the ministry of Methodist women came to a head during the decade of 1761 to 1771. Up to this point women had been engaged in many areas of leadership within the movement, but none had really moved fully into a public sphere. It may have been the celebration of Methodist love-feasts during this period—essentially services of testimony and prayer—that provided the impetus for women to speak more openly in a public way. Indeed, in 1761 Wesley encouraged some of the women in Birstall, a Methodist stronghold in Yorkshire, to exercise their gifts more freely at these assemblies. "The very design of the love-feast is a free, and familiar conversation," he wrote, "in which every man, yes, every woman,

---

2. Also known by her married name, Mary Taft.

3. Wesley, "Witnessing Women," 118–19.

4. For a discussion of early exchanges on these texts, see Chilcote, *Wesley and Women Preachers*, 118–23.

has liberty to speak whatever may be to the glory of God."[5] The line between testimony, exhortation, and preaching was very thin, and the more women engaged in activities such as these, the closer they came to boundaries that they themselves often feared to cross. Sarah Crosby emerged as the test case in this regard. At an event in Derby, when two hundred rather than thirty arrived to participate in a meeting she had scheduled, she felt overwhelmed both by the response and the responsibility of such a serendipitous challenge. Through a famous exchange of letters with John Wesley, she felt encouraged to continue in this ministry and, indeed, received his authorization as the first woman preacher of Methodism.[6] Despite the fact that Wesley was very reticent at this point to describe their activities as "preaching," a group of women revolving around Crosby and Mary Bosanquet engaged in these practices more and more.

During the summer of 1771, in a letter to John Wesley (Document 2), Mary Bosanquet provided the first defense of women's ministry in Methodism, closely following the template provided by Fell.[7] In this document she carefully considered the classic "prohibitions" and addressed a wide range of "objections." She emphasized the need to understand the biblical texts in context, concluding that the so-called prohibitive passages refer to specific situations in which particular women were being disruptive and therefore do not apply to women in general or preaching in particular. She pointed to the internal contradiction in St. Paul's own statements, barring them from speaking at one point and admonishing them to cover their heads while prophesying at another (1 Cor 11:5). Limiting the speaking of women to times of "peculiar impulse" placed too severe a limitation, she believed, on the gracious activity of God. She rejected the notion that women's preaching is "immodest," pointing to the examples of Mary, the woman of Samaria, the handmaid of 2 Samuel 20, and Deborah, all of whom were characterized by purity and humility yet publicly declared the message of the Lord. To the claim that all these instances were extraordinary calls, she acknowledged: "If I did not believe so, I would not act in an extraordinary manner—I praise my God, I feel him very near, and I prove his faithfulness every day." Bosanquet argued that, on the basis of her examination of Scripture, women were occasionally called by God to preach in extraordinary situations. The examination of her own conscience led her to believe, moreover, that she had received an "extraordinary call." Her letter proved to be a significant turning

5. Wesley, *Works*, 21:336.

6. See Chilcote, *She Offered Them Christ*, 62–66; cf. Baker, "Wesley and Crosby."

7. Crosby, *MS Letterbook*, 55–61; cf. Chilcote, *Wesley and Women Preachers*, 299–304.

point in John Wesley's own process of learning as he observed, reflected upon, and evaluated women's preaching, and its circulation affected many women as well.[8] As a consequence, he not only permitted such activities based upon an "extraordinary call," but increasingly emboldened women who felt compelled to exercise such a vocation. While Wesley's natural inclination was to conform to the church, its regulations, and traditions, as Frank Baker observed, he had his eyes "so firmly fixed on his spiritual goal that he never realized how far he had strayed from the remainder of the column."[9]

Over the remaining score of years in Wesley's life he wrote letters of encouragement to all the women preachers. His endorsements frequently found their way into subsequent defenses of the ministry of women. When Ann Gilbert (1733–90), the first Cornish woman preacher, sought his advice on the subject of her speaking in public, Wesley replied tersely: "Sister do all the good you can."[10] To Eliza Bennis (1725–1802) (Document 4), his coworker and advisor on Irish affairs, he insisted, "See that your talent rust not."[11] He encouraged Martha Chapman (fl. c. 1774) (Document 5) to speak out boldly and with courage regardless of the opposition.[12] Wesley's exhortation to Elizabeth Ritchie (1754–1835) (Document 6) reflects something of his spiritual pragmatism and the motivation for his support of women: "I want you to be (like me) here and there and everywhere. Oh what a deal of work has our Lord to do on the earth! And may we be workers together with him!"[13] In 1778 he wrote to Elizabeth Hurrell, one of the so-called women of Israel in Yorkshire, viewing her work as equal to any of his male itinerants: "It is well you spent a little time at poor Beverley. The little flock there stands in need of all the help we can give them."[14] When the ministry of Mary Bosanquet began to expand following her marriage to Wesley's lieutenant, John Fletcher, he expressed great satisfaction at hearing "that the work of our Lord prospers in your hands."[15] In a letter to a Cotswold preacher, Penelope Newman (fl. c. 1776–1782), on the eve of her marriage, he observed: "I have often been concerned at your being cooped up in a corner; now you are

---

8. For the influence of this apology on other women, see McInelly, "Mothers in Christ."

9. Baker, "Wesley's Churchmanship," 273.

10. Taft, *Holy Women*, 1:49.

11. Telford, *Letters of the Rev. John Wesley*, 6:23 (April 1, 1773).

12. Ibid., 6:74 (February 25, 1774).

13. Ibid., 6:84 (May 8, 1774).

14. Ibid., 6:331 (December 9, 1778).

15. Ibid., 7:128 (July 12, 1782).

likely to have a wider field of action."[16] In a sequence of letters to Sarah Mallet in the late 1780s (Documents 7–9) he advised her concerning opposition she experienced, empathized with regard to male jealousy, and mentored her in the best practices of the ministry. The ministry of Alice Cambridge (1762–1829) stands out as one of the great legacies of Irish Methodism. In a letter just within weeks of his death (Document 10), John Wesley advised her on how to navigate her relationship with male colleagues, recommending that she obey her superiors as much as conscience permitted. But he concluded without reservation: "It will not permit you to be silent when God commands you to speak."[17]

Three women stand out in terms of their influence in early Methodism and the ministry of women: Sarah Crosby, Mary Bosanquet, and Sarah Mallet. Crosby, as we have seen, was the first to receive John Wesley's authorization to preach; Bosanquet, who later married John Fletcher, was the most widely recognized early Methodist woman throughout the course of the eighteenth century; and Mallet was the first to receive the official authorization of the Methodist Conference to function as an itinerant. All three women figure prominently in apologies for the ministry of women well into the twentieth century, so some of their often-quoted statements and narratives related to their work play an important role in the evolving defense of their successors. In 1774 Sarah Crosby wrote an important letter to her friend and aspiring preacher, Elizabeth Hurrell (Document 11). In this letter she described the essential interrelationship of her religious experience and the divine imperative to preach God's grace. Despite the fact that many clamored for her to "hold her peace," she testified to the fact that shining her light was the only thing that brought her genuine happiness. Her words to an aspiring woman preacher (Document 12) reflect her indomitable spirit: "Speak and act, as the spirit gives liberty, and utterance; fear not the face of man."[18]

Mary Fletcher recorded the first sermon text (Dan 3:16) of an early Methodist woman in her journal.[19] Her sermon on Acts 27:29 remains the only extant sermon of a woman from that period.[20] After her marriage, she and her husband functioned essentially as the first "clergy couple" of Methodism. At one point in her ministry, however, speaking in public created so much personal anxiety that she set apart a full day to fast and pray in order

16. Ibid., 7:143 (October 1, 1782).

17. Ibid., 7:258–59 (January 31, 1791).

18. Taft, *Original Letters*, 66–67 (June 20, 1790).

19. Moore, *Mary Fletcher*, 98; cf. Chilcote, *Wesley and Women Preachers*, 318.

20. See Chilcote, *Wesley and Women Preachers*, 321–27.

to determine what she should do about it. Her reflections on that day of discernment reveal something of the anguish she experienced:

> It cannot be expressed what I suffer. It is only known to God what trials I go through in that respect. Lord, give me more humility, and then I shall not care for anything but thee! There are a variety of reasons why it is such a cross. The other day one told me, "He was sure I must be an impudent woman; no modest women, he was sure, could proceed thus!" Ah! How glad would nature be to find out—You, Lord, do not require it![21]

She did persevere and left behind a fascinating record of her ministry in her journal. One account of her preaching at Huddersfield (Document 13) became a mainstay in the defense of women preachers, offering simultaneously a spiritual justification and a personal testimony.

Three documents in this collection relate additionally to Sarah Mallet. The first (Document 14) is the most terse excerpt in this volume—the formal note of authorization approving her as a Methodist itinerant from the 1787 Conference at Manchester. Future apologists hearkened back to this piece of documentary evidence repeatedly in hopes of reminding Methodists of a heritage lost in their own time. Two excerpts from her journal (Documents 15–16) include an explicit description of her preaching and method and an implicit defense of her labors. Two men—Clarke and Pawson—who were present and engaged in the defense of her ministry at the authorizing conference exerted tremendous influence on others with regard to this issue at the turn of the eighteenth century. Adam Clarke (1760?–1832) was a Methodist theologian and biblical scholar of high renown. His biblical commentary, which was twenty years in the making, served as a primary Methodist theological resource for two centuries. On April 28, 1784, he heard Mary Sewell (c. 1758–86) preach on the classic Wesleyan text Ephesians 2:8. While he confesses to the fact that he had not been a proponent of women's preaching, he found himself compelled to admit freely that he found her ministry both scriptural and sound (Document 17). At approximately the same time, he came under the influence of another woman preacher, Mrs. Proudfoot (fl. c. 1780–90), and acknowledged God's vindication of her calling (Document 18). John Pawson (1737–1806), another highly esteemed contemporary of Wesley's, became sympathetic to the defense of women's ministry through his connection with the circle of women that revolved around Sarah Crosby in Leeds. Later marrying one of these women, Frances Mortimer, Pawson both promoted and defended their calling. As early as 1775 he offered the preaching house in Leeds, if they ever had need, to their

---

21. Moore, *Mary Fletcher*, 107.

use for their services.[22] In 1802 he prepared a letter of introduction for Mary Barritt (Document 19) hoping to stem the tide of opposition. His letter rehearses the defense of women and the role played in this by Wesley: "I have long thought that it is far more difficult to prove that women ought not to preach," he avers to the leaders at Dover, "than many imagine."[23] Although brief, this letter is the most significant male defense of women in ministry from earliest Methodism.

Methodist women in the eighteenth century defended their ministry and justified a preaching vocation on the basis of an "extraordinary call." While they challenged traditional interpretations of biblical texts that seemed to silence women, none called for a radical, egalitarian revolution in the life of the church. Moreover, their male counterparts "defined women who stepped beyond the boundaries of accepted female roles as exceptional," claims Jennifer Lloyd, "making it easier to neutralize their impact and justify their exclusion from positions of power and responsibility."[24] Developments following the death of John Wesley demonstrate this dramatically.

DOCUMENT 1

Sermon "On Visiting the Sick" (1786)
John Wesley
Source: Wesley, *Works*, 3:395–96

"But may not *women*, as well as men, bear a part in this honorable service?" Undoubtedly they may; nay, they ought; it is meet, right, and their bounden duty. Herein there is no difference; "there is neither male nor female in Christ Jesus." Indeed it has long passed for a maxim with many that "women are only to be seen, not heard." And accordingly many of them are brought up in such a manner as if they were only designed for agreeable playthings! But is this doing honor to the sex? Or is it a real kindness to them? No; it is the deepest unkindness; it is horrid cruelty; it is mere Turkish barbarity. And I know not how any woman of sense and spirit can submit to it. Let all you that have it in your power assert the right which the God of nature has given you. Yield not to that vile bondage any longer! You, as well as men, are rational creatures. You, like them, were made in the image of God; you are equally candidates for immortality; you too are called of God, as you have

22. Taft, *Holy Women*, 2:84.
23. Letter of October 25, 1802, in Pawson, Autograph Letters and Manuscripts.
24. Lloyd, *Women and British Methodism*, 3.

time, to "do good unto all men." Be "not disobedient to the heavenly calling." Whenever you have opportunity, do all the good you can, particularly to your poor, sick neighbor. And every one of *you* likewise "shall receive *your* own reward, according to *your* labor."

DOCUMENT 2

Letter of Mary Bosanquet to John Wesley (1771)
Source: Chilcote, *John Wesley and the Women Preachers*, 299–304

Cross Hall, near Leeds, 1771

Very Dear and Honored Sir,

Various have been my hindrances in writing, but none sufficient to have kept me so long silent to you, had I not been at a loss on one particular subject. I wanted your advice and direction in an important point, viz., to know if you approved my light in it. Yet I have been tossed between the temptations of Satan and the arguments of men, that I really could not tell what I thought myself nor how to state the case fairly at all. But, at present, I think both outward and inward circumstances tend to bring me to a crisis, and my light being clearer, I will now open all my mind. And I feel in faith, God will make you my director in this thing, so as to remove my scruples one way or the other.

My soul desires peace and would follow after it with all, especially with God's children, and more particularly with those that act as heads among us. I would hold up their hands in every point that lays within the short limits of my power, and perhaps can say more strongly than many, I honor them for their works' sake. Yet that word of the prophets has often come to my mind, "Woe is me that my mother has borne me a man of contention." How painful is it to be forced to contend with those with whom one desires above all things to live in peace, is well known to you, sir, by experience. My present situation is very peculiar.

When we first settled at Leytonstone, Sister Ryan and I began with little kind of prayer meetings, and they were productive of a blessing. Afterwards, on coming into Yorkshire, Sister Crosby, Brother S. and I did the same now and then, till the people, desiring us to come to such and such of their houses, the number of these meetings increased so as to return sometimes three or four times a week. The number of persons that came to them increased also, hundreds of carnal persons coming to them, who would not go near a preaching-house. And it is enough to say God was with us and made it known by the effects in many places.

However, about a month ago, one of our preachers began to express great dislike to it many ways. We conversed on it in a friendly manner and I asked him if my abstaining from any more meetings in a particular place would satisfy him (though Mr. Oliver had desired me to come there). He said no. He thought it quite unscriptural for women to speak in the church and his conscience constrained him to prevent it. We had a good deal more conversation but got no nearer, though were very friendly. Afterwards some others conversed with me on the same point, alleging the same objections and Satan strongly persuaded me to swallow them down altogether, and I found it very comfortable and easy to nature.

However, on weighing the thing before the Lord, I think it appears to me thus: I believe I am called to do all I can for God, and in order thereto, when I am asked to go with Brother Taylor to a prayer meeting, I may both sing, pray, and converse with them, either particularly, or in general, according to the numbers. Likewise, when Brother Taylor goes to preach in little country places, after he has done, I believe I may speak a few words to the people and pray with them. Twice it has happened, through the zeal of the people, that they gave out a meeting in a preaching house because they had no private house that would hold the people nor one quarter of them. When we came I was sorry, but could not tell what to do. Hundreds of unawakened persons were there, and my heart yearned over them. I feared my Master should say, "Their blood will I require of you." So after Brother Taylor had preached, I spoke to them. I believe I may go as far as I have mentioned above. But several object to this in our own round, and out of it, saying, "A woman ought not to teach, nor take authority over the man." I understand that text to mean no more than that a woman shall not take authority over her husband, but be in subjection, neither shall she teach at all by usurping authority; she shall not meddle in church discipline, neither order nor regulate anything in which men are concerned in the matters of the church. But I do not apprehend it means she shall not entreat sinners to come to Jesus, nor say, Come, and I will tell you what God has done for my soul.

Objection. But the Apostle says, "I suffer not a woman to speak in the church, but learn at home." I answer, was not that spoke in reference to a time of dispute and contention, when many were striving to be heads and leaders, so that his saying, "She is not to speak" here seems to me to imply no more than the other; she is not to meddle with church government.

Objection. No, but it meant literally, not to speak by way of edification while in the church or company of promiscuous worshipers.

Answer. Then why is it said, "Let the woman prophesy with her head covered," or can she prophesy without speaking? Or ought she to speak, but not to edification?

Objection. She may now and then, if under a peculiar impulse, but never else.

Answer. But how often is she to feel this impulse? Perhaps you will say, two or three times in her life; perhaps *God* will say, two or three times in a week, or day. And where shall we find the rule for this? But the consequences (here I acknowledge is my own objection, that all I do is *lawful*, I have no doubt, but is it expedient? that, my dear sir, I want your light in), but what are the consequences feared?

Objection. Why, for forty that comes to hear the preaching, one hundred and fifty will come to your meetings. Will not this cause their hands to hang down?

Answer. That only forty comes to preaching, I am sorry for, but that perhaps a hundred careless carnal sinners comes to our meetings (who would not otherwise hear at all) I am not sorry for, neither should I think this would make the hands of any sensible, gracious man hang down. He must know it is no excellence in us that draws them, but the novelty of the thing. And does it not bring many to preaching, let any impartial person judge.

Objection. But a worse consequence than this is to be feared. Will not some improper woman follow your example?

Answer. This I acknowledge I have feared. But the same might be said of preachers than come out; will not some improper man follow them?

Objection. But if an improper man comes out, the church has power to stop his mouth, but you will not let yours be stopped.

Answer. Yes, on the same condition I will. You would not say to him, no *man* must speak, therefore be silent, but only *you* are not the proper man. Now allowing women may speak, prove to me it is not my personal call, and I will both lovingly and cheerfully obey.

Objection. But is it safe to trust women to teach? Does not the Apostle say, "She was first in the transgression, therefore let her take no authority," and does not Mr. Wesley observe, She is more easily deceived, and more easily deceives?

Answer. He does, and there is much truth in it. On this supposition, the man's understanding is stronger, and his passions harder, consequently, not so easily wrought on. And on the other hand, supposing the woman's understanding weaker and her passions more tender, she is certainly more liable to be deceived, and probably speaking more to the affections than to the understanding, she is more like to deceive; so far I allow. But may not all this objection be removed by this single caution. Let no woman be allowed to speak among the people any longer than she speaks and acts according to the Oracles of God. And while she speaks according to the truth she cannot lead the people into an error.

Objection. Well, but is it consistent with that modesty the Christian religion requires in a woman professing godliness?

Answer. It may be, and is, painful to it, but I do not see it inconsistent with it, and that for this reason. Does not Christian modesty stand in these two particulars, purity and humility? First, I apprehend it consists in cutting off every act, word and thought that in the least infringes on the purity God delights in. Secondly, in cutting off every act, word and thought which in the least infringes on *humility*, knowing thoroughly our own place, and rendering to everyone their due. Endeavoring to be little and unknown, as far as the order of God will permit, and simply following that order, leaving the event to God. Now I do not apprehend Mary sinned against either of these heads, or could in the least be accused of immodesty when she carried the joyful news of her Lord's Resurrection and in that sense taught the teachers of mankind. Neither was the woman of Samaria to be accused of immodesty when she invited the whole city to come to Christ. Neither do I think the woman mentioned in the twentieth chapter of the 2 Samuel could be said to sin against modesty, though she called the general of the opposite army to converse with her, and then (verse 22) went to all the people, both heads and others, to give them her advice, and by it the city was saved. Neither do I suppose Deborah did wrong in publicly declaring the message of the Lord, and afterwards accompanying Barak to war, because his hands hung down at going without her.

Objection. But all these were extraordinary calls; sure you will not say yours is an extraordinary call?

Answer. If I did not believe so, I would not act in an extraordinary manner. I do not believe every woman is called to speak publicly, no more than every man to be a Methodist preacher. Yet some have an extraordinary call to it, and woe to them if they obey it not.

Objection. But do you believe you have this public call?

Answer. Not as absolute as some others, nevertheless, I feel a part of it, and what little I see to be my call, I dare not leave undone.

Objection. But if the people are continually coming to your meetings, they will not have time to attend the stated ones.

Answer. That I have often thought of, and therefore, I know no place except home where I meet more than once a month, and sometimes not that, as there are so many places to go to, and that caution, not to multiply meetings, I see very necessary.

Now, my dear sir, I have told you all my mind on this head, and taken the freedom to encroach a deal on your time and I find a liberty to say, I believe your exact direction I shall be enabled to follow, and shall be greatly obliged to you for the same.

Mr. Oliver is very desirous of our doing all the good we can; and indeed I am pained for the trouble he has had on our account. But it is not only on ours, for various difficulties have, I believe, interrupted some of his comfort this year. If he stays another year with us, I hope he will see more fruit of his labors. The Lord gives him a patient, loving spirit, and his preaching is very animating and profitable.

I praise my God I feel Him very near, and I prove his faithfulness every day. But I want to live as I do not, and to feel every moment that word, My God and my all.

DOCUMENT 3

Letter of John Wesley to Eliza Bennis (April 1, 1773)
Source: Telford, *Letters of the Rev. John Wesley*, 6:23

I fear you are too idle: This will certainly bring condemnation. Up and be doing! Do not loiter. See that your talent rust not: rather let it gain ten more; and it will, if you use it.

DOCUMENT 4

Letter of John Wesley to Martha Chapman (February 25, 1774)
Source: Telford, *Letters of the Rev. John Wesley*, 6:74

If you speak only faintly and indirectly, none will be offended and none profited. But if you speak out, although some will probably be angry, yet others will soon find the power of God unto salvation.

DOCUMENT 5

Letter of John Wesley to Elizabeth Ritchie (May 8, 1774)
Source: Telford, *Letters of the Rev. John Wesley*, 6:84

You give me a pleasing account of the work of God which seems to be dawning about Tavistock. I am not content that you should be pinned down to any one place. That is not your calling. I want you to be (like me) here and there and everywhere. Oh what a deal of work has our Lord to do on the earth! And may we be workers together with him!

DOCUMENT 6

Letter of John Wesley to Sarah Mallet (August 2, 1788)
Source: Telford, *Letters of the Rev. John Wesley*, 8:77–78

But you are in far greater danger from applause than from censure; and it is well for you that one balances the other. But I trust you will never be weary of well doing. In due time, you shall reap if you don't faint. Whoever praises or dispraises, it is your part to go steadily on, speaking the truth in love. I do not require any of our preachers to license either themselves or the places where they preach.

DOCUMENT 7

Letter of John Wesley to Sarah Mallet (February 21, 1789)
Source: Telford, *Letters of the Rev. John Wesley*, 8:118–19

My Dear Sister,

As your speaking at Mr. Hunt's was not a premeditated thing, I see no harm in it, and indeed you were so hedged in by a concurrence of circumstances that I do not know how you could well avoid it. Perhaps there was some end of divine providence (not known to us) to be answered thereby. Therefore I am not at all sorry that it so fell out. But you must expect to be censured for it.

But I was a little surprised a while ago when one speaking of you said, "Sally Mallet is not so serious as Betty Reeve." I thought Sally Mallet was serious as any young woman in Norfolk. Be wary in all your actions and you will never want any assistance which is in the power of, my dear Sally, Yours affectionately, John Wesley

DOCUMENT 8

Letter of John Wesley to Sarah Mallet (December 15, 1789)
Source: Telford, *Letters of the Rev. John Wesley*, 8:190

It gives me pleasure to hear that prejudice dies away and our preachers be-
have in a friendly manner. What is now more wanting in order to recover
your health you yourself plainly see. Be not at every one's call. This you may
quite cut off by going nowhere without the advice of Mr. Tattershall. Never
continue the service above an hour at once, singing, preaching, prayer, and
all. You are not to judge by your own feelings, but by the word of God. Never
scream. Never speak above the natural pitch of your voice; it is disgustful to
the hearers. It gives them pain, not pleasure. And it is destroying yourself.
It is offering God murder for sacrifice. Only follow these three advices, and
you will have a larger share in the regard of, my dear Sally, Yours affectionately, John Wesley

DOCUMENT 9

Letter of John Wesley to Alice Cambridge (January 31, 1791)
Source: Telford, *Letters of the Rev. John Wesley*, 8:258–59

I received your letter an hour ago. I thank you for writing so largely and so
freely; do so always to me as your friend, as one that loves you well. Mr. Bar-
ber has the glory of God at heart; and so have his fellow laborers. Give them
all honor and obey them in all things as far as conscience permits. But it will
not permit you to be silent when God commands you to speak: Yet I would
have you give as little offence as possible; and therefore I would advise you
not to speak at any place where a preacher is speaking at the same time, lest
you should draw away his hearers. Also avoid the first appearance of pride
or magnifying yourself. If you want books or anything, let me know; I have
your happiness much at heart.

DOCUMENT 10

Letter from Sarah Crosby to Elizabeth Hurrell (July 2, 1774)
Source: Crosby, *MS Letterbook*, 69–71

I hope my dear friend will be glad to hear that our Lord continues to pour out his Spirit amongst us. And what is astonishing even to ourselves is that our Lord is doing this great work by the most simple means. Many are thirsting for full salvation in L— and various other places.

As for myself my dear I know not what to say, but that the immeasurable comfort swells my own transported breast! For he renews my strength as the eagle. I live in a holy astonishment before my God while he fills my soul with divine power and the simplicity of a little child, and never was so continually filled, yes, overflowed with love before. Indeed my Lord shows me the reason was because I hearkened too much to the voice which said, hold thy peace; keep your happiness to yourself. (Though not enough to please them neither.) But he now forbids me to hide the light he gives under a bushel. And the more simply I witness for God, the more does he witness in my heart and others too. Glory be to his dear name forever. "O let my mouth be filled with thy praise, while all the day long I publish thy grace, etc."

DOCUMENT 11

Letter of Sarah Crosby to an Aspiring Preacher (June 20, 1790)
Source: Taft, *Original Letters*, 66–67

When we know we have our Lord's approbation, we should stand like the beaten anvil to the stroke, or lie in his hands as clay in the hands of the potter. Through evil report and good we pass, but all things work together for good to them that love God. Speak and act as the Spirit gives liberty and utterance; fear not the face of man, but with humble confidence, trust in the Lord, looking unto him who is able and willing to save to the uttermost all that come unto God by him.

DOCUMENT 12

The Journal of Mary Bosanquet (1776)
Source: Moore, *Life of Mrs. Mary Fletcher*, 117–19

Last Sabbath morning I went according to appointment to Goker. I arose early and in pretty good health. The day was fine though rather hot. About eleven we came to Huddersfield and called on Mrs. H—. She had asked me to lodge there on my return and have a meeting, saying, many had long desired it, and there would be no preacher there on that day. I felt immediately the people laid on my mind and that I had a message to that place, and said, "If the Lord permit, I will." She then said, "We will give it out at noon." We rode forward. Benjamin Cock met us and kindly conducted us over the moors. When we came to his hut all was clean and victuals enough provided for twenty men! But I was so heated with the ride (nearly twenty miles), and with the great fire on which they so liberally cooked for us, that I could not eat. My drinking nothing but water seemed also quite to distress them.

They said the meeting had been given out in many places and they believed we should have between two and three thousand people. That I did not believe, but there was indeed such a number and of such a rabble as I scarce ever saw. At one we went out to the rocks, a place so wild that I cannot describe it. The crowd which got round us was so great that by striving which should get first to the quarry (where we were to meet) they rolled down great stones among the people below us so that we feared mischief would be done. Blessed be God, none was hurt. I passed on among them on the top of the hill not knowing whither I went. Twice I was pushed down by the crowd, but rose without being trampled on.

We stopped on the edge of the spacious quarry filled with people who were tolerably quiet. I gave out that hymn, "The Lord my pasture shall prepare," etc. When they were a little settled I found some liberty in speaking to them and, I believe, most heard. As we returned into the house, numbers followed and filled it so full we could not stir. I conversed with them but could not get much answer. They stood like people in amaze and seemed as if they could never have enough. Many wept and said, "When will you come again?"

We then set off for Huddersfield. I felt very much fatigued and began to think how shall I be able to fulfill my word there? As we rode along Brother Taylor said, "I think I ought to tell you mind. I wish we could ride through Huddersfield, and not stop, for I know there are some there who do not like women to speak among them, and I fear you will meet with something disagreeable." I looked to the Lord and received, as it seemed to me, the following direction: If I have a word to speak for him, he will make my way; if not, the door will be shut. But few of the principal persons had any objection and the people much desired it. Beside, as it had been given out at noon, there would be a great many strangers whom it would not be well to disappoint. It was then agreed that we should have the meeting in the house where they usually had the preaching. But when we came here the crowd was very great and the place so hot that I feared I should not be able to speak at all.

I stood still and left all to God. A friend gave out a hymn during which some fainted away. Brother Taylor said, "I perceive it is impossible for us to stay within doors. The people cannot bear the heat and there are more without than are within." We then came out. My head swam with heat. I scarce knew which way I went, but seemed carried along by the people till we stopped at a horse block placed against a wall on the side of the street with a plain wide opening before it. On the steps of this I stood and gave out, "Come, ye sinners, poor and needy," etc. While the people were singing the hymn I felt a renewed conviction to speak in the name of the Lord. My bodily strength seemed to return each moment. I felt no weariness and my voice was stronger than in the morning while I was led to enlarge on these words, "The Lord is our Judge, the Lord is our Lawgiver, the Lord is our King. He will save us." Deep solemnity sat on every face. I think there was scarce a cough to be heard or the least motion, though the number gathered was very great. So solemn a time I have seldom known. My voice was clear enough to reach them all, and when we concluded I felt stronger than when we began.

DOCUMENT 13

The Manchester Conference Authorization of Sarah Mallet (1787)
Source: Taft, *Biographical Sketches of Holy Women*, 1:84

We give the right hand of fellowship to Sarah Mallet and have no objection to her being a preacher in our Connexion so long as she preaches the Methodist doctrines and attends to our discipline.

DOCUMENT 14

The Journal of Sarah Mallet (1787)
Source: Taft, *Biographical Sketches of Holy Women*, 1:84–85

My way of preaching from the first is to take a text and divide it and speak from the different heads. For many years, when we had but few chapels in this country, I preached in the open air and in barns—and in wagons. After I was married I was with my husband in the preachers' plan for many years. He was a local preacher thirty-two years and finished his work and his life well.

I am glad some of our preachers see it right to encourage female preaching. I hope they all will, both local and traveling preachers, think more on these words, "quench not the Spirit," neither in themselves nor others. "Despise not prophesying," no, not out of the mouth of a child—then would they be more like Mr. Wesley, and I think more like Christ.

DOCUMENT 15

The Journal of Sarah Mallet (1787)
Source: Hellier, "Some Methodist Women Preachers," 66

The same Lord that opened my mouth and endued me with power and gave me courage to speak his Word has through his grace enabled me to continue to the present day. The Lord has been, and is now, the comfort and support of my soul in all trials. And, thank God, I have not run in vain, neither labored in vain. There are some witnesses in heaven and some on earth.

DOCUMENT 16

The Journal of Adam Clarke (1784)
Source: Clarke, *Account of the Life of Adam Clarke*, 1:215–16

I have this morning heard Miss Sewell preach. She has a good talent for exhortation and her words spring from a heart that evidently feels deep concern for the souls of the people and, consequently, her hearers are interested and affected. I have formerly been no friend to female preaching, but my sentiments are a little altered. If God give to a holy woman a gift for exhortation and reproof, I see no reason why it should not be used. This woman's preaching has done much good and fruits of it may be found copiously in different places in the circuit. I can therefore adopt the saying of a shrewd man, who having heard her preach and being asked his opinion of the lawfulness of it, answered, "An ass reproved Balaam, and a cock reproved Peter, and why may not a woman reprove sin!"

DOCUMENT 17

The Journal of Adam Clarke (1784)
Source: Clarke, *Account of the Life of Adam Clarke*, 1:216

[Mrs. Proudfoot] spoke several pertinent things which tended both to conviction and consolation, and seems to possess genuine piety. If the Lord chooses to work in this way, shall my eye be evil because he is good? God forbid! Rather let me extol that God, who by contemptible instruments and the foolishness of preaching, saves those who believe in Jesus. You, Lord, choose to confound the wisdom of the world by foolishness and its strength by weakness that no soul may glory in your presence; and that the excellence of the power may be seen to belong to you alone. Had not this been the case, surely I had never been raised up to call sinners to repentance.

DOCUMENT 18

Letter of John Pawson to the Dover Society Leaders (October 25, 1802)
Source: Chilcote, *John Wesley and the Women Preachers*, 313–14

My dear unknown Friends,

It is now about thirty-three years since I was at Dover or any place in that neighborhood, so that I suppose there is no person now living who has any remembrance of me, yet nevertheless I cannot help wishing the prosperity of the work of God among you. It is but too well known that this has been for some considerable time at a very low ebb in Dover. I therefore could not help thinking that it was a kind providence that Mary Barritt was stationed among you and that by the blessing of God she might be the instrument of reviving this blessed work among you. Perhaps there never was an age in which the Lord so greatly condescended to the curiosity of mankind in order to do them good than in the present. He has been pleased to raise up and send forth all sorts of instruments—men, almost of all descriptions, poor men, rich men, learned and unlearned, yes black as well as white men, and if he is pleased to send by a woman also, who shall say unto him, "What are you doing?"

The late Mr. Wesley was very much opposed to women's preaching yet, when he saw that the Lord owned and blessed the labors of Mrs. Crosby, Mrs. Fletcher, and the late Miss Hurrell, he was obliged to allow that the Lord is pleased to go out of his common way sometimes for the good of his poor creatures. Therefore he would say nothing against women's preaching in extraordinary cases.

As to myself, I have long thought that it is far more difficult to prove that women ought not to preach than many imagine. Let anyone seriously consider, 1 Cor. 11:5. "Prophesies with her head uncovered." Now prophesying there has generally been understood as preaching. If then the women never did preach at all, why did the Lord by the Apostle give these instructions respecting their heads being covered or uncovered?

I have been no great friend to women's preaching among us, but when I evidently see that good is done, I dare not forbid them.

I seriously believe Mrs. Taft is a deeply pious, prudent, modest woman. I believe the Lord has owned and blessed her labors very much, and many, yes, very many souls have been brought to the saving knowledge of God by her preaching. Many have come to hear her out of curiosity who would not come to hear a man and have been awakened and converted to God. I do assure you there is much fruit of her labors in many parts of our Connexion. I would therefore advise you by no means oppose her preaching, but let her have full liberty, and try whether the Lord will not make her an instrument of reviving his work among you.

I am an old man and have been long in the work and I do seriously believe that if you yourselves do not hinder it, God will make Mrs. Taft the instrument of great good to you. Take care you do not fight against God. Many will come to hear her everywhere who will not come to hear your preachers. Let these poor souls have a chance for their lives. Do not hinder them.

Please to give this to your Leaders and Stewards [from J. S. Pipe].

My Dear Brethren,

From a pretty long acquaintance with Mrs. Taft, I most heartily unite with our honored Father, Mr. Pawson, in beseeching you not to hinder her exercising her talents among you; for I most assuredly believe that God has called her to declare the glad tidings of salvation to the world and that he has already honored her in the conversion of multitudes.

2

Zechariah Taft and the Wesleyan Protagonists

Introduction

John Wesley, who had been such a strong protagonist for the ministry of women and of women preachers in particular, died in 1791. In the final decade of the eighteenth century, the expansion of the public ministry of women seems to have approached its zenith. On the threshold of a new era, increasing numbers of women openly exercised their gifts in the ministry of preaching. These women, like their earlier counterparts, continued to struggle with a sense of call into the ministry, but they were strongly encouraged by a previous generation of models and mentors. At the close of his life, Wesley believed that prejudice against the women had severely declined within the Methodist societies, but he was seriously mistaken. As the ministry of women expanded, the question of women's preaching became a point of increasing contention and bitter controversy. The debate that ensued contributed substantially to early nineteenth-century schisms within Methodism. Protagonists, on one side, and detractors, on the other, marshaled their arguments for and against the practice, and many aspects of this debate reflected the larger crisis within the Methodist movement following Wesley's death. Would Methodism continue to embrace its identity as a movement of renewal or would it follow the typical trajectory leading to institutional consolidation with concomitant patriarchalization?

One of the most noteworthy women evangelists at the turn of the century, Mary Barritt, found herself in the epicenter of the controversy.

She received many invitations to preach from some of the most prominent ministers within Methodism and revival seemed to follow her wherever she spoke. Many of her proponents noted the biblical, balanced, and solid foundation of her preaching. Joseph Entwisle (1767–1841), an ascendant leader in Wesleyan Methodism, emerged as one of her nemeses. He expressed his antagonistic sentiments in a letter of 1802 to an itinerant colleague:

> We have *no female preachers* in this part of the country. I think women might with propriety exercise their gifts in a private way, or amongst their own sex; but I never could see the propriety of their being public teachers. Under the Patriarchal dispensation, the oldest male was the priest of the family. Under the Law, all the priests were men. The seventy preachers sent out by our Lord were all men. So were the twelve apostles. Nor do we ever read of a woman preaching, in the Acts of the Apostles. Hence I conclude, women are not designed for public teachers.[1]

Entwisle made it his goal to silence women and to do all in his power to end the ministry of women within Methodism. "Thus at the beginning of the new century women's ministry had become a focus of the continuing tension between pastoral discipline and evangelism," observes Jennifer Lloyd, "and a cause of anxiety to Methodist leadership. For the first time since Wesley's death Methodist leaders reconsidered the legitimacy of female preaching."[2]

At the turn of the century Methodism was a movement in search of a coherent doctrine of church and ministry. The evolution of this federation of societies into a church involved a concomitant transformation in self-understanding as Wesley's successors thought of themselves increasingly as ordinary ministers rather than extraordinary preachers or evangelists. Their inflated and elevated conception of pastoral authority was foreign to the democratic spirit and leveling sentiment that pervaded many of the societies and encouraged women's ministry. At the Dublin Conference for Irish Methodism in 1802 a serious debate arose over the question of women's preaching, revolving, in particular, around the pioneering ministry of Alice Cambridge. Hostility there to female peaching had become so strong that the Irish leaders took extreme and decisive action to suppress the work of the women.

> It is the judgment of the Conference, that it is contrary both to scripture and prudence that women should preach, or should exhort in public: and we direct the Superintendent to refuse a

1. Entwistle, *Memoir*, 231.
2. Lloyd, *Women and British Methodism*, 50.

> Society Ticket to any woman in the Methodist Connexion who preaches, or who exhorts in any public congregation, unless she entirely cease from so doing.[3]

In light of this action, the storm swirling around Mary Barritt in English Methodism intensified. Having recently married the active itinerant, Zechariah Taft (1772–1848), Mary traveled with her husband to Dover, where he had been newly appointed in the Wesleyan Methodist circuit. Anticipating opposition to his wife's ministry, Taft published a defense of his practice of "occasionally suffering a female to officiate for me."[4] This document, *Thoughts on Female Preaching*, is the earliest formal Methodist apology for the ministry of women subsequent to Mary Fletcher's defense.[5] Lloyd rightfully describes Taft as "the first Methodist man to argue systematically for female preaching."[6]

He relied heavily on the biblical exegesis of Adam Clarke, the most noteworthy Methodist scholar of his generation, in order to deal with the purportedly prohibitive biblical texts. He cited more instances of the ministry of biblical women and provided more biblical exposition than Fletcher cited in her letter to Wesley. He defended the position that "prophesying" in Scripture means "preaching," an interpretation argued consistently by most of the subsequent Methodist apologists, harkening back to the defense of Margaret Fell of the Society of Friends (Quakers). His view that the Joel 2:28–29 prophesy—the pouring out of the Spirit on all flesh—was fulfilled at Pentecost functioned as the anchor for his proactive argument. But he also addressed the common objections drawn from the writings of St. Paul, namely, 1 Corinthians 14:34–35 and 1 Timothy 2:12. He argued for a contextual, as opposed to a prescriptive, reading of these texts and even claimed with the philosopher John Locke that these texts "were never designed or intended to hinder women from praying or prophesying, with an audible voice, in the congregation or church."[7] His defense is both succinct and direct.

The opponents of female preaching, however, went to the English Conference of 1803, held in Manchester, with the action of the Irish Conference in the forefront of their minds, hoping that similar action might

3. *Minutes of the Methodist Conferences in Ireland 1802*, 152.

4. Taft, *Thoughts on Female Preaching*, 2.

5. Given the fact that Taft later expanded this tract in *The Scripture Doctrine of Women's Preaching* (Document 2 below), published in 1820, it has not been reproduced here because of the redundancy.

6. Lloyd, *Women and British Methodism*, 48.

7. Cited in ibid., 49.

be taken in their part of the church. When the question whether women should be permitted to preach was posed, only minimal debate ensued and the Conference responded with the following resolution:

> We are of the opinion that, in general, they ought not. 1. Because a vast majority of our people are opposed to it. 2. Because their preaching does not at all seem necessary, there being a sufficiency of Preachers, whom God has accredited, to supply all the places in our connexion with regular preaching. But if any woman among us think she has an extraordinary call from God to speak in pubic, (and we are sure it must be an *extraordinary* call that can authorize it,) we are of opinion she should, in general, address her *own sex*, and *those only*. And, upon this condition alone, should any woman be permitted to preach in any part of our connexion; and, when so permitted, it should be under the following regulations: 1. They shall not preach in the Circuit where they reside, until they have obtained the approbation of the Superintendent and a Quarterly Meeting. 2. Before they go into any other Circuit to preach, they shall have a *written* invitation from the Superintendent of such Circuit, and a recommendatory note from the Superintendent of their own Circuit.[8]

This prohibition hardly affected the women who had gained such prominence in the movement during Wesley's lifetime and were held in high esteem by so many. Many of these women, like Mary Fletcher and Mary Taft, for example, indulged with impunity in "irregular preaching." John Lenton has demonstrated that three main groups of women preachers—the Madeley, Taft, and Boyce circles—continued their work unabated until mid-century when that generation passed from the scene.[9] These supportive networks sustained the women in their various ministries. "Instead of seeking male validation," claims Carol Blessing, Mary Tooth (1774–1843), the protégé of Mary Fletcher in Madeley, "looked to other preaching women in order to help justify her own work."[10] To spite these women some of the Methodist leadership sought to strengthen the 1803 ban and the penalties related to women's ministry. On the threshold of the 1809 Conference, Jabez Bunting (1779–1858), president of the Wesleyan Conference in 1820, 1828, 1836, and 1844 and a dominant figure in early nineteenth-century Methodism, declared that female preaching was unscriptural and a disgrace to

---

8. *Minutes of the Methodist Conferences*, 2:188–89.

9. Lenton, "Support Groups," 138–45; cf. Lenton, "Labouring for the Lord."

10. Blessing, "Oh That the Mantle," 166.

increasingly respectable Wesleyanism. In an effort to counter the arguments of this powerful figure, Zechariah Taft distributed a printed circular to many of his ministerial friends prior to Conference, which may have slowed the momentum of this growing antagonism momentarily.

Taft continued his efforts to support the female preachers and enlarged his role as the most outspoken proponent of women in ministry by means of additional publications. Almost immediately after the 1809 Conference was adjourned, the misogynist editor of the *Methodist Magazine*, Joseph Benson (1749–1821), published a scathing criticism of the women preachers written by James McKnight. Taft reacted vehemently, and having had the publication of his own views in response denied by the editor, he published a small pamphlet independently (Document 19). In this tract, *Thoughts on Women's Preaching*, he opened with a lengthy letter to the *Methodist Magazine* editor (nearly half the document), raising concerns about the way in which he had been silenced and addressing some immediate issues. His response to McKnight's objections, however, present a more sustained biblical argument in which he advocated a contextual reading of the prohibitive passages, argued that prophesying means preaching, and emphasized the defense of women's preaching by prominent figures of authority in early Methodism, including John Wesley.

Having been involved in the debate over women's ministry for several decades, Taft published his definitive apologetic in 1820, *The Scripture Doctrine of Women's Preaching* (Document 20). Essentially, he expanded the small tract he had prepared earlier in 1803. Unlike his diatribe against McKnight, which was reactive in nature, in this larger work he assumed a proactive posture, more for the benefit of the women he sought to encourage than against their detractors. As the title indicates, Taft developed an argument for the ministry of women on the basis of scriptural evidence. His defense is primarily biblical and spiritual, but also exhibits practical concerns in the life of the church. In 1825 he published the first volume of *Biographical Sketches of Holy Women*, a compilation of spiritual narratives, memoirs, and correspondence of noteworthy women preachers; the second volume followed in 1828. While these volumes contained no defense of the women per se, Taft permitted the women to speak for themselves, the autobiographical material providing a powerful defense of the ministries into which they had been called.[11]

Disney Alexander (fl. c. 1795–1825), a lesser-known Methodist physician and lay preacher from Halifax, carried on the legacy of Taft. Attracted to

11. These two volumes contain large amounts of invaluable material in the form of correspondence and journals, "of which almost no manuscripts survive" (Lenton, "Support Groups," 145).

Methodism during the lifetime of the Wesleys, he served as an apologist for the movement in the North, publishing small tracts with titles like "Reasons for Methodism Briefly Stated." It is difficult to date with precision exactly when he took up the cause of the women or why, but in 1827 he published *A Scriptural View of Female Privileges in the Church of Christ* (Document 21). Not uncommon for this period, and perhaps even mirroring the dialogical device frequently employed by John Wesley, Alexander created the fictitious antagonist, Philotheos, over against whom he developed his arguments. He devoted nearly nine pages of this twelve-page tract to a defense of Methodism against this critic's charge of "enthusiasm"—meaning religious fanaticism. In his apologetic material related to women he repeated much of the biblical evidence marshaled by Taft. Written in something of a florid style and dispatching his foil with apparent ease, Alexander emphasized the positive evidence for women's ministry in Scripture and the fulfillment of Joel's prophecy; the egalitarian impulse of Galatians 3:28 figures prominently in his approach.

In the opening decades of the nineteenth century, for the rising generation of women who felt called to ministry, the prohibitions of the 1803 Conference and the increasing censure that followed in its wake shattered their hopes and dreams. Given these dramatic changes, increasing numbers of aspiring women preachers found it necessary to sever their ties with the parent body of Methodism. Many found sanction for their activities within the larger Methodist family, in particular among the later Primitive Methodists (1811) and Bible Christians (1815). Others found welcome outside the parameters of Wesleyan Christianity among the Society of Friends or other movements of renewal. Those who remained within Wesleyan Methodism and decided to comply with the severe restrictions found it increasingly difficult to assert their more charismatic view of ministry over against the increasingly authoritarian spirit of the leadership. Not even the continuing claim to an "extraordinary call"—the primary defense of their champions—found welcome among the primary leaders of the new institution. Within Wesleyan Methodism in Britain, the question of women in ministry never really became a live issue again until the 1920s, and it took another half century before women's ministry was fully recognized in 1974.[12] The Conference was never pressed to change its mind until the changing winds of culture and church pressed the matter with renewed force.

---

12. See Field-Bibb, *Women Towards Priesthood*, 25–37; cf. Brake, *Policy and Politics in British Methodism*, 314–28..

DOCUMENT 19

Thoughts on Women's Preaching (1809), iii–iv, 6–14
Zechariah Taft

My heart's desire and prayer to God is that the preachers may not grieve the minds of multitudes of pious souls, and above all God's Holy Spirit, by attempting to stop those pious useful women whom God has so remarkably owned from using their talents in the church. I write this in the fear of God under a conviction of my duty, and I am happy to say were the eminently, holy, useful men of God now living, Mather, Pawson, Crook, and Shaw, to whom the name of Wesley may be added, that they would be like minded with myself and stand by me in so doing. Whether women ministered in holy things in the primitive church regularly or only when under the immediate influence of the spirit, whether they did this veiled or unveiled, whether they did it to their own sex only or to mixed companies of men and women, whether there were many of these women or only a few, I am not about to contend. My argument is "That God did in the primitive church and does to this day occasionally call, qualify, and commission his handmaids, or daughters to prophesy in his name in the sense St. Paul explains the word" (1 Cor 14:3). I will venture to assert that the late Mrs. Crosby and the present Mrs. Fletcher (the latter of whom has preached for nearly half a century) were both called of God to prophesy or preach the gospel. And there are multitudes of seals to such a ministry in different parts of Lancashire, Yorkshire, Lincolnshire, Nottinghamshire, Derbyshire, and beyond.

McKnight observes, "Let your women be silent in the churches. The prohibition standing in the connection implies that they were not to pray and prophesy in the church as teachers on pretense of being inspired and unable to restrain the motions of the spirit. Next the reasons mentioned by the Apostle show that the prohibition was absolute and general. Christ had not permitted women to speak in the church as teachers of the men. The Apostle, therefore, considered women's praying and prophesying in the church as a renouncing of their subjection to the men." Now if this is not anti-Methodist, I must confess I do not know what is.

McKnight says, "that the Corinthian women were not to pray and prophesy in the church as teachers on pretense of being inspired and unable to restrain the motions of the spirit." Mr. Wesley says on the same passage, "unless they are under an extraordinary impulse of the spirit."

"That the prohibition was absolute and general," that is, they were not to pray and prophesy at all in the church on any pretense whatever. But have not the Methodists and do they not still continue to suffer and encourage the women to pray, yes, and to exhort and speak in the church, both to men and women in their respective band meetings and love feasts for their edification and comfort? I have in my possession a multitude of letters, both from preachers and others in favor of women's preaching and among them several very valuable ones from the late venerable and useful ministers of the gospel, Messrs. Pawson, Mather, Crook, and others. Some of these I should have sent as being well worthy a place in your valuable *Magazine*, but I did not wish to provoke a controversy.

The first is extracted from a letter written by the late Mr. Pawson to some friends in the South of England, in which he says, "The late Mr. Wesley was very much opposed to women's preaching, yet, when he saw that the Lord owned and blessed the labors of Mrs. Crosby, Mrs. Fletcher, and the late Miss Hurrell, he was obliged to allow that the Lord is pleased to go out of his common way sometimes for the good of his poor creatures. Therefore he would say nothing against women's preaching in extraordinary cases. As to myself, I have long thought that it is far more difficult to prove that women ought not to preach than many imagine."

The other is a single sentence taken out of a long letter written by the late pious and useful Mr. Alexander Mather to a female preacher in which he says, "Your call is of God. I would have you go in at every open door, but do not wait until the door is thrown wide open. Go in if it be on the jar."

If St. Paul forbids women to speak in the church in the sense in which McKnight understands it, surely he must forbid their writing for the church for their edification and comfort, as this is one method and most excellent one of teaching. Nevertheless we have had several of these female writers. The writings of the celebrated Miss Hannah Moore, Miss Rowe, and several others have been justly held in high estimation. And if I mistake not, your very valuable correspondent S. B. is a female writer, and I have no doubt but her motive is to instruct and edify the church. How she can reconcile this with what she calls important arguments against women's preaching? I know not, and more especially with St. Paul, "I suffer not a woman to teach, nor to usurp authority over the man" (1 Tim 2:12), if St. Paul must be understood as forbidding all women from prophesying, speaking, or teaching in the church, even supposing their motive is only for its edification and comfort.

Again, what would these good people say who are so much afraid of women attempting to instruct or comfort the church had they lived when a woman was made (under Christ) the head of the Protestant church and defender of the faith? Surely they would have thought that this looked like suffering a woman to usurp authority over the man. But in the present question there is no usurping authority wherever women are properly invited to exercise their talents. It is done in perfect submission to discipline. And the fruit which has followed women's preaching, if not a positive, it is at least a presumptive proof that those highly useful and laborious instruments are called of God to publish salvation by Jesus Christ. That there have been and now are such instruments I assert in the name and fear of God. If required I can produce a cloud of signatures and witnesses to confirm it, and some of the seals to female ministry are now among the Methodist itinerant ministers, and vast many more are acting as local preachers, and others as class leaders among us. The late pious and useful Mr. Jonathan Coussins was awakened by hearing Miss. Penelope Newman, afterwards his wife. Hence he would often pleasantly say that he married his mother.

The usefulness of these women, not only in the conversion of souls but in every other way which concerns the comfort and prosperity of the church is in my judgment incalculable. That there are but few women who think themselves called of God to publish salvation to sinners is very clear. But as God is pleased to own the labors of some of those few in an extraordinary manner in the conversion of sinners and the edification of believers, it is conclusive in my judgment that their call is of God.

Arguments

First, that the silence which the Apostle enjoins in not asking questions in the church is evident from a great variety of particulars as well as from the context. Please read the chapter treating of the gift of tongues and of persons prophesying one after another. It is evident in these public assemblies they were people of different nations, as on the day of Pentecost, and that one minister had the gift of one tongue and a second of another, in the same diversity as they had the other miraculous gifts. That they all had not a universal knowledge of all languages is clear from the Apostle Paul's words, "I speak with tongues more than you all" (1 Cor 14:18). How reasonable then is this conclusion that there were a few inquisitive women in the assembly who, not understanding what the preacher was then delivering but prompted by curiosity (perhaps from a better motive), might ask questions to the interruption of the speaker and auditory? Therefore the Apostle gives the admonition, "Let your women, (that is wives) keep silence, and if they will learn anything let them ask their husbands at home" (1 Cor 14:35). This clearly shows that the prohibition was not a general one and that it must be confined to asking questions, for what had asking their husbands at home to do with their preaching? It seems a reflection on an inspired writer to suppose he wrote so inconsistently. I think, therefore, that the exposition I have given is easy and natural, does no violence to any part of the passage, and prevents one scripture from militating against another.

Secondly, if this comment be rejected how shall we reconcile the following scriptures with the common interpretation of that passage? "And it shall come to pass that I will pour out my spirit upon all flesh, and your sons and your daughters shall prophesy" (Joel 2:28). And "Philip had four daughters who prophesied" (Acts 20:9). The Apostle Paul respectfully mentions several women who "labored with him in the gospel" (Phil 5:2). And one he expressly styles a deaconess of a particular church: "I commend unto you, Phoebe our sister, a servant (it should be deaconess) of the church of Cenchrea" (1 Cor 16:1). No, if he forbids women to preach, how shall we reconcile the Apostle with himself? For he gives us particular directions respecting the manner of women's prophesying as he does of the men's. "Every man praying or prophesying, having his head covered, dishonors his head. But every woman praying or prophesying with her head uncovered, dishonors her head" (1 Cor 11:4–5). I would ask, why such particular directions about the mode of women's prophesying if it is unlawful for them to speak in the church?

Thirdly, to these striking, and I think unanswerable scriptures, the objector only proposes a very harmless question. But how do you prove that prophesying in any of these places means preaching?

I answer. This is begging the question. The proof lies at his own door. He should have proved that prophesying in any of these places does not mean preaching.

Fourthly, but as the whole is rested on this single point, I shall do it for him and prove that prophesying generally means preaching, and that in those places we are more particularly concerned, it has no other signification.

The Apostle has joined praying and prophesying together, and as praying in a public assembly (for of such he was treating) is universally allowed to be a part and indeed a very principal part of the ministerial office, and women did exercise this part of the ministerial function in being the mouth of the people to God, we have here at least a presumptive proof that prophesying means preaching, a demonstration that the speaking in the church which the Apostle reproves in women must be wholly confined to asking questions, otherwise it would be a prohibition against their praying as well as preaching. For how could women pray in public if it were a shame for them to speak in the church in the sense wherein it is generally understood?

The Apostle, when he uses the word precisely fixes the meaning thereof: "He that prophesies speaks unto men to edification, and exhortation, and comfort" (1 Cor 14:3). "He that prophesies edifies the church" (1 Cor 14:4). "For you may all prophesy, one by one, (that is, all who were qualified for and called to the ministry) that all may learn and all may be comforted" (1 Cor 14:31). All may learn from those who prophesied, and women did prophesy. Therefore women were teachers by whom the church was exhorted, edified, and comforted.

We frequently find the word prophesy used in the Old and New Testament in this way: "Aaron your brother shall be your prophet, that is, shall speak unto Pharaoh" (Exod 7:1–2). "Judas and Silas, being prophets, exhorted the brethren with many words" (Acts 15:33). "Anna the prophetess, coming into the temple, gave thanks unto the Lord and spoke of him (Christ) to all them who looked for redemption in Israel" (Luke 2:38). "Zacharias prophesied, saying, 'Blessed be the Lord God of Israel who has visited and redeemed his people'" (Luke 1:67). In all these places prophesying has no other meaning than preaching, and among the preachers we have a female. This exactly agrees with the definition the Apostle Paul gives us of the word when he defines the nature and use of it: "He that prophesies, speaks unto men by doctrine and exhortation for the edification and comfort of the church" (1 Cor 14:3). That there was nothing of an extraordinary nature in the prophesying which the Apostle treats of throughout the whole chapter we have been considering, may be learned from the close of it, for the church was to judge of what was delivered. "Let the prophets speak, two or three; and let the others judge" (1 Cor 14:29).

If it is granted that it does not mean preaching, it makes the case worse, for then it must be something greater, as the Apostle informs us: "He that prophesies is greater than he that speaks with tongues" (1 Cor 14:5). And he exhorts them "To desire the best of gifts, but rather that you may prophesy" (1 Cor 14:1), hereby signifying that prophesying was above all the spiritual and miraculous gifts which abounded in that church. There is but this alternative, if they are not allowed to be ordinary, then we make them extraordinary ministers.

Some persons when they have been closely pressed have sought for refuge by granting that these women who prophesied were called to an extraordinary work, which I think is giving up the whole point at once, as it grants more than is contended for. And hence we may infer according to the well-established rule that he who is called to a greater may be called to an inferior work.

Besides, should it be granted that prophesying means foretelling things to come, an insurmountable difficulty yet remains, for if it was unlawful for women who had that gift to speak in the church, how were they to communicate what was revealed to them? If by speaking, what could this be termed but the most excellent preaching?

The simple fact seems to be this, that though prophesying sometimes means predicting or foretelling things to come, yet in the places which I have quoted it only means preaching in the common sense of the word. Whenever it is used in the former sense, it always includes preaching as publishing these predictions to those concerned.

DOCUMENT 20

The Scripture Doctrine of Women's Preaching (1820), iii, 5, 8–9, 11–24
Zechariah Taft

Dedication to Mrs. Mary Taft

It is now some time since the substance of the following pages was put together. It was written chiefly for the comfort and encouragement of an eminently pious female who thought it her duty to call sinners to repentance. Had something of this kind been put into your hand when you first entered upon your public work, it would no doubt have saved you from many painful anxieties and distressing fears. Indeed, such was your unwillingness to enter upon that work which God required at your hand, and such the condescension of the Almighty, it might literally be said that you were *thrust out.*

Let the case be fairly stated that *God did in the primitive church and does to this day occasionally call, qualify, and commission his handmaids, or daughters, to prophecy (that is to preach) in his name.*

As Dr. Clarke says, "The word prophecy signifies to teach and proclaim the great truths of God, especially those which concern redemption by Jesus Christ" (1 Cor 11:5).

"Help those women who labored with me in the gospel" (Phil 4:3). "In the Grecian and Asiatic countries women were kept much secluded and it was not likely that even the apostles had much opportunity of conversing with them. It was therefore necessary that they should have some Christian women with them who could have access to families and preach Jesus to the female part of them. The Apostle tells us that certain women labored with him in the gospel and were assistants to others also who had assisted him" (Dr. Clarke).

"I commend unto you Phoebe our sister who is a servant of the church which is at Centhrea" (Rom 16:1). A deaconess. They were ordained to the office by the imposition of the hands of the Bishop. Theodoret says, "The fame of Phoebe was spread throughout the world. She was known not only to the Greeks and Romans but also to the Barbarians," which implies that she had traveled much and propagated the gospel in foreign countries.

"Greet Priscilla and Aquila, my helpers in Christ Jesus" (Rom 16:3).

"And the same man (Philip, the evangelist) had four daughters, virgins, which did prophesy" (Acts 21:9). Probably they were no more than teachers in the church, for we have already seen that this is frequently the meaning of the word "prophecy." This is undoubtedly one thing meant by the prophecy of Joel. "If Philip's daughters might be prophetesses, why not teachers" (Dr. Clarke).

"Whom when Aquila and Priscilla had heard (Apollos) they took him unto them and expounded unto him the way of God more perfectly" (Acts 28:26). "This eloquent man, and mighty in the Scriptures, who was even a public teacher, was not ashamed to be indebted to the instructions of a Christian woman in matters that not only concerned her own salvation but also the work of the ministry in which he was engaged" (Dr. Clarke).

We have a most successful female preacher in the Samaritan woman, "Many of the Samaritans believed on him for the saying of the woman" (John 4:39). This woman was the first apostle for Christ in Samaria! She went and told her fellow citizens that the Messiah was come and gave for proof that he had told her the most secret things she had ever done.

Mary Magdalene is another instance of Christ's choosing whom he pleases to bear his commission. "Jesus said unto her," after his resurrection, "touch me not; for I am not yet ascended to my Father. But go to my brethren and say unto them, 'I ascend unto my Father and your Father, and to my God and your God'" (John 20:17). Magdalene is a new apostle and the first who was commissioned to preach Christ arisen. All her delight was to do the will of her master and she hastened, as it were, on the wings of love to execute her commission by making known his resurrection to his disconsolate disciples.

"Salute Tryphena and Tryphosa who labored in the Lord. Salute the beloved Persis who labored much in the Lord" (Rom 16:12). "Two holy women who it seems were assistants to the Apostle in his work, probably by exhorting and visiting the sick. Persis was another woman who, it seems, excelled the preceding. For of her it is said she labored much in the Lord. We learn from this that Christian women, as well as men, labored in the ministry of the word. In those times of simplicity, all persons, whether men or women, who had received the knowledge of the truth believed it to be their duty to propagate it to the utmost of their power. Many have spent much useless labor in endeavoring to prove that these women did not preach. That there were some prophetesses as well as prophets in the Christian church, we learn. That a woman might pray or prophesy provided she had her head covered, we know. That whoever prophesied spoke unto others to edification, exhortation, and comfort, St. Paul declares (1 Cor 14:3). That no preacher can do more, every person must acknowledge, because to edify, exhort, and comfort, are the prime ends of the gospel ministry. If women thus prophesied, then women preached" (Dr. Clarke).

Chrysostom and Theophylact take great notice of Junia, mentioned in the Apostles's salutations. In our translation it is, "Salute Andronicus and Junia, my kinsmen, and my fellow-prisoners, who are of note among the apostles" (Rom 16:7). By the word *kinsmen* one would take Junia not to have been a woman but a man. But Chrysostom and Theophylact were both Greeks, consequently, they knew their mother tongue better than our translators, and they say it was a woman. It should therefore have been translated "Salute Andronicus and Junia, my kinsfolk." The Apostle salutes other women who were of note among them, particularly Tryphena and Tryphosa who labored in the Lord, and Persis who labored much in the Lord. If we look into ecclesiastical history we shall find women very eminent in the church long after the days of the apostles, women who were distinguished for their piety, their usefulness, and their sufferings. Witness the story of Perpetua and Felicitas, martyrs for the Christian faith, which contains traits that touch the most insensible and cannot be read without a tear. Eusebius speaks of Potominia, Ammias, a prophetess in Philadelphia, and others, who were equally distinguished by their zeal for the love which they bore to Jesus Christ.

Justin Martyr, who lived till about AD 150, says in his *Dialogue with Trypho the Jew*, "that both women and men were seen among them who had the gifts of the Spirit of God, according as Joel the prophet had foretold, by which he endeavored to convince the Jew that the latter days were come. Manasseh Ben Israel tells us that all their wise men understood the times of Messias."

Dodwell, in his *Dissertations on Irenaeus*, says that "the extraordinary gift of the spirit of prophecy was given to others besides the apostles, and that not only in the first and second, but in the third century, even to the time of Constantine, men of all sorts and ranks had these gifts, yes, and women too." Therefore we may certainly conclude that the prophetic saying of the Psalmist was verified: "The Lord gave the word, and great was the company of those that published it" (68:11). In the original Hebrew it is "Great was the company of the women publishers, or women evangelists."

Objections

First "*Let your women keep silence in the churches, for it is not permitted unto them to speak; but they are commanded to be in silence, as also says the law. And if they will learn anything, let them ask their husbands at home: for it is a shame for women to speak in the church*" (1 Cor 14:34–35). "Evidently it is that they were to be silent unless they had an extraordinary revelation to communicate made to them by the Holy Spirit, which revelations were *chiefly* predicting future events (Joseph Benson). Mr. Benson admits that sometimes they might speak by way of edification, exhortation, and comfort, though only when under the immediate influence of the Holy Spirit, and it will be difficult to prove that the apostles themselves preached without that extraordinary influence of the Holy Spirit. But I am inclined to think the silence here enjoined by the Apostle signified that the women were *not to ask questions in the church*, which is evident from a great variety of particulars, as well as from the context. The prohibition was not a general one. It must be confined to asking questions. At least the silence here enjoined was never intended to prohibit those pious females from instructing and comforting the Corinthian church, to whom he had before given directions respecting their adorning while thus employed. For what has women preaching to do with *asking questions, wanting information, and asking husbands at home*? However, if understood in any other sense, it has nothing to do with *single women*, with *widows*, with *learned women*, with those that understand, are prepared, and called of God to teach the things of religion, as it refers to *married women*, and those married women *only*, that are ignorant about what they should say. I think the emphasis should be laid on *your women*, and on *let them ask their husbands at home*, then the meaning is plain. There were at Corinth, it appears, some married women who were frequently asking bold, impertinent questions, occasioning debates, contention, and confusion. Let such women keep silence, and ask their husbands at home, for it is a shame for such women to speak in church.

Second, "Let the women learn in silence, with all subjection. But I suffer not a woman to teach, nor to usurp authority over the man" (1 Tim 2:11–12). "Unless they are under an extraordinary impulse of the Spirit" (John Wesley). "*Sine garrita*, without chattering. This was a precept of the synagogue. It is not allowed, says Maimonides, for women to *whisper or trifle* because of the reverence they should have for the congregation."

The subjection which is due from women to men in general, and to their husbands in particular, recommended by St. Paul, does not relate to matters pertaining to her own personal salvation or what is her duty in order to promote the salvation of others. In matters of conscience, both of faith and practice, women as well as men stand accountable to God.

That St. Paul *allowed* women to *edify the church* by prophesying or preaching, or speaking unto others to *edification, exhortation,* and *comfort* we have before proved.

I think the passage ought to be read thus: *I suffer not a woman to teach by usurping authority over the man.*

Most enemies to women preaching understand from this passage, that no woman is to *teach*, and that all *teaching* by women is usurping authority over the man. But this grants too much in as much as it involves the following difficulties:

No woman is to keep a school.

No woman is to teach her children to knit, or sew, or cook, or read, or write.

No woman is to write books, for this is one excellent method of teaching.

No woman is to pray in public, for praying is one method of conveying instruction upon doctrinal, experimental, and practical religion.

No woman is to prophesy, even supposing the term applies only to fore-telling future events. While that knowledge lies hid in their own mind there is no teaching; but if God commands them to prophesy aloud and they obey him, by this they teach to others that knowledge which before lay hid in their own breasts.

If it is objected that the *teaching* here forbidden means only that they are not to teach the *science of religion,* still all the difficulties remain except the two first, for the things belonging to religion may be taught by the *pen* as well as by the *mouth,* on our knees as well as in any other position.

But if it is objected that the teaching here forbidden only means face to face (but I ask, is not this taking too great liberties with the text? St. Paul does not say that this is the only kind of teaching which he forbids—but supposing it was), then the apostle evidently contradicts himself. That he admits and encourages this kind of teaching is plain from 1 Corinthians 11:4. For in whatever sense we understand prophecy, it must of necessity, imply teaching. Again, the sense of the text "as objected" is contradicted in Acts 28:16. Aquila, a female, expounded the word of God to Apollos. I defy any man to split that hair and prove that expounding is not teaching. But all these difficulties will be removed by understanding the passage thus: "*I suffer not a woman to teach, by usurping authority over the man*," and pray who does? I have not heard of any such usurpation in the church.

Mr. Wesley, in the former part of his life, was opposed to women preaching, but never so much an enemy to it as he was to *lay preaching*. But no sooner was he convinced that God was with them, that sinners were converted by them, than he not only ceased to forbid them but gave them encouragement.

"In the first attempts of a layman to preach, Mrs. Wesley heard his discourses, Mr. John Wesley was at this time absent from London, but the thing being quite new and appearing extra-ordinary, he was immediately acquainted with it. He hastened up to London with a full determination to put a stop to so glaring an irregularity. He conversed with his mother on the subject and told her his intention. She said, "I charge you before God, take care what you do, for that man is as much called to preach the gospel as ever you were." This kept him from a hasty execution of his purpose, and it being found upon inquiry that good was done, the practice was suffered to continue."

The conversion of sinners by the preaching of any person, whether male or female, was a strong proof in Mr. Wesley's judgment of a divine call to the great and important work. This will appear from his most excellent sermon on Mark 9:38–39. It was no doubt from a conviction of the success attending the efforts of his mother, Mrs. Susanna Wesley, to promote the spiritual advantage of the inhabitants of Epworth, that caused him to say, "that *even she*, as well as her father and grandfather, her husband and three sons, *had been, in her measure a preacher of righteousness*." When Mr. Wesley's father was from home, Mrs. Wesley used to read sermons and pray with the people in the vicarage-house at Epworth on the Sunday evenings to as many as the room would contain. Sometimes there were two hundred present on these occasions, and much good was done.

What were Mr. Wesley's opinions of the preaching of Mrs. Johnson and Miss Sarah Mallet may be gathered from his journal: "At six, I preached in the Presbyterian meeting, a large and commodious building. And I was now with the most lively Society that I have seen for many days, owing chiefly to the *good providence of God bringing sister Johnson here*. She came, indeed, in an acceptable time, for J. W. and his wife, who for many years had been pillars, had left the Society. They had one child, a son about nineteen years old, of whom they were fond enough; Miss. Newman, afterwards his wife. Hence he would often pleasantly say that he had married his mother. The usefulness of these women, not only in the conversion of souls, but in every other way which concerns the comfort and prosperity of the church is in my judgment incalculable." It was from this conviction Mr. Alexander Mather writes to one of these female preachers: "Your call is of God, I would have you go in at every opening door, but do not wait until the door is thrown wide open; go in if it is on the jar." Mr. Samuel Bradburn says: "*For my own part, I must not hinder a woman herein* (from preaching) *when I clearly discover nothing contrary to genuine piety—when I discover far greater abilities than I do in very many traveling preachers—when thousands of good and wise people are for women's preaching, and when there is much good done by it wherever they go.*"

I would finish by observing that if we condemn all women's preaching or prophesying to edification, exhortation, and comfort in the church of Christ, we at once condemn that respectable body of people called Quakers who universally allow and approve of it. Thus all those women who labor among them in word and doctrine and who profess to be influenced by the Spirit of God will be branded as hypocrites and impostors having taken upon them an office that does not belong to them and whose profession is a lie to the Holy Ghost. And by such conduct we condemn those bodies of people that have broken off from us and who universally allow this practice. And with all the imperfections we discover among them, we must acknowledge that much good has been done, and that by the preaching of both men and women. By admitting the impropriety of women's preaching we condemn that most useful body of people called Methodists, both that part of them which allows women may be endowed with authority from on high to preach, as well as that part of them which totally denies all such authority, seeing the whole body of them allow and approve of women's speaking to edification and comfort. Witness their love-feasts, class and band meetings; they are all religious services, and I cannot see how we can allow the one and reject the other.

Lastly, let all those daughters and handmaidens of the Lord who think it their duty to pray, prophesy, or preach in his name exercise the talent God has given them to his glory. As long as you are sensible that your hearts are sincere, your intentions pure, your lives holy, that you have no other end in view than gaining proselytes to Jesus Christ, continue to follow the openings of providence and the immediate teachings of his Spirit. If devils are cast out, souls saved, and the people willing to hear you, let no man stop you without producing his authority from the King of Heaven and giving you good and *sufficient* security that he will answer for your neglect of service in the church of Christ at the divine tribunal in the day of awful and righteous retribution. Let the case of Miss Mallet be ever fresh in your memory. And if it should happen that the preachers and stewards are opposed to your prophesying or speaking unto the people by way of exhortation, *do not, I beseech you, hastily leave the Connexion as some have done.*

Above all, do not attempt to speak at these seasons or in those places where the regular preachers preach, but rather speak in some private house to those who are willing to hear you and at a time when there is no meeting held in the neighborhood. From what has been advanced, I think it appears (at least to me) that female preaching in some extraordinary cases (and this is all I contend for) is both reasonable and lawful, consonant to Scripture, and the practice of primitive times. I certainly think if any person could so far divest himself of any preconceived opinion on this subject so as to weigh impartially in the balances of the sanctuary the scriptures cited in this pamphlet, would be convinced to decide in the same way. But I hope I am no bigot. All my differing brethren have an equal right to their opinion with myself. I conceived it my duty to publish this tract at *this time*, and I am satisfied with my motive. I have no sinister ends to serve, no party to please, no system that must be supported, because it has long been established by men. I trust I am endeavoring to follow *scriptural truth* wherever it may lead me. I know the conversion of sinners is the work of God—it is *his* to *begin, carry on*, and establish it. It is his to choose the instruments and means of doing it. And all the glory must be ascribed to him. I commend the reader to God and to the word of his grace, praying that both he and the writer may be led into all saving truth here, and at last brought into his eternal kingdom. Amen.

DOCUMENT 21

A Scriptural View of Female Privileges in the Church (1827), 9–14
Disney Alexander

It is strange that a writer of Philotheos's cast should discover the nakedness of his mind so much and take pains to spread it before meridian day by selecting those texts of Scripture that above all others serve to refute his opinions concerning female privileges in the church of Christ.

"But every woman that prays or prophesies with her head uncovered, dishonors her head, for that is even all one as is if she were shaven, for if a woman be not covered, let her also be shorn; but if it be a shame for a woman to be shorn, or shaven, let her be covered" (1 Cor 11:5–6). Now to use the words of Philotheos, "none but the willfully ignorant," the dupes of carnal blindness, could construe and contort these portions of Scripture in order to support his favorite and illiberal doctrine of debarring females from those privileges which God himself has vouchsafed them, and also from the eminent rank to which they are entitled on the great scale of human intellect. True, in some barbarous countries where the dark places of the earth are full of the habitations of cruelty, the fairer part of the creation are kept in a state of vassalage and degradation, even to cruelty. But it is worthy of observation that in proportion as the influence of the gospel prevails, female worth is prized, and they have not only been disentangled from the shackles that ignorance, superstition, and brutality have cast upon them, but they have secured that dignity, affection, and esteem which they so imperatively claim as their right, and as companions and helpmates for man to soften his cares alleviate his sorrows and sympathize in his woes. It is plain to an enlightened mind that the Apostle does not prohibit females from praying or prophesying in the church of God. He only forbids them to pray and prophesy with their heads uncovered.

"But every woman that prays" (1 Cor 11:5). Whatever may be the meaning of praying and prophesying in respect to women, so that some women at least as well as some men might speak to others to edification and comfort, this kind of prophesying or teaching was predicted by Joel, "And it shall come to pass afterward, that I will pour out my spirit upon all flesh, and your sons and your *daughters* shall prophesy, and your young men shall see visions, and your old men shall dream dreams" (2:28). And had there not been such gifts bestowed on women, the prophecy could not have had its fulfillment. The only difference marked by the Apostle was that the man had his head uncovered because he was the representative of Christ and the woman had hers covered because she was placed by the order of God in subjection to the man. It was a custom both among the Greeks and the Romans, and among the Jews an express law, that no woman should be seen abroad without a veil. This was and is a common custom throughout all the East, and none but the public prostitutes go without veils. So if a woman should appear in public without a veil, she would dishonor her head (her husband). We know that a woman suspected of adultery was ordered by the law of Moses to be stripped of her veil (Num 5:18).

"And if they will learn anything, let them ask their husbands at home, for it is a shame for a woman to speak in the church" (1 Cor 14:35). The Jews would not suffer a woman to read in the synagogue, though a servant, or even a child, had this permission. But the Apostle refers to irregular conduct, such conduct as proved they were not under obedience.

"Let your women keep silence in the churches" (1 Cor 14:34). This was a Jewish ordinance. Women were not permitted to teach in the assemblies or even to ask questions. The rabbis taught that a woman should know nothing but the use of her staff. The saying of the Rabbi Eliezer is both worthy of remark and execration: "Let the words of the law be burned rather than that they should be delivered to women." This was their condition till the time of the gospel when, according to the prediction, the Spirit of God was poured out on women as well as on men, that they might prophesy, i.e. teach. And that they did prophesy or teach is evident from what the Apostle says in 1 Cor 11:5 where he lays down rules to regulate this part of their conduct while ministering in the church.

But does not what the Apostle says here contradict that statement, and that the words in Chapter 11 should be understood in another sense? For here it is expressly said that women should keep silence in the church for it was not permitted for a woman to speak. Both places seem perfectly consistent. It is evident from the context that the Apostle refers here to asking questions in the synagogue, but this liberty was not allowed to any woman. St. Paul confirms this in reference to the Christian church. He orders them to keep silence, and if they wished to "learn anything, let them enquire of their husbands at home" because it was perfectly indecorous for women to be contending with men in public assemblies on points of doctrine or cases of conscience. But this by no means intimated that when a woman received any particular influence from God to enable her to teach that she was not to obey that influence. On the contrary, she was to obey it, and the Apostle lays down directions in chapter 11 for regulating her personal appearance when thus employed. All that the Apostle opposes is their *questioning or finding fault* in the Christian church, as the Jewish men were permitted to do in their synagogues, together with the attempt to usurp any authority over the men by setting up their judgment in opposition to them. For the Apostle has in view special acts of disobedience and arrogance of which no woman would be guilty who was under the influence of the Spirit of God. From this it is evident that it was the disorderly and disobedient that the Apostle had in view, and not any of those on whom God had poured out his Spirit.

I would say, can any forbid that women should prophesy when God pours out his Spirit upon them, but Philotheos with one sweeping stroke cuts off the doctrine of inspiration in this age. "*This is much more necessary now,*" he says, "*as there are no meetings where inspired persons are teachers.*" No marvel that this star of divinity (Philotheos) endeavors to degrade the female part of humanity by denying them the favors that God has vouchsafed them in degree in common with men. When he supersedes the influence of the Holy Ghost on the hearts of believers, he proves that he is a stranger not only to the conversion of the soul, but to this great and sublime doctrine of the Scripture. I shall reference a few passages relative to this supernatural and consolatory work on the heart of man. "If any man be in Christ Jesus, he is a new creature." If any man does not have the Spirit of Christ, he is none of his. "Except a man be born of water and of the Spirit, he cannot see the kingdom of God; that which is born of the flesh is flesh and that which is born of the spirit is spirit." "There is a Spirit in man, and the inspiration of the Almighty gives him understanding."

And I would say by the same analogy that neither man nor woman can preach, exhort, or pray to edification or the conversion of sinners unless a portion of the divine Spirit is poured out upon him or her. Hence the exclamation, "you have run and I have not sent you, therefore you shall not profit my people." Without me (says Christ) you can do nothing. I would ask what Philotheos means by inspiration? Does not every good and perfect gift come down from above? Hence every good desire, thought, expression, and beneficent action is the bright effluence of that great Spirit that spoke through the prophets, evangelists, and martyrs, and that now speaks through all his *called, faithful* ministers and servants, male and female.

3

Defenders of Women in Revivalist Methodism

Introduction

After the death of John Wesley, some of his followers continued to embrace the revivalist vision of the movement that, in their minds, had led to its phenomenal success. According to the proponents of this view, the itinerant preacher was an "extraordinary messenger," the term Wesley had coined in his sermon on "Prophets and Priests," which argued for the exceptional nature of his movement within the Church of England.[1] In his definitive study of this *Age of Disunity*, John H. S. Kent observed that the eighteenth-century Methodist minister under Wesley "existed simply as the agency of a special mission, and required no complicated background of 'ordination' or 'succession.' The minister was essentially an itinerant evangelist."[2] Some held on to this view tenaciously in the face of growing authoritarianism and respectability. Margaret Batty has described the situation with great clarity:

> The Methodist leaders tried to make Methodism respectable. Outspoken local preachers were expelled, those who tried to establish a means of mutual education and support were snubbed, Women preachers, who had become a joke to magazine editors,

1. Wesley, *Works*, 4:79, 82.
2. Kent, *Age of Disunity*, 68.

59

were banned. Any growth in new forms of religious expression, like camp meetings, was suppressed.[3]

While some—even women preachers like Mary Fletcher and Mary Taft—chose to remain within the ranks of Wesleyan Methodism, others found the new attitude to be intolerable and sought out ways to reclaim the vision and mission of the primitive movement.

In the opening decades of the nineteenth century two "offshoots" of Wesleyan Methodism, in particular, attempted to recover the more flexible, free, and egalitarian ethos that they believed had characterized the original movement. These new dissident groups—Primitive Methodists and Bible Christians—emphasized evangelistic revival and employed women preachers, and defended their right to do so.[4] Hugh Bourne (1772–1852), cofounder of the Primitive Methodists, was enamored with the ministry of Lorenzo Dow (1777–1834), an eccentric American evangelist who had transported his mission to the British Isles. Strikingly similar to Wesley's "field preaching" events but with an American frontier twist, his camp meetings were generally daylong open-air meetings that involved public prayer, preaching, and even Methodist love feasts. Convinced that he should organize a mass evangelistic event of this nature, Bourne held the first camp meeting in England on May 31, 1807, at Mow Cop in the West Midlands. William Clowes (1780–1851), having attended the inaugural event, became an ardent supporter of the movement with a following of his own. Both were expelled from Wesleyan Methodism—Bourne in 1808 and Clowes in 1810—because of their association with camp meetings, and they joined forces to establish the Primitive Methodist Connexion in 1811.[5] Sharing some of the same concerns but in a very different context in Cornwall and Devon, another Methodist preacher, William O'Bryan (1778–1868), began a movement of "cottage gatherings." Intimate fellowship, simplicity of style and life, a strong missionary impulse, and the extensive use of female preachers characterized these Bryanites, as they were called.[6] In 1815 O'Bryan formally separated from Wesleyan Methodism to establish the Bible Christian Church.[7] At the

3. Batty, "Local Preaching," 5.

4. While Jennifer Lloyd has demonstrated the promotion of women preachers in other Methodist sectarian groups like the Magic, Independent, and Arminian Methodists, only the PM and BC traditions produced apologetic documents that have survived; see Lloyd, *Women and British Methodism*, 42–84.

5. On female traveling preachers in Primitive Methodism, see Graham, *Chosen by God*.

6. For an incisive discussion of cottage religion of female preaching, see Valenze, *Prophetic Sons and Daughters*.

7. For a full discussion of the history of these two movements, see Milburn,

originating conference of the Bible Christians in 1819, fourteen of the itinerant preachers were women;[8] the minutes of the first Connexional Conference of the Primitive Methodists note six female traveling preachers.[9]

According to Jennifer Lloyd, it was Bourne's association with Dow and
other more radical Methodist secessionist groups that "led him to consider
the question of women's roles in Methodism."[10] The domestic setting of
many of their meetings, like earliest Methodism, provided a comfortable
space in which women could exercise their gifts freely. The cottage gathering
dynamic of O'Bryan's ministry had the same effect. The leveling sentiment
of the camp meeting was conspicuous. Not only were Bourne, Clowes, and
O'Bryan inclined to support women, given the general ethos of their similar movements, they were also pragmatists. They were all familiar with the
stunning success of female preachers like Mary Dunnel (fl. c. 1807–12), who
worked with Bourne in north Staffordshire, and "their encounters with effective female evangelists predisposed them to allow them to continue their
work."[11] Any personal doubts that O'Bryan had with regard to the ministry
of women were swept away when he slipped in unnoticed to hear his future
wife speak and he was immediately convinced of her call. "The fervent at-
mosphere of the Primitive Methodist camp meeting or the intimacy of Bible
Christian cottage gatherings," Lloyd avers, "created circumstances in which
women felt called to preach and emboldened to act on that call."[12]

In 1808, several years before the formal incorporation of the Primitive
Methodist Church, the leadership of the Independent Methodist Conference invited Bourne to prepare a statement in defense of female preachers.
His *Remarks on the Ministry of Women* (Document 22), published that same
year, follows the same pattern we have seen in the other contemporary defenses. It is quite likely that he was aware of Taft's earliest apology of 1803.
Like Taft, the prophecy of Joel figured prominently and his exegesis of the
critical biblical texts demonstrated his dependence on Adam Clarke. He
marshaled the same arguments for the contextuality of the prohibitive passages, the prominence of biblical women leaders, and the support of Wesley
and other authority figures within early Methodism. Like almost all the other defenses, he reminded his reader that with reference to women, "God has

---

Exploring Methodism, and Shaw, *The Bible Christians.* The most critical study of the
woman preachers among the PMs is Graham, *Chosen by God.*

8. Reported in Chilcote, *She Offered Them Christ,* 121.

9. Reported in Lloyd, *Women and British Methodism,* 71.

10. Lloyd, *Women and British Methodism,* 68.

11. Ibid., 71.

12. Ibid., 77.

chosen the foolish things of the world to confound the wise" (1 Cor 1:27). Exceptionalism remained a primary defense in this extremely brief tract.[13]

It had not escaped either Bourne or O'Bryan's notice that they had come to the same conclusions about the ministry of women independent of one another. In an issue of the *Primitive Methodist Magazine* Bourne included a lengthy letter he had requested from O'Bryan explaining how he had come to support female preaching. Reflecting the same judgment and spirit, O'Bryan articulated the formal position of the Bible Christians in the minutes of their first Conference held in 1819 (Document 23). According to Lloyd, "He published the defense as an extended article in the *Arminian Magazine*, the Bible Christian's official publication, and then much later as a pamphlet"[14] (Document 24). His treatise is really nothing more than an extended discourse on the Joel 2:28 text with arguments embedded in it that are virtually identical to his predecessors. Lloyd, however, rightfully notes a couple striking differences.[15] First, rather than focusing on the meaning of the term "prophesy" in the Joel text to secure its definition as preaching, he interpreted the citation of this statement in Acts as a sign of the approaching millennium. In other words, he linked the expanding ministry of women to the impending return of Christ. This is the first connection of the defense of women among the Methodist protagonists to millenarianism, a theme that later protagonists exploit as well. As Rosemary Radford Ruether and Eleanor McLaughlin have documented, "millennial expectation places the church in a 'liminal' relation to normative society and allows it to set aside social distinction."[16] Second, unlike Bourne and many of the other apologists, O'Bryan makes no reference to 1 Corinthians 1:27, associating the prophetic ministry of women with God's use of foolish or inferior instruments. Adam Clarke had even drawn a parallel in his biblical commentary between women and Balaam's ass—not intentionally demeaning women, but inferring God's use of any means of proclamation in exceptional situations. Nothing of this appears in O'Bryan's defense. As Lloyd observes, "Throughout his life O'Bryan remained convinced that women could equal or surpass men as preachers, and that their ministry was both vital and justified."[17]

13. Only the opening paragraphs are reproduced here, given the fact that the remainder of the document marshals exactly the same arguments, particularly against the conventional objections, discussed previously.

14. Lloyd, *Women and British Methodism*, 75. Not the *Arminian Magazine* of the Wesleyan Methodists.

15. Ibid., 75–76.

16. Ruether and McLaughlin, *Women of Spirit*, 21.

17. Lloyd, *Women and British Methodism*, 76.

John Stamp (c. 1808–47) became a Primitive Methodist local preacher around 1831, partnering in his ministry with two successive wives, who were both effective preachers.[18] He and his first wife gained a reputation for being successful revivalists in Louth. Concerning Stamp's last year as a Primitive Methodist itinerant, Robert Glen reports that "he became involved in increasingly acrimonious conflicts with connexional authorities, and as a result, he was expelled from the connexion at the conference held in Reading in June 1841. He soon moved to Hull where he established the Primitive Methodist New Connexion."[19] That same year he published *The Female Advocate* (Document 25) in which he articulated a well-ordered defense of the ministry of women. Glen speculates that the declining interest among the Primitive Methodist leaders to continue to appoint female itinerants around 1840, in particular, may have contributed to Stamp's alienation from that community, but precisely how his advocacy of women affected this relationship remains unclear. In one of the most thorough defenses of women in this early period, Stamp divided his forty-three-page treatise into eight substantive sections demonstrating the scriptural, historical, and practical justification of women's ministry. He answered objections, demonstrated inconsistencies among his detractors, and provided practical advice. Some parts of his defense are drawn directly from O'Bryan's "Discourse." Stamp indicated that his primary interest was to encourage women called to preach to embrace their God-given vocation.

At its onset, revivalist Methodism in the opening decades of the nineteenth century had significant apologists for the ministry of women, but within a generation, even within these movements, the doors of opportunity for women began to close and would not open again until another century. In her examination of the origins of Primitive Methodism, Sandy Calder draws an interesting conclusion about the place of women preachers in this movement as opposed to parent Wesleyan Methodism. "While the Primitive Methodist Church boasted of its embrace of untutored and women preachers," she argues, "in practice it restricted them to a niche role fairly early and phased them out rapidly. In contrast, the Wesleyans claimed to have ruled out their use early but quietly continued to employ them for some decades. Rhetoric, as so often in Primitive Methodist Church/Wesleyan Methodist comparisons diverged much more than reality."[20]

18. I am most grateful to John Lenton, Dorothy Graham, Robert Glen, and D. Colin Dews for their helpful communications on the life and ministry of John Stamp, June 21, 2016.

19. Glen, "Writings of Stamp," 5–6.

20. Calder, *Origins of Primitive Methodism*, 123.

DOCUMENT 22

Remarks on the Ministry of Women (1808), 1–2
Hugh Bourne

Agreeably to my promise I shall endeavor to give you a few remarks on the subject of women's ministry, though I have not been accustomed to study this controversy for the following reasons, which have been established among a few of us.

1. If persons who exercise in the ministry are of good report and the Lord owns their labors by turning sinners to righteousness, we do not think it our duty to endeavor to hinder them; but we wish them success in the name of the Lord without respect to persons.

2. We do not think it right to be the cause of any one's going to hell through a proud and fond desire of establishing our own (perhaps vain) opinions.

3. Instead of stopping to reason about various things, we find it best to be pressing on.

4. In general, instead of engaging in useless controversy, we find it more profitable to continue giving ourselves to God and spending the time in prayer. But my friends from time to time have spoken to me on this subject and from their observations and from other remarks I shall endeavor to answer your friend's propositions and objections.

DOCUMENT 23

Minutes of the First Conference of the Bible Christians (1819), 4–6

Q. 4. What are our thoughts on female preaching?

A. First, we believe God can enable a woman as well as a man to "Speak to edification, and exhortation, and comfort."

Secondly, God has promised or declared that females shall prophesy in his name (Joel 2:28–29). Thus we see divine inspiration of females, and female prophesying, was to accompany the great outpouring of the Spirit of God which had its dawn on the day of Pentecost and was to shine to a perfect day, not to be confined to the nation of the Jews *only*, but to extend to all and in the end to fill the whole earth. This is plainly the sense to which

Peter applied it. "And it shall come to pass in the last days, says God, I will pour out of my Spirit upon all flesh, and your sons and your daughters shall prophesy, and your young men shall see visions, and your old men shall dream dreams; and on my servants and on my handmaidens I will pour out in those days of my Spirit and they shall prophesy" (Acts 2:17–18).

Thirdly, it has been practiced in different ages.

Fourthly, in our days as well as heretofore, the Lord has owned their labors in *turning many to righteousness* through their word, and what but this is the end of all preaching? Namely, that sinners may be converted to God and eternally saved. We believe we ought to praise God that the kingdom of darkness is shaken and the kingdom of the Redeemer is enlarged whoever be the instruments God is pleased to use. We dare not be so insolent as to dictate to him who he shall employ to accomplish his gracious purposes.

Q. 5. But do not many object to female preaching?

A. Yes, and we are sorry on the part of the detractors that they have so far committed themselves as to oppose it without ever producing an argument (worth being called an argument) against it. We have seen a *little* tract or hand bill, printed at Helston, and sold by a Mr. H—signed *Methodius*, most probably his own compiling, which is *every way* so *little* that we thought it beneath our notice to answer it in any other way than by silent contempt, as the common sense of the reader would be a sufficient reply.

Q. 6. What is the chief objection to women's preaching?

A. Their strong fort, or (as they suppose) impregnable castle, are the words of Paul: "Let your women keep silence in the churches, for it is not permitted unto them to speak, but they are commanded to be under obedience, as also says the law. And if they will learn anything, let them ask their husbands at home, for it is a shame for women to speak in the church" (1 Cor 14:34–35). This is argued as if given to be a positive rule, strictly to forbid *all* female speech in public assemblies. But how inconsistent with this their *avowed opinion* do most of those objectors act! At the same time they allow women to *sing* in their public assemblies, others allow them to *pray* vocally, and some do allow them to *teach* and *instruct* the Societies (or those in church fellowship) also, which is in the strictest sense of the word the "church!" The church is always considered to be those in *church fellowship*. For in all the churches that we have any knowledge of, they allow their women either to sing, or pray, or instruct the church; yes, in some places they permit them to exercise in all these, and yet say, *Women ought to keep silence in the churches!!!* What a heap of inconsistencies!!! "If I build again the things which I destroyed, I make myself a transgressor" (Gal 2:18).

Q. 7. But does the above scripture (1 Cor 14:34–35) prohibit women from giving pious public instruction?

A. Surely not. Paul was too *pious* to oppose *piety* and too *wise* to *oppose himself* which he must have done if he had opposed pious women speaking on pious subjects to the edification of others. We never hear him saying that any *woman* preached out of envy and strife, but it appears as though some men did (Phil 1:15). Thinking to add to his afflictions, yet even concerning such he says, I will rejoice that Christ is preached. We may observe here that he did not desire to monopolize the preaching of the gospel to himself, to make merchandise of it, but rejoiced at the spread of truth by *whomever* it was published. Moreover if he had opposed women's preaching in this place, in the same Epistle he advises: "Every woman who prays or prophesies with her head uncovered dishonors her head; Let her be covered" (1 Cor 11:5–6). Which at least must amount to an approval of her praying and prophesying, which praying and prophesying, in this place, is applied *equally* to the *woman* as to the *man*.

DOCUMENT 24

"A Discourse in Vindication of Females" (1823), 405–11, 413–14, 418–25
William O'Bryan

And it shall come to pass afterwards that I will pour out my Spirit upon all flesh; and your sons and your daughters shall prophesy (Joel 2:28).

That these words refer to the gospel dispensation is beyond a doubt, but how far their meaning extends is what we have now to consider. And may the Holy Spirit at this time reveal the things of God and show them unto us.

In the first place, let us consider the nature of the promise contained in the text.

Secondly, consider the manner of its fulfillment.

Thirdly, take notice of the instruments which were foretold should be employed therein.

First, the promise contained in the text was a promise of the Holy Ghost which in the latter days should be given to mankind, or in others words, *to all flesh*. The term *afterwards* is by Peter in the second chapter of the Acts of the Apostles called *the last days*, which is the gospel dispensation, or as some term it, *the days of the Messiah*. The gospel dispensation being the last dispensation before the millennium (and under the reign of the Messiah all shall be endued with the Holy Spirit, all then being Christians, all will know the Lord). Christ is to believers what Adam was to his posterity. Adam through his sin separated all his posterity from God; Christ by His righteousness unites them to God. Adam by his transgression was separated from God and broken off as a branch is broken from the tree. Of consequence, all those souls that were contained in his loins were broken off also; but that no one shall be everlastingly lost for Adam's sin, God sent His Son into the world that the world through him might be saved. And Christ says, "Lo, I come to do your will, O God." Now those that are lost are not lost because Adam sinned, but because they would not be saved agreeable to God's method of salvation through faith in his Son Jesus Christ. Through this true believers receive the Holy Ghost and become *one Spirit with the Lord* (1 Cor 6:17) and so are again united to God.

Secondly, that this may appear more plainly I would consider the manner in which God is pleased to work.

None can be saved from death hereafter (or the second death) but those who are saved from death here in this world. To be saved from death in this world is to obtain the Holy Spirit, which is the Spirit of life by Christ Jesus (Rom 8:2–10). None can receive the Spirit of life except those who believe in Christ in a right way, or as the Apostle Paul expresses it, "With the heart unto righteousness" (Rom 10:10). Christ received the Spirit without measure (John 3:34). He imparts this Spirit to whom he will and in what measure he pleases according to the unerring counsel of infinite wisdom. By the Spirit of Christ, which is the Spirit of God, lost man is brought back and united to God through Christ and through Christ only.

Hereby, man is made one with Christ, and Christ is one with God. This is a great mystery to the carnal man, but no more great than gloriously true. Hereby believers become spiritually one with Christ, as mankind were naturally one in Adam, and are restored not only to the favor but also to the image of God being made *partakers of the divine nature* (2 Pet 1:4).

There have been different measures of the Spirit, or spiritual influences, given to the children of men under different dispensations and in different ages, and in different degrees to different persons in the same age. In one place, it is compared to dew (Hos 14:5). In another place, to showers (Ezek 34:26). But here it is spoken of as a flood or stream. God says, I will pour out my spirit upon all flesh, which implies an extraordinary degree of the presence and power of God in the soul, in such a manner and measure as had not been given before. This dispensation was to be marked with an abundance of peace, love, and joy, in the Holy Ghost. Enlarged views, clear manifestations, and understanding of the ways of God with men all combined with qualifications to declare this to others for their edification. This may be gathered from all previous promises and confirmed by that promise which was given on the day of Pentecost. Before the day of Pentecost it is said, *He that believes on me, as the Scripture has said, out of his belly shall flow rivers of living water* (John 7:38). *But he spoke this of the Spirit which they that believe on him should receive: for the Holy Ghost was not yet given; because Jesus was not yet glorified* (v. 39). Again, Jesus said to his disciples, *I tell you the truth. It is expedient for you that I go away, for if I go not away the Comforter will not come unto you. But if I depart, I will send him unto you* (John 16:7).

It is also plain from what followed the outpouring of the Spirit on the day of Pentecost that it was such as they had not hitherto known: *The multitude were confounded at it and were all amazed and marveled* (Acts 2:6–7). It is particularly noticed that the disciples were all filled with the Holy Ghost. They were cleansed from sin before the crucifixion. Jesus said, *Now ye are clean through the word which I have spoken to you* (John 15:3), but they were not *filled* with the Holy Ghost until the day of Pentecost. Then it was said that they were all *filled* with the Holy Ghost. They had been made clean through the word but were afterwards *filled with the Spirit*. It will be well to keep this in memory as being two distinct operations on and in the soul. Taking notice of this may prevent many mistakes. Being filled with the Holy Ghost was the great qualification for the ministry. Jesus said unto the disciples, *Behold I send the promise of my Father upon you, but tarry in the city of Jerusalem until you are endued with power from on high* (Luke 24:49). This was fulfilled on the day of Pentecost.

They were *all filled* with the Holy Ghost and spoke with other tongues as the Spirit gave them utterance. It should be noted here that the speaking in a different tongue from their own was for the profit of those present whose language that was. It is not necessary now for either the man or the woman to speak a language the people do not understand in order to be rendered useful. On the contrary, they must speak so the hearers may understand. Yet, in another sense now, all that are filled with the Holy Ghost speak with new tongues. Their language, which before was carnal and earthly, is now spiritual and heavenly. Their tongues are loosed to tell of that grace, and mercy, and love of God to which before they were strangers. It is this unction of the Holy One that is given to teach the teachers of mankind.

This fullness of the Spirit is the nature of heaven. It is this which makes the children of God so happy under the dispensation of the Spirit, and the nearer the millennium draws on the more of this may we expect, and the more this is experienced, the more will those who publish the glad tidings of the gospel increase. For more thereby will be prepared for the great work of the ministry. I believe hundreds more would be sent forth to publish salvation if they lived close to God and enjoyed this Christian privilege. This is like leaven which a woman took and hid in meal till the whole was leavened.

As the leaven leavens the meal, and that leavened meal leavens other meal, so those who receive the Spirit of God reveal it to others and point out to them the way to obtain it. As they spread the knowledge of the truth, the Spirit is given and as the Spirit is given, so some are qualified and sent to spread the knowledge of the truth. Christ calls this gift of the Holy Ghost the *power from on high* (Luke 24:49), by which divine power, or Holy Ghost sent down from heaven, the gospel was preached in the apostolic age (1 Pet 1:12) and stands as a directory for future ages.

Thirdly, this leads us more particularly to notice the instruments which God foretold should be employed in this great work of preaching the gospel or prophesying.

There, our text says, shall be *your sons and your daughters*—the sons and daughters of men or both *men* and *women*. Then it follows that women, as well as men, may prophesy. The Scripture declares in unequivocal terms that they did in the days of the apostles, *Phillip the evangelist—the same man had four daughters, virgins, which did prophesy* (Acts 21:8–9). The sacred historian is very particular in the reference to this subject. The number of the names of the *disciples* together were about an hundred and twenty (Acts 1:15), and in the second chapter it says that they were *all* in one place. And they were all filled with the Holy Ghost and began to speak as the Spirit gave them utterance.

Doubtless there were women who belonged to the church as well as men. Some women went to the sepulcher and were the first that were favored with a proof of the resurrection of Jesus, whom he commissioned to bear the tidings to the apostles (Matt 28). Mark and Luke bear testimony to the same, only Luke is a little more express. In recording the conversation which passed between Jesus and the disciples going to Emmaus (Luke 24:22) he mentions the disciples calling those women who went to the sepulcher, *certain women of our company*, which certainly means women belonging to the company of the disciples. Therefore they were counted in the number. Then it follows they too were filled with the Holy Ghost which is the great qualification for preaching the gospel of glad tidings to others. For who is so well qualified to describe a thing to another as he that has experienced it himself. Then it follows, if women have the gift of the Holy Ghost, women have *power from on high*. It is plain by the context that this gift was to enable them to publish Christ in Spirit and with power. It also follows that women may publish Christ in Spirit and with power, that is, women may prophesy as well as men. Christ makes no exceptions anywhere in the Bible against women publishing the glad tidings of the gospel. Though some have dared to oppose it, yet it is a dangerous presumption for man to do so. On the contrary, Christ permitted and sent women at different times to publish the gospel of glad tidings while he was here on earth. It was the gospel or glad tidings which Christ permitted the woman of Samaria to publish to its inhabitants. It was the gospel of glad tidings which Christ sent the women to publish at his resurrection. It is true, we do not find that Christ appointed them to elegant chapels, lofty pulpits, and fine soft cushions with those high sounding titles of Reverend, or Right Reverend, or most Reverend attached to them. Nor do we find that he ever ordained such for the men. But God expressly says, *daughters* (that is females) who had received his Spirit should prophesy—this is clear and cannot be denied.

So, under this brighter dispensation, the dispensation of the Spirit, he has at different times chosen those of both sexes, the sons and daughters of men, whom he has seen fit. He enabled them to declare his word and will to mankind. Having known the terrors of the Lord themselves, they have persuaded others. Having been converted themselves, they have strengthened their brethren. Having received the gift of the Holy Ghost themselves, they have been enabled to cry to others, "Behold the Lamb of God which takes away the sins of the world," and have been enabled to set to their seal that God is true. They have testified that God gives life to the dead—His Holy Spirit to them that ask him. Have men done this? Yes. And so have women too with much success, and God has owned the work for his. This, in brief, is what I understand by prophesying, let it be, either by men or by women, it does not matter if God be the author and the salvation of souls be the end.

I admire the wisdom of God in calling women to preach the gospel. The woman was first in the transgression and through her God gave his Son to the world. The serpent deceived the woman and the seed of the woman (not the seed of the man) bruised the serpent's head. Nevertheless the man and woman mutually brought sin into the world and the promise is that they shall be mutual instruments in spreading the knowledge of that salvation which shall at last prevail against sin and root it out of the world. The gospel prepares the way for the millennium. In the millennium, sin shall be destroyed, everlasting righteousness brought in, and all shall know the Lord from the least to the greatest. And the nearer the millennium draws on, most likely, the more will women preachers increase. I have long since thought Joel had a view of the very day in which we live and the work now going on; the more women preachers increase the more, I hope, will the life, power, and simplicity of the gospel spread.

To conclude let me address a few words to those who may have been opposed to women's preaching. On what ground did you oppose it? Was it because they have done harm by their preaching? I believe not. I never yet met with anyone who brought this as an argument against it, that they any more than men, have done any harm this way. It is possible that women, as well as men may run before they are sent, but this argument does not apply to women more than to men. Some have said women have not so strong intellectual powers as men have. Perhaps in general they have not. But some women have minds as well informed as the generality of men: witness Queen Elizabeth. Was she not in her day counted one of the first politicians in Europe? Under whose reign the English nation arrived to such importance as it seems it never had known before. Has every man who is called to preach natural abilities sufficient to govern a kingdom? If he has not, that objection falls to ground, for we find some women have had abilities for rule and government.

Time and limits fail me to recite the multitude of women who in sacred and profane history are famous for their wisdom, discretion, eloquence, and learning. And how weak the argument that women have not good sense enough to prophesy, to do that work which God has declared he has appointed them to do! I hope in future men will not display *their* want of *good sense* by again raising this pitiful objection. Then if women have had abilities to fill the place of kings, judges, and advocates, may they not have ability to speak of what they themselves experience of the things of God? But let it be remembered, it is not human wisdom, not the wisdom of this world nor of the princes of this world that converts souls. *Not by might nor by power, but by my Spirit, says the Lord of Hosts. Jesus says, The Spirit of truth which proceeds from the Father, He shall testify of Me* (John 15:26). And again, *He shall take of mine and shall show it unto you* (John 16:15). Agreeable herewith Paul prays, *The grace of our Lord Jesus Christ, and the love of God, and the communion of the Holy Ghost, be with you all, Amen* (2 Cor 13:14). It is by the communications of the Holy Spirit that anyone can prophesy or be a mouth for God. Therefore it is not human wisdom, but the Spirit of God, that does the work. And it is by this Spirit that holy men and holy women have spoken in the name of the Lord. And the Lord says, I will pour out my Spirit upon them and they shall prophesy.

From this I argue that whenever God qualifies and sends women to prophesy, it is their duty to obey, and stand forth, and bear witness to the truth. We know in courts of judicature that women, as well as men, are admitted as witnesses even in cases of life and death. God calls those whom he chooses to declare his name, his *witnesses* (Isa 43:10). In the instructions which our Lord gave to the disciples after his resurrection concerning their future proceedings in the ministry, he calls them *witnesses*. He opened their understanding that they might understand the Scriptures and said unto them, *Thus it is written, and thus it behooved Christ to suffer and to rise from the dead the third day; and that repentance and remission of sins should be preached in his name among all nations, beginning at Jerusalem. And you are witnesses of these things* (Luke 24:45, 48). Matthew records Jesus adding to the commission of the disciples, *And lo, I am with you always, even unto the end of the world* (Matt 28:20). This proves that all to the end of the world who are employed in like manner are witnesses for Jesus and witnesses for the truth. They must experience the truth themselves. And though all who experience the truth are not altogether in the same sense witnesses (they being only such as God shall think fit to select and send forth), yet all witnesses must experience the same truth—repentance, remission of sin, and the gift of the Holy Ghost.

We shall see this more clearly by comparing the above text in Luke 24:46–48 with Acts 1:8. *But you shall receive power after the Holy Ghost is come upon you. And you shall be witnesses unto me both in Jerusalem and all Judea and in Samaria and unto the uttermost part of the earth.* By this it appears clear that the preachers of the gospel or the Lord's *witnesses* are those, whether men or women, who have experienced themselves that salvation which they preach to others the substance of which is repentance, faith and holiness. True witnesses are not those who speak by the vague report of others, but those who testify from *their own knowledge*, what they have heard, or seen, or felt themselves. As women have experienced repentance toward God, and the forgiveness of sins, and the gift of the Holy Ghost, as well as men, and it cannot be denied, I see no reason why they may not bear witness to these truths as well as men. Had women been improper witnesses of the truth, surely Jesus would have pointed them out as such in the Bible (our complete rule both in faith and practice). But on the contrary, as had been already proved, he sent them forth after his resurrection, his witnesses, and he still uses them as such, hundreds know. Therefore they are not to be rejected, but received as the messengers of Christ.

In advocating the cause of women's preaching, I would not be misunderstood to mean that women should run before they are sent and counterfeit the gift of God by learning others' sermons. They should not learn skeletons and attach thereto a few passages from commentators and by much labor and art frame a fine discourse to please their hearers, gain loaves and fishes, acquire applause, and shine in stolen raiment, as too many *men* do. "Stealing the word of the Lord everyone from his neighbor" is not prophesying or preaching, but reciting as children do their lessons at school. No, I do not mean that women should act in this way. First they need to gain an experimental knowledge of the things of God, and if God sends them forth to declare his righteousness to others, not to be disobedient. They should then go and preach the preaching that he bids them as the

Spirit shall give them utterance. According to this rule, God has declared they shall speak or prophesy, and this is all that I contend for.

Would not the time of those who oppose the zealous efforts of holy women in bringing souls to Christ be better employed in striving to bring souls to Christ also? Or would it not be wiser in them to oppose that sort of preaching, so called, that moves by worldly interest and which is fraught with human policy? Surely we ought to countenance that of which God is the author and set our face against that which he abhors. There are at present, I believe, above a hundred women in our Connexion who speak in public. I do not know that they learn the sermons of others and repeat them in the pulpit for their own. Nor should I like for them ever to attempt to carry on this sort of traffic. But it is well known that some *men* learn skeletons by heart and attach borrowed or rather stolen pieces to them and vend them for sermons of their own. A pious friend of mine, being one day in Cornwall, went to hear preaching and heard a sermon that he was acquainted with before, having heard the clergyman of his parish read it in the church. Afterwards going into a friend's house and taking up a book, he saw the same sermon. Having heard it so often, he was well acquainted with it and knew it to be the same. A very near relation of mine, one Lord's Day heard a sermon delivered as if it were an *extempore* one. After preaching, her uncle with whom she returned took a volume of sermons which he had in his house and read the same sermon nearly word for word.

These are not the only instances of the kind that have been discovered. Perhaps these sort of preachers, or rather *reciters*, do not know how often they are talked of and what others think of them. Few are faithful enough to tell them of it. I have heard of a woman that once, after preaching, commended the preacher's memory and naming the author of the sermon told the reciter that he had done the author justice for he had missed only one word in the discourse. No wonder that those who only feed the people with words and preach to amuse their hearers, fall asleep and their congregations too. In time it becomes an old tale, dry and stale like a "moldy crust," containing neither life nor power. From such pastors, O Lord deliver us! I recommend my readers to read Jeremiah 23:9. There appears to have been some such in his day on which account he was heartbroken. The Lord is against such, no matter how much they may be esteemed by those who like to sleep in their sins undisturbed. *Therefore, behold, I am against the prophets, says the Lord, that steal my words everyone from his neighbor* (Jer 23:30). The Lord is against such and declares he will feed them with wormwood and make them drink the water of gall.

Therefore, this is what every good man should be set against, that which God is so much against, namely, the lulling souls asleep in their sins by amusing them with words instead of crying aloud and urging on them the necessity of a speedy turning to God. This is what every good man should be against: instead of opposing those, who at the command of the Lord, are striving to save souls from hell, and who for this purpose have submitted to that painful part of the cross of leaving their homes, families, near and dear friends. They have gone forth and exposed themselves to hunger, cold, toil and labor, night and day, purely to do the will of God. Is it possible that a good man can be hostile to these? I believe it is impossible.

To conclude, I address a few words to my female friends who labor in the gospel. My dear *sisters* whom the Lord has called and sent forth to be witnesses for Himself. Fear not, nor be dismayed at the reviling of men, for God, even your God, will come and save you. Only be faithful and keep up the communion between God and your souls so as always to live under the sweet influences of His Holy Spirit. This is your strong hold. This is what you have to trust to. Everything short of this will fail you. This is the salt that seasons others. This is the true leaven which a woman took, and blessed be God, many *women*, as well as men, have taken. Use it wisely and carefully, By and by we shall see the whole lump of mankind leavened. For the earth shall be full of the knowledge of the Lord as the waters cover the sea. Then there will be no need to preach (to say to our neighbor, know the Lord) for all will know Him from the least to the greatest. Then the faithful cross-bearers shall be glorious crown-wearers. Then they that turn many to righteousness shall shine as the stars; yes, at last, shine as the sun in the kingdom of their Father.

Thus after a little toil you shall enjoy an eternal rest. Fear not little flock for it is your Father's good pleasure to give you the kingdom. Remember, Jesus says "Lo I am with you always." He will be with you all in the end. The Rock of living water will follow you. Also he says, "Where I am, there shall my servant be, to behold the glory that I had with the Father before the world was." Remember, the seed of the woman was once a preacher; and a despised, laborious preacher. Take courage, my sisters, you will soon be with him for ever and ever. And the more souls you win for Christ, the more glorious will your crown be. Eternal glory will be a good reward for a little affliction and toil here below.

May God of his infinite mercy enable each of us to fulfill the good pleasure of his will, and at last hear the welcome word, "You have been faithful over a few things, I will make you ruler over many things; enter into the joy of the Lord. Amen and Amen."

DOCUMENT 25

The Female Advocate; or, The Preaching of Women (1841), 1, 13, 15,
18–19, 25, 34, 39–40, 42–45
John Stamp

I am a staunch advocate of female preaching, and if in this I err, I err with
prophets, apostles, martyrs, fathers, Wesley, Clarke, Pawson, Fletcher,
Bramwell, and nearly all the fathers of the Methodists, the Quakers, Bible
Christians, Primitive Methodists, Wesleyan Association New Connexion,
and tens of thousands of the Wesleyans; yes, more, with Jesus Christ and the
whole of the Bible. Therefore, I shall endeavor to prove:

That female preaching is scriptural.

That it was the usage of the primitive church.

I am to show that female preaching is in accordance with old
Methodism.

Nearly all the first race of Methodist preachers were favorable to female preaching, not merely winked at it, but were strong advocates of it.

I am now to show, that God has owned their labors.

It is well known that the Bible Christians are most staunch advocates
of female preaching. They employ nearly twenty of them as itinerants and
many more as local preachers. God has owned their labors not a little. Some
years ago Miss Ann Corey, a preacher in that Connexion, visited different
parts of Kent and God slew sinners by heaps under her. Mrs. O'Bryan and
the two Miss O'Bryans were the means, in God's hand, of the conversion of
hundreds. Most persons of any standing in the religious world have heard
of the great success attending the labors of the late Miss Carr and Miss Williams, who have been itinerating throughout the kingdom for nearly thirty
years. Thousands, no doubt, will bless God through all eternity that ever
they heard them. They are still preaching. Dorothy Ripley crossed the Atlantic ten times, and hundreds, yes, thousands, were saved under her ministry
in America.

Mrs. Zilpha Elaw, a lady of color, has traveled throughout America
as a kind of evangelist during the last eighteen years, preaching amongst
different sections of the church. She is a Wesleyan preacher. In 1840 she
visited England bringing with her credentials properly signed by preachers,
stewards, and leaders. She spent twelve weeks with me in my circuit in Kent

and God owned her word as he had done in her father's land. She intends visiting the principal towns in England, God willing, before she returns.

I have now to show that it is the duty of all Christians to help females in this important work to which God has called them. If it be asked, how are we to know if they are called of God to preach, we answer that we must judge the same way as we do the call of men. Is God with them and souls saved by them? Are devils cast out, and men, women, and children turned from sin to holiness and from Satan to God? Have they gifts, grace, and fruit? If so, it is at your peril that you stop them. You will go to the bar of God covered with the blood spots of guilt. But it is not sufficient that you let them alone. No! You must encourage them. They need encouragement. Paul helped them and often urged his companions in the ministry to do the same. In one place he says, "Help those beloved women who labored with me in the gospel, who have labored with Clement, and with others, my fellow-laborers, whose names are in the book of life." *Help them! Help them! Help them!* was the cry of the Apostle. If Paul, under the influence of the Holy Ghost, wrote, "Help them!" who dare refuse? These women labored with Paul and the other apostles in the *gospel*. Observe that! *in the gospel!* Not in mending stockings, carrying water, sweeping the house, and making beds, as a reverend divine sneeringly said, but laboring with the Apostle. What did he do? He preached, and they helped him.

John Wesley helped women in their labor of love as did most of the old Methodist preachers as these pages have already testified. We dare not say to the modest and pious female, "You shall not declare the word of the Lord," when we believe that, from an infinitely higher authority, there is issued a directly opposite injunction: "You shall go to all that I shall send you, and whatsoever I command you, you shall speak."

I purpose to answer the objections of certain individuals to female preaching.

I am now to show the inconsistency of those persons who forbid females' preaching, but permit them to sing, lead class, write books, or in any other way have a voice in the church.

I am now to conclude by making an application of the whole. In doing this, let me address a few words to those, first, who oppose female preaching, and second, to those handmaids who feel called of God to labor in his vineyard.

A few words to those who oppose female preaching. Let me ask, then, on what grounds do you oppose it? Is it because they do harm by their preaching? I believe not. I never met with one who ever brought this as an argument against it. Some of them may have done harm by running before they were sent with poor talent, little fruits, or unholy lives; but all these things will apply to men with equal propriety. Why, then let me ask, do you oppose them? Is it out of pure love to their souls, fearing they are endangering their immortal all, by taking upon them an office to which they are not called by God, and lying to the Holy Ghost and telling him he had thus called them to preach? Do you observe those handmaids who thus speak for God to be women of light trifling spirits? Do you see them high-minded, dressy gossips, in a general way? I am sure you do not. Why then, let me ask again, do you oppose them? Is it because you are so very sure that it is anti-scriptural for them to win souls, then, are you the men, and is wisdom sure to die with you? Be not be overly dogmatic. Remember that many ministers more holy and much more learned than you have been staunch supporters of a female ministry. When you have proved yourself superior to John Wesley and Dr. Adam Clarke and have refuted all they have said, your assertions then, perhaps, will have more weight with the public. Until then, pause, pray, and ask your conscience why you have opposed them when you could not help seeing that much good is done everywhere they go by their preaching.

I hope it is not envy, because God gave them so many souls for their hire, that such numbers flocked to hear them, or so many spoke well of them. Did they draw some of your hearers away and at times leave you with almost empty chapels? I admit that it is trying, but it will not do to give way to a bad spirit and instead of preaching the gospel to those who stand by spend your time in declaring how wicked it is for them to preach, and more wicked still for your hearers to leave such a man of talent as you are and go and hear them. I hope you are not offended because they get such good collections to help on the cause they have espoused. Remember you employ women to collect and praise them to the sky on the platform when they do well. The great Dr. Clarke says, "One woman is worth seven and a half men in the way of collecting."

Let me tell you, many of them can preach better than hundreds of men who have been trained for the ministry. As a proof, the writer upon good authority asserts that a clergyman of the present day of great celebrity in London has the principle part of the sermons which he reads on the Sabbath day composed by his wife. In soul saving many of them excel most men and as far as mortals can see are much more self-denying and holy than many men who have hundreds a year for preaching. And do not forget that most of the women labor for nothing. And those who are paid often only receive their traveling expenses, just enough to keep them, and not in affluence. No! They do not say put me into the priest's office for a piece of bread. Love to God and souls induced them to face the storm of persecution from wicked men, the devil, insinuations from some part of the church, and their own weakness. Yet God is with them. His right arm leads them on. And it is quite clear that as the millennium approaches, their numbers will increase. If one section of the church gets too proud to let women save souls, God will, yes, he does raise up others. Thus his handmaids shall prophesy. The army of preaching women increases daily. As one of old said of the Apostle, so say I in reference to female preaching that if this work is of men or devils, it will come to naught; but if it be of God, (and tens of thousands of wise and holy men verily believe it is), you cannot overthrow it.

Second, to those handmaids who feel themselves called to labor in God's vineyard.

My dear sisters and fellow laborers, will you suffer the word of exhortation from one who was brought to God under one of your own sex and has often seen the arm of God made bare through them more than ever he did under men. Will you pardon my asking the following questions?

Are you at this moment in the possession of an indwelling God?

Are you clear in the blessing of entire sanctification?

Have you a clear call from heaven to preach?

Do you convert sinners, not try, but do it? Where do the spiritual children live that God has given you? Can you call them by name? Women's preaching is something extraordinary. If nothing extraordinary follows, what proof have you that the Spirit has called you to so important an office in the church of God?

Do you fix your eye on God's glory in all you say or do?

If you can answer these questions in the affirmative, All hail! Then, in spite of men and devils go on, go on. Let no man, nor number of men, however high they may stand in the church, stop you, unless they can present you a certificate signed by Jesus saying that he will hold you guiltless at the day of doom. Look then, my dear sisters, at your own responsibility. Eternity is looking with all its eyes at you. Let me tell you in love and in deep toned pity that there is for you no middle destiny. It is a solemn thing to stand so near that holy Lord God!

My dear sisters, if you would swell the chorus of eternity, strike one of heaven's sweetest lyres, take your everlasting station among apostles, martyrs, confessors, and enjoy God increasingly forever. Be faithful. Preach without restraint. Intercede warmly. Invite powerfully. Persuade forcibly.

Urge incessantly the blood-bought salvation which, thank God, is as free as the air, full as the ocean, strong as the pillars of eternity's throne, and measureless as everlasting ages.

Keep in mind the thousands of souls God saved under Ann Cutler and Mary Barrett. He is the same. Expect great things, aim at great things, and believe for them, and you shall have them. Do something—*do it, do it, do it,* and do it quickly.

To serve the present age, your calling to fulfill,

Oh, may it all your powers engage, to do your Master's will.

So prays one, who deeply feels for you.

4

Autobiographical Apologetics

Introduction

Women figured prominently in the establishment of Methodist societies in the American colonies when the movement crossed the Atlantic in the 1760s with a wave of emigration from the British Isles. Through the course of the First and Second Great Awakenings, these women both shaped and were shaped by the unfolding history and culture of this new context. In a chapter related to women evangelists in *Methodism and the Shaping of American Culture*, Catherine Brekus concludes that three factors combined, in particular, to enhance the possibility of public ministry by women in this new environment: a general shortage of preachers, a belief that God could speak directly to and through any person, and a theology that stressed the spiritual equality of all believers."[1] Her research revealed more than twenty women who engaged in itinerant ministries of preaching and evangelism from 1784—the year the Methodist Episcopal Church was founded in the new republic—to the middle of the nineteenth century. While many of these women have been forgotten, Brekus claims that "they caused a sensation among Methodists in early national and antebellum America."[2] Four African American women preachers stand out among their sisters and brothers during the nineteenth century: Jarena Lee, Zilpha Elaw, Julia A. J. Foote, and Amanda Berry Smith. These women are remembered, in part, because they

1. Brekus, "Female Evangelism."
2. Ibid., 152.

left behind remarkable autobiographical accounts of their indefatigable labor. These publications functioned as apologies for the ministry of women.[3]

Jarena Lee (1783–1850?) launched black women's autobiography in America with the publication of her *Life and Religious Experience* in 1836 (Document 26).[4] Although Lee never defined this memoir explicitly as a defense of women in ministry, William Andrews notes that she argued for "women's spiritual authority that plainly challenged traditional female roles as defined in both the free and slave states, among whites as well as blacks."[5] Born free in New Jersey in 1783, Lee joined Philadelphia's Bethel African Methodist Episcopal Church (AMEC) after her conversion in 1804. Following a period of severe emotional and spiritual struggle—including three episodes of suicidal inclinations—she prayed for and experienced sanctification. Priscilla Pope-Levison notes that she was the first African American woman to record this experience for others to read.[6] About five years later, in 1811, she felt called to preach and sought to obtain a preacher's license, but was rebuffed by the founding pastor of Bethel Church, Richard Allen. In 1819 she demonstrated her gift and call dramatically by exhorting the same congregation extemporaneously after having interrupted the inept preacher in the pulpit. This time, instead of chastising her, Bishop Allen endorsed her call and encouraged her expanding ministry. Lee embarked on the "lonely, self-sacrificing life of an itinerant evangelist"—to borrow Brekus's phrase—that carried her from Philadelphia into New York and Maryland, and as far west as Ohio.[7] The editors of *The Methodist Experience in America* report that "in one year in the 1820s, she claimed to have traveled more than two thousand miles and preached more than one hundred seventy-five sermons."[8] Constantly besieged by opponents of female preachers, Lee recounted confrontational incidents on almost every page of the expanded edition of her *Life*, published in 1849.

Like Lee, Zilpha Elaw (c. 1790–1846?), also a free black woman, was drawn to the Methodists and joined one of the small societies outside

---

3. See Andrews, *Sisters of the Spirit*, for the full accounts of Lee, Elaw, and Foote; cf. Houchins, *Spiritual Narratives*.

4. On Lee, her ministry, and autobiography, see Haynes, *Radical Spiritual Motherhood*; Foster, "Neither Auction Block nor Pedestal"; and McKay, "Nineteenth-Century Autobiographies." The excerpts from Lee's autobiography reprinted below are taken from the expanded 1849 edition.

5. Andrews, *Sisters of the Spirit*, 2.

6. Pope-Levison, *Turn the Pulpit Loose*, 27.

7. Brekus, "Female Evangelism," 135.

8. Richey, Rowe, and Schmidt, *Methodist Experience in America*, 1:150.

Philadelphia in 1808 as a consequence of seeing a vision of Jesus.[9] Having moved with her husband to New Jersey, in 1817 she attended her first camp meeting, fell into a trance, and received the gift of sanctification. Reminiscent of medieval women like Julian of Norwich and Hildegard of Bingen, during an extended illness of two years she experienced what she considered to be angelic visitations. After her recovery she resumed an evangelistic ministry of expanding proportions despite her husband's attempts to thwart her. After the death of her husband in 1823 she opened a school for black children in Burlington, but soon thereafter felt called to a ministry preaching among the slaves in Maryland and Virginia. In 1840 she responded to God's call to ministry in England, where she preached over a thousand sermons in London and the Midlands. It was in some measure due to the hostility and heavy criticism she received from Anglican clergy who opposed women in ministry that she published her *Memoirs* (Document 27) in London in 1846.

Julia A. J. Foote (1823–1901) joined the African Methodist Episcopal Zion Church (AMEZC) in Boston soon after her move there with her new husband in 1841.[10] In parallel fashion to the spiritual narratives of her female colleagues, Foote linked her sense of calling to her experience of holiness. When she began to exercise her ministry, however, she immediately encountered resistance, even to the holding of meetings in her own home, and was removed from the membership list of her church on the charge of schism. Persevering through opposition related to her gender, race, and spiritual eccentricities at nearly every turn, she preached as an itinerant holiness evangelist for half a century. She published her autobiography, *A Brand Plucked from the Fire*, in 1879 (Document 28). The title, alluding to Zechariah 3:2, may have been a veiled reference to the providential rescue of John Wesley as a child, whom his mother Susanna described thereafter as a "brand plucked from the burning." In 1894 Bishop Hood, one of the few bishops supporting the ministry of women, ordained her as the first female deacon in the AME Zion Church; just prior to her death in 1900 she was ordained an elder, only the second to hold this office in her denomination.

In his examination of the lives of these three women, Andrews discerned a clear consequence of the experience of conversion they all held in common. This spiritual transformation provided "a very real sense of freedom from a prior 'self' and a growing awareness of unrealized, unexploited

---

9. On Elaw, her ministry, and autobiography, see Douglass-Chin, *Preacher Woman*, and LaPrade, "Pens in the Hand of God."

10. On Foote, her ministry, and autobiography, see Sawyer, "Julia Foote," and Douglass-Chin, *Preacher Woman*.

powers within."[11] Moreover, the connection of their call to the subsequent experience of sanctification fueled their passion for faithfulness in response to the work of the Holy Spirit. As Andrews describes it, their experience of sanctification bestowed a serene confidence and "ample sanction for acts that many, especially men, would judge as rebelliously self-assertive and destructive of good order in the church."[12] Sanctification conferred a sense of total harmony with God's will, self-worth and ultimate value, and spiritual power oriented toward the liberation of others, as well as the ability to trust the promptings from God they received in their daily lives from the Spirit. This interrelationship of sanctification, the Holy Spirit, and ministerial vocation loomed large, as well, in the holiness movement of the nineteenth century of which they were a part.

Amanda Berry Smith (1837–1915), a younger contemporary of Foote and an AME preacher, owed much to the holiness movement as well, having felt her call to preach during the holiness revivals that sprung up at the time of the American Civil War.[13] Jualynne Dodson describes her as "the most internationally known of the AME preaching women between 1868 and 1900."[14] A native of Maryland, this former slave did not unite with the Methodists until after the Civil War in 1865. By 1869 she had been widowed twice and began an entrepreneurial itinerant preaching ministry in New Jersey and New York. She preached in camp meetings in the Northeast until experiencing a call to carry the gospel to other parts of the world. In 1876 she was invited to preach and sing in England by those who had heard about her ministry. Having completed a successful ministry there, she embarked for India and then Africa, where she spent eight years evangelizing and organizing churches. Having become something of a sensation in this wide-ranging ministry and upon her return to the United States in 1890, she began work on her autobiography, subsequently published in 1893 with the title *The Story of the Lord's Dealings with Mrs. Amanda Smith, the Colored Evangelist* (Document 29). "Her powerful preaching and her singing," claim Carl and Dorothy Schneider, "won her repute not only in the United States but also in Europe and Africa."[15]

11. Andrews, *Sisters of the Spirit*, 12.

12. Ibid., 14.

13. On Smith, her ministry, and autobiography, see Haynes, *Radical Spiritual Motherhood*, and Israel, *Amanda Berry Smith*.

14. Dodson, "Nineteenth-Century A.M.E. Preaching Women," 283.

15. Schneider, *In Their Own Right*, 81.

Brekus notes that in this era "the similarities between men's and women's memoirs are striking."[16] But there is a striking difference in the women's autobiographical apologies. While often portraying themselves as weak in the "surface plot" of their narratives, in the "submerged plot" each emerges as "a commanding prophet whose authority had come directly from God."[17] In addition, they employed a range of explicit arguments in defense of their ministries. Susan Lindley discerns at least three apologetic strategies in the autobiography of Jarena Lee.[18] (1) She appealed to an authority higher than any human institution or cultural expectation; God's direct call authenticated her ministry. (2) She pointed to the results of her preaching and the large numbers of sinners who were converted and turned to God. (3) She identified biblical precedence for the work in which she was engaged in an effort to silence those who used the Bible as a weapon against women. These three arguments appear in the other three publications as well.

Brekus provides a highly textured and nuanced study of these women's narratives and the defenses they marshaled against their opponents.[19] She argues, for instance, that all of these women developed elaborate justifications for their "right to preach." They referred to biblical heroines, argued for Mary's priority as the one to first proclaim the resurrection, countered the typical biblical prohibitions in Paul with the fulfillment of Joel's prophecy at Pentecost, laid claim to special divine revelation, and used the language of "Mothers in Israel" to defend their actions. She observes:

> Drawing on both biblical imagery and the language of republican motherhood, they both reinforced and undermined common ideas about women's domesticity. On the one hand, they seemed to root their religious authority in their traditional domestic roles as mothers and sisters, but on the other, they also identified themselves with some of the most powerful women in the Bible. . . . Mothers in Israel and Sister in Christ mixed "feminine" tenderness with "masculine" strength; they were loving nurturers, but also "bold soldiers" for Christ.[20]

But they marshaled these arguments and made these professions without transgressing the boundaries of authority established by men. "Because female preachers combined their belief in women's spiritual equality with

16. Brekus, *Strangers & Pilgrims*, 170.

17. Ibid., 180.

18. Lindley, *You Have Stept Out*, 181–82.

19. Brekus, "Female Evangelism."

20. Ibid., 160. The term "mother in Israel" was first applied to Deborah in Judges 5:7.

political conservatism, they can best be described as biblical rather than secular feminists. Instead of demanding equality with men, they continued to accept women's 'natural' subordination."[21]

Elizabeth Grammer also analyses these autobiographical defenses and demonstrates incisively how this genre functioned both to defend the women and subvert misogynist biblical interpretation.[22] In *Some Wild Visions* she illustrates from most of these sources. Julia Foote, for example, reassures her readers that some of the antipathy toward women was the consequence of poor biblical translation. The same word when used in reference to Phoebe is translated "servant," but when applied to the male Tychicus is rendered "minister."[23] In Jarena Lee's account of Richard Allen's rejection of her request for formal recognition, she portrays him "as an enemy seeking to thwart God's plan for her life," and Lee utilizes an image from the prophet Jeremiah (20:9) to indicate the way in which she was being smothered.[24] In another contentious encounter with a critic, Lee employs particularly masculine metaphors from both Testaments to present herself "as a Christian soldier doing battle with her culture's basic assumptions."[25] Along the same line as Grammer's conclusions, Mitzi Smith demonstrates how Zilpha Elaw, as a black woman struggling against constraints placed upon her by others, negotiated power relations with her own voice and pen. Rather than rejecting Pauline texts used to restrict her activities, Elaw exploits images and language from St. Paul's call narratives and reinterprets them in terms of her own spiritual experiences.[26]

The same forces related to institutionalization and the desire for respectability that led to the repression of earlier Methodist women's voices also mitigated women's ministry in these African American traditions. Jarena Lee's experience related to the publication of an expanded edition of her autobiography demonstrates this devolution. The very church leaders who had supported her in earlier years began to shun her during the 1840s when concerns for respectability and gentility were on the rise. In 1845, she requested the Book Committee of the AMEC to publish the new version of her previously successful *Life*. They responded with disdain, indicating that her autobiographical account was unintelligible. In 1849 she defied her own church, therefore, by publishing the enlarged edition at her own expense.

21. Ibid., 162.
22. Grammer, *Some Wild Visions*.
23. Ibid., 52.
24. Ibid., 98.
25. Ibid., 99.
26. Smith, "Unbossed and Unbought."

Despite the cycle of institutionalization that degenerated from affirmation to rejection, even in the case of these women, one of the threads that knit them closely together was their elevated view of the Holy Spirit and the gospel mandate of sanctification. Women found renewed support in the holiness movement that rediscovered these links.

DOCUMENT 26

The Life and Religious Experience of Jarena Lee, a Coloured Lady (1836), 10–13, 23, 38–40
Jarena Lee

Between four and five years after my sanctification, on a certain time, an impressive silence fell upon me and I stood as if someone was about to speak to me, yet I had no such thought in my heart. But to my utter surprise there seemed to sound a voice which I thought I distinctly heard, and most certainly understand, which said to me. "Go preach the gospel!" I immediately replied aloud, "No one will believe me." Again I listened and again the same voice seemed to say—"Preach the gospel. I will put words in your mouth and will turn your enemies to become your friends."

At first I supposed that Satan had spoken to me, for I had read that he could transform himself into an angel of light for the purpose of deception. Immediately I went into a secret place and called upon the Lord to know if he had called me to preach and whether I was deceived or not, when there appeared to my view the form and figure of a pulpit, with a Bible lying thereon, the back of which was presented to me as plainly as if it had been a literal fact.

In consequence of this, my mind became so exercised that, during the night following, I took a text and preached in my sleep. I thought there stood before me a great multitude while I expounded to them the things of religion. So violent were my exertions and so loud were my exclamations that I awoke from the sound of my own voice which also awoke the family of the house where I resided. Two days after I went to see the preacher in charge of the African Society, who was the Rev. Richard Allen, the same before named in these pages, to tell him that I felt it my duty to preach the gospel. But as I drew near the street in which his house was, which was in the city of Philadelphia, my courage began to fail me. So terrible did the cross appear, it seemed that I should not be able to bear it. Previous to my setting out to go to see him, so agitated was my mind that my appetite for my daily food failed me entirely. Several times on my way there I turned back again, but as often I felt my strength again renewed, and I soon found that the nearer I approached to the house of the minister, the less was my fear. Accordingly, as soon as I came to the door my fears subsided, the cross was removed, all things appeared pleasant—I was tranquil.

I now told him that the Lord had revealed it to me that I must preach the gospel. He replied by asking in what sphere I wished to move in? I said, among the Methodists. He then replied that a Mrs. Cook, a Methodist lady, had also some time before requested the same privilege, who, it was believed, had done much good in the way of exhortation and holding prayer meetings and who had been permitted to do so by the verbal license of the preacher in charge at the time. But as to women preaching, he said that our Discipline knew nothing at all about it—that it did not call for women preachers. This I was glad to hear because it removed the fear of the cross—but no sooner did this feeling cross my mind than I found that a love of souls had in a measure departed from me, that holy energy which burned within me as a fire began to be smothered. This I soon perceived.

O how careful ought we to be lest through our by-laws of church government and discipline we bring into disrepute even the word of life. For as unseemly as it may appear now-a-days for a woman to preach, it should be remembered that nothing is impossible with God. And why should it be thought impossible, heterodox, or improper for a woman to preach? Seeing the Savior died for the woman as well as for the man.

If the man may preach because the Savior died for him, why not the woman, seeing he died for her also. Is he not a whole Savior, instead of a half one, as those who hold it wrong for a woman to preach would seem to make it appear?

Did not Mary first preach the risen Savior, and is not the doctrine of the resurrection the very climax of Christianity—hangs not all our hope on this, as argued by St. Paul? Then did not Mary, a woman, preach the gospel? She preached the resurrection of the crucified Son of God.

But some will say that Mary did not expound the Scripture, therefore, she did not preach in the proper sense of the term. To this I reply, it may be that the term preach in those primitive times did not mean exactly what it is now made to mean. Perhaps it was a great deal more simple then than it is now—if it were not the unlearned fishermen could not have preached the gospel at all as they had no learning.

To this it may be replied by those who are determined not to believe that it is right for a woman to preach, that the disciples, though they were fishermen and ignorant of letters too, were inspired so to do. To which I would reply that though they were inspired, yet that inspiration did not save them from showing their ignorance of letters, and of man's wisdom. This the multitude soon found out by listening to the remarks of the envious Jewish priests. If then to preach the gospel by the gift of heaven comes by inspiration solely, is God constrained? Must he take the man exclusively? May he not, did he not, and can he not inspire a female to preach the simple story of the birth, life, death, and resurrection of our Lord and accompany it too with power to the sinner's heart. As for me, I am fully persuaded that the Lord called me to labor according to what I have received, in his vineyard. If he has not, how could he consistently bear testimony in favor of my poor labors in awakening and converting sinners?

In my wanderings up and down among men, preaching according to my ability, I have frequently found families who told me that they had not for several years been to a meeting, and yet, while listening to hear what God would say by his poor female instrument have believed with trembling—tears rolling down their cheeks, the signs of contrition and repentance towards God. I firmly believe that I have sown seed in the name of the Lord, which shall appear with its increase at the great day of accounts when Christ shall come to take up his jewels.

At a certain time I was beset with the idea that soon or late I should fall from grace and lose my soul at last. I was frequently called to the throne of grace about this matter, but found no relief. The temptation pursued me still. Being more and more afflicted with it, till at a certain time, when the spirit strongly impressed it on my mind to enter into my closet and carry my case once more to the Lord. The Lord enabled me to draw nigh to him and to his mercy seat at this time in an extraordinary manner. While I wrestled with him for the victory over this disposition to doubt whether I should persevere, there appeared a form of fire about the size of a man's hand, as I was on my knees. At the same moment there appeared to the eye of faith a man robed in a white garment from the shoulders down to the feet. From him a voice proceeded, saying: "You shalt never return from the cross." Since that time I have never doubted, but believe that God will keep me until the day of redemption. Now I could adopt the very language of St. Paul and say that nothing could have separated me from the love of God which is in Christ Jesus. Since that time, 1807, until the present, 1833, I have not even doubted the power and goodness of God to keep me from falling, through the sanctification of the spirit and belief of the truth.

In the year 1811 I changed my situation in life having married Mr. Joseph Lee, pastor of a society at Snow Hill, about six miles from the city of Philadelphia. It became necessary therefore for me to remove. This was a great trial at first as I knew no person at Snow Hill, except my husband, and to leave my associates in the society, and especially those who composed the band of which I was one. None but those who have been in sweet fellowship with such as really love God, and have together drank bliss and happiness from the same fountain, can tell how dear such company is and how hard it is to part from them.

At Snow Hill, as was feared, I never found that agreement and closeness in communion and fellowship that I had in Philadelphia among my young companions, nor ought I to have expected it. The manners and customs at this place were somewhat different, on which account I became discontented in the course of a year and began to importune my husband to remove to the city. But this plan did not suit him. As he was the Pastor of the Society he could not bring his mind to leave them. This afflicted me a little. But the Lord showed me in a dream what his will was concerning the matter.

I dreamed that as I was walking on the summit of a beautiful hill that I saw near me a flock of sheep, fair and white, as if but newly washed. There came walking toward me a man of a grave and dignified countenance dressed entirely in white, as it were, in a robe and looking at me, who said emphatically, "Joseph Lee must take care of these sheep or the wolf will come and devour them." When I awoke I was convinced of my error and immediately, with a glad heart, yielded to the right spirit in the Lord. This also greatly strengthened my faith in his care over them, for fear the wolf should by some means take any of them away. The following verse was beautifully suited to our condition, as well as to all the little flocks of God scattered up and down this land:

> Us into thy protection take,
>> And gather with Thine arm;
> Unless the fold we first forsake,
>> The wolf can never harm.

I now returned to Philadelphia where I stayed a short time and went to Salem, West Jersey. I met with many troubles on my journey, especially from the elder who like many others was averse to a woman's preaching. And here let me tell that elder, if he has not gone to heaven, that I have heard that as far back as Adam Clarke's time, his objections to female preaching were met by the answer—"If an ass reproved Balaam, and a barn-door fowl reproved Peter, why should not a woman reprove sin?" I do not introduce this for its complimentary classification of women with donkeys and fowls, but to give the reply of a poor woman who had once been a slave. To the first companion she said, "Maybe a speaking woman is like an ass—but I can tell you one thing, the ass seen the angel when Balaam didn't."

I was invited by one of the Trustees of the Old Methodist Church to pay them a visit on the ensuing Sabbath morning. I made the appointment for said day. I left Georgetown on the morning early. Half past ten o'clock we arrived in Milford. The church bell was ringing. We were conducted into the church. A local preacher was in the pulpit and had prayed but was asked to come down by another who invited me there. I spoke for them and afterwards they gave out for another appointment at night, but it caused a controversy among themselves and they threw it on him to come and see if I would fill it. Previous to this the colored preachers told me there was controversy about woman preaching. But he came and asked me how long I had been preaching the gospel. I answered, rising five or six years. He said it was something new. I told him it seemed to be supposed so. I referred him to Mrs. Fletcher of England, an able preacher and wife of Mr. Fletcher, a great and worthy minister of the parish. He asked why I did not go to the Quakers. I told him I was sent to the Methodists. I asked if he had a sister in the church and she witnessed a Christian life and was called and qualified to preach, do you think you would be justified before God to stop her? He has not answered me yet. I found it was prejudice in his mind. He talked as if he had not known what the operation of the Spirit of God was. We may say with propriety he had not tarried at Jerusalem long enough.

I met a camp meeting of the African Methodist Episcopal Church at Denton. The Elder was much encouraged in commencing the camp. Although in a slave State, we had everything in order, good preaching, a solemn time, and long to be remembered. Some of the poor slaves came happy in the Lord. Some walked from twenty to thirty, and from that to seventy miles, to worship God. Although through hardships they counted it all joy for the excellence of Christ. Before day they, or a number of them, had to be at home, ready for work. Some said they came as sinners before God but went away as new creatures in Christ, and they could not be disputed. My heart glows with joy while I write; truly God is inscrutable.

The Elder gave me an appointment and collection and I returned to Philadelphia. And on Sunday morning Bishop Allen gave me an appointment in Bethel Church and we had a shout in the Camp of Israel.

DOCUMENT 27

Memoirs of . . . Mrs. Zilpha Elaw, an American Female of Colour (1846), 126–27, 139–43
Zilpha Elaw

Having taken apartments in Well-close-square, in the evening I attended at the Countess of Huntingdon's chapel in Pell Street and heard a discourse which afforded some encouragement to the heart of a female stranger in a foreign land. Some days elapsed ere I met with any of the Methodist family, but going on the Wednesday evening again to Pell Street Chapel, as I was passing a window I caught sight of a lady whose appearance powerfully arrested my attention, and it appeared that the feeling of surprise and interest was mutual.

I turned back and spoke to her and inquired if she was acquainted with any section of the Methodist body? She said that her daughter should on the following evening conduct me to the Wesleyan Chapel of St. George, which she did accordingly. I found that several class meetings were held on that evening. On that occasion I met with Mr. A— who introduced me to Mr. C—, one of the local preachers. I was admitted into the class led by him and enjoyed a very sweet time of refreshing from the presence of the Lord.

I became also acquainted with Mrs. I—, a true sister in the Lord, who has since fallen asleep in Jesus and was introduced to a gentleman who interested himself greatly on my behalf, very considerably enlarged the circle of my acquaintance, and even ushered me before the committees of the peace and anti-slavery societies. I found my situation rather awkward in reference to the later body.

I was first received by a deputation of three gentlemen and afterwards admitted before the board. It was really an august assembly. Their dignity appeared so redundant that they scarcely knew what to do with it all. Had I attended there on a matter of life and death I think I could scarcely have been more closely interrogated or more rigidly examined. From the reception I met with my impression was that they imagined I wanted some pecuniary or other help from them, for they treated me as the proud do the needy. In this, however, they were mistaken.

Among many other questions they demanded to be informed whether I had any new doctrine to advance that the English Christians are not in possession of, to which I replied, no. But I was sent to preach Christ and Him crucified, unto the Jews a stumbling block and unto the Greeks foolishness (1 Cor 1:23). They also wished to be informed how it came about that God should send me, to which I replied that I could not tell. But I knew that God required me to come hither and that I came in obedience to His sovereign will, but that the Almighty's design therein was best known to Himself. But behold, said I, "I am here!"

Pride and arrogance are among the master sins of rational beings. A high look, a stately bearing, and a proud heart are abominations in the sight of God, and ensure a woeful reverse in a future life. Infidels will indulge in pomposity and arrogance, but Christians are and must be humble and lowly. As a servant of Jesus I am required to bear testimony in his name who was meek and lowly, against the lofty looks of man and the assumptions of such lordly authority and self-importance.

Before this work meets the eye of the public, I shall have sojourned in England five years and I am justified in saying that my God hath made my ministry a blessing to hundreds of persons. Many who were living in sin and darkness before they saw my colored face have risen up to praise the Lord for having sent me to preach his gospel on the shores of Britain. Numbers who had been reared to maturity and were resident in localities plentifully furnished with places of worship and ministers of the gospel, and had scarcely heard a sermon in their lives, were attracted to hear the colored female preacher, were enclosed in the gospel net, and are now walking in the commandments and ordinances of the Lord. I have traveled in several parts of England and I thank God He has given me some spiritual children in every place wherein I have labored.

Soon after my arrival I met with a gentleman who advised my immediate return to my own country, adding that if he had been in America before my departure and had known my intention, he would have advised me better. I replied that I had no will of my own in the matter, but my heavenly Father commanded and I durst not confer with flesh and blood, but obeyed and came. But like other men destitute of faith in God, he did not comprehend this kind of argument and persisted in his worldly reasoning, saying that people did not give away their gold here and I had much better return.

It is to be deplored that there are so many Christians of this person's kind who are of the world, speak in accordance with its principles and sentiments, and walk according to its course. Instead of having little faith, they discover none at all. Ignorant of the Scriptures and of the power of God, the love of the Father is not in them. Having parted with this Laodicean gentleman, I called upon Mrs. H— in Princes Square. My mind being somewhat damped, I sat a few minutes in silence, which Mrs. H— broke by an affectionate inquiry into my circumstances, at the same time presenting me with a handsome donation telling me not to be discouraged for the Lord would open my way and sustain me. My mind was cheered and my faith strengthened by this opportune proof of the power of God to furnish succor and raise up friends for his people even in a land of strangers.

DOCUMENT 28

A Brand Plucked from the Fire (1879), 77–81, 112–16
Julia A. J. Foote

Women in the Gospel

Thirty years ago there could scarcely a person be found in the churches to sympathize with anyone who talked of holiness. But, in my simplicity, I did think that a body of Christian ministers would understand my case and judge righteously. I was, however, disappointed.

It is no little thing to feel that every man's hand is against us and ours against every man, as seemed to be the case with me at this. I had constant access to God and a clear consciousness that he heard me, but I did not seem to have that plenitude of the Spirit that I had before. I realized most keenly that the closer the communion that may have existed, the keener the suffering of the slightest departure from God. Unbroken communion can only be retained by a constant application of the blood which cleanses.

Though I did not wish to pain anyone, neither could I please anyone only as I was led by the Holy Spirit. I saw, as never before, that the best men were liable to err, and that the only safe way was to fall on Christ, even though censure and reproach fell upon me for obeying his voice. Man's opinion weighed nothing with me, for my commission was from heaven and my reward was with the Most High.

I could not believe that it was a short-lived impulse or spasmodic influence that impelled me to preach. I read that on the day of Pentecost the scripture was fulfilled as found in Joel 2:28–29. It certainly will not be denied that women as well as men were at that time filled with the Holy Ghost because it is expressly stated that women were among those who continued in prayer and supplication, waiting for the fulfillment of the promise. Women and men are classed together, and if the power to preach the gospel is short-lived and spasmodic in the case of women, it must be equally so in that of men. And if women have lost the gift of prophecy, so have men.

We are sometimes told that if a woman pretends to a divine call and thereon grounds the right to plead the cause of a crucified Redeemer in public, she will be believed when she shows credentials from heaven, that is, when she works a miracle. If it is necessary to prove one's right to preach the gospel, I ask of my brethren to show me their credentials, or I cannot believe in the propriety of their ministry.

But the Bible puts an end to this strife when it says: "There is neither male nor female in Christ Jesus." Philip had four daughters that prophesied or preached. Paul called Priscilla, as well as Aquila, his "helper," or, as in the Greek, his "fellow-laborer" (Rom 15:3; 2 Cor 8:23; Phil 2:5; 1 Thess 3:2). The same word which in our common translation is now rendered a "servant of the church" in speaking of Phoebe (Rom 19:1) is rendered "minister" when applied to Tychicus (Eph 6:21). When Paul said, "Help those women who labor with me in the gospel," he certainly meant that they did more than to pour out tea. In 1 Corinthians 11 Paul gives directions to men and women how they should appear when they prophesy or pray in public assemblies, and he defines prophesying to be speaking to edification, exhortation and comfort.

I may further remark that the conduct of holy women is recorded in Scripture as an example to others of their sex. And in the early ages of Christianity many women were happy and glorious in martyrdom. How nobly, how heroically too, in later ages, have women suffered persecution and death for the name of the Lord Jesus.

In looking over these facts I could see no miracle wrought for those women more than in myself.

Though opposed, I went forth laboring for God, and he owned and blessed my labors and has done so wherever I have been until this day. And while I walk obediently, I know he will, though hell may rage and vent its spite.

As I left the Conference, God wonderfully filled my heart with his love so that as I passed from place to place, meeting one and another of the ministers, my heart went out in love to each of them as though he had been my father. The language came forcibly to my mind: "The trial of our faith is much more precious than of gold that perishes, though it is tried by fire" (1 Pet 1:7). Fiery trials are not strange things to the Lord's anointed. The rejoicing in them is born only of the Holy Spirit. Oh, praise his holy name, for a circumcised heart teaching us that each trial of our faith hath its commission from the Father of spirits. Each wave of trial bears the Galilean Pilot on its crest. Listen. His voice is in the storm, and winds and waves obey that voice. "It is I. Be not afraid." He has promised us help and safety in the fires, and not escape from them.

A Word to My Christian Sisters

Dear Sisters: I would that I could tell you a hundredth part of what God has revealed to me of his glory, especially on that never-to-be-forgotten night when I received my high and holy calling. The songs I heard I think were those which Job, David, and Isaiah speak of hearing at night upon their beds, or the one of which the Revelator says "no man could learn!" Certain it is, I have not been able to sing it since, though at times I have seemed to hear the distant echo of the music. When I tried to repeat it, it vanished in the dim distance. Glory! glory! glory to the Most High!

Sisters, shall not you and I unite with the heavenly host in the grand chorus? If so, you will not let what man may say or do keep you from doing the will of the Lord or using the gifts you have for the good of others. How much easier to bear the reproach of men than to live at a distance from God. Be not kept in bondage by those who say, "We suffer not a woman to teach," thus quoting Paul's words, but not rightly applying them. What though we are called to pass through deep waters, so our anchor is cast within the veil both sure and steadfast? Blessed experience! I have had to weep because this was not my constant experience. At times, a cloud of heaviness has covered my mind, and disobedience has caused me to lose the clear witness of perfect love.

One time I allowed my mind to dwell too much on my physical condition. I was suffering severely from throat difficulty and took the advice of friends and sought a cure from earthly physicians instead of applying to the Great Physician. For this reason my joy was checked and I was obliged to cease my public labors for several years. During all this time I was less spiritual, less zealous, yet I was not willing to accept the suggestion of Satan that I had forfeited the blessing of holiness. But alas! the witness was not clear, and God suffered me to pass through close trials, tossed by the billows of temptation.

Losing my loving husband just at this time, I had much of the world to struggle with and against.

Those who are wholly sanctified need not fear that God will hide his face if they continue to walk in the light even as Christ is in the light. Then they have fellowship with the Father and the Son, and become of one spirit with the Lord. I do not believe God ever withdraws himself from a soul which does not first withdraw itself from him, though such may abide under a cloud for a season and have to cry: "My God! My God! Why have you forsaken me?"

Glory to God, who gives us the victory through our Lord Jesus Christ! His blood meets all the demands of the law against us. It is the blood of Christ that sues for the fulfillment of his last will and testament, and brings down every blessing into the soul.

When I had nearly despaired of a cure from my bodily infirmities I cried from the depths of my soul for the blood of Jesus to be applied to my throat. My faith laid hold of the precious promises (John 14:14; Mark 2:23; 11:24). At once I ceased trying to join the iron and the clay—the truth of God with the sayings and advice of men. I looked to my God for a fresh act of his sanctifying power. Bless his name! Deliverance did come with the balm, and my throat has troubled me but little since. This was ten years ago. Praise the Lord for that holy fire which many waters of trial and temptation cannot quench.

Dear sisters in Christ, are any of you also without understanding and slow of heart to believe as were the disciples? Although they had seen their Master do many mighty works, yet, with change of place or circumstances they would go back upon the old ground of carnal reasoning and unbelieving fears. The darkness and ignorance of our natures are such that, even after we have embraced the Savior and received his teaching, we are ready to stumble at the plainest truths! Blind unbelief is always sure to err; it can neither trace God nor trust him. Unbelief is ever alive to distrust and fear. So long as this evil root has a place in us, our fears cannot be removed nor our hopes confirmed.

Not till the day of Pentecost did Christ's chosen ones see clearly or have their understandings opened. Nothing short of a full baptism of the Spirit will dispel our unbelief. Without this we are but babes—all our lives are often carried away by our carnal natures and kept in bondage. Whereas, if we are wholly saved and live under the full sanctifying influence of the Holy Ghost, we cannot be tossed about with every wind, but like an iron pillar or a house built upon a rock, prove immovable. Our minds will then be fully illuminated, our hearts purified, and our souls filled with the pure love of God, bringing forth fruit to his glory.

DOCUMENT 29

An Autobiography (1893), 79–80, 198–200, 203–4, 321
Amanda Berry Smith

And when they sang these words, "Whose blood now cleanses," O what a wave of glory swept over my soul! I shouted glory to Jesus. Brother Inskip answered, "Amen, Glory to God." O, what a triumph for our King Emmanuel. I don't know just how I looked, but I felt so wonderfully strange, yet I felt glorious. One of the good official brethren at the door said as I was passing out, "Well, Auntie, how did you like that sermon?" But I could not speak. If I had, I should have shouted, but I simply nodded my head. Just as I put my foot on the top step I seemed to feel a hand, the touch of which

I cannot describe. It seemed to press me gently on the top of my head, and I felt something part and roll down and cover me like a great cloak! I felt it distinctly. It was done in a moment, and O what a mighty peace and power took possession of me! I started up Green Street. The streets were full of people coming from the different churches in all directions. Just ahead of me were three of the leading sisters in our church. I would sooner have met anybody else than them. I was afraid of them. Well, I don't know why, but they were rather the ones who made you feel that wisdom dwelt with them. They were old leading sisters, and I have found that the colored churches were not the only ones that have these leading consequential sisters in them. Well, as I drew near, I saw them say something to each other, and they looked very dignified. Now, the devil was not so close to me as before. He seemed to be quite behind me, but he shouted after me, "You will not tell them you are sanctified."

"No," I said, "I will say nothing to them." But when I got up to them I seemed to have special power in my right arm and I was swinging it around, like the boys do sometimes! I don't know why, but O I felt mighty as I came near those sisters. They said, "Well, Smith, where have you been this morning?"

"The Lord," I said, "has sanctified my soul." And they were speechless! I said no more, but passed on, swinging my arm! I suppose the people thought I was wild, and I was, for God had set me on fire! "O," I thought, "if there was a platform around the world I would be willing to get on it and walk and tell everybody of this sanctifying power of God!"

> Of victory now o'er Satan's power,
> Let all the ransomed sing,
> And triumph in the dying hour
> Through Christ the Lord our King.
> Oh! it was love,
> 'Twas wondrous love,
> The love of God to me,
> That brought my Savior from above,
> To die on Calvary.

Somehow I always had a fear of white people—that is, I was not afraid of them in the sense of doing me harm or anything of that kind—but a kind of fear because they were white, and were there, and I was black and was here! But that morning on Green Street, as I stood on my feet trembling, I heard these words distinctly. They seemed to come from the northeast corner of the church, slowly, but clearly: "There is neither Jew nor Greek, there is neither bond nor free, there is neither male nor female, for you are all one in Christ Jesus" (Gal 3:28). I never understood that text before. But now the Holy Ghost had made it clear to me. And as I looked at white people that I had always seemed to be afraid of, now they looked so small. The great mountain had become a mole hill. "Therefore, if the Son shall make you free, then are you free, indeed." All praise to my victorious Christ!

> He delivered me when bound,
> And when wounded, healed my wound.
> Sought me wandering, set me right,
> Turned my darkness into light.
> Hallelujah! Hallelujah! Praise the Lord!

In May 1870 or 1871 the General Conference of the AME Church was held at Nashville, Tennessee. It was the first time they ever held a General Conference south of Mason-Dixon line. I had been laboring in Salem where the Lord first sent me and blessed me in winning souls. The people were not rich. They gave me a home and something to eat, but very little money. So before I could get back to New York, my home, I took a service place at Mrs. Mater's in Philadelphia—corner of Coach and Brown Streets—while her servant, Mary, went to Wilmington to see her child. She was to be gone a month, but she stayed five weeks, and now the Annual Conference was in session at the AME Union Church nearby where I was, so I had a chance to attend.

The election of delegates to the General Conference the next year was a very prominent feature of the Conference. Of course every minister wanted or hoped to be elected as a delegate. As I listened my heart throbbed. This was the first time in all these years that this religious body of black men with a black church from beginning to end was to be assembled south of the Mason-Dixon line.

But the great battle had been fought and the victory won. Slavery had been abolished. We were really free. There were enthusiastic speeches made on these points. Oh, how I wished I could go, and a deep desire took possession of me. But then, who was I? I had no money, no prominence at that time, except being a plain Christian woman, heard of and known by a few of the brethren as a woman preacher which was to be dreaded by the majority, especially the upper ten. Fortunately I had a good friend in Bishop Campbell knowing him so well years before he was elected to this office. Also Bishop Wayman, Bishop Brown, and Bishop Quinn were friends of mine. I believe I always had their sympathy and friendship. But there was no opportunity for me to speak to them personally. So I ventured to ask one of the brethren who had been elected delegate to tell me how much it would cost to go to Nashville. I would like to go if it did not cost too much.

He looked at me in surprise mingled with half disgust—the very idea of one looking like me to want to go to General Conference. They cut their eye at my big poke Quaker bonnet, with not a flower, not a feather. He said, "I tell you, sister, it will cost money to go down there, and if you ain't got plenty of it, it's no use to go," and turned away and smiled. Another said: "What does she want to go for?" "Woman preacher; they want to be ordained," was the reply. "I mean to fight that thing," said the other. "Yes, indeed, so will I," said another. Then a slight look to see if I took it in. I did. But in spite of it all I believed God would have me go. He knew that the thought of ordination had never once entered my mind, for I had received my ordination from Him Who said, "You have not chosen Me, but I have chosen you and ordained you that you might go and bring forth fruit, and that your fruit might remain."

I spoke to some of the good sisters who were expecting to go. They said they did not know what it would cost. So I went home and prayed and asked the Lord to help me, and the conviction that I was to go deepened, and yet it seemed so impossible. Just before the Conference closed I ventured to ask another good brother who had been elected delegate and whom I knew very well, and he was so nice, I thought he would tell me. "Brother S.," I said, "how much do you think it will cost?" This was the uppermost thought then—the cost to go to Nashville. "Oh, my sister," he replied, "I don't know. It will take all of a hundred dollars." And with a significant toss of the head, he shot through the door. I saw him no more till I met him next year at Nashville—and that was a surprise—but he managed to speak to me as we both stopped at the Sumner House and sat at the same table.

I was quite a curiosity to most of the visitors, especially the southern brethren, in my very plain Quaker dress. I was eyed with critical suspicion as being there to agitate the question of the ordination of women. All about, in the little groups that would be gathered talking, could be heard, "Who is she?" "Preacher woman." "What does she want here?" "I mean to fight that thing." "I wonder what day it will come up?"

Of course, I was a rank stranger to most of them. The bishops and all those whom I did know had all got there before me and were settled, and I was not going to trouble them for anything. Then those of the ladies whom I knew, wives of ministers or bishops, were dressed to the height of their ability. I could not rank with them, so I was all alone. No one but God knows what I passed through the first three days. God, in answer to prayer, had marvelously opened my way.

The meeting was opened in the usual way—an address by one of the bishops, then a song by the choir, singing as they could sing. Miss Sheppard spied me in the audience and told Prof. White. He looked and looked and could not see me at first. Then he went and spoke to Miss Sheppard again. Then she pointed out the plain bonnet. Then he spied me and quickly came down and shook hands, and was so glad. They all looked astonished. Holding me by the hand he escorted me to the platform and introduced me to the large audience, who in the midst of overwhelming amazement, applauded. Then the good professor told how they had met me in Boston and how I sang the grand old hymn, "All I want is a little more faith in Jesus," and what a burst of enthusiasm it created. And of all the surprised and astonished men and women you ever saw, these men and women were the most so.

While he was making these remarks, I prayed and asked God to help me. Then he said, "I'm going to ask Mrs. Smith to sing that same song she sang in Boston, and the Jubilee Singers will join in the chorus."

If ever the Lord did help me, He helped me that day. And the Spirit of the Lord seemed to fall on all the people. The preachers got happy. They wept and shouted "Amen! Praise the Lord!" At the close, a number of them came to me and shook hands and said, "God bless you, sister. Where did you come from? I would like to have you come on my charge." Another would say, "Look here, sister, when are you going home? God bless you. I would like to have you come to my place." And so it went. So that after that many of my brethren believed in me, especially as the question of ordination of women never was mooted in the Conference.

But how they have advanced since then. Most of them believe in the ordination of women, and I believe some have been ordained. But I am satisfied with the ordination that the Lord has given me. Praise His name!

I had no trouble after I had Prof. White's and Prof. Spence's kind recognition, and I had the pleasure of spending a week or more at the university with those good people. And as I would talk at several of the meetings the Lord blessed the dear teachers and students. I also spent a week at Dr. Braden's. They were very kind, and the Lord gave us blessing in some meetings. They have done and are doing a grand work among my people. May God bless them all.

I give this little story in detail to show that even with my own people, in this country, I have not always met with the pleasantest things. But still I have not backslidden nor felt led to leave the church. His grace has ever been sufficient. And all we need today is to trust Him.

Simply trusting every day,

Trusting through the stormy way,
Even when my faith is small,
Trusting Jesus, that is all.

Saturday, 22nd. Arrived at Bangalore late in the afternoon. Stopped with Brother Carter, pastor of the Methodist Church.

But the good Plymouth Brethren were much disturbed because I was a woman and Paul had said, "Let your women keep silence in the churches." So they had nice articles in the daily papers. Then they wrote me kind letters and bombarded me with scriptural texts against women preaching, pointing out some they wished me to preach from. I never argue with anybody—just say my say and go on. But one night I said I would speak on this subject as I understood it. Oh, what a stir it made. The church was packed and crowded. After I had sung I read out my text: "Let your 'men' keep silence in the church," quoting the chapter and verse (1 Cor 14:28) where Paul was giving directions so as not to have confusion—one to speak at a time, while the others listened. And then one was to interpret, and if there was no interpreter, they should keep silence in the church. So I went on with my version of it. We had an excellent meeting, and the newspaper articles stopped, and the letters stopped, and I went on till I got through.

I have wondered what has become of the good Plymouth Brethren in India since the Salvation Army lassies have been so owned and blessed of God. Their work has told more practically on the strongholds of heathenism than all that holy conservatism would have brought to bear in a thousand years.

Oh, that the Holy Ghost may be poured out mightily! Then shall the prophecy of Joel be fulfilled. For are we not living in the last days of this wonderful dispensation of the Holy Ghost?

5

The Early Holiness Movement
and Phoebe Palmer

Introduction

In 1853 Antoinette Brown Blackwell (1825–1921) was the first woman to be ordained by an established Protestant denomination in the United States. Despite the fact that she was a Congregationalist, the Wesleyan Methodist Luther Lee (1800–1889) was invited to deliver the sermon at her ordination in South Butler, New York, undoubtedly because of his passionate and vocal advocacy of women's ministry, abolition, and holiness. "Logical Lee," as he was known, had joined with other Methodist abolitionists to form the Wesleyan Methodist Connexion a decade earlier and had become a leader in that new denomination. According to Beverly Zink-Sawyer, he "never hesitated to engage in debates concerning theological or social issues."[1] His sermon, entitled *Woman's Right to Preach the Gospel* (Document 30), which is essentially a lengthy discourse on the exegesis of all the pertinent biblical texts, demonstrates that he was anxious to exploit this auspicious occasion to wage war against those who stood in opposition to the ministry of women. He took as his text St. Paul's maxim for equality, Galatians 3:28. The common themes of abolitionism and holiness combined in Lee to form a unique and potent defense of women's ministry.

Abolitionism had led to a new antislavery interpretation of the Bible. According to Donald Dayton, "Those persons who concluded that the spirit of the Bible was antislavery even though the letter of some passages seemed

1. Zink-Sawyer, *From Preachers to Suffragists*, 70.

to condone slavery found that the form of the argument allowed them to make a similar case that the spirit of the Bible was for the liberation of women."[2] Indeed, the very text from which Lee preached was the Magna Carta of the antislavery movement. In parallel fashion to abolitionism, the first women's rights convention, held in the Wesleyan Methodist Church in Seneca Falls, New York, just five years earlier in 1848, had intimate connections with the holiness movement. Zink-Sawyer reports that the final resolution unanimously adopted at this watershed event "expressed the realization that women had been too long excluded from ministry as well as other professions."[3] Concern for the emancipation of women in both church and society was an extension of both abolitionism and holiness, and Lee's sermon rang the changes on these themes; as in Wesley's original vision, Lee's holiness embraced concern for social justice.

The holiness movement of the nineteenth century, in fact, rooted itself deeply in the Wesleyan conception of sanctification, or holiness of heart and life. John and Charles Wesley sought to recover a biblical vision of the Christian life that stretched beyond the sufficiency of God's forgiveness of sin to the plenitude of God's love filling the soul. During the first half of the nineteenth century, and with the American frontier as the backdrop, some Methodists began to question whether they had abandoned this emphasis and believed they needed to reclaim it as their defining feature. The contemporary Second Great Awakening, characterized by large-scale revivalism and the camp meeting, fueled this concern and helped to restore the centrality of holiness and Christian perfection. While basing their theology on the teachings of John Wesley—articulated in his *Plain Account of Christian Perfection*—these new advocates of holiness placed a high value on entire sanctification as a "second blessing," an instantaneous work of the Holy Spirit that both purified and perfected the believer. A devout Methodist woman occupied the center of this movement of revitalization.

Phoebe Palmer (1807–74) can be described properly as the mother of the holiness movement in the United States and the higher life movement in Britain.[4] In New York City in the 1830s she and her sister facilitated what came to be known as the Tuesday Meeting for the Promotion of Holiness. Priscilla Pope-Levison observes that on what Palmer called her "day of days," July 26, 1837, "she experienced sanctification, 'the full assurance of faith,' for

---

2. Dayton, *Higher Christian Life*, ix–x.

3. Zink-Sawyer, *From Preachers to Suffragists*, 73.

4. On Palmer's life and ministry, see White, *Beauty of Holiness*; Raser, *Phoebe Palmer*; and Heath, *Naked Faith*.

which she had been searching."[5] This experience catapulted Palmer into a range of ministries that came to define her life as a holiness theologian, author, missioner, evangelist, and preacher. As Janette Hassey notes, "Palmer's life symbolized the link between John Wesley's Evangelical revival in Britain and the American holiness movement."[6] In all, Palmer wrote eighteen books of "practical theology, biography and poetry."[7] In 1859 she published one of her most important books in response to the mounting criticism she had received as a female preacher over the course of the previous two decades. *The Promise of the Father*, a four-hundred-page manifesto, presented several well-researched and carefully thought out arguments demonstrating that women had a mandate to proclaim the gospel. In 1869 she published a new edition of this monumental work, a pamphlet retitled *Tongue of Fire on the Daughters of the Lord* (Document 31), which retained and presented the substance of her arguments in greatly abbreviated form.[8]

According to Thomas Oden, three primary characteristics of Palmer's *Tongue of Fire* stand out: (1) it is her own concise, definitive statement of the crucial importance of the gifts (charismata) of women in the service of the church; (2) it reveals her proto-feminist, critical method of exegesis, her pungent rhetorical style, and her spirited mode of argument; and (3) it shows clearly how Phoebe Palmer remains a major spiritual forerunner not only of the spirituality of the modern Wesleyan family of churches but also of the charismatic movement and the worldwide Pentecostal fellowship.[9] In this pamphlet, Palmer attributed the long-standing prohibitions against women in the church to two things in particular: a faulty interpretation of the Bible and a distorted and unchristian view most men had of women. She concluded that women, acting in their legitimate sphere, were more likely than men to exhibit true piety.

Palmer's two published defenses of women's ministry revolved around the central portion of the Pentecost account (Acts 2:17–18) that celebrates the fulfillment of Joel's prophetic vision of Christian egalitarianism. "Phoebe considered this the paradigmatic verse," according to Pope-Levison, "because it encapsulated the *promise of the Father* who has imparted to women, in the last days of this present age, the power to bear witness to the saving

---

5. Pope-Levison, *Turn the Pulpit Loose*, 63.

6. Hassey, *No Time for Silence*, 97.

7. White, *Beauty of Holiness*, 233.

8. For one of the best discussions of this tract, see Hogan, "Negotiating Personhood."

9. Oden, *Phoebe Palmer*, 31–32.

and sanctifying gospel of Jesus Christ."[10] On the basis of this reading of the text, Palmer not only believed women had the privilege to proclaim the gospel, but believed they should be expected and, perhaps, even compelled to pray, prophesy, and preach. Harold Raser discerns the influence of the theological writings of Mary Fletcher's husband, John, in Palmer's defense:

> The central thread throughout is the "argument from Pentecost," which was based on Fletcher's doctrine of dispensations. According to Palmer, the present age is the "dispensation of the Spirit," which was inaugurated at Pentecost with "signs and wonders," the chief of these being the power to "prophesy," which Palmer understands to mean to "herald the glad tidings [of Jesus] to others" or to proclaim "to every creature . . . the love of God to [humanity] through Jesus Christ."[11]

Due to the pervasive influence of Palmer's book, C. S. Cowles argues that "this became the principal scriptural justification for women preachers throughout the 19th and 20th centuries."[12]

Palmer indicated that the impetus for writing *The Promise of the Father* was the experience of witnessing a distraught young woman who was torn between testifying to her experience of sanctification and respecting the boundaries that restricted women's speech. As a so-called evangelical feminist who did not seek to challenge the natural sphere of women's activity and did not even "intend to discuss the question of 'Women's Rights' or of 'Women's Preaching,'" Palmer argued tenaciously nonetheless for the responsibility of all believers "to testify to their own regeneration in order to prompt the regeneration of others."[13] Anne Loveland points out that for Palmer, "the proper sphere for most women was the home" and that a public ministry was something "a few exceptional women" might do.[14] Rather than staking her claim on a foundation of women's rights, an evangelistic mandate undergirded her stance of radical obedience. Moreover, as Susan Lindley has argued, two theological convictions supported her position:

> First, if the sanctified believer did not testify publicly to what God had done, God would revoke the gift; for women, as well as men, response to God's call in public witness was not a matter of preference but a necessity. Second, Palmer was convinced (as

---

10. Pope-Levison, *Turn the Pulpit Loose*, 66.
11. Raser, "Holding Tightly," 178.
12. Cowles, *Woman's Place?*, 169.
13. Zink-Sawyer, *From Preachers to Suffragists*, 81.
14. Loveland, "Domesticity and Religion," 48.

were many other American Christians) that she was living in the "last days," and that it was critical that the church neither neglect nor repress the gifts of the Spirit, even or especially when they are bestowed on women.[15]

She was one of the first to introduce this millenarian element into her argument alongside the panoply of arguments that had become standard by this time.

Nancy Hardesty, Lucille Siler Dayton, and Donald Dayton, historians of the holiness tradition, suggest six factors that help to explain the receptivity of those within this movement to the ministry of women: (1) a theology centered in experience, (2) a doctrine of holiness rooted in Scripture, (3) an emphasis on the work of the Holy Spirit, (4) a freedom to be experimental, (5) an emphasis on perfection and holiness with its implicit critique of the status quo, and (6) a sectarian bent.[16] Jennifer Lloyd has also emphasized "holiness theology's endorsement of spontaneity in religion, the lack of emphasis on original sin, and its insistency on the possibility of instantaneous conversion" as elements that encouraged the ministry of women.[17]

While some contemporary and later Methodist apologists challenged Palmer's biblical hermeneutic and reframed arguments using different lenses, Palmer's influence remained pervasive. Hassey observes that her ministry and writing directly affected three particularly prominent figures in the defense of women in ministry: "Catherine Booth heard Palmer preach during a British evangelistic tour and received encouragement for her own public ministry. Frances Willard professed sanctification during a Palmer revival, while B. T. Roberts experienced conversion through her ministry."[18] The apologetic works of all three will be examined in subsequent chapters.

DOCUMENT 30

Woman's Right to Preach the Gospel (1853), 3–5, 22
Luther Lee

"There is neither male nor female, for you are all one in Christ Jesus." (Gal 3:28)

15. Lindley, *You Have Stept Out*, 120.

16. Hardesty, Dayton, and Dayton, "Women in the Holiness Movement," 241–48; cf. Hardesty, "Holiness Movements."

17. Lloyd, *Women and British Methodism*, 178.

18. Hassey, *No Time for Silence*, 99.

The thinking portion of the assembly has by this time reasoned within themselves, "that is a singular text from which to preach an ordination sermon." This may render it proper for me to remind my hearers, just at this point, that the text is no more unusual as the basis of an ordination sermon than the occasion is unusual upon which I am called to preach it.

The ordination of a female, or the setting apart of a female to the work of the Christian ministry is, to say the least, a novel transaction in this land and age. It cannot fail to call forth many remarks and will, no doubt, provoke many censures.

It is to be presumed that the parties concerned in this transaction believe their course to be right and that they have their reasons for so believing. And I feel assured that there can be no time nor place more appropriate for an exhibition of such reasons than the time and place of the transaction which breaks in upon long established opinions and usages. And as I have been called upon to deliver the discourse on the occasion, I should deem it out of place, tame and cowardly, for me to deliver an ordinary sermon setting forth the duties and responsibilities of a Christian minister without taking hold of the peculiarity of the occasion and vindicating the innovation which we this hour make upon the usages of the Christian world.

It is with these views, and under these impressions, that I have selected the text which I have read as the basis of my discourse. "There is neither male nor female, for you are all one in Christ Jesus."

What does this text mean? What was the Apostle's design in uttering these words? Whatever the text means, or does not mean, its application is to be limited to what is clearly and specifically Christian. It is in Christ Jesus that there is no difference, and that the sexes become one. There may be differences of rights and positions growing out of incidental relations and conventional rules and usages in matters which do not affect the fundamental rights of humanity, which I need not discuss. But when we come to consider those rights and privileges which we claim as Christians, and which belong to us as believers in Christ, there is no difference. We are all one in Christ Jesus. On this occasion, without even presuming to discuss the questions of civil and political rights, the text amply sustains me in affirming that in a Christian community, united upon Christian principles, for Christian purposes—in other words, in the Church of which Christ is the only head—males and females possess equal rights and privileges. Here there is no difference, "there is neither male nor female, for you are all one in Christ Jesus!" I cannot see how the text can be explained as to exclude females from any right, office, work, privilege, or immunity which males enjoy, hold, or perform. If the text means anything, it means that males and females are equal in rights, privileges, and responsibilities upon the Christian platform.

I am very frank to confess that I had never very thoroughly investigated the question until called upon to preach on this occasion, though I have held an opinion loosely on the subject for many years. In my own estimation this call laid me under obligation to do one of two things, either step forward and assist this church, or decline to do so for good and satisfactory reasons. I might have evaded the question by declining for want of time or some other fictitious reason, but that would not only have been in bad keeping with my general character, but would have been false to Christianity and my brethren. If those inviting me here are right in proposing to ordain a female to the gospel ministry, they needed my help and were entitled to it. If they were wrong, they needed my reproof and reasons for it, and it was due to my own fidelity and to truth that I should administer it. But to do either required thought beyond what I had ever bestowed upon the subject. You may then suppose me to have asked myself, "If I decline, what reason can I give for so doing? So far as I know there is no want of moral, mental, or educational qualification on the part of the candidate. If it be right to ordain any female, it is right to ordain this female."

At this point, the text which I have selected for the occasion presented itself to my mind and I reasoned thus: I acknowledge the candidate to be in Christ, to be with me a sister in Christ. If I deny her the right to exercise her gifts as a Christian minister, I virtually affirm that there is male and female and that we are not all one in Christ Jesus by which I shall contradict St. Paul. I am then brought to this conclusion which I will state in the form of a proposition as the consequence of the text:

Females have a God-given right to preach the gospel.

I take it upon myself, as my portion of the effort on this occasion, to defend and substantiate the above proposition. To make any distinction in the church of Jesus Christ, between males and females purely on the ground of sex, is virtually to strike this text from the sacred volume, for it affirms that in Christ there is no difference between males and females, that they are all one in regard to the gospel of the grace of God. If males may belong to a Christian church, so may females. If male members may vote in the church, so may females. If males may preach the gospel, so may females. If males may receive ordination by the imposition of hands or otherwise, so may females, the reason of which is found in my text: "There is neither male nor female, for you are all one in Christ Jesus."

We are here assembled on a very interesting and solemn occasion, and it is proper to advert to the real object for which we have come together. There are in the world, and there may be among us, false views of the nature and object of ordination. I do not believe that any special or specific form of ordination is necessary to constitute a gospel minister. We are not here to make a minister. It is not to confer on this our sister a right to preach the gospel. If she has not that right already we have no power to communicate it to her. Nor have we met to qualify her for the work of the ministry. If God and mental and moral culture have not already qualified her, we cannot by anything we may do by way of ordaining or setting her apart. Nor can we by imposition of our hands confer on her any special grace for the work of the ministry. Nor will our hands, if imposed upon her head, serve as a special medium for the communication of the Holy Ghost as conductors serve to convey electricity. Such ideas belong not to our theory, but are related to other systems and darker ages. All we are here to do and all we expect to do, in due form and by a solemn and impressive service, is to subscribe our testimony to the fact that in our belief our sister in Christ, Antoinette L. Brown is one of the ministers of the New Covenant, authorized, qualified, and called of God to preach the gospel of his Son Jesus Christ. This is all, but this even renders the occasion interesting and solemn. As she is recognized as the pastor of this flock, it is solemn and interesting to both pastor and flock to have the relation formally recognized. But as a special charge is to be given to both by others, I forbear to open the subject of their mutual responsibilities, and will conclude by invoking the blessing of the Father and of the Son and of the Holy Ghost upon both preacher and people. Amen.

DOCUMENT 31

Tongue of Fire on the Daughters of the Lord (1869)
Phoebe Palmer

1. Female Prophesying; or, Daughters of the Lord Almighty

When the founder of our holy Christianity was about leaving his disciples to ascend to his Father, he commanded them to tarry at Jerusalem until endued with power from on high. And of whom was this company of disciples composed? Please turn to the first chapter of the Acts of the Apostles. We see the number assembled in that upper room was about one hundred and twenty. Here were Peter, James, John, Andrew, Philip, Thomas, Bartholomew, Matthew, James the son of Alpheus, and Simon the Zealot, and

Judas the brother of James. "These all continued with one accord in prayer and supplication, with the women, and Mary, the mother of Jesus, and with his brethren" (Acts 1:14).

Let us observe that here were both male and female disciples, continuing with one accord in prayer and supplication, in obedience to the command of their risen Lord. They are all here waiting for the promise of the Father.

And did all these waiting disciples, who thus with one accord continued in prayer, receive the grace for which they supplicated? It was the gift of the Holy Ghost that had been promised. And was this promise of the Father as truly made to the daughters of the Lord Almighty as to his sons? "And it shall come to pass afterward that I will pour out my Spirit upon all flesh; and your sons and your daughters shall prophesy, your old men shall dream dreams, your young men shall see visions. And also upon the servants and upon the handmaids in those days will I pour out my Spirit" (Joel 2:28–29). When the Spirit was poured out in answer to the united prayers of God's sons and daughters did the tongue of fire descend alike upon the women as upon the men? How emphatic is the answer to this question.

"And there appeared unto them cloven tongues like as of fire, and it sat upon *each of them*" (Acts 2:3). Was the effect similar upon God's daughters as upon his sons? Mark it: "And they were all filled with the Holy Ghost and began to speak as the Spirit gave utterance." (Acts 2:4). Doubtless it was a well-nigh impelling power which was thus poured out upon these sons and daughters of the Lord Almighty, moving their lips to most earnest, persuasive, convincing utterances. Not alone did Peter proclaim a crucified, risen Savior, but each one, as the Spirit gave utterance, assisted in spreading the good news. And the result of these united ministrations of the Spirit, through human agency, was that three thousand were in one day pricked to the heart. Unquestionably, the whole of this newly baptized company of one hundred and twenty disciples, male and female, hastened in every direction under the mighty constraining of that perfect love that casts out fear, and great was the company of them that believed.

And now, in the name of the head of the church, let us ask, Was it designed that these demonstrations of power should cease with the day of Pentecost? If the Spirit of prophecy fell upon God's daughters alike as upon his sons in that day, and they spoke in the midst of that assembled multitude as the Spirit gave utterance, on what authority do the angels of the churches restrain the use of that gift now? Who can tell how wonderful the achievements of the cross might have been if this gift of prophecy in woman had continued in use as in apostolic days? Who can tell but long since the gospel might have been preached to every creature?

Evidently this was a specialty of the last days, as set forth by the prophecy of Joel. Under the old dispensation, though, there was a Miriam, a Deborah, a Huldah, and an Anna who were prophetesses. The special outpouring of the Spirit upon God's daughters, as upon his sons, seems to have been reserved as a characteristic of the last days. "This," says Peter, as the wondering multitude beheld the extraordinary endowment of the Spirit falling alike on all the disciples, "this is that which was spoken by the prophet Joel: 'And also upon my servants and upon my handmaidens will I pour out my Spirit'" (Acts 2:16–17).

And this gift of prophecy bestowed upon all was continued and recognized in all the early ages of Christianity. The ministry of the word was not confined to the apostles. When, by the cruel persecutions of Saul all the infant church were driven away from Jerusalem, except the apostles, these scattered men and women of the laity went everywhere preaching the word—that is, proclaiming a crucified, risen Savior. And the effect was that the enemies of the cross, by scattering these men and women who had been saved by its virtues, were made subservient to the yet more extensive proclamation of saving grace.

Impelled by the indwelling power within, these Spirit-baptized men and women, driven by the fury of the enemy in cruel haste from place to place, made all their scatterings the occasion of preaching the gospel everywhere. And believers were everywhere multiplied, and daily were there added to the church such as should be saved.

Justin Martyr, who lived till about AD 150, says in his *Dialogue with Trypho the Jew* "that both *women* and *men* were seen among them who had the gifts of the Spirit of God according as Joel the prophet had foretold, by which he endeavored to convince the Jew that the *latter days* were come. For by that expression Manasseh Ben Israel tells us all their wise men understood the times of Messias.

In his dissertations on Irenaeus, Dodwell says that "the extraordinary gift of the spirit of prophecy was given to others besides the apostles, and that not only in the *first* and *second* but in the *third* century, even to the time of Constantine, men of all sorts and ranks had their gifts; yes, and *women* too." Therefore we may certainly conclude that the prophetic saying of the Psalmist was verified: "The Lord gave the word and great was the company of those that published it" (68:11). In the original Hebrew it is "Great was the company of women publishers, or women evangelists." Grotius explains, "The Lord gave the word, that is, plentiful matter of speaking, so that he would call those which follow the great army of preaching women, viz., victories, or female conquerors."

The Hebrew scholar Rev. J. Benson, in his voluminous and deeply spiritual commentary, says the clause here given, "The Lord gave the word, great was the company of those that published it," literally translated is, "*Large was the number of women who published the glad tidings.*" The eminent linguist, Dr. Adam Clarke, quotes the original text and follows it with the literal reading, "*of the female preachers there was a great host.*" And then, as though he anticipated the incredulity with which this literal rendering would be received, and resolved on relieving himself of the responsibility of a non-reception of it, he affirms, "Such is the literal translation of the passage," and leaves it with the reader to make the application with the exclamation, "The reader may make of it what he pleases."

But though this excellent commentator suggests that the reader make what use of it he please, it certainly ought to be assumed that all sincere Christians, whether male or female, will in their Scripture searching make it their highest pleasure to ascertain the mind of the Spirit, adopting the Bible mode of interpreting the Scriptures by comparing scripture with scripture. Fearful that he may be compelled to the sustainment of some unpopular theory, is not in a state of mind to warrant the belief that he shall know of this or any other doctrine, whether it be of God. Schaff's *History of Christ's Church* says, "Woman, among the early Christians, had the fullest freedom in the house of worship, and the consequence was not only that she added vastly to the success of Christianity in those times, but her own character was wonderfully elevated and her genius developed by this equality of right. It is said that Libanius, on seeing the mother of St. Chrysostom, a most noble woman, exclaimed, "What women these Christians have!"

Eusebius speaks of Potominia Ammias, a prophetess in Philadelphia, and others who were equally distinguished by their zeal for the love which they bore to Jesus Christ.

Chrysostom and Theophylact take great notice of Junia, mentioned in the apostle's salutations. In our translation it is, "Salute Andronicus and Junia, my kinsmen and my fellow-prisoners, who are of note among the apostles" (Rom 16:7). By the word *kinsmen*, one would take Junia not to have been a woman, but a man. But Chrysostom and Theophylact were both Greeks, consequently they knew their mother-tongue better than our translators, and they say it was a woman. It should therefore have been translated, "Salute Andronicus and Junia, my kinsfolk." The apostle salutes other *women* who were of note among them, particularly Tryphena and Tryphosa, who labored in the Lord, and Persis who labored much in the Lord.

We could refer to many women who in the apostolic age used this gift to the edification of the church, particularly Phoebe, the *servant of the church*, or deaconess, as the Greek word signifies, of the *church at Cenchroea*.

Deaconesses were ordained to the office by the imposition of the hands of the bishop. Theodorus says, "The fame of Phoebe was spread throughout the world, and she was known, not only to the Greeks and Romans, but also to the barbarians." This implies that she traveled much and propagated the gospel in foreign countries. "It is reasonable to suppose, in view of her being a succor of many," says the Rev. Mr. Benson, "that this acknowledged servant of the church was a person of considerable wealth and influence, or we may suppose the appellation, "servant of the church," was given her on account of the offices she performed as a deaconess. Says another able divine on this subject, "There were deaconesses in the primitive church, and it is evident that they were ordained to this office by the imposition of the hands of the bishop. The form of prayer used on the occasion is still extant in the apostolic constitution." And this order was continued for several centuries in the church, *until the reign of the man of sin* commenced.

The Christian churches of the present day, with but few exceptions, have imposed silence on Christian woman so that her voice may but seldom be heard in Christian assemblies. And why do the churches impose it? The answer comes from a thousand lips and from every point, "The head of the church forbids it, and the churches only join in the authoritative prohibition, 'Let your women keep silence in the churches'" (1 Cor 14:34). And here we come fairly at the question: If the head of the church forbids it, this settles the question beyond all controversy.

But under what circumstances was this prohibition given? Was it not by way of reproving some unseemly practices which had been introduced into the Corinthian church, and which in fact seem to have been peculiar to *that* church? For it is in connection with this and kindred disorders which had been introduced among the Corinthian believers, in connection with the exercise of the gift of prophecy, that Paul says, "We have no such custom, *neither the churches of God,*" that is, the other churches of God over which the Holy Ghost had made him overseer. It is evident that the irregularities here complained of were peculiar to the church of Corinth, and in fact, not even applicable to other Christian churches of Paul's day, much less Christian churches of the present day as no such disorders exist. The irregularity complained of was not the prophesying of women, for this the Apostle admits, and directs how the women shall appear when engaged in the duty of praying or prophesying. The prohibition was evidently in view of restraining women from taking part in those disorderly debates which were not unusual in the religious worship of those days. In the Jewish synagogue it was a matter of ordinary occurrence for persons to interrupt the speaker by introducing questionings which frequently resulted in angry altercations. It was in reference to this reprehensible practice that Paul enjoins silence, and not in reference to the exercise of the gift of prophecy, which, in connection with this subject, he so plainly admits. Otherwise the Apostle's teachings were obviously contradictory.

But if Paul's prohibition, "Let your women keep silence in the churches," is to be carried out to the letter in relation to the prophesying of women— that is, her speaking "to edification, exhortation, and comfort"—regardless of explanatory connections and contradictory passages, why should it not be carried out to the letter in other respects? If the Apostle intended to enjoin silence in an absolute sense, then our Episcopalian friends trespass against this prohibition at every church service in calling out the responses of women in company with the men in the liturgy, and when they repeat our Lord's Prayer in concert with their brethren. And thus also do they trespass against this prohibition every time they break silence and unite in holy song in the church of God of any or every denomination. And in fact we doubt not but it were less displeasing to the head of the church that his female disciples were forbidden to open their lips in singing, or in church responses, than that they should be forbidden to open their lips when the spirit of prophecy has been poured out upon them, moving them to well-nigh irrepressible utterances.

But Paul also says, "I suffer not a woman to teach, nor usurp authority over the man" (1 Tim 2:12). It will be found by an examination of this text, with its connections, that the sort of teaching here alluded to stands in connection with usurping authority. As though the Apostle had said, "The gospel does not alter the relation of women in view of priority. For Adam was first formed, then Eve. And though the condition of woman is improved, and her privileges enlarged, yet she is not raised to a position of superiority, where she may usurp authority and teach dictatorially, for the law still remains as at the beginning."

But the sort of teaching to which the Apostle here alludes, in connection with usurping authority, cannot be the same to which he refers in 1 Cor 14. Here Paul admits the prophesying of women in public assemblies. He could have had no intention in his Epistle to Timothy to forbid that sort of teaching which stood in connection with the exercise of the gift of prophesy which arose from the immediate impulses of the Holy Ghost. This is rendered abundantly plain by another passage in his Epistle to the Corinthians in which he notices the public prophesying of females and gives particular directions respecting their conduct and appearance while engaged in that sacred duty. "Every man *praying* or *prophesying*, having his head covered, dishonors his head. But every woman that prays or prophesies with her head uncovered dishonors her head (1 Cor 11:4–5).

With respect to the prophesying to which the Apostle here alludes, as exercised by both men and women in the churches of the saints, he defines its nature (see 1 Cor 14:3). The reader will see that it was directed to the "edification, exhortation, and comfort of believers," and the result anticipated was the conviction of unbelievers and unlearned persons. "Such," says the author of an excellent work, "were the public services of women which the apostle allowed. And such was the ministry of females predicted by the prophet Joel and described as a *leading* feature under the gospel dispensation. Women who speak in assemblies for worship under the influence of the Holy Spirit assume thereby no *personal authority* over others. They are instruments through which divine instruction is communicated to the people."

But by whom has the exercise of the gift of prophesy in woman been most seriously resisted? Has not the use of this endowment of power been withstood mainly by those whose lips should keep knowledge? Have not the people who have sought to know the law on this important topic been met with the dissuasive teachings, as though God's ancient promise had not been fulfilled? We cannot resist the conviction that the restraining of the gift of prophecy as given to woman in fulfillment of the promise of the Father involves far greater responsibilities than has been apprehended. The subject of which we treat stands in vital connection with the salvation of thousands, and if so, may we not anticipate that he whose ceaseless aim is to withstand the work of human salvation in every variety of form, as an angel of light will withstand the reception of truth on this subject?

Again we repeat that it is our most solemn conviction that the use of a gift of power delegated to the church as a specialty of the last days has been neglected, a gift which, if properly recognized, would have hastened the latter day glory. We believe that tens of thousands more of the redeemed family would have been won over to the world's Redeemer if it had not been for the tardiness of the church in acknowledging this gift. We believe it is through the workings of the Man of Sin, whose aim it is to withstand the up-building of Christ's kingdom on earth, that this deception has been accomplished. We believe that he who quoted Scripture to our Savior has in all deceit quoted Scripture to pious men—men who would not wickedly wrest the Scriptures to their own destruction, but who from a failure in not regarding the scriptural mode of interpretation, by comparing scripture with scripture, have unwittingly followed the traditions of men. They have thereby been guilty of the egregious error of making the inspired teachings appear contradictory and of withstanding the workings of the Holy Spirit in accordance with those teachings in the hearts of thousands of the daughters of the Lord Almighty.

We believe that the attitude of the church in relation to this matter is most grievous in the sight of her Lord, who has purchased the whole human family unto himself, and would fain have every possible agency employed in preaching the gospel to every creature. He whose name is Faithful and True has fulfilled his ancient promise and poured out his Spirit as truly upon his daughters as upon his sons.

God has, in all ages of the church, called some of his handmaids to eminent publicity and usefulness. When the residue of the Spirit is poured out and the millennium glory ushered in, the prophecy of Joel being fully accomplished in all its glory, probably then there will be such a sweet blending into one spirit—the spirit of faith, of love, and of a sound mind. With such a willingness to receive profit by any instrument—such a spirit of humility, in honor preferring one another—the wonder will then be that the exertions of pious females to bring souls to Christ should ever have been opposed or obstructed.

The earnestly pious of all denominations seem now disposed to recognize Wesley as having been greatly instrumental under God in the revival of primitive Christianity. To those acquainted with the history of the church at the time this great reformer was raised up, we need not say that the reception of the full baptism of the Holy Ghost was but faintly, if at all, recognized as the privilege of the believer. But as soon as this primitive flame again revived, just so soon this gift of power—anciently promised as a specialty of the last days—was newly recognized. What a host of laborers together in the gospel were quickly raised up! And who that has read the correspondence and journal of Wesley has not marked his special recognition and appreciation of this endowment of power? No more appreciatively did an ancient Apostle regard "those women that labored with him in the gospel" than did this modern apostle and his coadjutors.

A recognition of the full baptism of the Holy Ghost as a grace to be experienced and enjoyed in the present life was the distinguishing doctrine of Methodism. And who can doubt that it was this specialty that again brought out a host of Spirit-baptized laborers as in the apostolic days? And the satisfaction with which this apostolic man recognized and encouraged the use of this endowment of power is everywhere observable throughout his writings. As one says, "Mr. Wesley pressed into the service of religion all the useful gifts he could influence." He well knew that in the ratio in which the devoted female, or any other instrumentalities, were calculated to be useful, to just that degree would the grand adversary raise up opposing agencies to withstand.

To his friend Miss Briggs, he writes, "*undoubtedly* both you and Philothea, and my dear Miss Perronet, are now more particularly called to speak for God. In so doing, you must expect to meet with many things which are not pleasing to flesh and blood. But all is well. So much more will you be conformed to the death of Christ. Go in his name and in the power of his might. Suffer and conquer all things." Over a century has rolled away, and still we may thankfully record that this ancient flame, though not cherished as it might have been, has not died out.

In his journal Mr. Wesley introduces the name of one of his female helpers, Miss Sarah Mallet, afterwards Mrs. Boyce: "I was strongly importuned by our friends at Long Stratton to give them a sermon. I had heard of a young woman there who had uncommon fits, and of one that lately preached. But I did not know that it was one and the same person. I found her in the house to which I went and talked with her at large. I was surprised. Of the following relation which she gave me, there are numberless witnesses.

"Some years since it was strongly impressed upon her mind that she ought to call sinners to repentance. This impression she vehemently resisted, believing herself quite unqualified, both by her sin and ignorance, till it was suggested, 'If you do it not willingly, you shall do it, whether you will or no.' She fell into a fit, and while utterly senseless, thought she was in the preaching-house of Lowestoft where she prayed and preached for nearly an hour to a numerous congregation. She then cried out 'Lord I will obey thee. I will call sinners to repentance!' She has done occasionally from that time and her fits returned no more."

Perhaps this was intended to satisfy her own mind that God had called her to publish salvation in the name of Jesus to perishing sinners and to incline her to take up that cross which appears to have been more painful to her than death itself, and also to convince others that *even now* God has poured out his Spirit upon his handmaids and upon his daughters that they may prophesy or preach in his name the unsearchable riches of Christ.

The author of *The Heroines of Methodism* says, "Probably the experience of this young woman and the wonderful dealings of the Lord with her greatly helped to enlarge the views of John Wesley upon the subject of female preaching. It is very evident from his letters and conduct towards her that he believed her, as a preacher, to be doing what the Lord required at her hands."

Says Miss Mallet, "At thirteen I became member of the Methodist Society, and the Lord made known to me what he would have me do. But oh, how unfit did I see myself to be! From that time, the word of God was an unsealed book. It was my companion day and night. My love to God and souls increased. I have been often led to cry out in the bitterness of my soul, 'O Lord! I am but a child. I cannot preach your word.' But the more deeply was it impressed on my mind, 'Woe is me if I preach not the gospel,' till my distress of soul destroyed my body.

"In my twentieth year the Lord answered my prayer in a great affliction and made known to others, as well as to myself, the work he would have me do and fitted me in the furnace for his use. From that time I began my public work. Mr. Wesley was to me a father and a faithful friend. I have not, nor do I seek, either ease or wealth or honor, but the glory of God and the good of souls. And, thank God, I have not run in vain nor labored in vain. There are some witnesses in heaven and some on earth. When I first began to travel, I followed Mr. Wesley's counsel which was to let the voice of the people be to me the voice of God, and where I was sent for to go. To this counsel I have attended to this day. But the voice of the people was not the voice of some of the preachers. Mr. Wesley, however, soon made this easy by sending me a note by Mr. Joseph Harper from the conference held at Manchester in 1787. The note was as follows: 'We give the right hand of fellowship to Sarah Mallet and have no objection to her being a preacher in our connection so long as she preaches the Methodist doctrine and attends to our discipline.'"

We believe that hundreds of conscientious, sensitive Christian women have actually suffered more under the slowly crucifying process to which they have been subjected by men who bear the Christian name than many a martyr has endured in passing through the flames. We are aware that we are using strong language, but we do not use it in bitterness, but with feelings of deep humiliation before God that the cause of truth demands the utterance of such sentiments. We conscientiously believe, and therefore must speak.

Thousands are in this day enduring this crucifying process perhaps as never before. God has given the word, and in this wonderful season of the outpouring of the Spirit, great might be the company who would publish it. This, in a most emphatic sense, is the day of which the prophet spoke— when God would pour out his Spirit on his sons and daughters. Though many men have in these last days received the baptism of fire, still greater, as in all revivals, has been the number of females. These constitute a great company—witnesses for Christ—who wish desperately to publish the glad tidings of their own heart experiences of his saving power, at least in the social assembly.

A large proportion of the most intelligent, courageous, and self-sac-rificing disciples of Christ are females. Many women followed the Savior when on earth. And compared with the dearth of male disciples, many women follow him still. Were the women who followed the incarnate Savior earnest, intelligently pious, and intrepid, willing to sacrifice that which cost them something in ministering to him of their substance? In like manner, there are many women in the present day, earnest, intelligent, intrepid, and self-sacrificing, who, were they permitted or encouraged to open their lips in the assemblies of the pious in prayer, or speaking as the Spirit gives utterance, might be instrumental in winning many an erring one to Christ. We say, were they permitted and encouraged; yes, encouragement may now be needful. So long has this endowment of power been withheld from use by the dissuasive sentiments of the pulpit, press, and church officials that it will now need the combined aid of these to give the public mind a proper direction and undo a wrong introduced by the "man of sin" centuries ago.

But more especially do we look to the ministry for the correction of this wrong. Few, perhaps, have really intended to do wrong, but little do they know the embarrassment to which they have subjected a large portion of the church of Christ by their unscriptural position in relation to this matter. The Lord our God is one Lord. The same indwelling Spirit of might which fell upon Mary and the other women on the glorious day that ushered in the present dispensation still falls upon God's daughters. Not a few of the daughters of the Lord Almighty have, in obedience to the command of the Savior, tarried at Jerusalem. The endowment from on high having fallen upon them, the same impelling power which constrained Mary and the other women to speak as the Spirit gave utterance impels them to testify of Christ.

"The testimony of Jesus is the spirit of prophecy" (Rev 19:10). And how do these divinely baptized disciples stand ready to obey these impelling influences? Answer, you thousands of heaven-touched lips, whose testimonies have so long been repressed in the assemblies of the pious! Yes, answer you. thousands of female disciples of every Christian land, whose pent-up voices have so long, under the pressure of these manmade restraints, been uttered in groaning before God!

But let us conceive what would have been the effect had either of the male disciples interfered with the utterances of the Spirit through Mary or any of those many women who received the baptism of fire on the day of Pentecost. Suppose Peter, James, or John had questioned their right to speak as the Spirit gave utterance before the assembly, asserting that it was unseemly and out of the sphere of woman to proclaim a risen Jesus in view of the fact that there were men commingling in that multitude. How do you think that He who gave woman her commission on the morning of the resurrection, saying "Go, tell my brethren," would have been pleased with an interference of this sort?

But are not doings singularly similar to these being transacted now? We know that it is even so. However unseemly on the part of brethren, and revolting to our finer sensibilities, such occurrences may appear, we have occasion to know that they are not at all unusual in religious circles. We will refer to a Christian lady of more than ordinary intellectual endowments, of refined sensibilities, and whose literary culture and tastes were calculated to constitute her a star in the galaxy of this world.

2. A Life-Picture

I have seen a lovely female turn her eye away from the things of time and fix it on the world to come. Jesus, the altogether lovely, had revealed himself to her. And the vision of her mind was absorbingly entranced with his infinite loveliness, and she longed to reveal him to others. She went to the assembly of the pious. Out of the abundance of her heart, she would fain have spoken, so greatly did her heart desire to win others over to love the object of her adoration. Had she been in a worldly assembly and wished to attract others with an object of admiration, she would not have hesitated to have brought out the theme in conversation, and attracted listeners would have taken her more closely to their hearts and been won with the object of her love.

But she is now in the assembly of the pious. It is true many of them are her brothers and sisters, but cruel custom sealed her lips. Again and again she goes to the assembly for social prayer and the conference meeting, feeling the presence and power of an indwelling Savior enthroned uppermost in her heart and assured that he would have her testify of him. At last she ventures to obey God rather than man. And what is the result? A committee is appointed to wait on her and assure her that she must do so no more. Whisperings are heard in every direction that she has lost her senses. Instead of sympathizing looks of love, she meets averted glances and heart repulses. This is not a fancy sketch. No, it is a life-picture. You who have aided in bringing about this state of things, how does this life-picture strike you?

3. Who Was Rejected?

Think of the feelings of the Christian lady who has thrown herself in the bosom of your church community in order that she may enjoy the sympathies of Christian love and fellowship. Had grace divested her of refined sensibilities? No! Grace has only turned those refined sensibilities into a sanctified channel and given her a yet more refined perception of everything pure and lovely and of good report. What must be the sufferings of that richly-endowed, gentle, loving heart? But was it not her loving, gentle, indwelling Savior who desired for her to testify for him? In rejecting her testimony for Jesus, did not Jesus, the head of the church, take it as done unto himself?

Just as we were about to close the preceding paragraph, the activities of our pen were interrupted by the call of a valued minister of the gospel whose early religious training was in the bosom of a sect where the testimony of Jesus from the lips of women was not permitted in the church. We will introduce him to our readers. He tells us of an experience in connection with the theme of our work with which some husbands may sympathize. But we will let him speak for himself.

4. The Seal Broken

Never shall I forget the conflicting emotions of my poor heart when, for the first time, the voice of my wife was heard in a religious meeting. She had been trained from childhood in the Congregational Church, her father having been a deacon in the same for fifty years. I had been born and raised and educated for the ministry in the Episcopal Church. All know the oppressive silence imposed on woman's lips by both these denominations in their social meetings for prayer and Christian conference. But the voice of my wife, now for the first time, breaks upon my ear. We had only joined the Methodist Church the evening previous. I had anticipated some things in the new church not altogether in harmony with my views and tastes. But never had it entered my heart that my wife should so far forget custom of silence among females in the house of God.

My mortification for a few moments was indescribably keen. I would have dissolved our union with the church instantly and retraced our steps had it been possible. Such license, such disobedience to custom, I felt for the moment intolerable. My mortification arose not from a conviction that God was dishonored, Christ displeased, or the Holy Ghost grieved, but that the community, our former friends in the church we had just left, would be grieved and some point the finger of scorn. It was not a care for God's pleasure so much as a dread of violating long-established customs, wounding the hearts of old friends, that troubled me.

It was suggested to my mind that I had not religion enough to allow my wife to do what she deemed to be a duty to her Savior, that my prejudices must be her standard of activity. I at once saw the injustice both to my wife and to my Savior of thus thrusting my feelings and preferences between her and the cross. I was deeply humbled and, lifting up my heart to God in prayer, forgiveness was at once bestowed. I was made happy and blessed to enjoy woman's voice, in spite of former prejudices, in prayer and prophesying.

"I would have consulted you, my dear husband, had I imagined before going to church such a duty would have been impressed upon me," said my wife.

"It is well you did not, for my consent could not have been obtained. It is done now. It nearly killed me for a moment, but I have the victory and your testimony both rebuked and encouraged me. Henceforth, please Christ and not your husband."

I have often thought since then how cruel to woman it is to compel her to stifle her convictions, to grieve the Holy Spirit, to deny the Savior the service of her noble gifts because the pleasure of the church (not surely the world, for it favors woman's liberty) must be regarded above that of God.

The Church a Potter's Field where the gifts of women are buried! And how serious will be the responsibilities of that church which does not hasten to roll away the stone and bring out these long buried gifts! Every church community needs aid that this endowment of power would speedily bring. And what might we not anticipate as the result of this speedy resurrection of buried power! Not, perhaps, that our churches would be suddenly filled with women who might aspire to occupy the sacred desk. But what a change would soon be witnessed in the social meetings of all church communities! God has eminently endowed woman with gifts for the social circle. He has given her the power of persuasion and the ability to captivate. Who may *win* souls to Christ if she may not?

And how well-nigh endless her capabilities for usefulness, if there might only be a persevering effort on the part of the ministry to bring out her neglected gifts, added to a resolve on the part of women to be answerable through grace to the requisition. Our friend speaks too truly of the church as the only place where woman's gifts are unrecognized—that is, the church estranges herself from woman's gifts. To doubt whether woman brings her gifts into the church would be a libel on the Christian religion.

Let us contemplate that lovely, fascinating lady, whose cultivated tastes, richly endowed mind, and unrivalled conversational powers made her the soul and star of every worldly circle in which she moved. Did she move in the festive hall or the refined social circle, charmed worldlings irrespective of sex, gather around her and, as they greeting her gifts by unrestrained manifestations of approval, acknowledged themselves won by her endowment of power over mind?

Surely there has been no tardiness of the children of this world in acquainting themselves with her gifts. But the Holy Spirit comes to the heart of this interesting worldling bringing to her remembrance that she is not her own but bought with the price of her Redeemer's blood. She now apprehends through the enlightening influences of the Holy Spirit that all her various gifts have been purchased at an infinite price and must all be brought into the Lord's storehouse in order that they may be used for his glory.

Sin has its short-lived pleasures and she has enjoyed the pleasure of securing the smiles of an appreciative world. But the Holy Spirit assures her that she must come out from the world and be separate, and she sees that she must renounce the world and sin and through Christ give herself up to God and his church if she would become a member of the household of faith and secure life everlasting. How crucifying to flesh is the struggle! But she has revolved rather to endure the death of nature than to perish everlastingly. The struggle is severe. Nature, unreproved by God, will often suffer intensely in passing through the struggle which ensues in emerging from the death of sin to a life of holiness. God will not reprove because he knows that nature clings to earth. But the struggle past, the emancipated soul, with all its redeemed powers is at once taken to the heart of infinite love. This point gained, it is the divine order that all the issues of future life should flow out upon a redeemed world in unison with the head of the church. The church militant is Christ's visible body.

And now these gifts, so often in requisition and so prized in the social assembly of the children of this world, have been brought into the church. We said it were a libel on the religion of Jesus to assert that natural gifts of a high order, bestowed by the God of Nature, are recalled or buried when the possessor becomes a recipient of grace and a child of the kingdom. The God of Nature is also the God of all grace. Whatsoever was lovely becomes now more lovely. That which was of good report becomes of far better report through the refining of grace, and far more effectual for good.

Now that these endowments of power which were so captivating and commanding and so appreciatively recognized in worldly assemblies are laid as a sacrifice on the altar of the service of the church, what becomes of them? Does the church acquaint herself with these gifts? No! She is both a stranger to them and estranges herself from them. In most church organizations, she authorizes no church assemblies where she brings her sons and daughters together to call out these gifts for mutual edification and comfort. What means of grace does she acknowledge where her female members, in common with her male members, may use the gift of utterance with which God has endowed her? If the church authorizes no means by which she may acquaint herself with the gift which God has bestowed on women, what becomes of them? Why, of course they are buried. And where are the sepulchers in which they are entombed? Why, the church.

When the head of the church comes to receive his own with usury and demands that these buried gifts be brought forth, who will be required to meet the demand? Church communities are made up of individuals. Will it be some one individual member of that church session? Or will it be that minister who has failed to acquaint himself and his church session and other member of his flock of their responsibility before God in thus entombing an endowment of power which might have been instrumental in the spiritual life of thousands? What wonder, then, that our devoted friend said that the church is as a Potter's Field in which to bury strangers. For the church estranges herself from woman's gifts and buries them within her pale.

But the spirit of inspiration within us and around us, from every point, seems to say that the time is coming and now is when woman's gifts so long entombed in the church shall be resurrected. The command, "Come forth!" is already penetrating the sepulcher where these gifts have been buried. Faith sees the stone being rolled away. And what a resurrection of power shall we witness in the church when, in a sense answerable to the original design to God, women shall come forth—a very great army—engaging in all holy activities; when, in the true scriptural sense and answerable to the design of the God of the Bible, woman shall have become the "helpmeet" to man's spiritual nature! The idea that woman, with all her noble gifts and qualities, was formed mainly to minister to the sensuous nature of man is wholly unworthy of a place in the heart of a Christian.

In the name of the Lord Jesus who has purchased the church with his blood and has made abundant provision, not only for her purification, but for her beauty and strength, we implore those who minister at the altar of Christian churches to look at this subject. Christ would not have the church unseemly in the eyes of his enemies. How grievous in his sight that repelling influences should emanate from her whom he would call his beloved and whom he desires to stand without spot, wrinkle, or any such thing, so attractive in beauty and strength as to draw all men to her holy shrine!

Surely the church should present a model of all the blessed proprieties of grace. He, by whose forming hand she should be modeled, would have her inward construction and exterior surroundings all so truly in the *beauty* of holiness as to invite investigation and admiration. Why should she not be an embodiment of everything pure, lovely, and of good report? And such, in fact, she must be through Christ or her Lord can never receive her approvingly and say to her, "You are all fair, my love. There is no spot in you." Yet such she cannot be while she entombs in her midst the gift of prophecy entrusted to her daughters.

Oh the endless weight of responsibility with which the church is pressing herself earthward through the depressing influences of this error! How can she rise while the gifts of three-fourths of her membership are sepulchered in her midst? Would that we might speedily see her clothed in strength and coming up out of "the wilderness, leaning on her Beloved, fair as the moon, clear as the sun, and terrible as an army with banners!"

> Daughter of Zion, from the dust
> Exalt thy fallen head;
> Again in thy Redeemer trust:
> He calls thee from the dead.

6

Catherine Booth
and the Salvation Army

Introduction

Catherine Booth (1829–90), cofounder of the Salvation Army—an offshoot of Methodism in Britain—was one of those many women who fell under the influence of Phoebe Palmer, particularly her views on holiness and ministry.[1] In 1859, having just published her women's manifesto, Palmer preached her holiness doctrine at a revival in Newcastle-upon-Tyne, which had been an early epicenter of Methodism. While successfully winning many converts, this also exposed her to public ridicule as a "female ranter," with a particularly nasty pamphlet attack from the pen of Rev. Arthur Rees, Anglican curate of Sunderland. Pamela Walker reports that Rees "deplored the emotional services and disorderly, even hysterical, behavior revivalists encouraged."[2] But more to the point, he marshaled all the typical biblical arguments in a vicious diatribe against Palmer. An enraged Catherine Booth—who was beginning to explore her own call—wrote to her mother, "I am determined that fellow shall not go unthrashed."[3] She almost immediately published locally a pamphlet of her own, *Female Teaching*, reprinted in a slightly expanded second edition in 1861 by the Methodist printer G.

---

1. On Catherine Booth's life and ministry, see Green, *Catherine Booth*, and Read, *Catherine Booth*; cf. Eason, *Women in God's Army*.

2. Walker, "Gender, Radicalism, and Female Preaching," 175.

3. Reported in ibid., 176.

J. Stevenson in London. In 1870 yet a third edition surfaced under the title *Female Ministry; or, Woman's Right to Preach the Gospel* (Document 32).

Booth's defense reflected all of the apologetic trajectories related to women's ministry that Palmer had popularized. As Hassey points out, she "broke no new hermeneutical ground in her scriptural support for women's ministry."[4] Her arguments followed a pattern well established in the eighteenth century: evaluating difficult or problematic texts in their relation to other biblical passages and following what she described as a "common sense" approach to Scripture. She quoted and closely followed the reasoning and exegesis of Palmer's *Promise of the Father*. While concurring with Palmer's views on the 1 Corinthians 14 and 1 Timothy 2 texts, she considered them to be the wrong starting point for her defense, turning attention instead to the positive models of biblical women, the egalitarianism of Galatians 3:28, and the instrumentalism of Acts 2:17–18. She also challenged the corrupt nature of the church in which men had subjugated and silenced women simply to assert their power and legitimize authoritarianism. Ultimately, she judged a woman's call on the preeminent standard of the fruit her ministry bore. She broke no new ground in any of these arguments.

But in *Female Ministry*, Booth deviated in one particular and significant arena, not only from the holiness moorings, but also from the previous generations of British and American proponents of women—the area of "women's rights." Her concept of the woman's right to preach developed rapidly over the course of the 1850s.[5] According to Jennifer Lloyd, Booth "had been contemplating women's position in religion since 1855, when she sent a letter in reply to a Congregationalist minister's sermon on women's inferior nature, maintaining that until women had an equal education no one could know their natural abilities."[6] Her maturing view of women in ministry revolved around not only the scriptural texts that addressed women's ministry, but more importantly around the place of women in the natural order of the world.[7]

In this influential pamphlet, she established a new trajectory in terms of her argument against the natural subordination of women in creation, maintaining that Eve's subordination to Adam was an aspect of God's punishment and not God's original design. Walker concludes that "the most innovative and ultimately significant aspect of her thinking was her assertion that women could possess spiritual authority as women and could preach

---

4. Hassey, *No Time for Silence*, 99.
5. See Murdoch, "Female Ministry," which examines the history of this pamphlet.
6. Lloyd, *Women and British Methodism*, 180–81.
7. See Walker, "Chaste and Fervid Eloquence," 291.

as Christian women in their own voices as a part of the natural order."[8] This shift from preaching in exceptional circumstances under the impulse of the Holy Spirit to preaching as a "natural right" shaped most of the subsequent arguments related to the ministry of women. Walker succinctly identifies her most unique contribution:

Women's authority did not depend on the spontaneous outpouring of the Holy Spirit but was also based on the biblical text and could be part of the institutional church. Preaching, for Catherine Booth, was both the rational and systematic exegesis of Scripture and the outpouring of the Holy Spirit; it was part of the institutional church and it was inspired. She insisted that Christian women possessed the right to preach and that this right was based on their natural capacities and qualities. She therefore did not justify her claim by placing herself outside of social convention and order, but rather proclaimed her right to preach as a part of the covenant between God and humanity. She did not regard herself as a singular prophetic figure but rather as a dutiful Christian wife and mother.[9]

This claim for a woman's "right to preach," rooted in an affirmation of female virtue, reason, and natural independence, distinguished her from many of the other male and female apologists of her generation.

DOCUMENT 32

Female Ministry; or, Woman's Right to Preach the Gospel (1870)
Catherine Mumford Booth

The first and most common objection urged against the public exercises of women is that they are unnatural and unfeminine. Many labor under a very great but common mistake, viz., that of confounding nature with custom. Use or custom makes things appear to us natural which, in reality, are very unnatural. Novelty and rarity make very natural things appear strange and contrary to nature. So universally has this power of custom been felt and admitted that it has given birth to the proverb, "Use is second nature." Making allowance for the novelty of the thing, we cannot discover anything either unnatural or immodest in a Christian woman becomingly attired and appearing on a platform or in a pulpit. By nature she seems fitted to grace either. God has given to woman a graceful form and attitude, winning

---

8. Walker, "Gender, Radicalism, and Female Preaching," 178.

9. Ibid., 179.

manners, persuasive speech, and, above all, a finely-toned emotional nature, all of which appear to us eminent natural qualifications for public speaking.

We admit that want of mental culture, the trammels of custom, the force of prejudice, and one-sided interpretations of Scripture, have hitherto almost excluded her from this sphere. But before such a sphere is pronounced to be unnatural, it must be proved either that woman has not the ability to teach or to preach or that the possession and exercise of this ability makes her less natural in other respects, that as soon as she presumes to step on the platform or into the pulpit, she loses the delicacy and grace of the female character. We have numerous instances of her retaining all that is most esteemed in her sex and faithfully discharging the duties peculiar to her own sphere and, at the same time, taking her place with many of our most useful speakers and writers.

Why should woman be confined exclusively to the kitchen and the distaff any more than man to the field and workshop? Did not God, and has not nature, assigned to man his sphere of labor "to till the ground and to dress it"? If exemption is claimed from this kind of toil for a portion of the male sex on the ground of their possessing ability for intellectual and moral pursuits, we must be allowed to claim the same privilege for woman. Nor can we see the exception more unnatural in the one case than the other, or why God in this solitary instance has endowed a being with powers which he never intended her to employ.

There seems to be a great deal of unnecessary fear of women occupying any position which involves publicity, lest she should be rendered unfeminine by the indulgence of ambition or vanity. But why should woman any more than man be charged with ambition when impelled to use her talents for the good of her race? Moreover, as a laborer in the gospel her position is much higher than in any other public capacity. She is at once shielded from all coarse and unrefined influences and associations, her very vocation tending to exalt and refine all the tenderest and most womanly instincts of her nature. As a matter of fact it is well known to those who have had opportunities of observing the private character and deportment of women engaged in preaching the gospel that they have been amongst the most amiable, self-sacrificing, and unobtrusive of their sex.

"We well know," says the late Mr. Gurney, a minister of the Society of Friends, "that there are no women among us more generally distinguished for modesty, gentleness, order, and right submission to their brethren, than those who have been called by their divine Master into the exercise of the Christian ministry."

Who would dare to charge the sainted Madame Guyon, Lady Maxwell, the talented mother of the Wesleys, Mrs. Fletcher, Mrs. Elizabeth Fry, Mrs.

Smith, Mrs. Whiteman, or Miss Marsh with being unwomanly or ambitious? Some of these ladies we know have adorned by their private virtues the highest ranks of society and won alike from friends and enemies the highest eulogiums as to the devotedness, purity, and sweetness of their lives. Yet these were all more or less public women, every one of them expounding and exhorting from the Scriptures to mixed companies of men and women. Ambitious doubtless they were, but theirs was an ambition akin to his who, for the "joy that was set before him, endured the cross, despising the shame," and to his, who counted all things but dung and dross and was willing to be regarded as the off-scouring of all things that he might win souls to Jesus and bring glory to God. Would that all the Lord's people had more of this ambition.

Well, but say our objecting friends, how is it that these whose names you mention and many others should venture to preach when female ministry is forbidden in the word of God? This is by far the most serious objection which we have to consider—and if capable of substantiation should receive our immediate and cheerful acquiescence. But we think that we shall be able to show by a fair and consistent interpretation that the very opposite view is the truth. Not only is the public ministry of woman not forbidden; rather, it is absolutely enjoined by both precept and example in the Word of God.

First we will select the most prominent and explicit passages of the New Testament referring to the subject, beginning with 1 Corinthians 11:1–15: "Every man praying or prophesying, having his head covered, dishonors his head. But every woman that prays or prophesies with her head uncovered, dishonors her head; for that is all one as if she were shaven," etc. "The character," says a talented writer, "of the prophesying here referred to by the Apostle is defined in 1 Corinthians 14:3–4 and 31. The reader will see that it was directed to the 'edification, exhortation, and comfort of believers,' and the result anticipated was the conviction of unbelievers and unlearned persons. Such were the public services of women which the Apostle allowed, and such was the ministry of females predicted by the prophet Joel and described as a leading feature of the gospel dispensation. Women who speak in assemblies for worship under the influence of the Holy Spirit assume thereby no personal authority over others, they simply deliver the messages of the gospel which imply obedience, subjection, and responsibility, rather than authority and power."

Dr. Adam Clarke, on this verse, says, "Whatever may be the meaning of praying and prophesying in respect to the man, they have precisely the same meaning in respect to the woman! So that some women at least, as well as some men, might speak to others to edification, exhortation, and comfort. And this kind of prophesying or teaching was predicted by Joel

2:28 and referred to by Peter (Acts 2:17). And, had there not been such gifts bestowed on woman, the prophecy could not have had its fulfillment. The only difference marked by the Apostle was, the man had his head uncovered, because he was the representative of Christ, the woman had hers covered, because she was placed by the order of God in subjection to the man, and because it was the custom both among Greeks and Romans, and among the Jews an express law, that no woman should be seen abroad without a veil. This was and is a custom through all the East and none but public prostitutes go without veils. If a woman should appear in public without a veil, she would dishonor her head—her husband. And she must appear like to those women who have their hair shaven off as the punishment of adultery."

We think that the view above given is the only fair and common sense interpretation of this passage. If Paul does not here recognize the fact that women did actually pray and prophesy in the primitive churches, his language has no meaning at all. And if he does not recognize their right to do so by dictating the proprieties of their appearance while so engaged, we leave to objectors the task of educing any sense whatever from his language. If, according to the logic of Dr. Barnes, the Apostle here, in arguing against an improper and indecorous mode of performance, forbids the performance itself, the prohibition extends to the men as well as to the women, for Paul as expressly reprehends a man praying with his head covered as he does a woman with hers uncovered. With as much force might the doctor assert that in reproving the same church for their improper celebration of the Lord's Supper (1 Cor 11:20–21), Paul prohibits all Christians in every age celebrating it at all. "The question with the Corinthians was not whether or not the women should pray or prophesy at all—that question had been settled on the day of Pentecost—but whether, as a matter of convenience, they might do so without their veils." The Apostle kindly and clearly explains that by the law of nature and of society it would be improper to uncover her head while engaged in acts of public worship.

We think that the reflections cast on these women by Dr. Barnes and other commentators are quite gratuitous and uncalled for. Here is no intimation that they ever had uncovered their heads while so engaged. The fairest presumption is that they had not, nor ever would till they knew the Apostle's mind on the subject. We have precisely the same evidence that the men prayed and preached with their hats on as that women removed their veils and wore their hair disheveled, which is simply none at all.

We cannot but regard it as a signal evidence of the power of prejudice that a man of Dr. Barnes's general clearness and acumen should condescend to treat this passage in the manner he does. The doctor evidently feels the unfounded nature of his position and endeavors, by muddling two passages of distinct and different bearing, to annihilate the argument fairly deducible from the first. We would like to ask the doctor on what authority he makes such an exception as to the following: "But this cannot be interpreted as meaning that it is improper for females to speak or to pray in meetings of their own sex." Indeed! But according to the most reliable statistics we possess, two-thirds of the whole church is and always has been composed of their own sex. If then no rule of the New Testament is more positive than this, viz., that women are to keep silence in the churches, on whose authority does the doctor license them to speak to the larger portion of the church.

A barrister writing us on the above passage says, "Paul here takes for granted that women were in the habit of praying and prophesying. He expresses no surprise nor utters a syllable of censure. He was only anxious that they should not provoke unnecessary obloquy by laying aside their customary head dress or departing from the dress which was indicative of modesty in the country in which they lived. This passage seems to prove beyond the possibility of dispute that in the early times women were permitted to speak to the 'edification and comfort' of Christians and that the Lord graciously endowed them with grace and gifts for this service. What He did then may He not be doing now? It seems truly astonishing that Bible students, with the second chapter of the Acts before them, should not see that an imperative decree has gone forth from God, the execution of which women cannot escape. Whether they like or not, they 'shall' prophesy throughout the whole course of this dispensation, and they have been doing so, though they and their blessed labors are not much noticed."

Well, but say our objecting friends, hear what Paul says in another place: "Let your women keep silence in the churches, for it is not permitted unto them to speak; but they are commanded to be under obedience, as also says the law. And if they will learn anything, let them ask their husbands at home, for it is a shame for women to speak in the church" (1 Cor 14:34–35). Now let it be borne in mind this is the same Apostle, writing to the same church, as in the above instance. Will any one maintain that Paul here refers to the same kind of speaking as before? If so, we insist on his supplying us with some rule of interpretation which will harmonize this unparalleled contradiction and absurdity.

Taking the simple and common sense view of the two passages, viz., that one refers to the devotional and religious exercises in the church and the other to inconvenient asking of questions, and imprudent or ignorant talking, there is no contradiction or discrepancy, no straining or twisting of either. If, on the other hand, we assume that the Apostle refers in both instances to the same thing, we make him in one page give the most explicit directions how a thing shall be performed, which in a page or two further on, and writing to the same church, he expressly forbids being performed at all.

We admit that "it is a shame for women to speak in the church," in the sense here intended by the Apostle, but before the argument based on these words can be deemed of any worth, objectors must prove that the "speaking" here is synonymous with that concerning the manner of which the Apostle legislates in 1 Corinthians 11. Dr. Adam Clarke, on this passage, says, "according to the prediction of Joel, the Spirit of God was to be poured out on the women as well as the men, that they might prophesy, that is teach. And that they did prophesy or teach is evident from what the Apostle says (1 Cor 11) where he lays down rules to regulate this part of their conduct while ministering in the church. All that the Apostle opposes here is their questioning, finding fault, disputing, etc., in the Christian church, as the Jewish men were permitted to do in their synagogues (see Luke 2:46); together with attempts to usurp authority over men by setting up their judgment in opposition to them, for the Apostle has reference to acts of disobedience and arrogance of which no woman would be guilty who was under the influence of the Spirit of God."

The Rev. J. H. Robinson writing on this passage remarks: "The silence imposed here must be explained by the verb, to speak (*lalein*), used afterwards. Whatever that verb means in this verse, I admit and believe the women were forbidden to do in the church. But what does it mean? It is used nearly three hundred times in the New Testament and scarcely any verb is used with so great a variety of adjuncts. In *Schleusner's Lexicon* its meaning is traced under seventeen distinct heads and he occupies two full pages of the book in explaining it. Among other meanings he gives *respondeo, rationem reddo, præcipio, jubeo*—"I answer, I return a reason, I give rule or precept, I order, decree." In *Robinson's Lexicon* (Bloomfield's edition) two pages nearly are occupied with the explanation of this word. He gives instances of its meaning, "as modified by the context, where the sense lies, not so much in *lalein* (*lalein*) as in the adjuncts." *The passage under consideration is one of those to which he refers as being so "modified by the context."* Greenfield gives, with others, the following meanings of the word: "to prattle—be loquacious as a child—to speak in answer to answer, as in John 19:10; harangue. plead, Acts 9:29; 21. To direct, command, Acts 3:22." In *Liddel and Scott's Lexicon*, the following meanings are given: "to chatter, babble; of birds, to twitter, chirp; strictly, to make an inarticulate sound, opposed to articulate speech; but also generally, to talk, say."

"It is clear then that *lalein* may mean something different from mere speaking and that to use this word in a prohibition does not imply that absolute silence or abstinence from speaking is enjoined. On the contrary, the prohibition applies to an improper kind of speaking, which is to be understood, not from the word itself but, as Mr. Robinson says, from 'the context.' Now, 'the context' shows that it was not silence which was imposed upon women in the church, but only a refraining from such speaking as was inconsistent with the words, 'they are commanded to be under obedience,' or, more literally, 'to be obedient.' That is, they were to refrain from such questionings, dogmatic assertions, and disputations, as would bring them into collision with the men—as would ruffle their tempers and occasion an unamiable volubility of speech. This kind of speaking, and this alone, as it appears to me, was forbidden by the Apostle in the passage before us. This kind of speaking was the only supposable antagonist to and violation of 'obedience.' Absolute silence was not essential to that 'obedience.'"

"My studies in 'Biblical criticism,' have not informed me that a woman must cease to speak before she can obey, and I am therefore led to the irresistible conclusion that it is not all speaking in the church which the Apostle forbids and which he pronounces to be shameful. On the contrary, a pertinacious, inquisitive, domineering, dogmatic kind of speaking, which, while it is unbecoming in a man, is shameful and odious in a woman, and especially when that woman is in the church, and is speaking on the deep things of religion."

Parkhurst, in his lexicon, tells us that "the Greek word 'lalein,' which our translation renders speak, is not the word used in Greek to signify to speak with premeditation and prudence, but is the word used to signify to speak imprudently and without consideration, and is that applied to one who lets his tongue run but does not speak to the purpose, but says nothing." Now unless Parkhurst is utterly wrong in his Greek, which it is apprehended no one will venture to affirm, Paul's fulmination is not launched against speech with premeditation and prudence, but against speech devoid of these qualities. It would be well if all speakers of the male as well as the female sex were obedient to this rule.

We think that with the light cast on this text by the four eminent Greek scholars above quoted, there can be no doubt in any unprejudiced mind as to the true meaning of "lalein" in this connection. And we find from church history that the primitive Christians thus understood it; that women did actually speak and preach amongst them we have indisputable proof. God had promised in the last days to pour out his Spirit upon all flesh and that the daughters as well as the sons of mankind should prophesy.

And Peter says most emphatically, respecting the outpouring of the Spirit on the day of Pentecost, "This is that which is spoken of by the prophet Joel" (Acts 2:16–18). Words more explicit, and an application of prophecy more direct than this, does not occur within the range of the New

Testament. Commentators say, "If women have the gift of prophecy, they must not use that gift in public." But God says by his prophet Joel, they shall use it just in the same sense as the sons use it. When the dictation of men so flatly opposes the express declaration of the "sure word of prophecy," we make no apology for its utter and indignant rejection.

Presbuteros, a talented writer of the Protestant Electoral Union, in his reply to a priest of Rome says:

> Habituated for ages, as men had been, to the diabolical teaching and delusions practiced upon them by the papal "priesthood," it was difficult for them, when they did get possession of the Scriptures, to discern therein the plain fact, that among the primitive Christians preaching was not confined to men, but women also, gifted with power by the Holy Spirit, preached the gospel; and hence the slowness with which, even at the present time, this truth has been admitted by those giving heed to the word of God, and especially those setting themselves up as a "priesthood" or a "clergy."

As shown in page 66, "God had, according to his promise on the day of Pentecost poured out his Holy Spirit upon believers—men and women, old and young—that they should prophesy, and they did so. The prophesying spoken of was not the foretelling of events, but the preaching to the world at large the glad tidings of salvation by Jesus Christ. For this purpose it pleased God to make use of women as well as men. It is plainly the duty of every Christian to insist upon the fulfillment of the will of God, and the abrogation of every single thing inconsistent therewith. I would draw attention to the fact that Phoebe, a Christian woman whom we find in our version of the scripture (Rom 16:1) spoken of only as any common servant attached to a congregation, was nothing less than one of those gifted by the Holy Spirit for publishing the glad tidings or preaching the gospel. The manner in which the Apostle (whose only care was the propagation of evangelical truth) speaks of her shows that she was what he in Greek styled her a deacon (*diaconon*) or preacher of the word. Our translators speak of her (because she was a woman) only as 'a servant of the church which is at Cenchrea.' The men 'deacons' they styled ministers, but a woman on the same level as themselves would be an anomaly, and therefore she was to be only the servant of men ministers, who, in the popish sense, constituted the church!"

The Apostle says of her—"I commend unto you Phoebe our sister, who is a minister (*diaconon*) of the church which is at Cenchrea, that you receive her in the Lord as becomes saints, and that you assist her in whatsoever business she has need of you." To the common sense of disinterested minds it will be evident that the Apostle could not have requested more for any one of the most zealous of men preachers than he did for Phoebe! They were to assist "her in whatsoever business she" might require their aid.

Hence we discern that she had no such trifling position in the primitive church as at the present time episcopal dignitaries attach to deacons and deaconesses! Observe, the same Greek word is used to designate her that was applied to all the apostles and to Jesus himself. For example: "Now I say that Jesus Christ was a minister (*diaconon*) of the circumcision" (Rom 15:8). "Who then is Paul, and who is Apollos, but ministers (*diaconoi*) by whom you believed" (1 Cor 3:5). "Our sufficiency is of God; who also has made us able ministers (*diaconous*) of the new testament" (2 Cor 3:6). "In all things approving ourselves as the ministers (*diaconoi*) of God" (6:4). The idea of a woman deacon in the "three orders!"—it was intolerable, therefore let her be a "servant." Theodoret however says, "The fame of Phoebe was spoken of throughout the world. She was known not only to the Greeks and Romans, but also to the Barbarians," which implies that she had traveled much and propagated the gospel in foreign countries.

"Salute Andronicus and Junia, my kinsmen and my fellow prisoners, who are of note among the apostles, who also were in Christ before me" (Rom 16:7). By the word "kinsmen" one would take Junia to have been a man. But Chrysostom and Theophylact, who were both Greeks, and consequently knew their mother tongue better than our translators, say Junia was a woman. Kinsmen should therefore have been rendered kinsfolk. But with our translators it was out of all character to have a woman of note amongst the apostles and a fellow-prisoner with Paul for the gospel. Therefore let them be kinsmen!

Justin Martyr, who lived till about AD 150, says, in his *Dialogue with Trypho the Jew*, "that both men and women were seen among them who had the extraordinary gifts of the Spirit of God, according as the prophet Joel had foretold, by which he endeavored to convince the Jews that the latter days were come."

Dodwell, in his dissertations on Irenæus says, "that the gift of the spirit of prophecy was given to others besides the apostles, and that not only in the first and second, but in the third century—even to the time of Constantine—all sorts and ranks of men had these gifts; yes, and women too."

Eusebius speaks of Potomania Ammias, a prophetess in Philadelphia, and others, "who were equally distinguished for their love and zeal in the cause of Christ."

"The scriptural idea," says Mrs. Palmer, "of the terms preach and prophesy stands so inseparably connected as one and the same thing that we should find it difficult to get aside from the fact that women did preach, or in other words, prophesy in the early ages of Christianity, and have continued to do so down to the present time to just the degree that the spirit of the Christian dispensation has been recognized. And it is also a significant fact, that to the degree denominations who have once favored the practice, lose the freshness of their zeal, and as a consequence their primitive simplicity and, as ancient Israel, yield to a desire to be like surrounding communities, in a corresponding ratio are the labors of females discountenanced."

If anyone still insists on a literal application of this text, we beg to ask how he disposes of the preceding part of the chapter where it occurs. Surely, if one verse be so authoritative and binding, the whole chapter is equally so. Therefore, those who insist on a literal application of the words of Paul under all circumstances and through all time will be careful to observe the Apostle's order of worship in their own congregations.

But, we ask, where is the minister who lets his whole church prophesy one by one, and himself sits still and listens while they are speaking so that all things may be done decently and in order? But Paul as expressly lays down this order as he does the rule for women, and he adds, "The things that I write unto you are the commandments of the Lord" (verse 37). Why then do not ministers abide by these directions? We anticipate their reply—"Because these directions were given to the Corinthians as temporary arrangements and, though they were the commandments of the Lord to them at that time, they do not apply to all Christians in all times." Indeed, but unfortunately for their argument the prohibition of women speaking, even if it meant what they wish, was given amongst those very directions and to the Corinthians only. For it reads, "Let your women keep silence," and, for aught this passage teaches to the contrary, Christian women of all other churches might do what these women were forbidden to do. Until, therefore, learned theologians make a personal application of the rest of the chapter, they must excuse us declining to do so of the 24th verse and we challenge them to show any breach of the divine law in one case more than the other.

Another passage frequently cited as prohibitory of female labor in the church is 1 Timothy 2:12–13. Though we have never met with the slightest proof that this text has any reference to the public exercises of women, nevertheless, as it is often quoted, we will give it a fair and thorough examination. "It is primarily an injunction," says the Rev. J. H. Robinson, "respecting her personal behavior at home. It stands in connection with precepts respecting her apparel and her domestic position, especially her relation to her husband. No one will suppose that the Apostle forbids a woman to 'teach' absolutely and universally. Even objectors would allow her to teach her own sex in private. They would let her teach her servants and children, and perhaps, her husband too. If he were ignorant of the Savior, might she not teach him the way to Christ? If she were acquainted with languages, arts or sciences, which he did not know, might she not teach him these things? Certainly she might! The 'teaching,' therefore which is forbidden by the Apostle is not every kind of teaching any more than, in the previous instance, his prohibition of speaking applied to every kind of speaking in the church. It is such teaching as is domineering and involves the usurpation of authority over the man. This is the only teaching forbidden by St. Paul in the passage under consideration."

"If this passage be not a prohibition of every kind of teaching, we can only ascertain what kind of teaching is forbidden by the modifying expressions with which *didaskein* stands associated and for anything these modifying expressions affirm to the contrary, her teaching may be public, reiterated, urgent, and may comprehend a variety of subjects, provided it be not dictatorial, domineering, nor vociferous; for then, and then only, would it be incompatible with her obedience."

The Rev. Dr. Taft says, "This passage should be rendered 'I suffer not a woman to teach by usurping authority over the man.' This rendering removes all the difficulties and contradictions involved in the ordinary reading and evidently gives the meaning of the Apostle." "If the nature of society," says the same writer, "it's good and prosperity—in which women are jointly and equally concerned with men—if in many cases their fitness and capacity for instructors, being admitted to be equal to the other sex, are not reasons sufficient to convince the candid reader of woman's right to preach and teach because of two texts in Paul's epistles, let him consult the paraphrase of Locke, where he has proved to a demonstration that the Apostle in these texts never intended to prohibit women from praying and preaching in the church provided they were dressed as became women professing godliness and were qualified for the sacred office."

"It will be found," says another writer, "by an examination of this text with its connections that the teaching here alluded to stands in necessary connection with usurping authority, as though the Apostle had said, the gospel does not alter the relation of women in view of priority, for Adam was first formed, then Eve."

"This prohibition," says the before-named barrister, "refers exclusively to the private life and domestic character of woman and simply means that an ignorant or unruly woman is not to force her opinions on the man whether he will or no. It has no reference whatever to good women living in obedience to God and their husbands or to women sent out to preach the gospel by the call of the Holy Spirit."

If this context is allowed to fix the meaning of *didaskein* in this text, as it would in any other, there can be no doubt in any honest mind that the above is the only consistent interpretation. If it is, then this prohibition has no bearing whatever on the religious exercise of women led and taught of the Spirit of God. We cannot forbear asking on whose skirts the mischief resulting from the false application of this text will be found? Thank God the day is dawning with respect to this subject. Women are studying and investigating for themselves. They are claiming to be recognized as responsible human beings answerable to God for their convictions of duty, and urged by the divine Spirit they are overstepping those unscriptural barriers which the church has so long reared against its performance.

Whether the church will allow women to speak in her assemblies can only be a question of time. Common sense, public opinion, and the blessed results of female agency will force her to give us an honest and impartial rendering of the solitary text on which she grounds her prohibitions. Then, when the true light shines and God's words take the place of man's traditions, the Doctor of Divinity who shall teach that Paul commands woman to be silent when God's Spirit urges her to speak will be regarded much the same as we should now regard an astronomer who should teach that the sun is the earth's satellite.

Another argument urged against female preaching is that it is unnecessary, that there is plenty of scope for her efforts in private, in visiting the sick and poor, and working for the temporalities of the church. Doubtless woman ought to be thankful for any sphere for benefiting her race and glorifying God. But we cannot be blind to the supreme selfishness of making her so welcome to the hidden toil and self-sacrifice, the hewing of wood and the drawing of water, the watching and waiting, the reproach and persecution attaching to her Master's service, without allowing her a tittle of the honor which He has attached to the ministration of His gospel.

Here again, man's theory and God's order are at variance. God says, "Those who honor me I will honor." Our Lord links the joy with the suffering, the glory with the shame, the exaltation with the humiliation, the crown with the cross, the finding of life with the losing of it. Nor did he manifest any such horror at female publicity in his cause as many of his professed people appear to entertain in these days. We have no intimation of his reproving the Samaritan woman for her public proclamation of him to her countrymen, not of his rebuking the women who followed him amidst a taunting mob on his way to the cross. And yet, surely, privacy was their proper sphere. On one occasion he did say with reference to a woman, "Verily, I say unto you, wherever this gospel shall be preached in the whole world, what this woman has done for me will be told for a memorial of her" (Matt 26:12; see also Luke 7:37–50).

As to the obligation devolving on woman to labor for her Master, I presume there will be no controversy. The particular sphere in which each individual shall do this must be dictated by the teachings of the Holy Spirit and the gifts with which God has endowed her. If she has the necessary gifts and feels herself called by the Spirit to preach there is not a single word in the whole book of God to restrain her, but many, very many to urge and encourage her. God says she *shall* do so and Paul prescribes the manner in which she shall do it, and Phoebe, Junia, Philip's four daughters, and many other women actually did preach and speak in the primitive churches.

If this had not been the case there would have been less freedom under the new than under the old dispensation—a greater paucity of gifts and agencies under the Spirit than under the law. Fewer laborers when more work to be done. Instead of the destruction of caste and division between the priesthood and the people, and the setting up of a spiritual kingdom in which all true believers were "kings and priests unto God," the division would have been more stringent and the disabilities of the common people greater. Whereas we are told again and again in effect, that in "Christ Jesus there is neither bond nor free, male nor female, but you are all one in Christ Jesus."

We commend a few passages bearing on the ministrations of woman under the old dispensation to the careful consideration of our readers. "And Deborah, a prophetess, the wife of Lapidoth, she judged Israel at that time" (Jud 4:4–10). There are two particulars in this passage worthy of note. First, the authority of Deborah as a prophetess, or revealer of God's will to Israel, was acknowledged and submitted to as implicitly as in the cases of the male judges who succeeded her. Secondly, she is made the military head of ten thousand men, Barak refusing to go to battle without her.

Again, in 2 Kings 22:12–20, we have an account of the king sending the high priest and the scribe to Huldah, the prophetess, the wife of Shallum, who dwelt at Jerusalem in the college, to inquire at her mouth the will of God in reference to the book of the law which had been found in the house of the Lord. The authority and dignity of Huldah's message to the king does not betray anything of that trembling diffidence or abject servility which some persons seem to think should characterize the religious exercises of woman. She answers him as the prophetess of the Lord, having the signet of the King of kings attached to her utterances.

"The Lord gave the word, and great was the company of those that published it" (Psa 68:11). In the original Hebrew it is, "Great was the company of women publishers, or women evangelists." Grotius explains this passage, "The Lord shall give the word, that is, plentiful matter of speaking, so that he would call those which follow the great army of preaching women, victories, or female conquerors." How is it that the feminine word is actually excluded in this text? No Hebrew scholar could possibly deny it. When applied to Phoebe, the translators preferred to leave "diaconon" out altogether. But the Lord gives the word and he will choose whom he pleases to publish it notwithstanding the condemnation of translators and theologians.

"For I brought you up out of the land of Egypt and redeemed you out of the house of servants; and I sent before you Moses, Aaron, and Miriam" (Mic 6:4). God here classes Miriam with Moses and Aaron and declares that He sent her before His people. We fear that had some of our friends been men of Israel at that time, they would have disputed such a leadership.

In the light of such passages as these, who will dare to dispute the fact that God did under the old dispensation endue his handmaidens with the gifts and calling of prophets answering to our present idea of preachers. Strange indeed would it be if, under the fullness of the gospel dispensation, there were nothing analogous to this, but "positive and explicit rules," to prevent any approximation thereto. We are thankful to find, however, abundant evidence that the "spirit of prophecy which is the testimony of Jesus," was poured out on the female as fully as on the male disciple, and "his daughters and his handmaidens" prophesied. We commend the following texts from the New Testament to the careful consideration of our readers.

"And she (Anna) was a widow of about fourscore and four years, who departed not from the temple, but served God with fasting and prayers night and day. And she coming in that instant, gave thanks likewise unto the Lord, and spoke of him to all them that looked for redemption on Jerusalem" (Luke 2:37–38). Can anyone explain wherein this exercise of Anna's differed from that of Simeon recorded just before? It was in the same public place, the temple. It was during the same service. It was equally public, for she "spoke of Him to all who looked for redemption in Jerusalem."

Jesus said to the two Marys, "All hail! And they came and held him by the feet and worshipped Him. Then said Jesus unto them, Be not afraid. Go, tell my brethren that they go before me into Galilee" (Matt 28:9, 10). There are two or three points in this beautiful narrative to which we wish to call the attention of our readers.

First, it was the first announcement of the glorious news to a lost world and a company of forsaking disciples. Second, it was as public as the nature of the case demanded and intended ultimately to be published to the ends of the earth. Third, Mary was expressly commissioned to reveal the fact to the apostles, and thus she literally became their teacher in that memorable occasion. Oh, glorious privilege, to be allowed to herald the glad tidings of a Savior risen! How could it be that our Lord chose a woman to this honor? Well, one reason might be that the male disciples were all missing at the time. They all forsook him and fled. But woman was there, as she had ever been, ready to minister to her risen as to her dying Lord—

> Not she with traitorous lips her Savior stung,
> Not she denied Him with unholy tongue;
> She, whilst apostles shrunk, could danger brave;
> Last at the cross, and earliest at the grave.

But surely, if the dignity of our Lord of his message were likely to be imperiled by committing this sacred trust to a woman, He who was guarded by legions of angels could have commanded another messenger. But, as if intent on doing her honor and rewarding her unwavering fidelity, He reveals himself first to her and as an evidence that he had taken out of the way the curse under which she had so long groaned, nailing it to his cross, he makes her who had been first in the transgression first also in the glorious knowledge of complete redemption.

"Acts 1:14 and 2:1–4. We are in the first of these passages expressly told that the women were assembled with the disciples on the day of Pentecost, and in the second that the cloven tongues sat upon them each and the Holy Ghost filled them all and they spoke as the Spirit gave them utterance. It is nothing to the point to argue that the gift of tongues was a miraculous gift, seeing that the Spirit was the primary bestowment. The tongues were only emblematical of the office which the Spirit was henceforth to sustain to his people. The Spirit was given alike to the female as to the male disciple, and this is cited by Peter (16, 18), as the peculiar specialty of the latter dispensation. What a remarkable device of the devil that he has so long succeeded in hiding this characteristic of the latter day glory! He knows, whether the church does or not, how eminently detrimental to the interests of his kingdom have been the religious labors of woman, and while her seed has mortally bruised his head, he ceases not to bruise her heel, but the time of her deliverance draws nigh."

"Philip the evangelist had four daughters, virgins, which did prophesy." From Eusebius, the ancient ecclesiastical historian we learn that Philip's daughters lived to a good old age, always abounding in the work of the Lord. "Mighty luminaries," he writes, "have fallen asleep in Asia. Philip, and two of his virgin daughters, sleep at Hierapolis. The others and the beloved disciple John rest at Ephesus."

"I entreat you also true yokefellow, help those women who labored with me in the gospel with Clement and with my other fellow laborers" (Phil 4:3). This is a recognition of female laborers, not concerning the gospel but in the gospel, whom Paul classes with Clement and other his fellow laborers. Precisely the same terms are applied to Timotheus, whom Paul styles a "minister of God and his fellow laborer in the gospel of Christ" (1 Thess 3:2).

Again, "Greet Priscilla and Aquila, my helpers in Christ Jesus; who have for my life laid down their own necks, unto whom not only I give thanks, but all the churches of the Gentiles" (Rom 16:3–4).

The word rendered helpers means a *fellow laborer, associate coadjutor* (Greenfield) working together, an assistant, a joint laborer, a colleague (Dunbar) in the New Testament, spoken only of a co-worker, helper in a Christian work, that is of Christian teachers (Robinson). How can these terms, with any show of consistency, be made to apply merely to the exercise of hospitality towards that apostle or the duty of private visitation? To be a partner, coadjutor, or joint worker with a preacher of the gospel must be something more than to be his waiting maid.

"Salute Tryphena and Tryphosa who labor in the Lord. Salute the beloved Persis who labored much in the Lord" (Rom 16:12). Dr. Clarke, on this verse, says, "Many have spent much useless labor in endeavoring to prove that these women did not preach. That there were prophetesses as well as prophets in the church we learn and that a woman might pray or prophesy provided that she had her head covered we know, and, according to St. Paul (1 Cor 14:3), whoever prophesied spoke unto others to edification, exhortation, and comfort, and that no preacher can do more every person must acknowledge. Because to edify exhort, and comfort, are the prime ends of the gospel ministry. If women thus prophesied, then women preached."

"There is neither Jew nor Greek, there is neither male nor female, for you are all one in Christ Jesus" (Gal 3:28). If this passage does not teach that in the privileges, duties, and responsibilities of Christ's kingdom all differences of nation, caste, and sex are abolished, we should like to know what it does teach, and wherefore it was written (see also 1 Cor 7:22).

As we have before observed, 1 Corinthians 14:34–35 is the only text in the whole book of God which, even by false translation, can be made prohibitory of female speaking in the church. How is it then that by this one isolated passage, which according to our best Greek authorities is wrongly rendered and wrongly applied, woman's lips have been sealed for centuries and the "testimony of Jesus which is the spirit of prophecy," silenced when bestowed on her? How is it that this solitary text has been allowed to stand unexamined and unexplained, no, that learned commentators who have known its true meaning as perfectly as either Robinson, Bloomfield, Greenfield, Scott, Parkhurst, or Locke have upheld the delusion and enforced it as a divine precept binding on all female disciples through all time?

Surely there must have been some unfaithfulness, "craftiness," and "handling of the word of life deceitfully" somewhere. Surely the love of caste and unscriptural jealousy for a separated priesthood has had something to do with this anomaly. By this course theologians and commentators have involved themselves in all sorts of inconsistencies and contradictions, and worse, they have nullified some of the most precious promises of God's word. They have set the most explicit predictions of prophecy at variance with apostolic injunctions, and the most immediate and wonderful operations of the Holy Ghost in direct opposition "to positive, explicit, and universal rules."

Notwithstanding however all this opposition to female ministry on the part of those deemed authorities in the church, there have been some in all ages in whom the Holy Ghost has wrought so mightily that, at the sacrifice of reputation and all things most dear, they have been compelled to come out as witnesses for Jesus and ambassadors of His gospel. As a rule these women have been amongst the most devoted and self-denying of the Lord's people, giving indisputable evidence by the purity and beauty of their lives that they were led by the Spirit of God.

Now, if the Word of God forbids female ministry, we would ask how it happens that so many of the most devoted handmaidens of the Lord have felt themselves constrained by the Holy Ghost to exercise it? Surely there must be some mistake somewhere, for the word and the Spirit cannot contradict each other. Either the word does not condemn women preaching or these confessedly holy women have been deceived. Will any one venture to assert that such women as Mrs. Elizabeth Fry, Mrs. Fletcher of Madeley, and Mrs. Smith have been deceived with respect to their call to deliver the gospel messages to their fellow creatures? If not, then God does call and qualify women to preach, and His word, rightly understood, cannot forbid what His Spirit enjoins.

Further, it is a significant fact, which we commend to the consideration of all thoughtful Christians, that the public ministry of women has been eminently owned of God in the salvation of souls and the edification of his people. Paul refers to the fruits of his labors as evidence of his divine commission (1 Cor 9:20). "If I am not an apostle unto others, yet doubtless I am to you, for the seal of mine apostleship are you in the Lord." If this criterion be allowed to settle the question respecting woman's call to preach, we have no fear as to the result. A few examples of the blessing which has attended the ministrations of females may help to throw some light on this matter of a divine call.

At a missionary meeting held at Columbia, March 26th, 1824, the name of Mrs. Smith of the Cape of Good Hope was brought before the meeting when Sir Richard Otley, the chairman, said, "The name of Mrs. Smith has been justly celebrated by the religious world and in the colony of the Cape of Good Hope. I heard a talented missionary state that wherever he went in that colony, at 600 or 1000 miles from the principal seat of government, among the natives of Africa, and wherever he saw persons converted to Christianity, the name of Mrs. Smith was hailed as the person from whom they received their religious impressions. Although no less than ten missionaries, all men of piety and industry, were stationed in that settlement, the exertions of Mrs. Smith alone were more efficacious and had been attended with greater success than the labors of those missionaries combined." The Rev. J. Campbell, missionary to Africa, says, "So extensive were the good effects of her pious exhortations that on my first visit to the colony, wherever I met with persons of evangelical piety, I generally found that their first impressions of religion were ascribed to Mrs. Smith."

Mrs. Mary Taft, the talented lady of the Rev. Dr. Taft, was another eminently successful laborer in the Lord's vineyard. "If," says Mrs. Palmer, "the criterion by which we may judge of a divine call to proclaim salvation is by the proportion of fruit gathered, then the commission Mrs. Taft received is preeminently unmistakable. In reviewing her diary, we are constrained to believe that not one minister in five hundred could produce so many seals to their ministry. An eminent minister informed us that of those who had been brought to Christ through her labors, over two hundred entered the ministry. She seldom opened her mouth in public assemblies, either in prayer or speaking, but the Holy Spirit accompanied her words in such a wonderful manner that sinners were convicted and, as in apostolic times, were constrained to cry out, 'What must we do to be saved?' She labored under the sanction and was hailed as a fellow helper in the gospel by the Revs. Messrs. Mather, Pawson, Hearnshaw, Blackborne, Marsden, Bramwell, Vasey, and many other equally distinguished ministers of her time."

The Rev. Mr. Pawson, when President of the Wesleyan Conference, writes as follows to a circuit where Mrs. Taft was stationed with her husband, where she met with some gainsayers: "It is well known that religion has been for some time at a very low ebb in Dover. I therefore could not help thinking that is was a kind providence that Mrs. Taft was stationed among you, and that, by the blessing of God, she might be the instrument of reviving the work of God among you. I seriously believe Mrs. Taft to be a deeply pious, prudent, modest woman. I believe the Lord has owned and blessed her labors very much, and many, yes, very many souls have been brought to the saving knowledge of God by her preaching. Many have come to hear her out of curiosity, who would not have come to hear a man, and have been awakened and converted to God. I do assure you there is much fruit of her labors in many parts of our connection."

Mrs. Fletcher, the wife of the sainted vicar of Madeley, was another of the daughters of the Lord on whom was poured the spirit of prophecy. This eminently devoted lady opened an orphan house and devoted her time, her heart, and her fortune to the work of the Lord. The Rev. Mr. Hodson, in referring to her public labors, says, "Mrs. Fletcher was not only luminous but truly eloquent—her discourses displayed much good sense and were fraught with the riches of the gospel. She excelled in that poetry of an orator which can alone supply the place of all the rest—that eloquence which goes directly to the heart. She was the honored instrument of doing much good and the fruit of her labors is now manifest in the lives and tempers of numbers who will be her crown of rejoicing in the day of the Lord." The Rev. Henry Moore sums up a fine eulogy on her character and labors by saying, "May not every pious churchman say, Would to God all the Lord's people were such prophets and prophetesses!"

Miss Elizabeth Hurrell traveled through many counties in England preaching the unsearchable riches of Christ and very many were, through her instrumentality, brought to a knowledge of the truth, not a few of whom were afterwards called to fill very honorable stations in the church.

From the Methodist Conference held at Manchester in 1787, Mr. Wesley wrote to Miss Sarah Mallet, whose labors, while very acceptable to the people, had been opposed by some of the preachers: "We give the right hand of fellowship to Sarah Mallet and have no objection to her being a preacher in our connection so long as she preaches Methodist doctrine and attends to our discipline."

Such are a few examples of the success attending the public labors of females in the gospel. We might give many more, but our space only admits of a bare mention of Mrs. Wesley, Mrs. Rogers, Mrs. President Edwards, Mrs. Elizabeth Fry, Mrs. Hall, Mrs. Gilbert, Miss Lawrence, Miss Newman, Miss Miller, Miss Tooth, and Miss Cutler, whose holy lives and zealous labors were owned of God in the conversion of thousands of souls and the abundant edification of the Lord's people.

Nor are the instances of the spirit of prophecy bestowed on women confined to bygone generations. The revival of this age, as well as of every other, has been marked by this endowment, and the labors of such pious and talented ladies as Mrs. Palmer, Mrs. Finney, Mrs. Wightman, Miss Marsh, with numberless other Marys and Phoebes, have contributed in no small degree to its extension and power.

We have endeavored in the foregoing pages to establish what we sincerely believe, that woman has a right to teach. Here the whole question hinges. If she has the right, she has it independently of any man-made restrictions which do not equally refer to the opposite sex. If she has the right and possesses the necessary qualifications, we maintain that, where the law of expediency does not prevent, she is at liberty to exercise it without any further pretensions to inspiration than those put forth by that male sex. If, on the other hand, it can be proved that she has not the right, but that imperative silence is imposed upon her by the word of God, we cannot see who has authority to relax or make exceptions to the law.

If commentators had dealt with the Bible on other subjects as they have dealt with it on this, taking isolated passages, separated from their explanatory connections, and insisting on a literal interpretation of the words of our version, what errors and contradictions would have been forced upon the acceptance of the church, and what terrible results would have accrued to the world. On this principle the Universalist will have all men unconditionally saved because the Bible says, "Christ is the Savior of all men." The antinomian, according to this rule of interpretation, has most unquestionable foundation for his dead faith and hollow profession seeing that St. Paul declares over and over again that men are "saved by faith and not by works." The Unitarian also, in support of his soul-withering doctrine, triumphantly refers to numerous passages which, taken alone, teach only the humanity of Jesus.

In short, "there is no end to the errors in faith and practice which have resulted from taking isolated passages, wrested from their proper connections, or the light thrown upon them by other scriptures, and applying them to sustain a favorite theory." Judging from the blessed results which have almost invariably followed the ministrations of women in the cause of Christ, we fear it will be found in the great day of account that a mistaken and unjustifiable application of the passage, "Let your women keep silence in the churches," has resulted in more loss to the church, evil to the world, and dishonor to God, than any of the errors we have already referred to.

And feeling, as we have long felt, that this is a subject of vast importance to the interests of Christ's kingdom and the glory of God, we would most earnestly commend its consideration to those who have influence in the churches. We think it a matter worthy of their consideration whether God intended woman to bury her talents and influence as she now does, and whether the circumscribed sphere of woman's religious labors may not have something to do with the comparative non-success of the gospel in these latter days.

7

Free Methodist Perspectives

Introduction

The Free Methodist Church stands squarely in the holiness tradition of the Wesleyan family of churches, tracing its roots back to figures like Phoebe Palmer. B. T. Roberts (1823–93) was converted under Palmer's ministry and became the storm center of several interrelated conflicts that reflected deep cultural changes within the Methodism Episcopal Church during the second half of the nineteenth century.[1] In particular, he opposed "pew rental" policies (thus, the eventual "Free" Methodist title) because of its commercialization of the church and its discrimination against the poor. But his ardent abolitionism and his desire to restore entire sanctification, or holiness, to its proper place in the life of the Christian disciple also aggravated the increasingly respectable leadership of the church. In 1860 Roberts liberated himself from his Methodist Episcopal moorings and founded his "Free" church on the principles of freedom in church, freedom from slavery, and freedom in Christ that leads to a wholly sanctified life.[2]

Roberts also believed in freedom for women. As someone deeply entrenched in the holiness movement, his approach to women's ministry reflects the same six fundamental emphases associated with Palmer, his theological mentor: experiential theology, scriptural holiness, spiritual fruit, experimental freedom, social critique, and sectarian ambiance. Roberts declared that Christians should build their lives upon the central standard of

---

1. Hassey, *No Time for Silence*, 103.
2. On Roberts's life and work, see Snyder, *Populist Saints*.

Galatians 3:28, emphasizing the liberation of women and the unity of all in Christ.[3] He had argued from the outset of Free Methodism for the full participation of women in the ministry of the church. In 1872 he published a twenty-four-page pamphlet entitled *The Right of Women to Preach the Gospel*, a title borrowed, perhaps, from Luther Lee's ordination sermon for Antoinette Brown Blackwell.[4] He argued that "women's ordination is not merely consistent with the gospel; it is *required* by it.[5] In 1890 he presented a formal resolution to this effect to the General Conference, which his church rejected.[6] The following year, therefore, at this own expense he published *Ordaining Women* (Document 33), an extended essay—strikingly similar in content and approach to Lee's sermon—constructed upon the dual pillars of abolitionism and perfectionism.[7] An ardent proponent for the ordination of women, he fought unsuccessfully to his dying day for his church's approval of what he considered to be a woman's right. "In this issue," as Benjamin Wayman laments, "Roberts was a prophet without honor in his own denomination."[8]

In seventeen chapters and around 150 pages, Roberts addressed the prejudices and objections of the detractors and provided the evidence in support of women's ministry, but built his argument primarily upon a biblical foundation. While his defense contains all the usual biblical arguments—which do not need to be reproduced here—his approach to the biblical texts may reflect a contribution more profound than has been assumed. In an article entitled "More Radical than First Wave Feminism?: The Gospel According to B. T. Roberts," Wayman contrasts the approach to the Bible reflected in Robert's *Ordaining Women* with that of his contemporary Elizabeth Cady Stanton (1815–1902), famed American suffragist. While the "egalitarian hermeneutic" of Stanton's *Women's Bible* and Roberts's "galatian hermeneutic" both championed women's equality, Wayman believes that Roberts's reverence for Scripture, his role as a church leader, and his focus on Galatians 3:28 enabled him to help reshape nineteenth-century readings of Scripture more widely because his reading reinforced rather than undermined the authority of the Bible.[9] The principal point, as Mark Chaves

---

3. Zikmund, "Protestant Women's Ordination," 945.

4. Wayman, *Ordaining Women*, xvii.

5. Ibid., xix.

6. Hassey, *No Time for Silence*, 103.

7. See ibid., and Dayton, *Higher Christian Life*, x.

8. Wayman, *Ordaining Women*, xi.

9. Wayman, "More Radical," 11.

avers, is the fact that Roberts promoted "the principle that women have an equal right with men to religious positions."[10]

The substance of Roberts's argument rested on six summative propositions—published as a conclusion to his book—the first one of which defined his teaching most succinctly: Man and woman were created equal, each possessing the same rights and privileges as the other. Janette Hassey, in *No Time for Silence*, compares and contrasts the essential approach of Roberts with three other great women's advocates who also stood within the heritage of holiness: Palmer, Booth, and Willard.[11] (1) Willard and Roberts stressed egalitarian marriage, not the submission of wives taught by Palmer and Booth. (2) Willard and Roberts advocated women's ordination, with the implication of a woman's authority to govern, whereas Palmer promoted only the right of women to preach. (3) Only Roberts emphasized the parallels between slavery and the issue of women's ministry. He could not separate the hermeneutics that liberated the slave from the freedom of women in Christ. Perhaps this last point is the most poignant. In Wayman's words, Roberts "saw the barring of women from ordination as akin to racism."[12]

Following the death of Roberts, the efforts to secure women's ordination in the Free Methodist Church seemed to stall. But a new advocate quickly assumed the mantle of the fallen apologist. In 1898 the Free Methodists adopted an episcopal organization and appointed four bishops. One of these men, Walter Ashbel (W. A.) Sellew (1844–1929), ardently defended the right of women to ordination. Four years before his elevation to the episcopacy—just one year after Roberts's death—in 1894 he published *Why Not?: A Plea for the Ordination of Those Women Whom God Has Called to Preach the Gospel* (Document 34). Subsequently, he was one of the primary architects of legislation that led to the ordination of women as deacons in 1911. The resolution read, in part: "Whenever any annual conference, shall be satisfied that any woman is called of God to preach the gospel, that annual conference may be permitted to receive her on trial, and into full connection, and ordain her as a deacon, all on the same conditions as we receive men into the same relations."[13] Concerned to maintain the momentum that led to this significant victory, he reprinted his defense in 1914. In the foreword of this second edition he identified the two primary reasons for this action: (1) many had joined the Free Methodists since the original publication of his book and he wanted to make sure they were fully aware of

10. Chaves, *Ordaining Women*, 72–73.
11. Hassey, *No Time for Silence*, 105.
12. Wayman, *Ordaining Women*, xv.
13. Marston, *From Age to Age*, 419.

the biblical foundations of the decision to ordain women, and (2) he wanted to forestall any attempts to repeal the 1911 action.[14]

Sellew's defense lacked Roberts's passion but made up for it in logic. His arguments were somewhat more driven by the cultural and political context; he was shrewd to discern that political equality would soon be guaranteed for women and he wanted to make sure the church stayed abreast of potential constitutional changes. But his defense differed from that of Roberts in two critical ways. First, instead of maintaining that God created men and women as equals, he emphasized the inherent gender differences and framed the call of women as something extraordinary, a view that can only be viewed as regressive given Roberts's radical egalitarianism and the evolution in argumentation over the course of the nineteenth century. Secondly, he attempted to reassure his male readers that the ordination of women would not lead to a dismantling of male authority in the life of the church. It would take the Free Methodist Church nearly a century before they approved the full ordination of women as elders in 1974.[15]

DOCUMENT 33

Ordaining Women (1891), 118–20, 123–28, 130, 132–36, 158–59
B. T. Roberts

Chapter 13: Required

"Why ordain women as long as the right to preach is quite generally conceded to them? Why should they not be satisfied with the privileges they now enjoy?" Reader, will you consider candidly our answers to these questions? The last, great command of Christ requires that they who make converts should be invested with authority to administer the sacrament of baptism. "Go, therefore, and make disciples of all nations baptizing them in the name of the Father, and of the Son, and of the Holy Ghost; teaching them to observe all things whatsoever I have commanded you, and lo, I am with you always, even unto the end of the world. Amen" (Matt 28:19–20).

Notice the close connection of teach and baptize in this important text: Go, therefore, and make disciples of all the nations, baptizing them. This certainly implies that those who make disciples for Christ—convert sinners—should, as a rule, baptize them. The same persons who are

---

14. Sellew, *Why Not?*, 4.
15. See Hardesty, Dayton, and Dayton, "Women in the Holiness Movement," 238.

commanded to make disciples are commanded to baptize them. Till they have done this, their work is not complete. The one is a part of their mission as well as the other. They who catch the fish may string the fish. These revivalists must be proved first (1 Tim 3:10), but if found worthy and reliable, they should be clothed with authority to administer the sacraments to those whom they get converted.

If a woman, then, is permitted to hold revivals—to do the work of an evangelist—she should, when properly tried, if found duly qualified, be ordained. The churches must either stop her work or allow her to complete her work. Woman must either be permitted to baptize or she must not be permitted to make converts. By the present arrangement the churches separate what God has joined together. "Must, then, everyone who gets a sinner converted, baptize him?" We do not affirm this. But if he keeps on getting sinners converted and is evidently called of God to make this the business of life, then the church, when it is satisfied of this, should authorize him to administer the sacraments. Whoever makes full proof of a call to the ministry should, in due time, be invested with the full functions of the ministry. In oriental countries where women are kept in great seclusion, it is necessary that women should be authorized to administer baptism to their female converts.

Is a woman permitted to teach a primary class in our schools? Then may she, when qualified, teach Latin and Greek and Algebra, become Principal and even school Superintendent. The highest scholastic honors are not withheld from her simply because she is a woman. Dartmouth and Columbia, two of our renowned colleges, each conferred the title of LLD on Maria Mitchell, one of the greatest astronomers of the age. When the captain and owner of a Mississippi river boat suddenly died, his wife assumed command, and when the civil authorities, after a rigid examination, found that she possessed the necessary qualifications, they promptly licensed her as a captain. Her sex did not debar her from promotion in a calling for which men are specially adapted. Nor was the precedent considered dangerous. The gallant sailors did not fear that they would be superseded by women as commanders of ships. Is a woman permitted to conduct a trial in a justice's court? She may also be admitted to practice in the higher courts. There is, in the aggregate, quite a number of women lawyers in the several states. Yet the men of the world do not appear to have any apprehension lest they should be crowded out of the legal profession.

Woman owes her elevation to Christianity. She shows her appreciation by rallying around the cross of Christ. Justice, then, demands that all barriers placed by men in the way of the elevation of woman to any office in the gift of the church be removed. "Even if we could do without them," writes John Stuart Mill, "would it be consistent with justice to refuse to them their fair share of honor and distinction, or to deny to them the equal moral right of all human beings to choose their occupation (short of injury to others) according to their own preferences, at their own risk? Nor is the injustice confined to them. It is shared by those who are in a position to benefit by their services. To ordain that any kind of persons shall not be physicians, or shall not be advocates, or shall not be members of parliament, is to injure not them only, but all who employ physicians or advocates, or elect members of parliament, and who are deprived of the stimulating effect of greater competition on the exertions of the competitors, as well as restricted to a narrower range of individual choice."

Chapter 14: Fitness

Naturally, to say the least, woman is equally qualified with men for the ministry of the gospel. A celebrated skeptic bears the following testimony to the character of woman: "I tell you women are more prudent than men. I tell you, as a rule, women are more truthful than men. I tell you that women are more faithful than men—ten times as faithful as men. I never saw a man pursue his wife into the very ditch and dust of degradation and take her in his arms. I never saw a man stand at the shore where she had been morally wrecked, waiting for the waves to bring back even her corpse to his arms. But I have seen woman do it. I have seen woman with her white arms lift man from the mire of degradation and hold him to her bosom as though he were an angel." Dr. Lardner says of the women of Jerusalem in the days of Christ: "The number of women who believed in Jesus as the Christ and professed faith in him was not inconsiderable. Many of these had so good understanding and so much virtue as to overcome the common and prevailing prejudice. Without any bias or passion or worldly interests, and contrary to the judgments and menaces of men in power, they judged rightly in a controverted point of as much importance as was ever debated on earth.

Christ very plainly told the twelve that he would rise again the third day. But they did not seem to understand it. But the women appeared to understand it. At early dawn on the third morning "came Mary Magdalene and the other Mary to see the sepulcher." They were on the lookout, and to them Christ first showed himself after his resurrection. It was a woman that he commissioned to go to his disciples and foretell them of his ascension. Woman entered readily into the spirit of his words. It was in the apostolic church that woman began to teach the teachers of the Christian religion.

Fettered as she has been, Christianity owes much to her for the progress it has already made. If woman has done so much under the restrictions placed upon her in the days of barbarism under the reign of force, and which have been perpetuated to our day, what might she not have done had all restrictions on account of sex been removed and she been free to exert her abilities to the utmost in the cause of Christ?

Woman has a special aptitude for teaching. This is acknowledged by the general selection of women to teach in our public schools. They succeed as teachers. In the work of the ministry, so far as they have been permitted to attempt it, women have acquitted themselves as creditably as men. Where they have labored, prejudices have been removed.

To the objection that such cases are exceptions, we reply in the words of John Stuart Mill: "Many women have proved themselves capable of everything, perhaps without a single exception, which is done by men and of doing it successfully and creditably."

The practical turn of woman's mind specially fits her for the work of the gospel ministry. Women generally are not given to abstractions. They make the most of the realities about them. Cases occur where the father of a family, overwhelmed with misfortune, dies in despair. The mother, though unused to the management of affairs, gathers up the fragments, gradually retrieves their fortunes, and raises her family in respectability and honor. This disposition of woman to look at the present and make the best of existing circumstances would be of great benefit to the cause of Christianity if all restrictions on account of sex were removed and she were left free to do good according to her inclination and ability.

Women are not wanting in the courage and fortitude essential to the minister of the gospel. The bold Peter denied Christ, but the New Testament gives us no account of any woman who opened her mouth against him in the face of danger. The annals of the church, in the days of persecution, tell us of many a noble, tender, gentle woman who met death in its most terrific form rather than deny Christ.

Chapter 17: Conclusion

In the preceding pages the following propositions have been clearly proved.

1. Man and woman were created equal, each possessing the same rights and privileges as the other.

2. Because she was first in the transgression in the fall, woman was made subject to her husband as a punishment.

3. Christ re-enacted the primitive law and restored the original relation of equality of the sexes.

4. The objections to the equality of man and woman in the Christian church based upon the Bible rest upon a wrong translation of some passages and a misinterpretation of others. The objections drawn from woman's nature are fully overthrown by undisputed facts.

5. In the New Testament church, woman filled the office of apostle, prophet, deacon, or preacher, and pastor as well as man. There is not the slightest evidence that the functions of any of these offices, when filled by a woman, were different from what they were when filled by a man.

6. Woman took a part in governing the apostolic church.

We come, then, to this final conclusion: *The gospel of Jesus Christ, in the provisions which it makes and in the agencies which it employs for the salvation of mankind knows no distinction of race, condition of sex, therefore no person evidently called of God to the gospel ministry and duly qualified for it should be refused ordination on account of race, condition, or sex.*

DOCUMENT 34

Why Not? (1894), 3, 5–11, 13–19, 21–22, 32–37
W. A. Sellew

This tract is intended chiefly for the members of the Free Methodist Church to which the author belongs. That church believes and holds that there are some women as well as men called to preach the gospel. The object of this tract is to convince the members of this church that those women whom they believe God has called to preach the gospel should be ordained the same as the men whom God has so called. The question of the right of some women to preach is not herein discussed, but is taken for granted, as those to whom it is addressed have deliberately, after years of discussion and consideration, with scarcely a dissenting voice, agreed that some women are called of God to preach, and when so called have just the same right as men to do so. So this tract is written only for a limited few. Yet the author trusts that it may prove neither uninteresting nor unprofitable to all who may be interested enough in women's work in the church to peruse its pages. It is written simply for the love of the truth and if there are any errors of statement or any flaws in the logic no one will be more pleased than the author to have the truth prevail at his expense.

Shall we ordain these women whom God has called to preach the gospel?

Ever since Eden the relation of women to men and to things has been a bone of contention. The devil early took a prominent part in this and has ever since managed some way to hold a place in this controversy.

It cannot be claimed that man and woman were created equal in every respect, as the absolute equality of any two persons associated together is a constitutional impossibility. A fundamental law of association, even when applied to only two persons, is that of superiority and inferiority. In the beginning, however, man and woman were created with equal rights. In the word we read: "So God created man in his image, in the image of God created he him; male and female created he them." There were no distinctions as to their right to be blessed of God, to live, to eat, to rule whatever there was to be ruled. There is a vast difference between equality of rights and equality of relations. Rights are inherent, relations are results. Rights, though unacknowledged, trampled upon and seemingly destroyed, cannot perish or change. Relations are constantly changing. So it cannot be claimed that man and woman were created equal as to their relation to each other. In that respect they never have been equal. They never can be so. At the time of creation, this inequality of relation between man and woman had two prominent phases in both of which man was manifestly superior.

In point of time, man was created first. It is doubtful if this point of superiority has any bearing whatever on the subject now under consideration

In point of physical strength, man was and always has been superior to woman. To be sure there have been some women stronger than some men, but generally they have never been able to hold their own with the men in this respect. This inferiority of the woman has not been one of beauty of proportion or form, nor of intellectuality, nor even one of physical or mental endurance, but simply of physical force. So, the profession of war has usually been considered as belonging to the men. And the profession of pugilism has always been regarded as their exclusive property. In fact, this superiority in physical power of the man over the woman has always been the open secret of their complicated conditions. The men have possessed the power and they have taken the rights. But rights taken by force are rights still, and woman the world over has been patiently waiting—waiting with a patience only surpassed by her modesty—for the glorious gospel of love as taught by Jesus Christ and its attendant civilization, to restore to her these rights which have been taken from her by force. This it has been doing, not suddenly, not with noise, not with confusion, not by wars and blood as other rights have been regained, but with peace and with quietness has this most blessed salvation been returning to woman those social, business, and religious privileges which God designed she should freely enjoy. Yet it is a most curious fact that the prejudice against the religious rights and privileges of woman is more strongly entrenched than that against either her social or business rights, and yields the last of all, and then most reluctantly. He who has the property of another in his possession, selfishly detained against the will of the rightful owner, is not at all likely, by the very nature of the case, to see clearly the right relations existing between them. So, men, who for so long a time had held these varied rights in their possession, acquired by force, and with whom this principle of power had been for so long a time both judge and jury, law and gospel could not be expected to see their relations rightly. But life is motion. Inherent rights will not always be quiet, and the law of return operates here as in nature. The prejudice against the social rights of woman was this to begin to give way; but so long delayed was this that not till after the dark ages did the light of God begin to break through and reveal what ought to have been recognized long, long before, that woman in the social sphere was not only the equal but actually the superior of man. It has, however, come at last; and now in all Christian nations the social work of the world and of the church is largely, where it belongs, in the hands of women.

The religious prejudice is still very strong against women. So much so that, even today, except in a few favored localities, it largely controls the professed Christian church. But the wonderful freedom of religious work in the United States, and especially the remarkable missionary activities of the world, are working wonders in letting light shine on the word of God in relations to woman's work in converting the world.

The relations of women to Christianity and to Christian work can be noted under two heads.

First, those privileges or duties which result from simple membership in the church of Christ. These are principally singing, praying, teaching and visiting. The right of women to do any or all of them is now not questioned. No Protestant body now denies some women the right to do any or all of these publicly under certain circumstances. Allowing it to be done publicly under certain circumstances, yields the question and throws the burden of proof on those who deny them this same right under certain other circumstances, to show that what they deny them is wrong.

Secondly, after the rights resulting from church membership come those privileges and duties which result from some official relation to the church. These may be reduced to two heads.

Preaching the Gospel. There is great prejudice even now against women preachers. So great is it that many will listen to no reasons or arguments in favor of their preaching, nor will they even go to hear them preach. With such it is no use to attempt argument. A good woman preacher filled with the Spirit will convince more people that she has a right to preach and do it more quickly and easily than pages of argument. But the age of women preachers has come. As the Spirit is poured out on all flesh our daughters are prophesying, and the prophecy, "The Lord gives the word. The women that publish the tidings are a great host" (Psa 68:11–12), is being rapidly realized. Whatever position other religious bodies may take, the Free Methodist Church has unequivocally declared that women have the same right to preach the gospel as men. They believe that the right is based simply upon the call of God. The number of men called has nothing whatever to do with the call. If we admit that one single woman is called of God to preach the gospel, that would establish her right to do so; and the call of ten thousand other women would not increase in the slightest degree to right of the one first called to do so.

That this is the position of our church cannot be denied, as the three classes of preachers recognize by our discipline, local preachers, traveling preachers, and evangelists, now have women among them duly authorized to be there by our church authorities. As said action granting women their licenses was not only taken without appeal but without protest, our polity as to that question may be regarded as settled beyond dispute. So it may also be considered as settled that the objection to ordaining women does not have any bearing on their right to preach. It has been suggested that a spirit of opposition to women preaching is the secret of the objection made by some among us to the ordination of women and that those who object to their ordination have never yet fully consented in their minds to this position which we as a church have taken, that women have all equal right with men to preach the gospel. It is feared that there is some truth in this suggestion, and that a careful and searching examination of their motives will reveal to such persons that the root of their objection is here, though they may not have been conscious of it. Such a suggestion is not entitled to consideration. If it has any foundation in fact, it is simply a relic of prejudice and not a principle of church polity with us.

All other official relations aside from preaching, connected with membership in the church may be classed as governments or privileges and duties related to the government of the church as an organized body.

Right here many persons make a bold stand against women having anything to do with governing the church. Such persons hold that, admitting the right of women to preach the gospel, the Bible plainly declares against their governing or ruling in the church. This question may be one that has two sides, and it may also be that we as a church have taken the wrong side. But right or wrong, our position has been taken and the Free Methodist Church is now fully committed to the right of women to govern equally with the men in the organized church of Christ. The Free Methodist Church is a democratic body. All authority is derived from its members. All vested authority is in or with some official body. No individual has any but delegated authority and that, if continued, is subject to frequent accounting and reelection to the office horn which he receives that authority. To show that women have equal rights of governing in our church, it may be stated that they can now, equally with men, be a member of any official body having any vested, as well as delegated, authority recognized by our church. They can also, according to our discipline, be elected or appointed to nearly every official position inside the church.

If any should raise the objection to ordaining women that we do not want women for chairmen and superintendents, and therefore should not ordain them, it may be answered that after they are ordained we need not elect them to those positions unless we desire to do so. Simply because a woman had been ordained elder we are under no more obligations to elect her chairman or superintendent than we now are to elect a man to these positions who possess no executive ability. It is an imputation on all concerned to say that we must have persons in these positions we do not want. Is not the right of ballot free and unrestricted? The Free Methodist Church is purely democratic. She knows whom and what she wants and she will have them, or she will know the reason why. *She can be trusted.*

If it should be argued that, because women are already allowed so many privileges in the Free Methodist Church, there is no necessity for their ordination, it will be readily admitted that women have already all the rights and privileges for religious work in our church that she needs or can well use. The above list of bodies to which she may belong and positions which she may fill is, of itself, a standing proof that no organized church offers to woman a greater field of usefulness or more opportunities for working for God and for the salvation of souls than the Free Methodist Church. No woman filled with the love of God and possessed with a burning desire to do something for the salvation of souls could ask for better opportunities than she finds here. This plea for her ordination is not made for her advantage directly, or that she may have more opportunities of work for God. She now has in our church all such openings she needs, and more than she uses. Ordination for woman is not asked for her benefit, but for the benefit of the church. She can now, as heretofore, get on very well without it, but the time has come when the church demands it both for the thing itself and for the consistency of our position before the world and before God. The position of our church with reference to women will never be fully rounded out in consistency until this is done.

Having failed in the foregoing relations of woman to the church to find any good or substantial ground of objection to her ordination under certain circumstance, let us consider the subject of ordination in general for a short time. The question as to whether a person called of God to preach the gospel should be formally ordained by men has always been one of great controversy, not only as to the simple fact, but more especially as to who, when, how, and by whom. Opinion has swung from one extreme to the other. This, like other forms, ceremonies, and ordinances, which always clothe the soul of true spiritual worship, has been magnified and exalted by ecclesiastical formalism which is always death to the spirit until the nut has become nearly all shell. On the other hand, it has been belittled and despised by all egotistical insubordination, until the poor soul, self-exposed to the devil, has been withered and blasted by his fierce attacks. Formalism exalts ordinances to the point of worshiping them instead of God. Fanaticism rejects them that she may the more completely and unrestrainedly worship self. The devil is fully satisfied with either of these forms of idolatry.

In order to understand women's relation to ordination, it will be necessary to obtain a correct understanding of the teachings of the New Testament on the subject of ordination in general. There are two classes of passages which refer to this subject.

First, those which use the word "ordain."

Secondly, those which refer to the ceremony without using the word.

It is a curious fact, and one that shows clearly the tendency of men who themselves have been ordained, to unduly magnify its importance, that scriptural ordination depends entirely upon those passages which do not use the word ordain or ordination, and that, if it depended alone upon those passages in the King James Version where the word ordain is used, the whole ceremony would be swept from its foundation. It is now admitted that in every passage in the New Testament where the word ordain is used to express the ceremony of setting apart by imposition of hands a person called to the ministry, it is incorrectly translated. So that if the authority in the New Testament for ordaining men depended upon what men have tried to make of it, ordination as a ceremony would fail. It is, however, fully established as a warranted and authorized ceremony by those passages which refer to it without using the word "ordain." These passages clearly show that the ceremony of ordination is not the exalted affair that some would have us believe. The obliteration of the word "ordain" from the New Testament, and the fact that the ceremony we call ordination by laying on of hands is not commanded but only referred to in the above passages, shows conclusively that it is simply a prudential ceremony.

To further show the true nature of New Testament ordination and to strip it of some of its self-appropriated functions and importance, let us notice that nowhere can it be shown that the administration of the sacraments—Baptism and the Lord's Supper—was committed to ordained persons. In fact, the contrary impresses itself upon a careful, unprejudiced enquirer. There is nothing to show that any of the apostles had been ordained at the day of Pentecost when so many were baptized. Paul preached many years before his ordination as given in Acts 13:3, and then he seems to have been ordained more as a superintendent and missionary than as a preacher or administrator of sacraments, while there is no account of his ordination as elder, and nowhere is he distinctly called "elder;" and he may not have been one, though he probably was. There is no account of the ordination of any elder as such in the New Testament. Peter and John incidentally call themselves "elders," but when and where and by whom they were ordained elders we do not know. Neither do we know that a single individual, except Peter and John, was an elder in the apostolic church. Furthermore we only know by the New Testament that elders had but two functions or prerogatives.

First, some of them ruled or presided, probably elected to do so.

Secondly, they were authorized to anoint and pray for the sick. Nowhere are they authorized to baptize or administer the Lord's Supper. While this is so, it has always been considered as wise and prudent to commit the administration of the sacraments to ordained persons, but their right to administer the sacraments was not based upon their ordination, but primarily upon their call to preach.

Christ laid hands on many persons and for many purposes, principally for healing, but never for ordination. Many other facts might be mentioned to show that this ceremony of ordination has been carried far above and beyond its original simplicity and importance by men who had ends to serve. It has been the storm center so long of the controversy about "apostolic succession" that its importance in theological controversy is not intrinsic, but artificial and deceiving.

Let no one suppose, however, that because it was so simple and was the result of the growth of the apostolic church rather than or divine revelation, it is of no importance. It occupies an important and honored place in the church. Though the intrinsic and official importance of ordination has always been denied by the Protestant church, yet its relative importance has always been recognized. It has always been considered as a recognition by the church of a call to preach already made by God, and the formal and permanent induction into a ministry to which the candidate has already been ordained by the Holy Ghost. The church makes nothing, creates nothing, imparts nothing. It simply recognizes. The functions of the church were not to bestow a gift, but simply to recognize and authenticate what has already been bestowed by the head of the church. For this reason they prayed that the Lord would show whom he had chosen, and they laid hands on him to express the co-operative action and the benediction of the church as to the choice already made by the Holy Ghost. "The Holy Ghost said: Separate me Barnabas and Saul for the work whereunto I have called them" (Acts 13:2).

Therefore, as the Free Methodist Church unequivocally recognizes the ministry of women, we are bound to recognize her right to ordination—to permit and encourage her to a public ministry, to travel a circuit, to organize classes, to have full charge of a station as a pastor, and year after year to do all the work as a minister that we ask or expect of a man. Then, after she does it all, to deny her ordination is inconsistent to say the least. We have gone too far or not far enough. If some should say that indeed we have gone too far, it may be answered, that is not now the question. When that question is raised we may consider it, but it has no place here or now. We are face to face with this issue. If we were of sufficient numbers or importance as a church to attract the attention of the secular or religious press, there would be some who would vigorously assail our position, allowing women the right to preach the gospel on an equality with man, and more, who would still more strongly attack our position allowing them official positions in the government of the church. But all persons of every creed or belief, of every name and nation, would join in ridiculing our inconsistency if, after allowing women these things already mentioned, we refuse them ordination. Those among us who object to the ordination of women are in this dilemma. They must either consent to their ordination on logical grounds or they must deliberately attempt to undermine our established and recognized position regarding woman's relation in our church. An open challenge is out to show a single passage of Scripture, or produce a single argument against ordaining women that will not apply with equal force either against their right to preach the gospel or against their right to govern in the church of Christ.

On the other hand, it can clearly be shown that in apostolic times not only were there women ministers or preachers, but that they were ordained to a distinct official relation to the church. It does not appear that there were a large number of them so ordained, probably only a few, but if it can be shown that there was one, it opens the way for others under similar conditions. What those conditions were or what they should be now if women are to be ordained is not now the question.

We conclude from these facts:

1. That there were deaconesses in the primitive church

2. That they were an established order of officials.

3. That many of them at least, if not all, were ministers or preachers. The fact that those in the diaconate, both men and women, *preached*, and that they *all* preached, is as clearly proven respecting the women as the men.

4. That women deacons were elected to this office and set apart to the ministry thereof by the imposition of hands, the same as the male deacons.

5. That the women deacons performed the same duties for and stood in the same relation to the women as the men deacons did for and to the men.

In view of these facts it is very difficult to see how we can consistently avoid the conclusion that to be consistent we must allow the ordination of women to the subordinate ministry of the diaconate.

Someone may ask, however; "How about women elders?" There are some good authorities who claim that there was a distinct order of women elders in the apostolic church, but it would be difficult to establish that fact by the Word, except by inference. To be sure it would not be an unreasonable inference to conclude that, because there were women in the subordinate ministry of the diaconate, some of these women were elevated to the eldership. But to prove it is another thing. It does not seem, however, that we are required to prove it. If it is admitted that women were elected and ordained to the diaconate, according to our view of the gospel ministry, the burden of proof is on those who deny their right to the eldership to show why women could be deacons and not as well be elders. It is admitted that there is not a single case of a woman elder mentioned by name as such in the New Testament, but this proves nothing. It will be admitted that there was a large number of men elders in the apostolic times, yet of all these only two are mentioned as such by name, and those merely incidentally. It is nothing strange, therefore, that no woman is mentioned as being an elder, even if there were some in the eldership.

Going to the very extreme and admitting that not a single woman was elevated to the superior order of ministers or elders, yet that does not prove they might not have been so promoted if the apostles and elders had thought best to do so. From the nature of the case we are warranted in concluding both that some of them might have been, and actually were, elevated to the eldership, unless those who oppose it show they were not entitled to it under any circumstances. This they will hardly attempt to do. Unless they do so, we are warranted in concluding that the reason there were not women elders, (if there were none, which is probable but by no means certain) must be one of two.

Either the prejudice against women was so strong that the authorities of the apostolic church did not consider it wise or prudent to elevate to the eldership some of those illustrious women whom Paul mentions as being so useful to him in the ministry, and whom the very highest authorities already quoted do not hesitate to say were ordained to the diaconate, or they did not consider any of them sufficiently noted for wisdom, ability and discretion to entitle them to sit with the men in the higher councils of the church. In either case it was simply a matter opinion. We now may and do think differently. Prejudice is not now so strong as then and women are quite as illustrious and much more generally and broadly informed. If it should be objected that women were ordained in apostolic times because of the peculiar social conditions prevalent then, and that the exclusiveness of woman's relations rendered ordained women an absolute necessity, it may be answered that this has nothing to do with this question because a necessity never creates a right. The right existed before the necessity and continues after the necessity ceases to exist. Whether the Oriental exclusiveness of the female is more conducive to purity and holiness than the present apparent laxity in the social relation of the sexes may be an open question, but it does not bear on our subject. It is not improbable however that there may be at some future time, more or less remote, a reaction on this subject and that public opinion may demand of religious bodies that they authorize women to perform for their sex some at least of the duties now discharged by male ministers. If so, would conference action in that direction create the right of woman to ordination? It would simply recognize what was already there and had been called out by an apparent necessity. Some may think, and not unreasonably, that the necessity for such action now actually exists. That is a matter of opinion. Whether it does or not, the right to it is inherited. Its recognition is all that is asked.

It has been urged that if we ordain women we will soon be ruled by women. It may be answered that we are now so ruled if it be true that the people are sovereign. Women have a majority in most of our societies and the real authority of the church is there. No person in our church can be started in the ministry without the recommendation of the society to which he belongs. The society elects its lay representative to conference. Now, it is a fact that, though the women have the real power and authority in the church by having the majority of the votes, yet she almost always uses it to delegate her power as a voter to some man whenever anyone suitable for the position can he found. How often do we find the women of a society struggling to find men enough who are eligible to fill the offices in the church? It is only when the men are manifestly unfit for the position, when some woman is preeminently qualified for it, that a woman is elected. If the men rule the Free Methodist Church today it is because the women have expressed by their votes a desire to have it so. This is no argument either way, but is favorable to the ordination of women rather than against it.

That other objection to the ordination of women which we sometimes hear, that men through feelings of gallantry or enthusiasm would vote some women into orders who were not worthy, has more foundation than the last. It is admitted that there is some danger in this respect, but not enough to entitle it too much consideration. There are quite a number of unworthy men ordained each year from one cause or another, and why should the men desire to monopolize all the unworthiness in this line? Ought not the women to have their rights in this as in other respects? Furthermore it may be noted that, while the women by having a majority in most of our societies have by virtue of that majority the right to say by their votes whom they think God has called to preach the gospel, they have delegated to the men the right to determine who shall be ordained. As it is altogether likely that comparatively few women will be ordained, and as practically not a single woman can be ordained except by the votes of the men to whom our women voters have delegated this right, we must trust these men to see to it that the few women who are ordained shall be every way well qualified and worthy of the high office to which they may be chosen.

It has also been urged that because some women seem to want to be ordained it is an objection to it. The only ground upon which it would be commendable for a woman to desire ordination is the same we would commend as the basis of a man's desire for ordination. That would be a desire to be permanently recognized by the church in a ministry to which such a person had already been called by God. To desire ordination for the honor it confers or for the privileges it grants would be regarded as unworthy in a woman as in a man, and no more so. In whatever light we view this question, we are forced—some of us reluctantly—to the conclusion that the present position of our church on this subject is entirely inconsistent. If a woman is called to preach the gospel she has the same right as a man to be ordained. If she is called to the pastorate it does not increase her right to ordination, but it places an imperative responsibility upon that body which recognizes that call to see to it that she is ordained. Such a body is bound to do so in honor, in justice, in right, in due respect, not for woman, but for themselves.

What shall we as a church do in this dilemma? Is not the past history of our denomination an answer to this question? Have we ever made a backward move? Has not God honored us in every one of the advances we have made along the lines of truth? Our present position as to woman's place and work in the church of Christ has been carefully and prayerfully taken. Her ordination may not have been seen or considered when this was done, but it was there, and is the only logical conclusion or completion of that position. Every argument, every vote, against her ordination, whether intended or not, is only an argument, is only a vote, against her present place, her position, her work in the church. It strikes most logically at what we have already done, to destroy our own work. Shall we tear down that which we have built at so great a cost? How much better to complete our work and remove the only inconsistency in the full application to our little Zion of that glorious passage, "There is neither Jew nor Greek, there is neither bond nor free, there is neither male nor female; for all are one in Christ Jesus."

8

"Woman's Right to Preach" in the Nazarene Tradition

Introduction

"From its earliest days," reports historian Rebecca Laird, "the Church of the Nazarene has officially recognized the ministerial rights of women!"[1] For Phineas F. Bresee (1838–1915), the primary founder of this holiness denomination, the church's affirmation of women's ministry was so fundamental that he saw no need to develop any formal defense of women as clergy. Even when some asked for the new denomination to make its affirmation of women explicit, Bresee and others assured them that the case had been made by the numerous women in ministry. The Constitution of Los Angeles Church of the Nazarene—the "mother congregation" of the denomination—did state definitively, "We recognize the equal rights of both men and women to all offices of the Church of the Nazarene, including the ministry."[2] But while categorical statements such as this one did guide the fledgling Nazarene communities, formal recognition did not always inform actual practice. Some of the older congregations from regional groups that joined in 1908 did not all have such a robust vision for women in leadership. But for those who lived into this ideal, according to Stan Ingersol, the Nazarene concept of apostolic ministry provided the justification for the acceptance of women's voices and gifts.[3] Essentially this meant that every

1. Laird, *Ordained Women*, 11.
2. Quoted in ibid.
3. See Ingersol, "Burden of Dissent" and "Holiness Women."

Christian belief and practice must conform to or reflect the belief and practice of the apostolic church. For those in positions of authority, the biblical evidence for the ministry of women was irrefutable; women's ministry, therefore, ought to be embraced and replicated in every age.

In her definitive study of the early Nazarene women preachers, Laird identifies five critical themes that characterized the life and ministry of these women:[4]

1. The women shared a deep conviction that they had been called of God and empowered to preach by the sanctifying grace of the indwelling Holy Spirit.

2. The women struggled with the call, knowing that it was often deemed inappropriate and out of step with family, church, and society expectations.

3. The women evidenced a willingness to go ahead and preach, wherever and whenever they could, not waiting for official sanction.

4. The women tended to plant the churches they served through their own evangelistic efforts.

5. The women formed informal support networks among themselves in order to sustain their various ministries.

"Inevitably, of course," as Timothy Smith pointed out, "questions concerning the propriety of women preachers arose, in part from the intense prejudice against them."[5] Passionate Nazarenes rose to the occasion, publishing most of their apologetic material in the opening decades of the twentieth century during the denomination's formative period. The several items collected in this chapter are unique in terms of diversity. One sample of this apologetic material is an excerpt from a Bible study, two are sermons, one is an autobiographical account, and one is a more conventional, systematic defense of the ministry of women. The sheer range of material reveals something about the importance, and even centrality, of women's ministry in this holiness tradition.

In 1897 James A. (J. A.) Murphree (fl c. 1890–1910) organized a church in Waco, Texas as part of the emerging New Testament Church of Christ, one of the many apostolic and Pentecostal movements in the Wesleyan spirit that would merge in the early twentieth century to form the Church of the Nazarene under Bresee. In 1899 Murphree became president of a small training center to prepare ministers for this gospel mission and launched

4. Laird, *Ordaining Women.* 189.

5. Smith, *Called Unto Holiness*, 122.

an eight-page monthly newspaper called *The Evangelist*, which championed the cause of holiness and the ministry of women.[6] This noteworthy biblical expositor and preacher published *Bible Readings and Teachings on Important Subjects* that same year. He included women's ministry among the four important topics identified in the subtitle of this work: "Living Without Sin, Entire Sanctification, Women Preaching, and Seventh of Romans All Explained and Harmonized." In the segment "On Women Preaching" (Document 35) he rehearsed the argument that "prophesying" means "preaching," countered the purported objections in 1 Corinthians and 1 Timothy, and left it to his readers to draw the obvious conclusions. His defense consisted essentially of laying out the principal scriptural texts about women. C. S. Cowles notes the preponderant number of women preachers in the New Testament Church of Christ when they united with the other groups to form the Church of the Nazarene in 1908.[7]

In their revivals, women preachers like Mary Lee Cagle, Donie Mitchum, and Annie May Fisher regularly preached a stock sermon defending their public ministry.[8] In 1903, Annie May Fisher (fl c. 1900–1920) published *Woman's Right to Preach* (Document 36), a twenty-six-page pamphlet based on a sermon she delivered at Chilton, Texas. In typical fashion, she exposed the misinterpretation of Scripture that led to the oppression of women and marshaled the positive evidence for the affirmation of women's ministry, emphasizing the prophetic witness of Joel in Acts 2 and the egalitarian foundations of St. Paul's epistles. She offered no unique twists or turns in her defense of women. As Ingersol notes, "it fell to Fannie McDowell Hunter [c. 1860–1935] to frame the issue in a way unique in the apologetics of female ministry."[9] Born in Missouri in about 1860, she was the granddaughter of a circuit-riding Methodist preacher to the Quapah people in the Indian Territory. Married to Prof. W. W. Hunter when she was nineteen and widowed just three years later, Hunter became a music evangelist and songwriter, noted for her gifts in piano and voice. After a brief evangelistic ministry with the Salvation Army, she engaged extensively in a revivalist ministry that carried her into several southern states. In 1904 she was host pastor of a council that merged the New Testament Church of Christ with the Independent Holiness Church to form the Holiness Church of Christ. Her composite document, *Women Preachers* (Document 37), was one of

6. Jernigan, *Pioneer Days*, 160.

7. Cowles, *Woman's Place*, 174.

8. See Ingersol, "Ministry of Cagle."

9. Ibid., 189.

the two books that appeared the following year in an effort to articulate the nature of this new denomination.

According to Ingersol, "*Women Preachers* differed from other works of its genre by its collective nature."[10] Exactly half the book summarized standard arguments for the ministry of women, developed in the previous half century and published in apologies by Phoebe Palmer, B. T. Roberts, Catherine Booth, and others. Despite this fairly conventional line of argument and marshaling of evidence, Letha Scanzoni and Susan Setta emphasize the fact that Hunter "called the Church to task for accepting women as foreign missionaries while denying women the right to preach."[11] This defense was distinguished from others of its kind by the narrative structure that comprised the second half of the book."[12] Hunter published nine autobiographical call narratives, which functioned, as has been discussed earlier, as apologies in their own right, including hers (Document 38). These autobiographical accounts affirmed the divine origin of women's authority in ministry against all prejudice to the contrary. One contributor, Jonnie Jernigan (1862–1940), was a fearless preacher and advocate of women from the Independent Holiness Church wing of the Holiness Church of Christ. Her narrative (Document 39), which included the story of her ordination at the same time as her husband, underscored the egalitarian impulse that governed this movement. In 1920 Jernigan expanded this original account in a thirty-eight-page pamphlet published under the title *Redeemed Through the Blood; or, The Power of God to Save the Fallen.*

Mary Lee Cagle (1864–1955) stands out as one of the most significant figures in early Nazarene history, particularly as it relates to the defense of women's ministry. She was converted at a Methodist evangelistic meeting when she was fifteen and sensed a call to Christian ministry. Bitter opposition within her family, however, quickly quelled her enthusiasm. As Priscilla Pope-Levison reveals, "her brother-in-law declared that if she ever preached, his children would not be allowed to acknowledge their aunt."[13] Later overcoming her doubts and fears, she emerged as an indefatigable evangelist, church founder, and prophetic leader. In his definitive study of her life, Ingersol describes the extent of her influence:

> Mary Lee Cagle's contribution was impressive. In the Nazarene period, she continued to carve an enviable role as a founder of

10. Ibid.

11. Scanzoni and Setta, "Women in Evangelical, Holiness, and Pentecostal Traditions," 238.

12. Ingersol, "Ministry of Cagle," 189.

13. Pope-Levison, *Turn the Pulpit Loose*, 147.

new congregations, taking a leading role in establishing churches in Abilene, Lubbock, and many smaller places. At least eighteen congregations were founded directly by her and dozens of
others with her assistance. In Lubbock, she and Henry Cagle
were founding co-pastors in 1909. With her oversight, this congregation erected a building seating over 500 people, praised as
the finest Nazarene facility in the Southwest at the time. Over
the next forty years, the Cagles held revivals from Tennessee to
Arizona and from El Paso north to Cheyenne, Wyoming.[14]

Her "choice of sectarian dissent became the logical means of resolving an
intense inner conflict," Ingersol contends, "between her sense of divine call
and Southern Methodism's uncompromising attitude against women's laity
and clergy rights—a dilemma that can be understood as her particular embodiment of the universal conflict between conscience and obedience."[15]

In the summer of 1895, Fannie Hunter took Mary under her wing,
mentoring her through the challenges of being an unmarried woman in
ministry. Throughout her life, Cagle directed her revivalistic ministry primarily toward those who struggled in life, and "her personal struggle to
overcome prejudice against her ministry solely on the basis of gender," claims
Ingersol, "gave her empathy with a broad range of marginalized and dispos-
sessed people."[16] In her autobiography, she published her stock sermon on
"Woman's Right to Preach" (Document 40). She demonstrated how in the
biblical witness women led public prayer meetings, prophesied, labored in
the gospel, served the church, proclaimed the resurrection, declared Jesus'
messiahship, and were authorized to preach. Cagle's central argument—as
well as that of the other Nazarene apologists—is encapsulated in her conviction that what women "were allowed to do when the New Testament was
written will be all right for them to do now."

DOCUMENT 35

"On Women Preaching" (1899)
J. A. Murphree
Source: Murphree, *Bible Readings*, 51–52

14. Ingersol, "Ministry of Cagle," 190.
15. Ibid., 179.
16. Ibid., 191.

Let us notice some of the many places that speak of women preaching, praying, testifying, and laboring in the gospel, and that by the man who is said to have forbidden it.

The first I call your attention to is Anna, a prophetess, which means a preacher (Luke 2:36–38).

The second is that of the Samaritan woman who testified of Christ to the men of her city, and many of them believed on him (John 4:28–30, 39).

Women preached on the day of Pentecost. For Peter said Joel's prophecy (Joel 2:28) *which said she should, was fulfilled* (Acts 2:14–18).

DOCUMENT 36

Woman's Right to Preach (1903), 3–4, 7–8, 12, 14, 20–22, 24–26
Annie May Fisher

A noted speaker once announced for his theme the greatest subject on earth, namely, "Man."

Another speaker, following, declared his subject to be the greatest, namely, "Woman." "For," said he, "woman is man, but man can never be woman."

Our subject for tonight is, as announced, "Woman's Right to Preach," and you will find our text in Romans 8: 31, "If God be for us, who can be against us!"

Let me call your attention to this fact: "Woman are in almost every occupation and profession in the world, and but very little is said about it; but if she dares to obey God and goes into the ministry, a great host will rise up and oppose her, declaring that she is out of her place and that she has no right to preach the gospel of Jesus Christ.

It is not our purpose to take woman out of her God-appointed sphere and place her above the man, but we simply wish to prove to you from the Bible that she has a part in the great work of God, and in proclaiming the gospel of his dear Son. And if in this we are successful, we would urge the question set forth ill our text, "If God be for us, who can be against us!"

We find that the Old Testament abounds in passages in support of our claims; and in the-face of these plain scriptures we would ask, If God be for us, who would dare be against us? Would you deny us the glorious privilege of crying with the daughters of Zion, "Behold your God!" For He said, "And I, if I he lifted up, will draw all men to me."

"Ah," say some, "you can lift him up without preaching." We will admit that to take our stand in the pulpit, announce a text, and preach a sermon, is not the only way to lift him up, but it is one of God's ordained ways that through the foolishness of preaching he might save them. And we believe the New Testament gives the woman the same privilege and right to preach him as it does the man.

Why is it that all churches are so willing to send out the woman missionary? What is the difference between preaching in foreign fields and preaching at home? It seems strange, but when a woman is called as a missionary to face the dangers that lie across the waters, they believe at once in woman's right to preach.

We are glad, however, that for the sake of Jesus and a lost world, when she is called she is willing, like Paul, to "gladly spend and be spent."

The second thought I want to present is, they not only had a right to pray, but also to preach . . .

If anyone in the world ought to preach the Christ, it certainly is the woman. We ought to go into every nation, crying aloud and sparing not; holding up to the world this sinners' Friend.

Say, did you know that if it were not for the religion of the Lord Jesus Christ, women would not be valued more than stock? You men would think more of those old horses hitched out there in front of the tabernacle than you would of a woman. Of course it is true; history proves it to be a fact. Oh, my sister, we owe our all to him. How we ought to love him, honor him, and give him our very best. In every nation womanhood has been crushed beneath the heel of heathen cruelty and oppression and has never found liberty and freedom except through the gospel of our Lord. I say we owe it to the gospel and to womanhood everywhere that we women do all in our power to preach this Christ who has done so much for us. It was a woman who opened the flood-gates of hell and let into the world the awful tide of ungodliness that has for ages been bearing on its surging billows of slime the poor, lost souls of men to be hurled into an unending gulf of eternal woe. I tell you, we women are under a tremendous obligation to go out and stem the tide of iniquity and persecution and preach the power of a risen Lord.

And listen here, did you know that a man had nothing whatever to do with the completion of the plan of redemption? Not a thing! But a woman did. It took God the Father, God the Son, God the Holy Ghost, and a frail little woman. But *man not in it*. If God so honored us, you have no right to fight and oppress us. We have more right to preach than anybody else, and I pray God to help us see the awfulness of trying to hinder a woman ill her obligations to God, and her heaven-born privilege.

We women are noted for our talent to talk. We are sometimes called talking machines. Why not let our machines run for the glory of God and the salvation of lost souls?

I sometimes hear a woman say, "Please excuse me; I can't talk in public." You can talk in a clubroom, high tea society, and all kinds of social gatherings; why not in the love feast and at prayer meeting? The Bible says, "Out of the abundance of the heart the mouth speaks." Whatever your heart is full of that is what you are going to talk about. Oh, that we may be so filled with his love that we shall love him and a lost world above everything else.

It is said that man is the head. "But," says George Stuart, "if man is the head, the woman is the neck, and it takes the neck to turn the head." Another said, "If man is the head, then woman is the heart of the home, and the home is the heart of the nation." Hence the power of a woman's influence.

Sister, let's put in every word possible for God, in our homes, in our social gatherings, in the prayer meetings; and if God calls on you to preach the gospel, do not shrink. He who calls you will not fail you.

No record can be given where woman ever treated the Christ as did man. It was man who betrayed him with a kiss. "And while he yet spoke, behold a multitude, and he that was called Judas, one of the twelve, went before them and drew near unto Jesus to kiss him. But Jesus said unto him, Judas, betrays the Son of man with a kiss?" (Luke 22: 47–48).

No one in the wide, wide world can love like a woman. Men can beat us preaching, and doing many other things, but can never love like we do. A woman can love to the very last. A father will love till threadbare, will advise and counsel until disheartened and discouraged, then turn around and kick his own boy out of his home. But the mother's heart still holds on. Though ever so vile, a voice whispers gently. "He's mother's child." No one can be as true to an object of love as a woman. And no one can be more true to a God-given call to the ministry of the gospel than a woman. Oppose as much as you like, yet woman goes preaching on. It may be, my friend, that by your opposition you will keep some soul from God, but you can never affect us in the least. For God said, "Preach," and preach we shall.

DOCUMENT 37

Women Preachers (1905), 5, 9–10, 34, 43, 95–98
Frances "Fannie" McDowell Hunter

Like the Psalmist David I may say, "I have believed, therefore have I spoken" in the pages of this little book. For it was born of profound conviction that the teaching set forth therein is in perfect harmony with the teachings of the Bible. And such conviction came from the prayerful study of the Bible.

"By what authority do you do these things? And who gave you the authority?" (Matt 21:23). This is the question propounded by many when a woman enters the pulpit, takes a text, and preaches a sermon. With a desire to prove from God's Word who gave her this authority, I have written these pages.

In my travels in the evangelistic field I have found that woman's right to preach is a much discussed subject. There are many views entertained concerning just what woman may or may not do in religious work.

I have reviewed the Scriptures carefully on this subject, consulting the best authorities for the original translation. I see no reason why it should not be considered as candidly as any other subject.

I ask a special favor of those who may have any prejudice against the public ministry of women and have decided not to agree with the position I have taken, that they will read before making any condemnatory remarks. I think the subject is worthy of patient and prayerful investigation.

The little book falls far below my ideal; but with all its defects, with an earnest desire to promote the glory of God, it is prayerfully sent forth on its mission of love.

That women are to take a prominent part in evangelizing the world is clearly taught in the Old Testament. The first great prophecy concerning woman declares that her seed "shall bruise the serpent's head" (Gen 3:15). It was by the seed of the woman—Christ—that our redemption was purchased.

It was predicted that woman was to have a part in publishing the glad tidings of salvation. "The Lord gave the word; great was the company of those that published it" (Psa 68:11). As this passage is rendered in the authorized version of the Bible, there does not appear anything out of the common order. Unfortunately our translators have covered up the gender in this verse. The Hebrew word is of feminine gender.

The gospel of Jesus Christ is the sweetest news ever brought to mortal ears—and why not woman (whom God said was made a little lower than the angels) be allowed to bear the glad tidings of Jesus' power to us?

Opposition to women preaching has largely grown out of ideas based on tradition, prejudice, and misunderstanding and misapplying these two passages of Scripture found in Paul's writings. We face the difficulty of truth finding its way out of the jungles of prejudice and ignorance. Many persons who are blinded by prejudice simply refuse to open their eyes. They remind us of the man of whom we heard a woman evangelist tell. It illustrates why some fail to get the right meaning to these texts.

"A man told John he would give him five dollars if he could show him fifty rats in five minutes. So he took him to the stable and instructed him where to stand to see the rats run out as he would be inside to scare them out. The man asked John if he saw the rats to which John replied in the negative. After repeating the question several times and receiving the same reply, he stepped outside and to his amazement found that John had his eyes *closed tight*, and of course could see no rats." So many of our opponents are doing just as John did—simply *will not* see the truth because they allow prejudice to close their eyes to it.

Consecrated women, in obedience to the divine call, have taken upon themselves all the essential functions (many have taken *all* the functions) of the ministry in so far as prayer, exhortation, and preaching are concerned.

In the face of the Bible teaching on the ministry of women, who would presume to silence one of the thousands of modest, Christian women; who are in homes, the church, school, or in the WCTU, and other organizations, being blessed of God in using their voices in his service? And yet there are some ecclesiastics who form resolutions against their efforts to preach the gospel.

The writer was once present when a large body of preachers were in annual session. During that year, one of their pastors had invited a woman preacher to assist him in the revival services on his charge. She was greatly used of God in bringing the lost to Him. This body of preachers was in very plain terms expressing their disapproval of his course and of a woman being allowed to fill any pulpit within "their bounds." Different suggestions and resolutions were offered in order to prevent the repetition of such a course. At last it was settled in this way: "It is the sense of this body that no woman be allowed to fill any pulpit within our bounds." Later on, before the session closed, the presiding officer introduces his wife to the audience, who, *standing in the pulpit*, proceeds to make a speech in favor of the "−−−−−− Society" of the church, and from the pulpit very pathetically pleads with men and women to support it with their means and prayers. She met with the approval and applause of every member of that body. She was allowed perfect freedom to explain from the pulpit, *the plan of their society* (organization). But a woman preacher must not be allowed the privilege of explaining the *plan of salvation* and plead with lost men and women to yield to Christ. This same body of men approve of women going as missionaries, for their Board of Missions is supporting some in the foreign field. "Consistency, you are a jewel."

While men meet to discuss, "How to reach the masses," women with divine authority are going down to the masses. Miss Jane Addams was recently introduced to an audience, as "a woman who has done more for the down-trodden and oppressed in Chicago than any one man or set of men."

This may be well called woman's age. She moves up and the world feels her power. She is invading every line of employment. The census of 1900 makes returns for 303 separate occupations, and only in eight of these do women workers fail to appear. If she has freedom to engage in secular employment, why not allow her freedom to engage her time and talents in telling the story of Jesus and his love?

It is true she was first in the transgression and thus opened the flood gates of damnation and brought the curse of sin, misery, and woe upon us. If she, under the influence of the Evil One, could do so much damage, why not allow her under the influence of the Holy Spirit to do all she can to rescue us from the curse?

Dr. Adam Clarke said: "An ass reproved Balaam, a cock reproved Peter, and why not woman reprove sin?"

It is a well-known fact that she has done more to advance the cause of temperance in the last twenty-five years than the men had done in a hundred years previous. When our country is sufficiently advanced in thought to give women the ballot, prohibition will soon be a settled question. She would soon abolish laws licensing saloons.

Truly Jesus is the woman's Friend. He conferred on her the right, to think, to worship and act—honored her specially. She was the first he turned aside from the Jews to give his benedictions. He knew what she would be to the world.

Rev. Herrick Johnson says: "The best example of self-denying liberality in the Bible is recorded of woman. The best example of loving service in the Bible is recorded of woman. The best example of conquering prayer in the Bible is recorded of woman. The gift was a widow's mite; the service was the anointing of Jesus with a box of ointment; the prayer was a mother's prayer for a daughter possessed with the devil. Jesus never let fall such words of royal commendation as concerning these women. Of the poor widow he said, 'She has cast in more than them all.' Of Mary he said, 'She has done what she could.' And to the Canaanite mother he said: 'O woman, great is your faith! Be it unto you even as you will.'"

A heathen woman on reading the Bible said: "This book must have been written by a woman. It says so many good things about her." We know without it and without the Savior, whom it teaches, the lot of woman is pitiable in the extreme.

Where Christ is preached, woman's sphere is not one of deep degradation as it is where he is not preached and as it was among the numerous kingdoms of ancient paganism. In this Christian land she is honored. Woman, representing the highest place in the civilization of the world, is placed on the dome of the Capitol of Washington, holding in one hand the sword representing justice, and in the other, the olive branch, representing peace.

She is also the money-controlling power. You will find her image stamped on every piece of silver.

Since woman owes her elevation to Christianity, may she show her appreciation by rallying around the cross and may the careless daughters hear God's call to *arouse* and his warning of the consequences of being careless. "Rise up women that are at ease; hear my voice, you careless daughters: give ear unto my speech. Tremble you women that are at ease; be troubled, you careless ones" (Isa 32:9–11). O, that many more of Christian women would say with Phoebe Palmer: "When I consecrated myself to God, my lips and voice were included."

"Rise up women," and do the bidding of your Master, although some of his disciples may become indignant and say: "To what purpose is this waste?" Let Jesus reply to them: "Why trouble the woman? For she has wrought a good work upon me" (Matt 26:10).

We come now to this final conclusion: That we women preachers will adopt the glorious motto given by Peter: "We ought to obey God rather than men" (Acts 5:29).

DOCUMENT 38

"An Autobiographical Sketch" (1905)
Frances "Fannie" McDowell Hunter
Source: Hunter, *Women Preachers*, 53–54, 56, 59–61

My entrance upon the evangelistic field was at the instance of an evangelist and wife of Kentucky who were constantly engaged in revival meetings. They discovered that God had given me a musical talent that had been sufficiently cultivated to fill the position of organist. They felt impressed that he would use me in the ministry of song and so invited me to assist them in revival work.

I rejoiced to go on this great and glorious mission. Most tender ties bound me to my home, but stronger ties of love and duty bound me to the service of my Master. With joy did I hail the privilege of throwing my entire being into sacrifice and service for him and mankind.

So my first work was to sing the gospel. I soon found that God had entrusted me with a key that unlocked many hearts that were impervious to all other appeals. Few hearts are such impregnable fortresses that they will not yield to assaults of love through the ministry of song. God has used me in this way to cheer many sad hearts and to brighten lives for him and to rescue lives from the service of Satan.

In all of my religious work, I have kept before me this exhortation: "As we have therefore opportunity, let us do good unto all men" (Gal 6:10). God had led me to sow the seed in the congregation, in the home, on the street, in the cars, in the temperance hall, anywhere, everywhere.

God has given me evidence of his approval of gospel messages given in open air meetings. I recall one incident of an infidel saloon keeper being reached in this way. After having talked from the text, "The eyes of the Lord are in every place, beholding the evil and the good" (Prov 15:3), I approached this man and talked to him about his soul's salvation and requested him to pray for himself before coming to the next service in the evening. After supper he retired to a secret place in the garden. When he knelt, he said: "Lord you know I don't know how to pray. Will you please excuse me for all the sins I've committed against you?" The sins of years were blotted out in answer to his petition offered in penitence.

God has led me by his loving hand and called me to different fields and I have joyfully gone forward to do his will in proclaiming a full gospel. I have welcomed the life of the evangelist with the ever ceaseless travel, living in a "trunk," body often so weary and worn that a garret would seem inviting to get alone for a rest. Many times on this battlefield I have had to wrestle with giants of difficulty, and I have met with opposition and persecution; but what matters if devils rage and human opposition be felt, so long as we have the smile and approval of our Master? The joy of bringing the lost to Jesus outweighs all the toil, privations, and suffering.

Often I have been tempted to discouragement, and when my body was almost exhausted, the suggestion would come to give up the work.

One time after an apparent fruitless effort in a revival meeting, I almost yielded to the suggestion. There was much opposition to the public ministry of women, and the hindrances to our having a successful meeting were many. I did not know of a soul being influenced by my ministry. When about decided to give it up, my heavenly Father gave me a dose of encouragement from his Word: "For consider him that endured such contradiction of sinners against himself, lest you be wearied and faint in your minds" (Heb 12:3). Two years after the time the above revival was held, I took the train to go to a camp meeting and I was being tempted again to discouragement. It was like our Father to teach his discouraged child a lesson so gently. I had not been seated long in the car when a preacher of my acquaintance spoke to me. He told me a gentleman friend of his desired to become acquainted with me. I assured him I would be pleased to meet his friend. After being introduced, the friend said: "Do you remember the meeting you assisted in in the town in Kentucky?" I replied, "Yes, quite well." "Well," he said, "I will tell you for the glory of God that as you sang a consecration hymn on your knees the last night of the meeting, I fully consecrated myself to God and he sanctified me. Since then I have been licensed to preach and am now preaching a gospel of full salvation."

I lifted my heart in thankfulness to God and promised him that if ever discouragement should dare to step into my life, I would quickly send it away and press on in the work he called me to. I feel that such results prove ample compensation for all self-denying toil. Truly the King's service has its rewards. Roses and lilies have kissed my feet as I would stoop to lift the fallen. The realization of the wonderful strengthening and girding power of the words: "Lo, I am with you" has cheered me and brought me out of trials that seemed like prison walls to be "more than conqueror."

I shall be fully repaid if I can only be permitted to bear golden fruit from my field of labor to the feet of my Master and hear him speak in loving appreciation of my services as he did Mary's: "She has done what she could."

Will not the reader join me in a prayer that many precious souls may be won to him as a result of the work that till remains for me to do?

DOCUMENT 39

"My Call to God's Work" (1905)
Jonnie Jernigan
Source: Hunter, *Women Preachers*, 79–83

The days of my childhood were not without tokens of the character of my future life and work.

Very early in life I felt impressions from the Holy Spirit upon my spiritual nature. An intense longing to tell the lost world of Jesus' love possessed my soul.

I was reared by Methodist parents, and any suggestion to them that a woman might be called of God to preach, was promptly pronounced un-Methodist, so I kept the longing a secret from everyone.

In my girlhood days I was thrown with some Catholics, who told me the story of devoted nuns and Sisters of Charity, who lived a life of seclusion in order that they might live holy, and give their lives to the ministry of the suffering and helping the needy. Stories of their devoted lives in plague-stricken districts fell into my hands. They were fascinating to my young, girlish heart. As I repeated them to my parents, my heart fairly burned with the desire to take the Catholic veil, thinking that I might be thus fitted to bear the story of the "Man of Sorrows" to suffering hearts. But my parents promptly gave me to understand that Roman Catholicism was a delusion, and only a snare to trap fickle-minded women.

I was utterly discouraged and my heart crushed, as it seemed no way was open to me to give my life to the service of God. The Methodist Church would not recognize a woman preacher, and to join the Catholics meant to disgrace my family name of which I was proud, and so, broken-hearted and discouraged, I sought relief by going to a solitary place in the orchard of our home place where I wept bitterly before God.

These conditions prevented me being converted until after I was a grown woman. All of the time I was resisting the call of God until my heart became hardened. My heart was filled with pride, although I was a poor girl. I became a devotee of fashion, and my occupation was that of a milliner and fashionable dressmaker. I bent every energy to please my customers; but many times as they walked away attired in the latest styles, assuring me that they were pleased with my work, there would steal into my heart an intense longing to polish the soul of the woman and make it shine for God as I had adorned her body to shine for the gaze of worldlings.

This awful struggle in my heart continued unknown to anyone but God and myself, until one day I read a thrilling story of a missionary who braved many dangers to carry the gospel to China's forbidden soil. The Holy Spirit again impressed the call to gospel work upon my spiritual nature.

I reasoned as follows: "If the Methodist Church will not allow a woman to preach the gospel in America, I will give my heart to God and go as a foreign missionary to China where they will allow a woman to preach."

I wondered why they would allow her to preach in China and not in America; and why the church would have a grand missionary rally on the return of a woman missionary from China and allow her freedom in the churches to tell of her foreign work, but would refuse the pulpit to a woman of America to preach the gospel.

Soon after this I yielded to God and was gloriously converted.

Not long after this occurred, I was married; and to my surprise soon discovered that my husband too, had a call to preach and was not obeying it, under the delusion that the best thing for him to do was to take a course in a medical college to fit himself for a physician.

The pride in my heart soon led me to imagine that I was a rich doctor's wife, driving fine horses, helping to minister to the needs of suffering humanity.

We built many "air castles" only for God to sweep away at one stroke and leave us with blasted hopes.

One bright Monday evening, my husband came home from his work with face all aglow, as he told me that he had obtained the experience of sanctification. He told me of his *entire consecration* to God. He was so filled with the Spirit that he looked like a new man and the change in him affected me as I felt the fire to begin to burn in my own heart.

He looked at me with such a radiant face as he said: "I told God that I would preach the gospel and I am ready to begin immediately." I said in my heart: "*There it is again—a call to preach.*"

All of the bright prospects of being a rich doctor's wife vanished immediately and I meditated thus: "I will be troubled again with that call to preach and no church will want a woman preacher."

I turned away from my husband with a sad, heavy heart. For two weeks I fasted and prayed until I was physically weak. At last I yielded to God, saying: "Here am I, send me. I am ready to report for orders, dear Master. Summon me and I will go on any errand of love for Thee." From that time I have done my best for Him who has done so much for me.

I felt that my call was to the ones no one else seemed to care for. I longed to tell the unfortunate girl the story of Mary Magdalene, who washed the feet of my Lord with her tears of penitence, while he washed her sins away with his own precious blood and commissioned her to preach the first sermon of the Resurrection.

I desired to go to the homes of poverty and tell them of the Babe born in an ox-stall and cradled in a manger. Of him who had no place to lay his head and no money to pay his taxes.

I longed to tell the broken-hearted of the "Man of Sorrows" who was acquainted with grief—who wept with those who wept—who offered garments of praise for a spirit of heaviness.

I desired to tell all who were bound with the chains of sin, that Jesus came to set at liberty the captives, and to open the prison doors and set free the prisoners of sin.

I desired to tell the nameless child of one who "made himself of no reputation," who was conceived of the Holy Ghost and born of a virgin.

I deem it a great privilege to carry the gospel to the despised and neglected of earth and it affords me great joy to watch the joy of God's salvation flood their souls. The united ministry of my husband and myself is honored of God in the salvation of precious, immortal souls.

I am so grateful to God for not only endowing me with the gift of preaching, but also with a love for home and children. I feel that I am honored to be the mother of six children—all of whom are with us but baby Rachel, who went to heaven a few months ago.

Home duties, the care of my precious children, and of an invalid mother, I have not neglected. God has enabled me to meet these obligations cheerfully. While I have recognized my first duty was to home and children, this has not lessened my zeal for lost souls, nor has it been a hindrance to my obeying the call to the ministry. When my presence has been required at home so that I was prevented going into the highways and hedges, God has sent the erring ones to my home to receive spiritual help. In my own home there have been precious, erring girls redeemed from a life of sin. To God be all the glory!

I often preach on rescue work and as a result more than a score of erring girls have been brought to Jesus.

God has also given me a message for mothers and wives. Many sad hearts have been comforted by this message.

By the grace of God I expect to continue in this work, so that I may at last hear Him say, "Well done!"

DOCUMENT 40

"Woman's Right to Preach" (1928)
Mary Lee Cagle
Source: Cagle, Life and Work, 160–63, 166–67, 169, 171–76

We are now taking up a much discussed and a very badly misunderstood subject—woman's right to preach.

I have decided that what we have been accustomed to all of our lives has more to do with our opinions than what the dear old Bible says. For example, if we had been accustomed all our lives to hear women preach, and had never heard a man preach, then if a big two-hundred pound man came along preaching we would all declare that he was out of his place and would feel like saying, "Let him keep silent."

This is pre-eminently a woman's age. They are slowly but surely pressing their way to the front. Go into the school rooms and you will find ten women teachers to one man teacher. Go into the wholesale and retail stores and you will find practically all of the clerks are women. Women are almost entirely operating the telephone offices. Women have entered the practice of law. Some are governors; some are judges; some are in the legislature, others are members of Congress and some have reached the Senate. Some of the best doctors of the country are women. A late census gave 5,000 women doctors in the United States, and among them are eye, ear, nose and throat specialists and some of the best of surgeons. Some of the finest dental work I ever had was done by a woman. In fact women are filling acceptably every place of responsibility and trust, and everyone seems to think that is all right; as at least none raise objection; I have about decided that the men do not care so very much what women do, just so they help to make the living. Let a woman get a lost world on her heart, the cries of the lost ringing in her ears, a call from God to go rescue the lost, and the realization that "Woe is unto me if I preach not the gospel," with one accord people begin to cry, "Let her keep silent, let her keep silent."

Now we are going to look into the Bible and see what it has to say on the subject. We are going to take this up entirely from a biblical standpoint and see what women were allowed and what they were not allowed to do. I am 'persuaded that what they were allowed to do when the New Testament was written will be all right for them to do now.

   1. They took part in public prayer meeting (Acts 1:13–14)

   2. They prophesied (Luke 2:36–38)

3. Philip's daughters (Acts 21:8–9)

4. They labored in the gospel (Phil 4:3)

5. They served the church. (Rom 16:1–2)

6. A woman was the first to preach Jesus after he arose from the dead (John 20:16–18)

7. Jesus first declared his Messiahship to a woman (John 4:25–26)

8. They are as divinely authorized to preach as men (Joel 2:28–29)

9. The grace of God knows no sex (Gal 3:28)

Why did God give women such a talent to talk, if not to be used for him? If God did not intend for women to use their tongues for him he certainly did give the devil a great advantage in the beginning, for women can talk. The men are generally our superiors; but there are some things that we can excel them in. And one of them is talking: You can put a half-dozen women in one room and they can all talk at once and no one listen, and yet when they get out of the room each one can tell everything the other said. Men could not do that if their lives depended upon it. They have to talk one at a time and then they can't tell it correctly across the street. How many men are there who never went down town and phoned back and asked the wife what it was she told him to get? All that never did that keep your seats. It is no wonder to me why the devil has tried and in a large measure succeeded in keeping women from using their tongues for God, for he knows that if the women get filled with the Holy Ghost and turn their tongues loose on him he will have to hunt cooler quarters, or in other words will have to vacate.

Woman brought sin into the world. Why not let her help put sin out of the world?

There are two scriptures that seem to contradict all that I have said, and some have hardly listened to the points I have made, for thinking of these two quotations. We will now notice them.

Now the truth of the matter is this: God made man and woman, not to be bosses one of the other, but to be helpmates one for the other. When God made woman he did not take a bone out of Adam's head and make a woman, signifying that he should run over her; neither did he take a bone out of his foot signifying that she should be trodden under foot; but he took a rib out of Adam's side right close up to his heart, and made a woman; signifying that she should stand right up by his side on an equal footing with him, and that they should love each other and be companions, one for the other, and he should shield and protect her with his strong right arm and that she should cling to and confide in him.

How beautiful! And when God's plan is carried out, the result will always be a happy home. If God's plan was carried out there would be an end to separations and divorce suits.

I was holding a revival meeting at a summer resort. There were crowds of people who attended; many I knew well. One afternoon as I was out getting some fresh air I met a lady who lived in the town where my home then was. She asked me to sit down as she wanted to talk to me; I gladly did so; her little daughter had been saved in the meeting. She told me that she had enjoyed my preaching, and it had been a great help to her; but still she believed that it was wrong for me to preach. I asked, "Why?" She replied it was because the Bible said, "Let your women keep silence in the churches." I knew that the lady taught a large class in Sunday school when at home. I asked, "Do you keep silent when you are teaching your class in Sunday school?" She said, "No. But that is not what it means. It means preaching." I replied, "It does not say preaching. It says keep silent. And you can no more teach a class in Sunday school and keep silent than I can preach and keep silent. One breaks the silence as much as the other." The lady got silent.

My first husband, Rev. Robert L. Harris, was once a missionary in Africa; and I heard him say that after leaving there he could better understand this scripture. He said that many times when he was preaching, some woman would get up and ask him to explain and while he was explaining to her another woman would arise and ask him what he was saying to the first woman; then another would ask him what he was saying to the second woman; and so on till there would be five or six all on their feet, all talking at the same time, till he would have to tell them to sit down and keep silent, and when they got home their husbands would make it all plain to them.

In the same chapter where it says, "Let the women keep silent," it also says, "Let the man keep silent."

9

Late Nineteenth-Century Female Apologists

Introduction

In her various works on female evangelism and preaching in America, Catherine Brekus has examined the factors that promoted the public ministry of women in Methodism in the nineteenth century.[1] Despite the way in which multiple factors elevated receptivity to women in these roles, the gains of women in the early nineteenth century yielded to increasing antagonism in the 1830s and 1840s. "As Methodism was transformed from a small, struggling sect into a powerful, middle-class denomination," Brekus concedes, "women were no longer allowed to preach or even exhort in public."[2] The same forces, essentially, that mitigated the ministry of women in British Methodism—patriarchal institutionalism and cultural reputability—shaped American Methodism increasingly in the second quarter of the nineteenth century. In addition to this familiar pattern, another broad development influenced attitudes about the place and role of women as well. Jean Miller Schmidt describes the first half of the nineteenth century as the age of "the true Methodist woman."[3] She borrowed this language from Barbara Welter's watershed study which identified the four cardinal virtues of "true

---

1. See Brekus, *Strangers & Pilgrims* and "Female Evangelism" in particular.
2. Brekus, "Female Evangelism," 165.
3. Schmidt, *Grace Sufficient*, 79.

womanhood" in this period: piety, purity, submissiveness, and domesticity.[4] The domestication of both women and the church figured prominently in the attitudes of both men and women in antebellum America. But as Brekus observes, the great irony in this development was the way in which it "fueled the rise of a new generation of educated, politically astute women who demanded full equality in the church."[5] A new breed of Methodist women arose to defend their ministry following the Civil War.

During the 1860s several events catalyzed women. In 1866 Helenor Alter Davisson (1824–76) was ordained a deacon in the Methodist Protestant Church, becoming the first ordained woman in the Methodist tradition.[6] Three years later, Methodist women birthed the Woman's Foreign Missionary Society and raised funds independent of the male-dominated Methodist Episcopal Church structures to send Isabella Thoburn (1840–1901), an educator, and Clara Swain (1834–1910), a doctor, to India. That same year Maggie Newton Van Cott (1830–1914) was the first woman to receive a license to preach. Following her husband's death in 1866, she engaged in evangelistic work at Five Points Mission in New York City—that seedbed of holiness, social action, and women's ministry so closely linked with Phoebe Palmer. Not so much concerned with her right to preach nor impressed by the blessing of Methodist officials, Van Cott was more impelled by God's call; she neither sought a license nor valued it very highly.[7] But as Carolyn Gifford acknowledges, this action "touched off a debate in the MEC over women's right to be ordained which lasted nearly a century," a debate fueled most certainly by the seventy or so women licensed to preach during the 1870s.[8] Given what seemed to be a new day, women and men apologists ratcheted up the debate. Schmidt notes that the issue of "licensing women as local preachers and exhorters refused to disappear after 1872."[9] As sociologist Mark Chaves has concluded, "As the nineteenth century moved on, but especially after 1870, the issue of female clergy came to be more and more understood as an issue of gender equality."[10]

This debate eventually revolved around two female graduates of Boston University School of Theology and came to a head in 1880. "No woman threatened male domination of clergy rights until the late 1870s," wrote

4. Welter, *Dimity Convictions*, 21–41.

5. Brekus, "Female Evangelism," 173.

6. Shoemaker, "Small Work;" cf. Schmidt, *Grace Sufficient*, 181.

7. See Everhart, "Van Cott."

8. Gifford, *Defense of Women's Rights*, 7.

9. Schmidt, *Grace Sufficient*, 179.

10. Chaves, *Ordaining Women*, 10.

Rosemary Keller, "when Anna Howard Shaw and Anna Oliver sought to be ordained by the New England Annual Conference."[11] Anna Oliver (1840–92) graduated from the School of Theology in 1876, the first woman in America to obtain a Bachelor of Divinity degree. That same year she was granted a license to preach and assumed pastoral responsibilities at the First Methodist Church of Passaic, New Jersey. Anna Howard Shaw (1847–1919), whose family had emigrated from the Methodist center of Newcastle-upon-Tyne in England when she was four years old, followed a parallel path. Completing her theological studies at Boston as well in 1878 (like Howard, the only woman in her class), she immediately accepted a pastoral appointment in Cape Cod. When both of these women petitioned in 1880 for membership in the New England Annual Conference of the Methodist Episcopal Church, the Conference Examining Committee could find no reason to deny their candidacy for ordination. In due course, however, Edward G. Andrews, the presiding bishop, refused to ordain them. They made their appeal, therefore, to the ensuing General Conference, which was scheduled to meet in May of that year in Cincinnati.

According to Ken Rowe, Anna Oliver "launched a Spring offensive on the Methodist Episcopal Church, hoping to press a test case on the ordination of women."[12] She made the long journey to Ohio with a suitcase filled with copies of a pamphlet she had prepared to defend her position, and she placed a copy of her "Test Case" (Document 41) on the desk of every delegate elected to the Conference. In this pamphlet she explained her motivation, described her call and ministry, and examined and challenged each objection to her ordination. In particular, she defended the natural gifts and graces that women possess in relation to pastoral ministry. She and her supporters petitioned the General Conference to have all distinctions on the basis of gender removed from the *Book of Discipline* in reference to ordination. Classmates and professors from the alma mater of Oliver and Shaw lobbied on their behalf. One of their most ardent supporters, Mary Griffith, drafted an appeal of her own (Document 42), which she published on the eve of the Conference in the *Daily Christian Advocate*, a critical and widely circulated Methodist periodical. Mark Chaves observes that Oliver's strategy—supported by appeals like those of Griffith and the plaintiffs' colleagues in ministry—illustrates "a common way in which this issue was raised in the 1880s: a very small number of women, already functioning as clergy, sought full status and thereby generated conflict over the issue of women's

11. Keller, "Creating a Sphere," 248–49.
12. Rowe, "Ordination of Women," 64.

ordination."[13] In response to this apologetic effort, the General Conference not only rejected the appeal related to the ordination of women and the efforts to modify the *Book of Discipline*, but took punitive action against the women. The Conference prohibited the future licensure of women and rescinded all preaching licenses that had been issued to women since 1869. "The decision of that 1880 conference," writes Keller, "defined, in large measure, the status and role of women in the heritage of The United Methodist Church until the mid-twentieth century."[14]

As might well be expected, all those involved in this controversy responded in their own way, and the test case set a precedent for others within the Methodist family as well. Oliver remained within the fold of the Methodist Episcopal Church and continued a ministry characterized by her long-standing commitments to holiness, education, temperance, and gender inclusiveness.[15] Shaw returned to her Cape Cod congregations and pursued ordination in the Methodist Protestant Church. She was ordained in that tradition on October 12, 1880, only to have the ordination declared invalid four years later at their General Conference. She served several more years in ministry but, after adding a medical degree to her credentials, eventually moved on to become one of the most significant leaders in the women's suffrage and temperance movements.[16]

As Chaves notes, "a very similar story was unfolding almost simultaneously in the African Methodist Episcopal Church."[17] Stephen Angell provides the parallel narrative related to the African American counterpart of Shaw and Oliver, Sarah Ann Hughes.[18] Even before Hughes's birth in 1849, AME women had petitioned their General Conference for the coveted preaching license. Following a failed effort in 1844, women formed an organization, the Daughters of Zion, for the promotion of women's rights within the denomination. Their efforts met with entrenched resistance every quadrennium until 1882, when Hughes pressed her claim as a candidate for a pastorate.[19] Two years later the Conference finally agreed to license women as local preachers, but even then, as Susan Lindley observes, the action seems to have been motivated more by a concern to control the

---

13. Chaves, *Ordaining Women*, 167.

14. Keller, "Creating a Sphere," 246.

15. Richey, Rowe, and Schmidt, *Methodist Experience in America*, 1:243–44.

16. See Zink-Sawyer, *From Preachers to Suffragists*.

17. Chaves, *Ordaining Women*, 166.

18. Angell, "Controversy over Women's Ministry;" cf. Dickerson, *Liberated Past*, 121–36.

19. Ibid., 96; cf. Dodson, "Nineteenth-Century A.M.E. Preaching Women," 280–82.

women than anything else.[20] Ordination remained elusive. The Methodist Episcopal Church South did not even countenance a debate and refused to either license or ordain women.[21] The only exception to this regressive and repressive pattern was the Church of the United Brethren in Christ, which in 1889 approved the ordination of women and ordained its first female seminary graduate, Ella Niswonger.[22]

In that same year, Frances Willard (1839–98), evangelical social activist and founder of the Woman's Christian Temperance Union, published her monumental *Woman in the Pulpit* (Document 43). This apology reflects her exasperation over the actions of the 1880 General Conference. It also illustrates what Zikmund identified as the inextricable link between the parallel quests for women's ordination and lay equality in the church.[23] Willard's strong defense of women's rights in the church emerged not only in response to the ordination controversy, but also to the refusal of the church leaders to seat her and four other women who had been properly elected as lay delegates to the General Conference of 1888. She attributed her thoughts on women to two coeducational institutions—Oberlin College and Northwestern University, including Garrett Biblical Institute—that had begun to admit women, and to the life and ministry of her heroine, Phoebe Palmer. A rudimentary examination of her publication demonstrates the pervasive influence of both Palmer and Booth.[24]

But her defense reflects a different era and a new set of emphases. Hassey identifies several of these shifts in her apology:

> First, Willard exposed in-depth the inadequate biblical exegesis of opponents of women's public ministry. Second, she strongly advocated women's ordination. Third, she rejected the concept of the wife's subordination in marriage implicit in both Palmer and Booth. Finally, Willard criticized non-inclusive language, complaining that preachers rarely refer to the women of their audiences. . . . While Palmer and Booth stressed the lay preacher's rights, Willard focused on ordained women in the pulpit.[25]

In her analysis of this document, Nancy Hardesty compares Palmer's rationale, which she describes as the "prophet model," with the "mother

---

20. Lindley, *You Have Stept Out*, 181.

21. Zikmund, "Winning Ordination," 341.

22. Chilcote, "Women in the Pietist Heritage," 193–96.

23. Zikmund, "Winning Ordination," 341.

24. See Hassey, *No Time for Silence*, 101.

25. Ibid., 102.

model" developed by Willard.[26] Consistent with her general strategy for social change, Willard often cloaked radical ideas in language that seemed innocuous to those who remained captive to their cultural bias and did not have ears to hear. "Instead of defending themselves on the basis of their individual rights," Brekus avers, "these women took the language of motherhood in revolutionary directions, claiming to be uniquely qualified to preach because of their maternal qualities of compassion and understanding."[27]

Carolyn Gifford identifies another fundamental difference between Willard and many of her precursors. "Willard had put her finger on the fundamental problem," she writes. "Men did not want to share power—especially sacred power—with women."[28] With this in mind, Gifford analyzes the method Willard employs in the defense:

> Normally Willard preferred to work within a power system, carefully suggesting, cajoling, working out compromises as she moved toward a rearrangement of power so that men and women could share it. Both format and content of most of *Woman in the Pulpit* reflect her usual approach to an issue. In it she presented the full range of arguments for women's right to preach and be ordained: scriptural justifications; claims of woman's natural aptitude for ministry by virtue of her inherent higher spirituality than man's or because of her mothering capacities; the notion of woman's extraordinary call from God; the great need for women's special gifts in the ordained ministry of the church; and the appropriateness of official recognition for tasks that women were already performing within the church. . . . [Yet] Willard made one of the most provocative threats of her career. If men continued to balk at ordaining women perhaps women should take matters into their own hands and ordain themselves, she suggested . . . if men stalled any longer at sharing power and authority within the MEC, women would leave the denomination and form their own, giving themselves full laity and clergy rights.[29]

In addition to presenting her own defense, Willard collected the endorsements of prominent male ministers.[30]

26. Hardesty, "Minister as Prophet?"

27. Brekus, "Protestant Female Preaching," 969.

28. Gifford, *Defense of Women's Rights*, 10.

29. Ibid., 11–13; cf. Gifford, "American Women and the Bible," in which she compares the biblical hermeneutics of Willard and Elizabeth Cady Stanton.

30. See Schmidt, *Grace Sufficient*, 195. The contribution of Luther T. Townsend is discussed in chapter 8 below.

In 1898 Anna Howard Shaw articulated her mature thoughts on the church and women in an article entitled "Women in the Ministry" (Document 44). Zink-Sawyer provides a detailed analysis of this document in her incisive study of women preachers who entered the suffragist movement. She notes that "Shaw's apologetic for women in ministry contains glimpses of the argument that characterized her suffrage rhetoric . . . her argument assumes that the essential nature of women is more suited than that of men to the pastoral responsibilities of ministry and more capable of uplifting individual souls and entire congregations to higher spiritual and moral ideals."[31] She also examines Shaw's attitude about late nineteenth-century industrialization vis-à-vis religious and cultural developments, demonstrating how Shaw correlated economic progress—with its concomitant emphasis on work and the accumulation of wealth—with social and moral decay. These concerns directly interfaced her defense of women ministers and their potential to restore genuine religious piety and morality. "As if to anticipate feminist criticism of her argument and its acceptance of woman's essential nature," writes Zink-Sawyer, "Shaw concluded her essay with appeals to the divine rights and human equality of women."[32] Brekus acknowledges the fact that women like Oliver, Shaw, Griffith, and Willard embraced the regnant theme of domesticity, using the image of motherhood for their own purposes, but in the long run this "gave them a powerful language of female uniqueness that made it possible for them to defend their right to vote, own property, and be ordained."[33]

DOCUMENT 41

The "Test Case" (1880), 3–6, 8
Anna Oliver

Miss Anna Oliver was recommended for Deacon's Orders in the Methodist Episcopal Church at the last session of the New England Conference. The Bishop declined to submit the matter to the vote of the Conference because, in his judgment, the law of the church does not authorize the ordination of women. From this decision Presiding Elder Thayer took an appeal to the ensuing General Conference.

Miss Oliver asks for ordination. Ought she to be ordained?

31. Zink-Sawyer, *From Preachers to Suffragists*, 100.
32. Ibid., 101.
33. Brekus, "Female Evangelism," 172.

The church tacitly allows women to preach and labor as evangelists. For this ordination is not thought necessary. But here is a woman who believes herself called not to evangelistic work, but to the pastorate. The following are Miss Oliver's reasons for the belief, substantially as expressed before the New England Conference:

I am sorry to trouble our dear mother church with any perplexing questions, but it presses me also, and the church and myself must decide something. I am so thoroughly convinced that the Lord has laid commands upon me in this direction that it becomes with me really a question of my own soul's salvation. If the Lord commands me to just the course I am pursuing, as only they that do His commandments have right to the tree of life, I have no alternative.

Among other reasons, the following induce me to hold that I am called to pastoral and not evangelistic work:

I do not believe in evangelistic work as usually carried on, i.e., to warm up cold churches and *start* revivals. The legitimate sphere of an evangelist, in my understanding, is to assist an overworked minister and church while the revival is advancing. But the only invitations I received were of the first description. I have served about two years thus with what others call success.

The work of an evangelist is unsuited to women—certainly to me. It is contrary to the instincts of my nature. An evangelist has no home, is tossed from place to place. Advertisements, embracing personal descriptions are used with other sensational methods to draw together the people. The evangelist arrives and is thrust before a crowd of strangers. As soon as she becomes a little acquainted and forms some attachments, her time expires. She is torn away and thrust before another crowd of strangers. Women are said to be timid and shrinking, and will our good mother church take these shrinking, delicate, modest, sensitive, home-loving, nestling, timid little things, and toss them about from Maine to California, or send them as missionaries to wild and naked barbarians at the same time forbidding them to engage in the motherly work of the pastorate?

Pastoral work is adapted to women for it is motherly work. The mother has her little group, the pastor the flock. As a mother spreads her table with food suited to the individual needs of her family, so the pastor feeds the flock. Each knows the sick ones, the weak ones, those that must be carried in the arms, and those strong enough to help others. I recognize this field as suited to my natural qualifications.

My interest begins with conversions. Then an evangelist leaves. And I always felt as though a whole nursery full of my own little ones were being turned over to the care of strangers. The experience was, in a word, fearful.

I cannot endure to preach old sermons. I have subjects in my mind that will not let me rest until I work them up. To do so would be better for my present and future usefulness and for my own growth in grace. But a person who is preaching every night in the week cannot prepare new subjects.

The longer I preached as an evangelist, the less interest I felt—no matter how crowded the houses, nor what the apparent success—until I became convinced that, if the pastorate were unalterably closed, the Lord had released me from preaching. But just at this point pastoral work opened to me.

As a pastor my interest daily increases. I would rather toil quietly in a corner with a handful of persons, seeing believers sanctified and families transformed, than with the greatest éclat otherwise.

In evangelistic work I always saw some harm done, even where the most good was accomplished. But in regular labor, however small the gains, there is no discount of harm.

In this connection I may mention that, as an evangelist, my own spiritual growth was hindered, and had I long continued, I am convinced, I would have backslidden. On the other hand, in my present charge and in Passaic, the Lord has visited me with wonderful manifestations of his presence, and I realize in myself spiritual progress.

When the Lord calls one to preach, he always calls persons to hear. So in this case. Others beside myself have recognized my adaptation to the pastorate. In less than two years thirteen churches desired me for their pastor. But the ecclesiastical authorities refused to appoint a woman, *preferring in some instances to close or sell the church buildings.*

God sanctions my pastoral work. In proof of this I appeal to the record in Passaic, NJ, and Brooklyn, NY. But it may be said, notwithstanding the reasons just given, that I am mistaken in my call. Then it is a very great pity *for myself* that I cannot be convinced that I am mistaken—a pity that I have lived in this delusion all these years. I have made almost every conceivable sacrifice to do what I believe God's will. Brought up in a conservative circle in New York City that held it a disgrace for a woman to work, surrounded with the comforts and advantages of ample means, and trained in the Episcopal Church, I gave up home, friends and support, went counter to prejudices that had become second nature to me, worked for several years to constant exhaustion, and suffered cold, hunger, and loneliness. The things hardest for me to bear were laid upon me. For two months my own mother did not speak to me. When I entered the house she turned and walked away. When I sat at the table she did not recognize me. I have passed through tortures to which the flames of martyrdom would be nothing, for *they* would end in a day. And through all this time and today, I could turn off to positions of comparative ease and profit. However, I take no credit to myself for enduring these trials, because at every step it was plain to me that I had no alternative but to go forward or renounce my Lord.

Now is it possible that I am, that I have been all these years mistaken? Is it possible that our Father would either lead or leave a child of his in such a delusion?—a child whom he knows, as he knows my heart, desires nothing else so much as to learn the Father's will *to do it*. In fact he has really given constant evidence that he sanctions my course. At every step he has met me. He opened avenues of self-support while I was pursuing my studies. When I resigned loved ones, the joy of his presence more than compensated, so that trials have been no trials, for at all times he has given me the victory. I have been enabled through all to rejoice evermore, and in everything to give thanks. And now he has restored all my friends. My family, who once thought I disgraced them, are proud of me now. My parents love me today, as I am sure they would never have done had I obeyed them instead of God. Does God thus encourage fanatics or enthusiasts?

The Methodist Episcopal Church is the church of *my choice*. I have no one under God with whom to advise but the Bishops and brethren of our Church. Therefore I ask you, Fathers and brethren, tell me, what would you do were you in my place? Tell me, what would you wish the church to do toward you were you in my place? Please only apply the golden rule and vote in Conference accordingly.

Finally, let not the sympathies of my friends in the Conference be taxed, imagining that I am, or under any circumstances will be, in the least discouraged. I encourage myself in the Lord my God. No one and nothing can harm me. In all I am more than conqueror through him to whom be all the glory. In the future I intend in the strength of God to go forward as in the past, *joyfully*. If helped by you my brothers, then God bless you! If hindered by you my brothers, the Lord forgive you! (I know he will for I'll ask him to.) But whether helped or hindered, with God's grace I will stand where he commands me to stand; I will speak what he commands me to speak because I cannot do otherwise and God takes all the responsibility.

At a Church and Society meeting, held April 19, 1880, the following was unanimously passed:

> *Resolved*, that we, the Willoughby Avenue ME Church, of Brooklyn, NY, of which Miss Anna Oliver is pastor, are loyal to the doctrines and discipline of the Methodist Episcopal Church, and that we will and hereby do petition the General Conference of 1880 to make such alteration or alterations in the *Discipline*

as they may consider necessary to remove the disability or disabilities in the way of the ordination of our pastor.

At a meeting of the Alumni of the Boston School of Theology, held March 1880, the following resolution was passed, with one dissenting vote:

> *Resolved*, that the Alumni of the Theological School of the Boston University memorialize the General Conference to ordain those women who have felt called to the gospel ministry, and who have taken the thorough preparations of our colleagues and theological schools, and who have shown by gifts, grace and usefulness that they have the essential qualifications for the Methodist ministry.

Resolution of the New England Conference, adopted by a large majority:

> *Resolved*, that our delegates to the next General Conference be and are hereby instructed to use their influence to remove all distinctions of sex in the offices and ordination of our ministry.

DOCUMENT 42

"Position of Women in the Methodist Episcopal Church" (1880)
Mary Griffith

It is historic that women have done much for Methodism. Today they are doing more than ever, and yet in the whole constitution and organization of the church women are ignored—not as lacking, or being in fault, but simply as women. Churches are built and supported largely by the labors and contributions of women, yet the property is owned and controlled by a board from which women are excluded, and in whose election they have no choice.

In all this, the church is losing—losing both directly, by failing to put the best talent in the best places, and indirectly because the women members—the two-thirds of the church—are not brought out, strengthened, and made to grow. Women are the bulk of the church; when they suffer, the church suffers of course. The church brings out its *men*—especially its *young* men—by encouragement, training, and practice. With women, but little of this care is taken.

Women are rising up all over the land who feel moved by the Holy Ghost to preach. They are flocking into our theological schools as fast as the doors are opened; and the church must face their plea. You cannot quote Scripture against it for, if you claim that the restrictions laid upon ignorant, childish, Oriental women, ages ago, in a totally different state of society, were designed for the cultured, devoted, respected women of today, you remand us all back to veil, subjection, and silence; you hush our voices in the prayer meeting room and Sunday school class. We have already referred to the superior spiritual endowments of women. Where should the highest spirituality find the appropriate place of action if not in the pulpit—and how can the pulpit afford to deprive itself of this powerful element? It has been beautifully said, "There are truths which only a woman's heart will conceive, and only a woman's lips can teach—truths, by chance, which have come to her when baby fingers have clung round her neck in the dark." Women are the *talkers* of the race. There is no trouble in having this admitted. "A woman's voice can tell a long history of sorrow in a single word." Refine and cultivate the talking gift, and you have *oratory*. We cannot afford to be blind to the drift of these things.

The final test of this question lies in the *call* of a woman to preach. As Methodists we believe in the direct operation of the Holy Spirit on the mind. Now, numbers of women testify that they have this burning zeal for souls, that constraining desire to tell the love of Christ, that sense of condemnation in silence and all those other indications and impressions which in *men* are recognized as a call to preach. They are also led providentially into those paths of usefulness, they speak with that acceptability, they realize that success, they are sealed with that evident approval of God,—both upon their own consciousness and in outward results—which in a brother's case would bring him help, encouragement, opportunities of education, and finally license and ordination. Have these women "gifts, grace and usefulness"? We will risk the answer with all those who have made any considerable observation on the success of women's gospel work; and in addition, will beg to remind you that hitherto women have worked without any special training or education, in the face of many difficulties.

To deny that many women realize the call of God to preach or speak the gospel is to put away all faith in the conscious impressions of the Holy Spirit on the mind. Then, if God calls, how can the church refuse to call without coming into controversy with the divine Master? License and ordination are merely the church's seal of approval on what it recognizes as God's will and plan. They are right and necessary for the success and convenience of the workman. If women are called, they need these seals of approval as much as men do and for the same reasons.

It may be said, "Women *are* permitted to speak and preach freely in the Methodist Episcopal Church; and since the work is the main thing, why ask for office and recognition?" It is true that women have great liberty with us as compared with other churches. Thank God, they are not doomed to utter silence! Our Methodism is grandly in advance on this line, as it is on most others. We have had women preachers since Wesley's time. Probably not one who reads this will deny that women may and should deliver the gospel message in one way or another. Why deny as a church what we admit as individuals? Why not, at least, grant the exhorter's or local preacher's license?

Is it not a solemn and fearful thing—is it not cruel beyond compare—to hinder a soul that is called of the Holy Ghost? Can the church afford this loss? Are the fields no longer white and are the laborers so many that we can spurn any away, especially when the Master summons? We ask license and ordination for women because it is necessary for them and for the work. Without these they are forced into the uncertain, exposed, wearing life of traveling evangelists, without either the moral or financial support of the church. Without these they are left in the dubious and embarrassing position of one who goes before he is sent. The church says, "Since you will work, go on, but we will not give our approval." Is this fair? Is this just or righteous? Nay, since the delicacy of the womanly organ is sometimes talked of, is it *chivalrous* to force them into these rough and lonely paths? We simply ask that, when a woman-worker measures up to the same standard as a brother-worker, she shall be accorded the same privileges and powers. We should not have to ask, for however pure the motive—however faultless the form of request—we are, by the very fact of asking laid open to unjust suspicion and criticism.

The church is supposed to be founded upon *spiritual* principles. Measured by a spiritual standard, women are the equals of men. In Christ's kingdom is neither bond nor free, male nor female. Does his church on earth fairly represent that kingdom when its constitution ignores women and its customs shut her out of its highest places of privilege?

It rests with you, members of the General Conference, to remedy these evils, in great part at least. You best know how it should be done. Will you not examine the *Discipline* and determine that this May, of 1880, shall see the end of some of these harmful distinctions?

As women we have no representatives in your midst. What can we do but appeal to your sense of truth and righteousness? Surely our blessed Methodism is too pure—the heroic age of our history too fresh upon us—to let us appeal to a lower motive.

In order that the matter may be clearly understood, we ask you to formulate the principle, in legal, disciplinary enactment, that the masculine nouns and pronouns used in the *Discipline of the Methodist Episcopal Church*, in referring to trustees, stewards, Sunday school superintendents, class-leaders, exhorters, and preachers—itinerant and local—shall not be construed as excluding women from these offices; and, further, that the word "male" be expunged entirely from the *Discipline*.

DOCUMENT 43

Woman in the Pulpit (1889), 5–6, 40–42, 45, 47–50, 52–53, 55–60, 62
Frances E. Willard

This book is the outgrowth of an article prepared by me in compliance with the request of my good friends the editors of *The Homiletic Monthly*.

Its length went beyond the prescribed limits, and it overflows into these pages, accompanied by testimony collected by me from men and women preachers, and enriched by the criticism of Dr. Van Dyke, the learned Presbyterian, who is replied to by Dr. Townsend, the equally learned Methodist theologian.

Wishing to learn the opinion of three ministers than whom none living are more devout, more gifted or renowned, I wrote asking what they thought about "Woman in the Pulpit." The following replies will be of interest to their millions of readers in all lands. I count myself fortunate to be able to introduce this little book with the approving and brotherly words of these great men, and I beg a patient and unprejudiced attention, not only to their words but to the words of all the witnesses that follow them. With an earnest prayer that Christ's blessed kingdom in the earth may be advanced a little by the considerations herein urged, I can but repeat the well-known and half-pathetic words, "Go, little book, I cast you on the waters, go your way."

Christ, not Paul, is the source of all churchly authority and power. What do we find him saying? How did he deal with women? In the presence of the multitude, he drew from Martha the same testimony that he required of his apostles, and she publicly replied, almost in Peter's very words, "Yes, Lord, I believe that you are the Christ, the Son of God, which should come into the world," He declared his commission to the woman at the well of Samaria, with an emphasis and a particularity hardly equaled in any of his public addresses, and her embassy was abundantly rewarded. What pastor would not rejoice to hear such words as these: "Now we believe, not because of your saying, for we have heard him ourselves, and know that this is indeed the Christ, the Savior of the world."

It is objected that he called no woman to be an apostle. Granted, but he himself said that he chose one man who had a devil; is this a precedent! One is half inclined to think so when one reads the long record of priestly intolerance, its culmination being the ostracism of Christ's most faithful followers from their right to proclaim the risen Lord, who gave to Mary the first commission to declare his resurrection. True, he did not designate women as his followers. They came without a call. From their sex he had his human origin. With the immeasurable dignities of his incarnation and his birth, only God and woman were concerned. No utterance of his marks woman as ineligible to any position in the church he came to found. But his gracious words and deeds, his impartation of his purposes and plans to women, his stern reproofs to men who did them wrong, his chosen companionships, and the tenor of his whole life and teaching, all point out precisely the opposite conclusion. Indeed, Luke explicitly declares that as "he went throughout every city and village, preaching and showing the glad tidings of the Kingdom of God," "the twelve were with him and certain women" among whom were" Joanna, the wife of Chuza, Herod's steward, and Susanna and many others, who ministered unto him of their substance" (8:1–3).

What a spectacle must that have been for the "Scribes and Pharisees, hypocrites." What loss of caste came to those fearless women who, breaking away from the customs of society arid traditions of religion, dared to follow the greatest of iconoclasts from city to village with a publicity and a persistence nothing less than outrageous to the conservatives of that day.

"Verily, Devotion, Thy Name Is Woman!"
Not she with trait'rous kiss her Savior stung;
Not she denied him with unholy tongue;
She, while apostles shrank, could danger brave,
Last at his cross, and earliest at his grave.

Christ's commission only is authoritative. To whom did he give it after his resurrection until which time the new dispensation was not fairly ushered in? If we are to accept specific statements, rather than the drift and spirit of the inspired book, as conclusive of a question involving half the human race, let us then here take our stand on our Lord's final words and deeds. It is stated that the two disciples to whom Christ appeared on the way to Emmaus "returned to Jerusalem, and found the eleven gathered together, and them that were with them saying, 'The Lord is risen, indeed, and has appeared to Simon" (Luke 24:33). Be it understood that women used this language, the women "who came with him from Galilee." It was "them that were with them" (i.e., with the eleven) who were saying, "The Lord is risen indeed."

Let not conservative ecclesiastical leaders try to steady the Lord's ark. Let them not bind what God has loosed. Let them not retain the bondage he has remitted, lest haply they be found to fight against God!

Men preach a creed; women will declare a life. Men deal in formulas, women in facts. Men have always tithed mint and rue and cummin in their exegesis and their ecclesiasticism, while the world's heart has cried out for compassion, forgiveness, and sympathy. Men's preaching has left heads committed to a catechism and left hearts hard as nether millstones. The Greek bishop who said, "My creed is faultless, with my life you have nothing to do," condensed into a sentence two thousand years of priestly dogma. Men reason in the abstract, women in the concrete. A syllogism symbolizes one, a rule of life the other. In saying this I wish distinctly to disclaim any attack upon the clergy, any alighting allusion to the highest and holiest of callings. I am speaking only of the intolerant sacerdotal element that has handicapped the church from the earliest ages even until now and which has been more severely criticized by the best element in the church than by any words that I have penned.

Religion is an affair of the heart. The world is hungry for the comfort of Christ's gospel and thirsty for its everyday beatitudes of that holiness which alone constitutes happiness. Men have lost faith in themselves and each other. Boodlerism and "corners" on the market, greed of gain, passion for power, desire for drink, impurity of life, the complicity of the church, Protestant as well as Papal, with the liquor traffic, the preference of a partisan to a conscientious ballot, have combined to make the men of this generation faithless toward one another. The masses of the people have forsaken God's house and solace themselves in the saloons or with the Sunday newspaper. But the masses will go to hear women when they speak and every woman who leads a life of weekday holiness and has the gospel in her looks, however plain her face and dress may be, has round her head the sweet Madonna's halo in the eyes of every man who sees her. She speaks to him with the sacred cadence of his own mother's voice. The devil knew what he was doing when he exhausted sophistry to keep woman down and silent. He knew that "the only consecrated place on earth is where God's Spirit is" and that a Christian woman's heart enshrines that Holy Ghost more surely than many a "consecrated" pulpit.

Men have been preaching well-nigh two thousand years and the large majority of the converts have been women. Suppose now that women should share the preaching power, might it not be reasonably expected that a majority of the converts under their administration would be men? Indeed, how else are the latter to have a fair chance at the gospel? The question is asked in all seriousness, and if its practical answer shall be the equipping of women for the pulpit, it may be reasonably claimed that men's hopes of heaven will be immeasurably increased. Hence, one who urges the removing of the arbitrary ruling which now excludes woman from a choice portion of her kingdom may well claim to have manifested especial considerateness toward the interests of men.

The entrance of woman upon the ministerial vocation will give to humanity just twice the probability of strengthening and comforting speech, for women have at least as much sympathy, reverence, and spirituality as men, and they have at least equal felicity of manner and of utterance. Why then should the pulpit be shorn of half its power?

To the exegesis of the cloister we oppose that of common life. To the Orientalism that is passing off the stage, we oppose modern Christianity. In our day, the ministers of a great church have struck the word "obey" out of the marriage service, have made women eligible to nearly every rank except the ecclesiastic, and are withheld from raising her to the ministerial office only by the influence of a few leaders who are insecurely seated on the safety valve of that mighty engine—progress. In our day, all churches except the hierarchical Presbyterian, Episcopal, and Roman Catholic have made women eligible as members of their councils, leaders in their Sunday school systems, in several cases have set them apart to the ministry, and in almost all have opened their pulpits to them, even the slow moving Presbyterian having done this quite generally in later years, and the Episcopal, in several instances, granting women "where to stand" in its chapels, outside the charmed arc of its chancel rail.

"Behold, I make all things new"; "the letter kills, the spirit gives life." These are his words who spoke not as man speaks. And how the letter kills today, let the sectarianism, the sacerdotalism, and the woman-silencing of the church bear witness. The time has come when those men in high places, dressed in a little brief authority "within the church of Christ, who seek to shut women out of the pastorate, cannot do so with impunity. Today they are taking on themselves a responsibility in the presence of which they ought to tremble. To an earnest, intelligent, and devout element among their brethren they seem to be absolutely frustrating the grace of God. They cannot fail to see how many ministers neither draw men to the gospel feast nor go out into the highways and hedges seeking them. They cannot fail to see that, although the novelty of women's speaking has worn off, the people rally to hear them as to hear no others, save the most celebrated men of the pulpit and platform. It is especially true that "the common people hear them gladly." The plea, urged by some theologians with all the cogency of physiological illustration, that woman is born to one vocation and one alone, is negated by her magnificent success as a teacher, a philanthropist, and a physician, by which means she takes the part of foster mother to myriads of children orphaned or worse than motherless. Their fear that incompetent women may become pastors and preachers should be put to flight by the survival of the church, in spite of centuries of the grossest incompetency in mind and profligacy in life, of men set apart by the laying on of hands. Their anxiety lest too many women should crowd in is met by the method of choosing a pastor, in which both clergy and people must unite to attest the fitness and acceptability of every candidate.

When will blind eyes be opened to see the immeasurable losses that the church sustains by not claiming for her altars these loyal, earnest daughters, who, rather than stand in an equivocal relation to her polity are going into other lines of work or taking their commission from the evangelistic department of the Woman's Christian Temperance Union? Or are they willing that woman should go to the lowly and forgotten but not to the affluent and powerful? Are they willing that women should baptize and administer the sacrament in the zenanas of India—that part of the house for the seclusion of women—but not at the elegant altars of Christendom? Are they aware that thousands of services are held each Sabbath by white-ribbon women to whom reformed men and their wives have said: "We will come if you will speak. We don't go to church because they have rented pews and because we cannot dress well enough; but we'll come to hear you?" Have they observed that WCTU halls, reading rooms, and tabernacles for the people are being daily multiplied in which the poor have the gospel preached to them? Do they know that the World's WCTU, with Margaret Bright Lucas, of England, at its head is steadily wending its way around the globe and helping women to their rightful recognition as participants in public worship and as heralds of the gospel?

To ministerial leaders who have been profoundly impressed by the difficulties of the question, "Shall women be ordained to preach?" another question is hereby propounded: "Shall women ordain themselves?" When Wesley urged the Bishop of London to send out a bishop to the Methodist societies in America, that functionary turned aside with disdain—the societies were so few and the country so far. Wesley, loyal churchman though he was, then yielded to demands he could no longer ignore and consecrated Thomas Coke a bishop, who in turn consecrated Francis Asbury, the first Methodist bishop in America. That decision of the intrepid founder of Methodism cost the Episcopal Church its future in the New World as time has proved. History repeats itself. We stand once more at the parting of the roads. Shall the bold, resolute men among our clergy win the day and give ordination to women, or shall women take this matter into their own hands? Fondly do women hope, and earnestly do they pray, that the churches they love may not drive them to this extremity. But if her conservative sons do not yield to the leadings of providence and the importunities of their more progressive brothers, they may be well assured that deliverance shall arise from another place, for the women of this age are surely coming to their kingdom, and humanity is to be comforted out of Zion as one whom his mother comforts.

The National Woman's Christian Temperance Union has a department of evangelistic work, of Bible Readings, of Gospel Work for railroad employees, for soldiers, sailors, and lumbermen; of prison, jail, and police station work, each of these departments being in charge of a woman called a national Superintendent who has an assistant in nearly every State and Territory, and she, in turn, in every local union. These make an aggregate of several thousands of women who are regularly studying and expounding God's Word to the multitude, to say nothing of the army in home and foreign missionary work and who are engaged in church evangelism. Nearly all of this "great host" who now "publish the glad tidings" are quite beyond the watchful care of the church, not because they wish to be so, but because she who has warmed them into life and nurtured them into activity is afraid for her own gentle, earnest-hearted daughters.

The spectacle is both anomalous and pitiful. It ought not to continue. Let the church call in these banished ones, correlate their sanctified activities with her own mighty work, giving them the same official recognition that it gives to men and they will gladly take their places under her supervision.

There is hardly an objector who does not say, "I would be willing to hear Mrs. or Miss Blank preach, but then they are exceptions; if we open the flood gates, we cannot tell what may happen." But have you ever opened the flood gates to men? And certainly your dread of the unseemly behavior of Christian women (the most modest and conservative of human beings!) will lead you to greatly increased caution when their cases are being passed upon. The dominant sex has proven itself able to keep women who are incapable out of the medical and the teachers' professions, and surely it will stand on guard with double diligence lest they invade the place where are declared the holy oracles. The whole difficulty is one of imagination and vanishes when individualized as it would necessarily be in practice by the separate scrutiny of Conference and Synod upon each separate case.

"Oh, it must come, and let it come, since come it must, but not in our day." Why not in yours my brother? The day ill which it comes will be the most glorious one since Christ started the church based on his resurrection by commissioning Mary to bear the gladdest tidings this dying world has ever heard: "Behold, he is risen!"

The time is hastening, the world grows smaller. We can compass it a thousand-fold more readily than could any previous generation. Within five years, so we are told by leading railroad authorities, we shall be able to go around the globe in forty days, and to go accompanied by all the security and comfort of our scientific and luxurious civilization. Women can do this just as readily as men. Then, let us send them forth fully prepared. Let us sound in their gentle ears the "Take authority" of the church's highest tribunal, that untrammeled and free they may lift up the standard of Christ's cross on every shore and fulfill that wonderful and blessed prophecy, "The Lord gives the word. The women that publish the tidings are a great host" (Psa 68:11).

But even my dear old mother church (the Methodist) did not call women to her altars. I was too timid to go without a call and so it came about that while my unconstrained preference would long ago have led me to the pastorate, I have failed of it, and am perhaps writing out all the more earnestly for this reason thoughts long familiar to my mind.

Let me as a loyal daughter of the church urge upon younger women who feel a call as I once did, to preach the unsearchable riches of Christ, their duty to seek admission to the doors that would hardly close against them now in any theological seminary save those of the Roman, Episcopal, and Presbyterian churches. And let me pleadingly beseech all Christian people who grieve over the world's great heartache to encourage every true and capable woman whose heart God has touched in her wistful purpose of entering upon that blessed gospel ministry, through which her strong yet gentle words and work may help to heal that heartache and to comfort the sinful and the sad, "as one whom his mother comforts."

DOCUMENT 44

"Women in the Ministry" (1898), 491, 494–96
Anna Howard Shaw

It is difficult to understand the attitude of a denomination which will re-fuse to ordain the inspired women whose evangelistic work has brought thousands into a religious life, and yet which gladly ordains every young stripling of a boy fresh from the theological seminary. Frances E. Willard always longed to be ordained and would have been one of the most brilliant and convincing preachers of all history. Although unmistakably destined by God as a great spiritual leader, she was never authorized by man to fulfill this mission and was not considered worthy even to sit in the high councils of the church she had chosen.

It is assumed that fewer men go to church where women are pastors, but from my own observation and from careful inquiry, I can assert that the reverse is true. This would be even more marked if the churches universally would open their pulpits to women so that neither the preacher nor the men attending her services would be conspicuous. Since the office of minister is no longer that of school master, and he is not so much a propounder of theological dogmas as a persuader of mankind toward a life of purity and righteousness, woman seems particularly adapted to the ministry. Her superior persuasive powers render her especially effective in leading men to higher thoughts and purer lives.

Men, wearied with the turmoil of life, harassed by the rush and clamor of the market place, attend religious services to be soothed and comforted, fed on holy thoughts, and encouraged by the inspiration of a diviner life. They seek to be shown that they are not mere human machines, but carry in themselves a spark of the divine which may be kindled into a sacred flame. Who so will as woman can bring rest to these tired hearts, peace to these sinful souls, and at the same time arouse the moral and spiritual nature to noble action? When the woman minister is untrammeled and allowed the fullest use of her highest powers she will be most successful in drawing men into the church. The few men present in the congregations of our large churches today where male preachers of unquestioned ability have offici-ated for years, demonstrate beyond question that women preachers could not make matters any worse in this direction. The logical mind is forced to conclude that a change of some kind is an imperative necessity.

The great proportion of church members at present are women and an important part of the minister's duty lies in pastoral calls, usually made at the homes. It will be admitted that women can enter more fully into sym-pathy with their own sex than can any man, no matter how tender-hearted. The relation of pastor to the life of children also makes this position pe-culiarly adapted to a woman, who intuitively comprehends the nature and needs of children more fully than is possible for a man. That it is natural for women to devote themselves to the spiritual teaching and training of children is proved by the fact that Sunday school work is almost entirely in their hands, and for generations they have rendered most valuable and wholly gratuitous services.

Many young women come to me for counsel in regard to entering the ministry as a life work, but I am unable to encourage them, because I know how unwelcome they will be to the orthodox churches—how difficult every step of the way will be made. Men find it hard to contend with "the world, the flesh, and the devil." And it is asking too much of women to add to these the church also. I think, however, it would be as undesirable to have only women ministers as it is now to have only men in that position. The church needs the two, and both can do better work together than either can do alone.

It is commonly observed that the parishes over which women preside are like a large family in their oneness of interests and the harmony of their meetings. It is said of one city where for many years a woman has been minister that the young men of her congregation can be distinguished anywhere on the street or in society by their beautiful deference to women. To listen to the teaching of one who leads a high spiritual life tends to inspire a respect and reverence for the teacher, and where men are accustomed to this week after week from a woman, it cannot fail to create in them a respect and reverence for all womankind.

I realize how impossible it is to predict with any degree of accuracy what will be the ultimate result of women's ministerial work. Their power in the pulpit and their especial fitness for the pastorate will be developed and shown in proportion as the church makes them free. So long as they are permitted to officiate only in small and poor parishes, so long as many denominations continue to oppose their preaching as contrary to the Scriptures and antagonistic to the best interests of the church, and so long as both internal and external influences combine to limit and dwarf to its greatest possible insignificance all that women do in this office, just so long will their real value as a pastor and preacher remain unknown. In exact proportion as the church limits the usefulness of its women along the lines of its own spiritual development and misdirects them into so-called "domestic duties," the spiritual advance of the kingdom of Christ will be hindered and delayed.

It will require many years of loyal and unflagging service in barren and untried fields before women will be able to prove to cold and skeptical denominations their capabilities for the ministry. Not only will they have to do the work fully as well as men, but they will be compelled to prove themselves superior before just recognition will be accorded them. They had to stand this crucial test in every other department of the world's work, and the church will prove no exception to the rule. The last of the learned professions to accord to women equal opportunities with men will be the ministry, and yet the church is founded upon the sublime declaration, "God is no respecter of persons," and "There is neither male nor female, for you are all one in Christ Jesus the Lord."

10

Late Nineteenth-Century Male Apologists

Introduction

In the late nineteenth century three men, in particular, sought common cause with women like Anna Oliver, Anna Howard Shaw, and Francis Willard in their efforts to promote the ministry of women. All three flourished in that unprecedented and precarious era for women in American Methodist history, 1880–1920—a phase characterized more than anything else by ambiguity with regard to women preachers.[1] All three men were held in extremely high esteem in their respective denominations. All three lived long and productive lives; all born in the 1830s and dying in the 1920s. It is somewhat difficult to identify a common theme in their apologetic writings, as each made a unique contribution to the evolving defense of women's ministry. Since Luther Townsend and William Warren represent the same northern Methodist tradition, and their writings have a closer affinity than with the work of W. B. Godbey, the three documents in this chapter will not be presented in chronological order. Godbey's defense—more conservative and rooted in the cultural context of the southern church—represents an approach at variance with the apologetic arguments of his northern counterparts.

William Baxter (W. B.) Godbey (1833–1920) was an influential albeit eccentric evangelist of the Wesleyan holiness movement in its formative

---

1. Troxell, "Ordination of Women," 123.

period.[2] A prolific author, he published over 230 books and pamphlets and wrote numerous articles for holiness periodicals. One of the most well-traveled Methodists of his era, he toured extensively across the continental United States and circled the globe five times. He promoted a premillennialist reading of the New Testament in various holiness communities across the South through lecture tours, preaching events, and pamphlet publication. While transdenominational in virtually every way, he chose to remain a lifelong member of the Methodist Episcopal Church, South. Given the inverse relationship between women's ministry and religious institutionalism, one of the most unique foundations of his defense of women was his principled rejection of respectability. In 1888 he published *Victory*, a pamphlet exploring the connection between Christ's second coming and the preaching ministry of women. Seizing upon Psalm 68:11, Godbey affirmed: "Glory to God for this prophetic vision of hosts and armies of women going forth preaching the gospel to all nations. The fulfillment of this vision is to bring the millennium."[3] In 1891 he published a booklet entitled *Woman Preacher* (Document 45), in which, in Letha Scanzoni and Susan Setta's words, "he urged women to 'get sanctified' and preach the gospel despite their churches' refusal to license them."[4]

Godbey's pamphlet echoed the style of his eccentric preaching. Essentially he preached women into the pulpit. His arguments broke no new ground, but reflected the primary themes of the holiness apologetic. First, he viewed the ministry of women as a prophetic calling. God intended to use all Jesus' faithful disciples in the great project of the redemption of the world, but specifically calls women as the instruments of salvation in the Pentecostal dispensation of the Holy Spirit. Second, his millennialism—including the understanding that God had delayed the return of Christ to provide more time for the response of faith—fueled his concern for more women to become active in this mission. Third, consistent with his rejection of respectability, he implored the women to forget about licensure and ordination. These issues—as important as they had become for some women and men—meant nothing to him because he coveted none of this for himself. Fourth, Godbey elevated the concept of women's spiritual superiority that was part and parcel of this age of "true womanhood." He encapsulated his argument for the ministry of women in this one simple statement: "We need millions of holy women right now to help us save the world." His defense

2. On the life and work of Godbey, see Hamilton, *Godbey*.

3. Godbey, *Victory*, 12.

4. Scanzoni and Setta, "Women in Evangelical, Holiness, and Pentecostal Traditions," 223.

included nothing approaching a robust defense of the equality of women; rather, it reinforced the concept of the female evangelist as an exceptional instrument of the Holy Spirit for "a time such as this."

When Frances Willard was preparing *Woman in the Pulpit* in 1888, she turned to one of her former seminary professors with the invitation for him to prepare a detailed and cogent rebuttal of a noteworthy diatribe against women's ministry. She intended to publish his response in her volume alongside multiple endorsements from other Methodist leaders. The inimical document had been written by well-known Princeton English professor and Presbyterian minister Henry Van Dyke, a formidable scholar whose arguments demanded a weighty response from a comparable Methodist women's advocate. Luther Tracy Townsend (1838–1922) fit the bill. A graduate of Dartmouth and Andover Theological Seminary—the oldest theological seminary in America—and a veteran of the Civil War, he was a Methodist theologian and biblical scholar with impeccable credentials and an agile mind equal to the challenge. Not only a respected faculty member of the Boston University School of Theology, he was also recognized throughout the Methodist Episcopal Church for his skill as a biblical expositor and preacher. More to the point, according to Carolyn Gifford, "he agreed with Willard that radical action was necessary in the face of men's refusal to grant women their rights."[5]

Willard published the full text of Henry Van Dyke's fourfold argument against the ministry of women immediately preceding Townsend's rejoinder (Document 46)—a response nearly three times the length of the so-called "Counter Argument" of the Presbyterian antagonist.[6] Townsend systematically dismantled the typical and worn arguments of his adversary: (1) Against the claim that women possessed no qualifications for ministry, he countered with a profound portrait of female aptitude, including women's sound thought and intuition, capacity for empathy, predisposition for pastoral care, and "mother nature." (2) He quickly dismissed arguments based on women's physical weakness and maternal diversion with a litany of evidence demonstrating the strength and fortitude of women. (3) Against the claim that women were not authorized to enter the Christian ministry, Townsend marshaled evidence from the New Testament noting how women were authorized, in fact, by Christ, by the apostles in Acts, by St. Paul, and by the prevailing custom of the early church. (4) He devoted nearly twenty pages to a detailed refutation of the view that the Bible expressly excludes and prohibits women from ministry. Addressing all the pertinent

5. Gifford, *Defense of Women's Rights*, 14.
6. Willard, *Woman in the Pulpit*, 113–28.

texts in the typical fashion of the female apologists, and alluding to the same scholars and sources, he argued that a common-sense reading of Scripture reveals a profound biblical egalitarianism. He concluded his response with a direct call for "irregular ordinations" of women if the church remained recalcitrant.

A close colleague and friend at Boston University School of Theology, William Fairfield Warren (1833–1929), was one of the most well-known Methodist leaders at the turn of the century. Having received his theological training at Andover Theological Seminary, like Townsend, but also at the Universities of Halle and Berlin in Germany, he entered the ministry of the Methodist Episcopal Church in 1855. During the Civil War he served as Professor of Systematic Theology in the Methodist Episcopal Missionary Institute at Bremen in Germany and thereafter had executive roles at Boston University as Acting President of the School of Theology (1866–73), President of the University (1873–1903), and Dean of the School of Theology (1903–11). When Boston University was chartered in 1869 he lobbied actively to make it the first university in the country to open its doors fully to women. As an active member of the New England Annual Conference, he was in the thick of the ordination controversy revolving around his alumnae Oliver and Shaw in the 1880s. They could not have hoped for an advocate with greater stature across the northern church and beyond.

In 1884 Warren presented a petition to the General Conference on behalf of Anna Oliver, who continued to plead her cause for ordination. This recommendation was once again "defeated in a committee chaired by James Monroe Buckley, outspoken opponent of women's rights in the MEC and editor of an influential denominational newspaper."[7] A decade later he published a volume in which he explored questions related to church law, including a section entitled "The Dual Human Unit" (Document 47). In this book he advanced a somewhat unique idea. He argued that God created males and females as partners whose primary purpose was to live as dual human units. He inferred that they would participate together in the full range of life, and that included Christian ministry. Gifford observes that "Warren did not draw the most radical conclusion possible from his thesis—that each church should have both a male and female pastor, suggesting instead that a male minister preside over the parish church and a female minister preside over the 'church in the home.'"[8] Despite this complementarian perspective, Warren introduced a new hermeneutical approach to Scripture, giving particular attention to God's intentions concerning the relationship between

7. Ibid., 15.
8. Ibid., 16.

men and women. His unique approach to this question stimulated a spirit of innovation among those who sought to promote social and ecclesial change, including the advancement of women's rights.

DOCUMENT 45

Woman Preacher (1891), 5–8, 9, 10–13
W. B. Godbey

This is what we mean when we say let the women preach. God wants to save, sanctify, fill with the Holy Ghost and arm with a tongue of fire every man, woman, and child, and send them out to conquer the world for his Son whom he promised long ages ago: "I will give you the heathen for your inheritance and the uttermost parts of the earth for your possession." The ends of the earth are upon us. The Lord delays his coming because of our tardiness. The world's redemption is overdue. Satan has had it far too long. It is high time for the apocalyptic angel to come down and chain him, cast him out, and lock him up in hell, and usher in the millennium.

Eighteen hundred and sixty-eight years ago our Lord positively commanded us: "Go into all the world and preach the gospel to every creature." It is a burning shame on the escutcheon of the church that there are more unevangelized heathens today than when the commission was given.

This technical, sermonic, steel-ribbed, ironbound, iceberg stuff you call preaching is the devil's counterfeit to freeze and ritualize the church to death and send the world to hell. No, I don't mean that the women are to do that. For I want all the men to quit it and the women never to begin. Now don't forget that what the Bible means and what we mean is simply to get emptied of sin and filled with the Spirit so you will run over the balance of your life with your Pentecostal tongue of fire loose at both ends, reading the Word, expounding it, exhorting, testifying, praying, and shouting as free for Jesus as a bird of paradise.

"Brother Godbey, I thought the preachers constituted an order distinct from and superior to the laity." If you mean the elders or bishops (which mean the same office), whom the church ordains to take the pastoral charge of the Lord's flock, and the deacons whom they ordain to attend to the temporal interest of the churches, we have no controversy. And I don't care a picayune whether you ordain a solitary woman or not. Perhaps we would better show our sisters courtesy by relieving them of pastoral charges and temporal burdens, unless it is in the foreign field where a lonely woman may be (as is now in some of Bishop Taylor's work) the only chance to look after, preach, baptize, and sacrament the people. In that case let her be ordained like Sister Phoebe of the church at Cenchrea.

"But what about the ministry as a separate and distinct order in all bygone ages?"

It was so under the law, but not under the gospel. In the former dispensation the people stood outside, the priests in the sanctuary, and the high priest in the *sanctum sanctorum*. When the plan of salvation was perfected by the crucifixion of Christ, God with His own hand tore down the veil and invited all his people right into the *sanctum sanctorum*. Thus the Aaronic priesthood was forever superseded by that of Melchizedek—"without father or mother," without special distinction, neither male nor female. So you see when the Holy Ghost dispensation came in, the priesthood was transferred to the membership of the gospel church in which we are all called to preach with diversities of gifts (1 Cor 12). Justification makes us priests and sanctification makes us high priests (1 Pet 2:5–9 and Rev 1:6).

God's word positively assures us that sanctification makes us not only priests but royal, that is, high priests unto God. This is the crowning glory of the gospel dispensation that we not only gain the spiritual eminence of the Aaronic priesthood, but are all invited to walk right in through the rent veil into the Holy of Holies and there abide amid the unutterable glories of the *shekinah*, feasting on the hidden manna in the golden pot while Aaron's rod—adorned with blooming flowers, growing and ripening fruits—is the constant memento of our wonderful growth in grace all the time. But does that include the women? It includes the entire membership of God's church. This fact, so well authenticated in the Word of God, sweeps from the field the last vestige of cavil as to the women preaching. Did not the high priest have a right to preach? Why, he was the tiptop of the ministry. So, woman, get sanctified, and you are not only a preacher but you stand at the very top of the ministry. Let devils howl and "dry bone" preachers croak, and still it is so. Now, women, what more do you want? They will not give me license. Go and preach along with the apostles, for not one of them ever got license. Jesus himself had none. The church he belonged to, instead of giving him license, put him to death. The servant is not above his Lord. You go and do likewise. What would you think of the high priest putting on a long face and holding back for license when his office put him amid the glories of an ever present Jehovah, a million miles above all license. Oh, woman, quit bothering your dead church about license. Go and preach like lightning till the stars fall.

"Brother Godbey, did the women preach side by side with the apostles?"

They certainly did. In Paul's letter to Romans we find seven women preachers in fifteen verses. Sister Phoebe a "deacon" of the church of Cenchrea (Rom 16:1–15). In Methodism, the deacons are all ordained preachers of the gospel. So you see I prove by Paul that she was a preacher and by the Methodist church that she was an ordained preacher. Then Priscilla, Mariam, Trypyhena, Tryphosa, Persis, the mother of Rufus, the sister of Nereus (Acts 16:13). During Paul's missionary tour in Europe he enjoyed his first opportunity to preach the gospel to our fathers and mothers in a woman's meeting. Neither was it fortified by Satan's false modesty against the women preaching, when all that keeps us out of heathen darkness today came in that way. It all started from a woman's meeting. No wonder Paul, writing back to them, remembers "Those women who assisted me in the gospel" (Phil 4:3). Did he mean that they cooked his dinner and washed his clothes? No. He meant just what he said, that "they assisted him in the gospel," i.e., helped him preach.

Acts 21:9 tells us about Paul in one of his missionary tours stopping with Philip, the evangelist, who had been sent out by the apostles to preach in that country. He had four daughters who prophesied. What do you think they did? Paul tells us, "They spoke to men edification, exhortation, and comfort" (1 Cor 14:3). Now don't you know that is precisely what the preacher does? If he does not do that, he would better quit, and if he does everything else, he would better quit. First Corinthians 11:5 reveals the women preaching right along there at Corinth. Paul puts it to record with full approval. Meanwhile, he advises them when they pray and preach to wear something on their heads because it was customary, and in so doing they would avoid unnecessary criticism. But he says in verse 13 that it was not a matter of authority, but a mere suggestion of his that the women put something on their head instead of preaching bare-headed like the men. When you remember that men and women in that country dressed alike, you will at once see the propriety of the woman wearing something on her head to designate her from a man. But the passage shows plainly that to see the women preaching was a matter of constant observation.

Remember that was none of your dead churches. They were not only converted and sanctified, but so endowed with the gifts of the Holy Ghost (1 Cor 12:8–11) that something had to be done to teach them quietude while the word was preached. It is no trouble to keep your graveyard churches quiet. Dead women don't talk. When they get flooded with the life of heaven, you don't have to beg them to talk.

Could you uncap hell, look down and see the multiplied millions of souls which have slidden into the pit, you would no longer need this little tract to stir you up to open your mouth for God. John Wesley knew nobody could get religion nor keep it without opening the mouth for God and keeping it open. Hence, he made the class meeting a most indefatigable mouth opener, the test of membership in the Methodist Church. The day Methodism gave up the class meeting as a test of membership, Satan wrote Ichabod on her escutcheon. That Hebrew word means, "The glory is departed."

Satan has no conscience. Give him an inch and he will take a mile. Suppose we should give up the right of the woman to preach (which I shall never do), the devil would shove right on and do what he has done all over this country—tell them they are not to pray or testify. Then they would all go to hell for the want of personal salvation.

The judgment day alone will reveal the responsibilities of the preachers in this matter. Thousands of preachers, by their false interpretation of this and other scriptures, have arbitrarily kept their women from getting and keeping religion enough to keep them out of hell.

In Galatians 3:28 Paul caps the climax and clinches the last nail: "In him there is neither male nor female." It needs no comment. We enter Christ in regeneration and are kept and established in him by sanctification. Farewell old controversy on the woman question. You have wrapped the church in sackcloth and given the devil the world the last fifteen hundred years. Here the *ipse dixit* of the Almighty by his servant Paul. This settles you forever. "In him there is neither male nor female." What does it mean? In the kingdom of grace and glory there is neither male nor female. Hence, we see beyond the possibility of cavil there is no such a thing as sexual distinction in the kingdom of grace and glory.

When we are born of the Spirit into the Kingdom of God, sexual distinction goes into eternal eclipse, forever perpetuated by sanctification and glorification. Hence, the matter is settled, Satan's trick exposed, and all controversy forever swept from the field. This enfranchisement of the sisterhood is the crowning glory of the present age. When the devil succeeded in sidetracking the church into antinomianism, i.e., sinning religion, about fifteen hundred years ago, he maneuvered to horn the sisters off the gospel platform. It is astonishing how long he has kept them horned off. Oh, how he roars when he sees them coming back. But sisters, just come along, don't be afraid of his roaring, for that is all Jesus will let him do. So if he roars from the iceberg pulpits of North Pole churches and from the tripods of anti-holiness papers, just let him roar. It will do you good. Jesus lets him roar to scare off the unworthy and inspire the elect.

When God made man he made him out of the dirt. When he made woman he made her out of man. So woman is a double refinement. She everywhere vindicates her superiority. A wise general always attacks the stronger citadel first. Man is physically stronger than woman. So is the lion stronger than man. But woman is morally stronger than man. Oh, what a victory Satan won when he so awfully paralyzed the larger, truer, and more efficient wing of the army.

Give the woman a chance—and they are taking it—and they will rob Satan of his whisky. Confront him on every ramification of the battle field, fill the saloons and brothels of Christendom, and the jungles of heathendom, with blood-washed and fire-baptized missionaries, march to the music of full salvation to the ends of the earth, belt the globe with the glory of God, and transform a world long groaning in sin and misery into a paradise.

The women are better by nature and by grace than the men. Hence, they are the more efficient wing of the army. They lingered last at the cross and hastened first to the sepulcher—first to greet the risen Savior and first to receive from his lips the commission of the full-orbed gospel to a despondent church and a lost world. She is first in every noble enterprise when the men will let her. Bishop Taylor, God's greatest living saint, says whereas he prefers a husband and wife, if he has to take a single person for a missionary station, give him a lonely woman rather than a single man. I doubt not but God has given him deeper insight into gospel work than any other man in the world. He gives his verdict in favor of woman. We need millions of holy women right now to help us save the world. Brethren, some of us are heartily ashamed we have done so little for the Master. I, for one, have settled the question; if I can do no more I will get out of the way of the women. Remember Aesop's Fable of the surly dog that would not eat the hay nor let the ox eat it. Oh, brethren, for the sake of the souls Jesus bought with this blood, let us get out of the way of the women.

Many of us have done more harm by discouraging the women than we have ever done good. Let us make a new departure and take a solemn vow to encourage all the men, women, and children as long as we live, to get all the religion they can and do all the good they can. Shame on you to put the brakes on the Lord's train instead of the devil's. Don't you know the New Jerusalem railway is all up grade and needs no brakes? So let us all turn firemen.

DOCUMENT 46

"Reply to Dr. Van Dyke's Counter Argument" (1889)
Luther T. Townsend
Source: Willard, *Woman in the Pulpit*, 129–34, 145–46, 152–53, 168–72

No questions are of such weight and solemnity as those of right and wrong. The question, therefore, of what is right or wrong for women to do, especially when considered upon ethical rather than prudential grounds, is of such grave importance that it is not by men to be trifled with. We may add that if it is morally wrong for a woman to do certain things, she assumes responsibilities when attempting to do them that are in many ways perilous, and she would be earnestly warned and entreated not to persist in her wrong doing.

But, on the other hand, if it is right for a woman to do certain things, it is no unimportant affair for one to throw obstacles in her pathway. Men especially better not assume too great a responsibility, indeed no responsibility at all, unless there are reasons that are well-nigh unquestioned. This responsibility, however, our esteemed friend, the author of the "Counter Argument," unhesitatingly has taken upon himself. That Miss Willard is all wrong and that he is all right to him seems clear as sunlight.

While the rhetoric of the "Counter Argument" may well receive commendation, and while the reasoning on account of its intended fairness is entitled to a candid reply, and while our worthy doctor has given us a defense of the so-called "ecclesiastical polity of all the Christian ages" as good perhaps as can at present be given, still the feeling of every reader, upon a few moments' reflection, must be that the writer of the "Counter Argument" is very far from being sufficiently impressed with the gravity of the subject discussed. Indeed, there is apparent throughout a sort of heedlessness or recklessness ill becoming the treatment of such a subject.

The "Counter Argument" is open to criticism in other respects. Those who carefully weigh the entire discussion will not fail of the conviction that Miss Willard's positions, in more than one instance, have not been fairly represented, that her words have been strained to mean what manifestly was never intended, and certainly the friends of Miss Willard will lay down the book with the feeling that the good doctor, through having the advantage of being the attacking party, has been by this earnest woman at every point out reasoned.

The four general divisions of the "Counter Argument" are:

1. *Women have no special qualifications for the work of the ministry.*

2. *Women have special disqualifications for the ministry.*

3. *Women are not authorized to enter the Christian ministry.*

4. *The word of God expressly excludes and prohibits women from the work of the ministry.*

These divisions are progressive and give to the argument an outward form of completeness. But the first and third divisions, as will be seen, being merely negative, are not entitled to any considerable weight. And it may be said that when in an argument two out of four of its main propositions on one side are stated negatively, that side betrays poverty of resources.

The "Counter Argument," as anyone can readily see, when critically analyzed and when positively and briefly stated, amounts merely to this: All women are constitutionally and scripturally disqualified from exercising the functions of the Christian ministry.

Is this proposition true? Is this the only question, so far as the "Counter Argument" is concerned, that needs to be examined and answered? Still, perhaps, the importance of the subject and a certain courtesy due disputants from each other, are such as hardly will allow the ignoring of either of the four propositions before us. Therefore we take them up one by one.

First. "Women have no special qualifications for the ministry." We hope the reader will weigh carefully what the doctor says under this proposition. There are nearly two pages of reading matter. But arguments and facts there are none. We find not one valid reason supporting this leading proposition. Our reply to it is, therefore, a flat denial of its correctness. And we offset our esteemed doctor's personal assertion by a personal assertion to match it, which is this: Women *have* special qualifications for the ministry.

If we should say no more upon this point, we should have done everything that the "Counter Argument" logically calls for. But we should be exposed to the very criticism we have made, of course, that of leaving a proposition unsupported by either argument or fact.

That women have special qualifications for the ministry is proved upon the ground of their peculiar endowments and of the work which they have already accomplished. The evidence of the special qualifications of women for the ministry, derived from their actual success in the work, will appear further on in the discussion.

Confining attention for a moment to their peculiar endowments, the claim we make is that, as a matter of fact, women have reason and profound thought, and they have more accurate and quicker intuitions than those of men. Women have voice, earnestness, and oratory, and they have emotions and eloquence (persuasive) at least equal to those of men. They have quicker and tenderer sympathies than those of men. Women have the gifts of the Spirit, a high moral and religious sense, and their mother nature gives them peculiar advantage in winning souls to Christ and in building up Christian character. In pastoral work they can enter many homes from which men are debarred and can enter sick chambers to administer religious consolation at times when no man save the physician and the husband can be present. And by whom can the doctrines of the Incarnation and the vicarious Atonement be so profoundly comprehended and so convincingly set forth as by those whose "lips have blanched with agony" while learning from experience the meaning of those fundamental doctrines of our faith? No wonder that Hawthorne exclaims: "Oh, in the better order of things, heaven grant that the ministry of souls may be left in charge of women!"

The second proposition of the "Counter Argument" is this: "Women have special disqualifications for the ministry."

The ground upon which this assertion is made to rest is threefold: (1) the mental make-up of women, (2) their mental methods, and (3) their physical constitution, connected with the fact that they can be mothers.

It appears, therefore, that the general proposition of the "Counter Argument," that women are specially disqualified for the ministry, is false in every particular. It is false in the light of woman's physical endurance, and it is false in the light of woman's maternity.

The third main proposition of the "Counter Argument" is this: "Women are not authorized to enter ministry."

Carefully analyzing the reasoning employed by Dr. Van Dyke, we discover that he offers the following proof in support of the foregoing proposition: (1) Christ did not choose women to be his apostles. (2) The Acts of the Apostles record no ordination of women. (3) The Pastoral Epistles were not addressed to women.

One cannot help feelings of surprise that a thoroughly educated clergyman should present arguments from the silence of the Scriptures. Certainly the writer of the "Counter Argument" must know that the method of reasoning he has employed, designated among logicians as *argumentum e silentio*, is not only unsatisfactory but is also exceedingly perilous. It is a sword with an edge on the back, whose edge sometimes runs round the entire handle. It is almost sure in some way to cut the man, however skillful, who uses it. We may illustrate. Christ chose none except Jews, and Jews of his own country, to be his disciples; therefore no African, Asiatic, European, or American should presume to take upon himself the sacred office of a Christian apostle. Jews may, but Gentiles cannot.

The statement of our worthy friend is this: Women are not authorized to enter the ministry. We deny out and out this assertion, and offset it with the counter assertion that women *are* authorized to enter the ministry.

They have gospel authority. Though Christ did not call women to stand among his original twelve traveling companions (he had respect to the existing customs of society and may thereby have escaped scandal), still in the presence of the multitude he drew from Martha the same testimony he required of the twelve. He declared his commission to the woman at the well of Samaria, with an emphasis and a particularity hardly equaled in any of his public addresses, and that woman became the first preacher of Christ outside the Jewish commonwealth. These were women whom angels from heaven and Christ himself first commissioned to preach the Lord's resurrection from the dead.

Women stood in his congregation and received the same solemn and sublime benediction as that conferred upon the other disciples and were authorized to be henceforth his witnesses.

While the Acts of the Apostles does not state in explicit terms that women were ordained by the laying on of hands, yet it is stated in the Acts of the Apostles that women received the same of gifts of the Spirit as were given to men and that they were as much authorized as were the men to preach the universal gospel of peace.

And while it is true that the Pastoral Epistles were not in form addressed to women, yet it is undeniably true that Paul, the author of these Epistles, expected women to preach, sent women out to preach, gave women directions how to preach, commended those who did preach, and gave the names of no fewer than twelve women whom he recognized as ordained ministers of the gospel of Christ, designating them by the same word, deacon, that was applied even to Paul and Apollos, and employing the same word, prophesy, in describing what women deacons were to do as was used in describing the preaching of the apostles.

Such is the evidence for the statement that women are authorized to enter the ministry. They are authorized by our Lord in the Gospels. They are authorized by the apostles in the Acts. They are authorized by Paul in his Epistles. They are authorized by the prevailing custom of the church throughout its early history. If in all this there is not authority, we would like to be informed as to the kind and amount of authority that would be satisfactory to those who, on these grounds, are fighting the admission of women to the Christian ministry.

The fourth proposition of the "Counter Argument" reads thus: "The Word of God expressly excludes and prohibits women from the work of the ministry." We insist that the fourth proposition of the "Counter Argument," in its general scope and in all its particulars, is incorrect, being antagonistic to the common sense of the world and to the entire spirit of the gospel of our blessed Lord and Master.

The Christian church will not continue to hold even to the end of the centuries the views of this subject that have been held. The old regimen is not to last. It ought not to last. It is contrary to the Bible and common sense and, therefore, cannot last. It is not lasting. Women are to be ordained and are being ordained. There is a louder call today for ordained women than ever before. In some heathen lands Christian converts cannot receive the ordinances of the church except at the hands of ordained women. This is what Dr. Thoburn says of India, and what Dr. Baldwin says of China. Bishop Taylor has been forced, by his boundless field and his scanty number of workers, to admit women, without ordination, to his mission conferences, and appoint them to charges in Africa.

If the only way in which those women in the zenanas who have been led to Christ by women can receive the ordinances of the church is to receive them at the hands of ordained women, then there is but one manly and Christian thing for the men who are in charge of those fields to do, provided the churches at home refuse to act, and that one thing is for them to pray and to place consecrated hands upon those women missionaries, and say to them, not by authority given by the Methodist Episcopal Church or the Presbyterian Church, but by authority given by the great head of the church, "Take authority to execute the office of a deacon in the Church of God, in the name of the Father, and of the Son, and of the Holy Ghost," and "Take authority to read the Holy Scriptures in the Church of God and to preach the same." After doing this, then let those godly missionaries report their grave misdemeanor to the ensuing General Conference.

And what is to be said as to the Christian women of America? In some instances they have remarkable spiritual and intellectual gifts. In other respects, too, they have exceptional qualifications to meet all the conditions required of men who enter the ministry. They have "gifts, labors, and usefulness." When, therefore, such women hear the command of God bidding them speak and preach, what are they to do? What right have they to be "disobedient to the heavenly vision"? Or what right have they to hide their candle under the bushel? These noble women should knock only once more at the doors of the Methodist General Conference, and if their signals and entreaties are again uncivilly disregarded, they should never knock again. They should call together some of the noblest Christian women of the land

and, in solemn convocation, by the laying on of hands and by prayer they should set apart for pulpit and parish work those who trust that they "are inwardly moved by the Holy Ghost to take upon themselves the office of the ministry in the church of Christ, to serve God for the promoting of his glory and the edifying of his people."

When that step is taken, if those women are willing to extend an invitation, they will be surprised at the number of clergymen who, with a noble Wesleyan spirit, will hasten to render assistance at the ordination.

DOCUMENT 47

"The Dual Human Unit" (1894)
William Fairfield Warren
Source: Warren, Constitutional Law Questions, 191–94, 198, 200–201, 205–18

My first proposition I take directly from Holy Scripture, for I desire to consider this theme primarily in the light of God's Word. It is that deep, wonderful, and wonderfully neglected declaration of St. Paul: "Neither is the woman without the man, nor the man without the woman, in the Lord. For as the woman is of the man, so is the man also by the woman; but all things are of God." What does this mean? I understand it to mean:

1. That all souls are "of God," and all Christian souls "in the Lord" Christ.

2. That, in God's sight, no woman ever existed out of vital relation to man and to God.

3. That, in God's sight, no man ever existed out of vital relation to man and to God.

4. That whether considered in relation to creation—that is, as being "of God"—or in relation to redemption—that is, as being "in the Lord"—the relation of man to woman is not identical with that of woman to male and vice versa.

5. That nothing short of one man and one woman, both considered as "of God," and as "in the Lord," can constitute, in the full Christian sense, the human unit; that is, the unit in whose one common unfolding experience is found the total of the experiences of the fullest and most normal human life.

6. That the total experience of a man in isolation from woman, or of a woman in isolation from man, is fractional, not even hemispherical, since the two, if added together at their close, do not give as a result the perfect globe—the all-inclusive total of the experiences of the fullest and most normal human life.

7. That the real globe, the perfect and all-inclusive normal human experience is unattainable, even so in the Lord, unless the two halves of the human unit live their one life in the vital oneness of an entire and reciprocal communion with each other and with that Lord in whom they live and move and have their common being.

Let us look at another declaration of Holy Scripture. It is the familiar one: "Adam was first formed, then Eve. And Adam was not beguiled, but the woman being beguiled has fallen into transgression." This has so often been used by brutal men as a club wherewith to beat godly women down into a totally unjust subjection to their husbands and spiritual rulers, that we all instinctively hate to hear it quoted and never think of looking into it in search of pregnant and soul-clarifying instruction. But let us think a little about it, taking with us this Scripture idea of the dual human unit.

But what, now, is the practical significance of these scientific and scriptural ideas? The true implication and moral of the whole is this, that in their divinely settled order, both constituents of the human unit may go—yes ought to go—wherever the human unit belongs. Both may participate—yes ought to participate—in all that is an expression of the normal life of humanity. In no department of human life is it good for man to be alone; in none is it good for woman.

I know not how better to state it than by saying: *In the sphere of equals the initiation of all cooperations of the dual human unit must be with the man, or with men; the consummation with the woman, or with women.* But someone will say: Does not your law, which in the sphere of equals always and everywhere gives to man the initiative, unduly honor the man and subordinate the woman? By no manner of means. If there is any difference it is in favor of the woman. It puts her exactly in the place in which the proverb places God. The proverb says: "Man proposes, but God disposes." That is it, exactly. Every time, in the individual sphere, in the social sphere, everywhere that equal men and women co-operate, the decision, the consummation of things falls to her. Hers is the lap into which the lot falls and, humanly speaking, the "whole disposing thereof" is of her and by her.

The Scripture doctrine of the dual human unit goes far toward making this whole question [the ministry of women] clear as sunlight. The ideal Christian minister is not a man or a woman, but a man and a woman. Hence Paul, describing by inspiration the necessary qualifications of the primitive presbyter-bishop, invariably places in the forefront that he should be the husband of one wife" (1 Tim 3:2; Titus 1:6). If any of my readers for a moment fails to see the divine reason for this arrangement—which seems to have been equally beautiful in the days of Zacharias and his Aaronic wife, Elizabeth—he will see it the moment I remind him that in every charge in Methodism there are, or should be, two churches to be provided with the ministrations of the Word and with ministers called of God to minister. The one is the church within the parsonage and the other is the church outside. Each needs at its head a man and a woman called of God to be ministers of Christ. In the parsonage church, built upon the New Testament model of the "church in the house," the chief burden, both of the teaching of the Word and also of the pastoral care, falls upon the woman, but the man can by no means be excused. In the parish church, on the other hand, the chief burden of the teaching of the Word, and also of the pastoral care, falls upon the man, but the woman can by no means be excused. In many a mission field one will find the church inside the parsonage far more truly an ideal Christian church than the one outside. Sometimes, indeed, through long years of patient sowing, it is the only church belonging to the charge. In it are preached all the sermons; in it alone are maintained all the stated ordinances. In such cases how beautiful is that undivided ministry maintained by the household's undivided head!

But is there no other way in which a woman may enter the holy ministry? If even the sparrow has found a house and the swallow a nest at God's altars, may not that Christian virgin or that Christian widow whose soul longs, yes even faints, for the courts of the Lord?

I dare not say No, and our church dares not say No. No one can read Paragraph 201 of our *Book of Discipline* and not admit that our deaconesses are as truly an order or class of Christian ministers as are our missionaries, *and more truly than our local preachers.* And any woman fully possessed of the natural and spiritual gifts and of the special training required of a deaconess is so superior to those *to whom she is set to minister* that even, if there be men among them, the law assigning among equal men and women the leadership to men does not apply; hence, with perfect scriptural and rational propriety she can go forward with her ministry.

A similar result is sometimes reached in another way if, indeed, it be another. I refer to the case where a holy woman by virtue of her singleness of eye and eminence of piety and perfection of judgment in some specialty unconsciously acquires such an ascendency over her associates that even the most eminent of men in the ministry sit gladly and profitably at her feet. Such a woman exercised an almost lifelong ministry in New York only a few years ago. In her congregation, in her well-known parlors, were often to be found, not only eloquent brethren in the ministry, but even learned theologians and bishops in the church of God. Here, also, the law of equals no longer held.

This form of a woman's ministry sometimes appears in unanticipated places. I have space for but a single example. A few years ago there was a clergy house in the heart of Boston. In it resided a hundred ministers, some elders, some deacons, some local preachers, all of them men. The only person in authority in the building was a woman of immense brain and heart and of a presence that worthily enshrined them. She had also great power with God, and consequently, although the most unassuming and modest of women, she had great power with men. It was a power that seemed to go out from her without the slightest consciousness on her part. Of course, there were other more strictly and formally ecclesiastical authorities to whom these men were accountable, but as none of these lived within miles of the clergy house in question. This godly woman was, to all intents and purposes, their resident bishop. Week by week applications from the adjoining cities and towns would come in for preachers, and week by week, with no advice or direction from men, she, in practical effect, stationed her not otherwise appointed preachers, according to demand through all eastern Massachusetts and parts of adjacent States. Week by week, year after year, these men looked to her for their appointments with the most absolute confidence that the allotment would be discriminating and in perfect accord with the will of God. All this time the name of this local bishop or presiding elder stood in the Minutes of no Conference, and she coveted not to see it even among those of the officers of that school of theology. All the same, she was the revered episcopal head and the chief confidential spiritual adviser in a diocese manned by one hundred ministers. If this bride of Christ was not in the ministry, I have never seen a human being who was. God bless her! The fragrance and power and beauty of her life are with us forever.

Not widely different from cases of this sort is another which cannot be passed unnoticed. It has many illustrations on a small scale, some on a scale of national and even cosmopolitan significance. It occurs when social aggregates more or less extensive have fallen into a state of moral decadence and, as a consequence, have gone into captivity to some sort of evil force or forces which mean death unless a speedy and mighty deliverance can be wrought as by a miracle. In such a social or national emergency the keen sensitiveness of woman, both to the evil suffered and to the moral enormities that have entailed it, qualify her in an eminent degree to become the minister extraordinary through whom God can send deliverance. And when a nation has reached the point where nothing short of the cry of a woman's heartbreak can rouse it, and nothing short of a woman's almost maniac clutch on God can steady it, then from out her closet of spiritual agony comes forth the Deborah, the Joan of Arc, the divinely commissioned woman that is to rouse up and rebuke, to arraign and judge, to instruct and reform her degenerate people. The consciousness of her heavenly calling, added to that greatness of soul and fierceness of conscience that fitted her for so vast a work, lifts her far above all ordinary and commonplace motives, and makes her utterances like words hot from the lips of God. How she towers above the besotted nobilities and aristocracies and hierarchies of her land-judging judges, commanding commanders, counseling counselors, ushering in a new and diviner day! That such a woman is not licensed of man is small marvel. For any microscopic Sanhedrin, or Synod, or Quarterly Conference to attempt to license such a prophetess of the new dispensation would be as great an impertinence as for the aldermen of Cambridge gravely to license Longfellow to sing the songs that are in him. The credentials of her office were formulated in heaven's chancery and they bear the sign of the Almighty.

Such, O gracious sisterhood, are some of the forms and fields of the Christian ministry to which Christ and the church invite you. Have you always, all of you, appreciated all of them aright? Have you coveted, for Christ's sake, to be a high priestess at the holy altar of one of his every day churches, that there you might offer a daily and hourly service, redemptive to men and well pleasing to God? Have you, in genuine sympathy with Christ, had agony of spirit to the end that you might bring your many sons unto glory? Have all of those among you whom God has permitted to dwell in his courts been fully and conspicuously worthy? Has it never been partly the fault of some of these parsonage sisters that the New Testament idea, the Aquila and Priscilla idea of the Christian pastorate, as the office of a dual unit, has so seldom been realized? Have all our Christian virgins and all our Christian widows, so far as permitted, longed and fainted for the courts of their God? Are they now, so far as their obstructive brothers permit, crowding into that already authorized diaconate ministry, whose duties are "to minister to the poor, visit the sick, pray with the dying, care for the orphan, seek the wandering, comfort the sorrowing, save the sinning, and, relinquishing wholly all other pursuits, to devote themselves in a general way to such forms of Christian labor as may be suited to their abilities?"

At this point it may be useful to inquire whether the scriptural and scientific doctrine of the dual human unit and of the fundamental law of all social co-operations of men and women as set forth in the opening paragraphs of this paper, do not furnish a foundation upon which all sensible persons that have advocated or that have opposed the eligibility of women to the General Conference can meet and stand together. My own belief is that it does.

Let us look at the fundamental principles of the advocate of woman's eligibility. They are as follows:

Before the law of the church, all full members, as such, should be equal.

In order to the highest and best growth of the church, there is needed in every department of its life the just co-operation of men and women.

Accordingly, to refuse to Christian women a joint participation with men in any department of the life of the church is at once a detriment to the total body and a wrong to them.

Consider right here again the helpful Scripture doctrine—scientific as well—of the dual human unit. Like the ideal Christian minister, the ideal church legislator is not a man nor yet a woman, but a man and a woman. These pastoral pairs are so perfectly one in aim and sympathy and action that, as Paul says, the woman is never without the man, nor the man without the woman in the Lord, so it would be well if in every department of our church government, and in every department of our State government, the lawmaker, the judge, the executor of law, were never an isolated, single man, never an isolated, single woman, but always a human unit, including in one personal manifestation the combined wisdom and sympathy and experience and will of a mutually complementary man and woman. Could this ideal be actualized, it would little matter which of the two voices uttered the one thought or which of the four hands registered the one will.

11

Two Distinctive Early Twentieth-Century Women

Introduction

In the years immediately following the First World War, two Methodist women contributed with unequaled force to the discourse surrounding women and the biblical foundations of their ministry. Katharine Bushnell developed a new perspective on women's ministry that was driven by a singular question: Did St. Paul really forbid women preaching? Lee Anna Star, similarly, devoted her considerable abilities to an examination of the biblical status of women in home and church. Both believed fervently that the church inhibited the ministry of women and society oppressed women on the basis of mistranslated, misinterpreted, and misapplied scriptural texts. Unlike previous apologists and biblical exegetes, these two women brought an innovative spirit to the discussion and an eagerness to chart new directions in the conversation. Whereas earlier defenses, all the way back to the eighteenth century, tended to emphasize a "common-sense" approach to controversial biblical texts—offering contextualized readings of the Pauline prohibitions, for instance, and heralding the presence and accomplishments of biblical women—Bushnell and Starr's apologetic charted new territory with regard to the equality and responsibility of women. They realized that the liberation of women would entail a full revision of biblical interpretation, beginning with Genesis. As Kristin Du Mez observes, "Through their retranslation and reinterpretation of the first chapters of Genesis, these two American Protestant women sought to provide a basis for a profound

re-visioning of Christian theology and thereby challenge the Victorian social order in which they lived."[1]

Katharine C. Bushnell (1855–1946), a multitalented missionary, doctor, feminist, Bible translator, and social reformer, dedicated all her energies
and experiences in these multiple fields to the defense of women as men's
equals in God's eyes.[2] Dana Hardwick, in an article on the biblical mission
of Bushnell, notes the crusader "was convinced that sex-biased translations
were at the root of the subordination and oppression of women."[3] Bushnell
studied classics and medicine at Northwestern University, which prepared
her to serve for three years as a medical missionary for the Methodist Episcopal Church in China. Upon her return to the United States, she engaged
in reform work alongside Frances Willard. Her investigation of the white
slave trade in the upper Midwest led to legislation that protected the lives of
women. Her work as a missionary among women, in particular, convinced
her that prejudice against women emanated from mistranslations of Scripture. After twenty years of fighting injustice against women, she concluded
that women would continue to be marginalized and abused around the
world unless Christians believed God valued women just as much as men.
Her singular task was "to devise an interpretation that would free women to
seek their proper 'place in the divine economy.'"[4]

A brilliant linguist, fluent in multiple languages, Bushnell mastered
Greek and Hebrew in order to undertake a painstaking study of the Bible
and its teaching on women. As early as 1908 she began to circulate her initial findings about aberrant biblical interpretation based on male bias as a
"mimeographed correspondence course for women."[5] In 1916 she privately
published *God's Word to Women* (Document 48)—all her materials on
this subject that were originally in loose single sheets and bound into two
volumes.[6] Janette Hassey notes the features unique to Bushnell's apologetic
methodology:

> Three characteristics of *God's Word to Women* immediately dis-
> tinguish it from the previous writings. First, Bushnell extensively

1. Du Mez, "Leaving Eden," 144.

2. On the life and work of Bushnell, see Du Mez, *New Gospel for Women*, and Hardwick, *Oh Thou Woman*.

3. Hardwick, "Man's Prattle, Woman's Word," 165.

4. Ibid., 175.

5. Scanzoni and Setta, "Women in Evangelical, Holiness, and Pentecostal Traditions," 252.

6. Du Mez, *New Gospel for Women*, 100–101. It is very difficult to determine
the initial publication date of this work since it was privately printed and constantly
revised. Du Mez considers 1916 the earliest possible date.

examined women's role in marriage as well as in church ministry. Second, she exegeted Old Testament passages in depth, devoting the first twenty lessons to explore Genesis 1–3. Third, Bushnell utilized Hebrew and Greek in such a way that her book became more than a popular exposition easily understood by church laity.[7]

This book—described by Mimi Haddad as "the most extensive biblical treatment of gender ever published"—was popularized by Jessie Penn-Lewis, a British evangelical and Keswick holiness activist.[8] In the same year that Bushnell published her volume in America, Penn-Lewis published *The Magna Carta of Woman* in England with her permission, an orderly and simplified distillation of Bushnell's massive and somewhat disorganized work, also drawing upon the apologetic writings of Catherine Booth.[9]

Lee Anna Starr (1853–1937), a local pastor and temperance leader, shared Bushnell's passion for a more comprehensive vision of the status of women in both the church and the world. Like her contemporary, she also shared a love of biblical languages and the use of these tools to better understand God's Word.[10] An early pioneer of the Woman's Christian Temperance Union, she spent time in prison for her participation in the Woman's Crusade of 1873–74, a direct action against saloon and liquor traffic. The first female graduate in 1893 of what would become Pittsburgh Theological Seminary, she was ordained in the Methodist Protestant Church, serving pastorates in Adrian, Michigan, and Chicago. In consequence of opposition she experienced in ministry, in 1900 she published a small pamphlet, *The Ministry of Women*, developing a biblical defense for woman's right to preach. Her passion was to rediscover a systematic and comprehensive narrative demonstrating biblical equality. As a Methodist located between the poles of Protestant liberalism and conservatism, as Du Mez has demonstrated, she espoused the authority of the Bible and the literal truth of the Scriptures, but sought to peel away centuries of male bias and uncover what Scripture truly revealed on the issues of gender, sexuality, and morality.[11] All these concerns coalesced in *The Bible Status of Woman* (Document 49), which she published in 1926. "Starr's work," claims Catherine Kroeger,

7. Hassey, *No Time for Silence*, 112.

8. Haddad, "Irrepressible Legacy," 10.

9. Baker-Johnson, "Life and Influence of Jessie Penn-Lewis," 26.

10. On Starr's life and work, see Du Mez, "Forgotten Woman's Bible."

11. See Du Mez, "Forgotten Woman's Bible."

"better organized and expressed than that of Bushnell, influenced a new generation of women, including feminist preacher Alma White."[12]

The principal insights of Bushnell and Starr shaped the discourse on women's rights and biblical equality throughout the course of the twentieth century. While both held to an extremely high view of Scripture—inspired, infallible, inviolable—and employed conservative interpretive methods, they were able to construct what Du Mez describes as "extensive proto-feminist revisions."[13] One of their most significant contributions was their detailed examination of the entirety of the biblical witness and their interpretation of particular texts within the context of a completely new biblical narrative concerning women. Their revision of the biblical narrative, based upon solid exegesis, and their challenge to a Victorian view of female virtue and women's sphere, based on trenchant analyses of the social subjugation of women, framed their apologetic for women's ministry. Three particular elements of their biblical vision influenced the defense of this sacred calling.

First, "The traditional interpretation of the Genesis narrative depicted an inferior Eve seducing Adam into tasting the forbidden fruit, leading to humanity's fall into sin and their expulsion from the garden," writes Du Mez. "But Bushnell and Starr offered a dramatically different account."[14] Their argument contesting male supremacy consisted in several unique and logical steps. They asserted the original equality of man and woman at creation. The "order of creation," they reasoned, appeared to be ascending rather than descending. Making her point through sardonic humor, Bushnell argued that since monkeys were created before human beings, men must be subordinated to monkeys. Along similar lines, both argued that the creation of Eve from Adam's rib might suggest her superiority rather than inferiority. Du Mez notes:

> To understand how the "very good" state of humanity became "not good," Bushnell suggested that the Hebrew expression traditionally translated as "alone" could also mean "in-his-separation." Adam, then, may have become separated from God, falling slightly from his original perfection even before the Serpent's tempting. In order to redeem the stumbling Adam, she explained, God created a helpmeet for him, taking Eve out of Adam.[15]

---

12. Kroeger, "Legacy of Bushnell," 3.

13. Du Mez, "Leaving Eden," 145.

14. Ibid., 149.

15. Ibid.

Both scholars pointed out that a traditional understanding of "help-meet" as an inferior assistant or mere afterthought could not be defended on the grounds of Hebrew etymology.[16] Other similar exegetical insights related to the creation narrative confirmed their vision of the biblical equality of men and women.

Secondly, not only were men and women equal at creation, according to Bushnell and Starr, the fall did not further impugn women and bring upon them a curse from God as had been argued traditionally. "By reassessing Eve's sin and the subsequent curse," Du Mez maintains, "they established the foundations for a profoundly different biblical narrative and a new vision for the social order."[17] Genesis 3:16, in their view, was the crux of women's subordination as understood through its conventional translation. Their tight argument, based on a meticulous analysis of the original language, cannot be summarized here; their conclusions turned the traditional exegesis on its head. They dismantled this keystone of the arch of doctrine subordinating women to men. They concluded that "male authority over women was nothing other than the fruit of man's original sin. And man's injunctions for women to be silent, submissive, and 'womanly' contradicted God's will and reflected man's original rebellion against God."[18]

Thirdly, the approach of Bushnell to the purportedly prohibitive statement of St. Paul in 1 Corinthians 14, in particular, illustrates her unique approach to arguments for women's ministry. She summarized previous attempts of exegetes to harmonize the apparent contradiction between 1 Corinthians 11 and 14—Paul's admonition for women to cover their heads when prophesying and his command to silence women. She discerned at least four different arguments that sought to reconcile this tension: (1) Paul's command to silence women was limited and contextual;(2) Paul changed his mind; (3) Paul prohibited blabbering, not prophesying or preaching; and (4) Paul discountenanced the interruptive questioning of women. Bushnell did not believe any of these explanations were satisfactory. Hassey provides a concise description of her alternative reading: "Translating the passage with different punctuation, Bushnell rejected each of these hypotheses, concluding that Paul in 1 Corinthians 14:34–35 gave not his own view, but quoted the false Judaizer position. Priscilla's arrival at Corinth provided the Judaizers with an occasion to attack women's public prophecy, which Jewish oral law prohibited."[19] In contrast to Bushnell, Starr understood 1 Corinthians 14 as St. Paul's own view and affirmed a more conventional

16. Ibid., 150.

17. Ibid., 152.

18. Ibid., 157.

19. Hassey, *No Time for Silence*, 113.

contextual reading of the text as the apostle's effort to settle disturbances in church worship. But despite their different approach to this text, they reflected the same concern. As Hassey concludes, "dismayed that 'modern' women might reject Christianity as a whole because of supposed biblical teachings on women's subordination, Bushnell and Starr sought to correct that misunderstanding in an intellectually viable way."[20]

The biblical foundation upon which Bushnell and Starr built their arguments affected their vision of society profoundly. In particular, it challenged the efforts to domesticate women that had characterized the latter half of the nineteenth century. "Their biblical revisions," claims Du Mez, "directly challenged key components of the Victorian social order. According to Victorian ideals, 'true women' exhibited purity, passivity, and an innate religiosity. A woman's special virtue, combined with her delicate weakness, equipped her for her role as wife and mother, placing her at the center of the Victorian family—which, in turn, served as the basis for Victorian society."[21] Bushnell and Starr unmasked the unbiblical platform upon which this vision was founded. They exposed the sex bias in multiple translations in the New Testament that supported the Victorian illusion. According to Du Mez, the most significant biblical text to which Bushnell turned to challenge the regnant conception of women was the story of the woman caught in adultery in John 8. This story, on the basis of their exposition, "not only dismantled any notion of a sexual double standard that had proved so damaging to women, but it also demonstrated Christ's compassion for women."[22]

The impact of Bushnell and Starr's biblical scholarship on the defense of women in ministry cannot be overestimated. Together they advanced a new vision for women's God-given sphere, which, in Starr's words, "is as wide as the earth's circumference, as high as the firmament and as deep as the sea."[23]

---

20. Ibid., 117.
21. Du Mez, "Leaving Eden," 158.
22. Ibid., 162.
23. Starr, *Biblical Status*, 21.

DOCUMENT 48

God's Word to Women (1916), Lesson 89 (¶¶723, 725–26, 731), Lesson 90 (¶¶732–38, 741), Lesson 91 (¶¶742, 744–46, 752–54, 756–58, 760)
Katharine Bushnell

Lesson 89: Women May Preach

723.[24] The church has often told woman we might say very loudly that Paul commanded her to "keep silence in the churches." The church has told woman very softly, or not at all, that Jesus Christ obliged one woman to *not keep silence*, but to proclaim before a great multitude, made up largely of men, that Christ had redeemed her from that very "curse," as it has been called, which is supposed by some to lie at the base of the doctrine of silence and subordination for women and which was the pretext for her original exclusion from service at the altar.

725. We have a lesson to learn from Christ's bringing the woman to the front to declare her own redemption from an infirmity, instead of his merely declaring it for her. It is not enough that Christ's teaching is plain on this subject, *we women must proclaim this*. It is not enough for women to modestly and quietly seek their own redemption they must proclaim it, even when that proclamation lays them open to the false charge of immodesty.

726. This brings us to another lesson that Christ taught when he caused yet another woman *not to keep silence*. This case is recorded in Luke 13:11–13. We can easily picture this poor deformed creature making her way wearily to the synagogue to hear the great prophet, climbing the steps to the stuffy little compartment behind a lattice, usually up in the gallery under the roof. How amazed she must have been to have the great prophet call out suddenly, "Mary, come here to me." The other women help her to descend as quickly as possible, and she walks up the aisle to the platform with trembling feet, and stands in a most unusual position, out in public, among all the men! Gently he spoke to her and "laid his hands on her," and behold not only is she "loosed from her infirmity" of a bowed back but also of a silenced tongue; "she was made straight and glorified God." This means, of course, that she broke the silence with her hallelujahs and with rapid tongue began to tell eagerly all about her former suffering, and healing, to all in the synagogue.

24. The Bushnell volume contains no pagination; rather, the author uses lesson and paragraph numbers.

731. On a third occasion the Master's words so stirred a woman's heart that she began to pour out blessings on his head. She "preached Christ" after her own fashion, interrupting him in his discourse to do so. Did Christ silence the woman? Not at all. He said "Amen" to what she uttered and added to her teaching (Luke 11:27). Yet apparently not one of these three incidents of sanctioned women speaking in public in Christ's presence has ever been sufficient to arrest the attention of expositors to the degree that they would consider whether Paul's one utterance, "*Let the women keep silence*," could not be brought into conformity with the precedent set by Jesus and with the Apostle's own words elsewhere. But if one such saying is pronounced sufficient to silence one half, yes, more than one half the church membership, why are not other sayings sufficient to silence the other half?

Lesson 90: Women Must Preach and Teach

732. Penance has no purpose except to expiate guilt. When women are taught that they must take a specially lowly position, that they must meet their husbands' sensual demands with unquestioning obedience (see Lesson 14), that they must be silent in church, that they must go veiled, that they must not teach or preach, that they must have no part in church government, and all because Eve sinned, they are taught to do penance and they are taught thereby that in some sense guilt adheres to them. The teaching of all these things (whether acknowledged or not) is precisely what Tertullian dared to say, namely, "God's verdict on the sex still holds good, and the sex's *guilt* must still hold also."

733. Now the question is, Will enlightened women accept this as "the gospel" men should preach to them? They will not, of course, if they honor their Savior as One who made a full and sufficient atonement for the sins of the whole world. Nor will they pass under the control of the incompetent or unworthy simply because such may be *males*. And so long as the church endorses such teachings, by practicing the custom of the male management of all its affairs, just so long will it see its more enlightened female membership diminishing.

734. There was a time when in civil government and every department of life men governed, but that day is passing everywhere, excepting where its existence is most incongruous, in the church. For long ago it was written, "*If you have respect of persons, you commit sin, and are convinced* (i.e. convicted) *of the law as transgressors*" (Jas 2:9). When the rule of the male was universal, woman could accept membership in a church without a change of status. She cannot today. An invitation to identify herself with any religious

society which carries with it the inference that she will turn backward into servitude will be declined with increasing frequency in days to come. And this attitude on the part of Christian women may not be justly ascribed to pride and want of sanctity. No mature human being has a right to yield unquestioning obedience to other than God Himself. The competent have no right to accept the leadership of the relatively incompetent, and women have fully demonstrated the fact that they cannot all be reckoned as less competent than men. Nor must the more righteous accept control by the less righteous.

735. But far and above all this, no Christian should ever dishonor the atonement of Jesus Christ. Nor can a Christian do this without sin. There is no place in this whole world for a Christian to seek to please God by doing penance. The acceptance of penance is *a denial* of the *sufficiency of the atonement* for our sins. We women refuse that attitude towards Jesus Christ. Jesus Christ's atonement did not fall short of reaching Eve by any means.

736. *Woe be it unto* (us women) *if we preach not the gospel*, for just to the extent that these other matters are taught Christ more than woman *is dishonored* and the world may perish for want of a knowledge of the fullness and sufficiency of the atonement of Jesus Christ unless we women challenge this false doctrine, by exhibiting in our lives the results of an atonement with *no sex limits on it*.

737. Again we ask, If one only expression, "*Let the women keep silence*" (1 Cor 14:34), which readily admits of a qualifying interpretation, is allowed to pass as forbidding one half of the human family forever from proclaiming the gospel of Jesus Christ, why may not other like expressions silence the other half forever?

738. There is such an offense as handling the Word of God deceitfully, as distorting it out of semblance to common sense. This is precisely what is being done by those who, in the face of a world perishing for the lack of the gospel of Jesus Christ and in an age when it is clearly to be seen that the present state of Christendom is a disgrace because of its utter failure to meet the requirements of Christian life, when the world is mangled and bleeding to death, starving and rotting in its social corruption, while male ministers of the gospel are as frequently discrediting Christ in their pulpits as honoring Him, as frequently attacking the Bible as explaining it, in such an age as this it is pertinent to ask the question whether women have any right to keep silent?

741. Shall we women, at such a time as this sit still and *remember our sex*? Never! We will brush aside the opposition of those who can think only in terms of *sex* and go up "*to the help of the Lord against the mighty.*" And

what must women preach? Review the history of the past few years and the answer must be plain to every Christian. Women must preach that "religion of blood" which the fastidious have affected to find so offensive to their aesthetic taste, the "blood of the Cross" of the Only One whose blood would have sufficed to spare that of millions of their sons who have been offered up as human sacrifices to Mars had its flow of "sorrow and love" been accepted on earth as an atonement and remedy for sin before sin begot its blood-thirsty brood. There is no alternative. It must be the "blood of the Cross" and self-immolation or else bloody wars for self-deification. Antichrist is at hand. Which shall it be?

Lesson 91: Women Were Witnesses, Too

742. Please center your thoughts on a little group of women who came out of Galilee with our Lord and followed him from place to place in his ministry. They are first mentioned clearly as *"Mary called Magdalene, Jo-anna the wife of Chuza, Herod's steward, Susanna, and many others"* (Luke 8:2–3). Those that are mentioned by name here are probably the women of comfortable means, *"who ministered unto him of their substance."* Three of the "many others" can be identified: *"Mary the mother of James and Joses; and the mother of Zebedee's children,"* whose children were James and John, and the mother's name Salome (Matt 27:56, Mark 15:40); and the mother of Jesus, frequently mentioned.

744. The women around Jesus must have witnessed most of his miracles, heard most of his discourses, seen his sufferings, and known his claims that he was the Messiah. These women had no more lofty ambition for themselves than to minister unto their Lord. To be sure, the mother of Zebedee's children, the aunt of Jesus Christ, is shown as asking for a high place for her sons in Christ's kingdom (Matt 20:21), but it is evident she was pressed into this service by her sons, since the Lord does not answer her but the sons: *"You know not what you ask"* and *"When the ten heard it they were moved with indignation against the brethren."* This shows that they did not hold the mother culpable. Mark does not even mention the mother as voicing the request of the sons (Mark 10:35). No, these women who followed the Lord had no wishes of their own to be gratified. Their service was a disinterested one.

745. When Jesus was about to be received up into heaven he gave his disciples a strict injunction *not* to go forth to witness for him until they received the spirit of prophecy (Acts 1:4–5, 8). It was to be given to them,

1) because they had witnessed his life on earth, 2) to enable them to give forth a recital of all they had witnessed with "power," and 3) the possession of that Holy Spirit was proof to others that they were witnesses chosen of God to give testimony. For these reasons it is said that *"the testimony of Jesus is the spirit of prophecy"* (Rev 19:10). That Holy Spirit was not poured out upon any on that day of Pentecost, save Christ's own chosen witnesses to his birth, life on earth, death, resurrection and ascension. These numbered one hundred and twenty persons (Acts 1:15; 2:3). Not each one was a witness of all these events, but each had a part to tell.

746. A witness has no other business as a witness except to give a simple recital of what the witness has seen. Jesus Christ would not, in fact could not, choose *as witnesses* for certain events in his career on earth those who had not witnessed those events. Imagine the anger of a judge who calls up a case in court to find that the complaining parties have not brought a single witness of that which had been complained of, only a lot of eloquent pleaders. He would say, "Away with these! One intelligent child is of more value to me than a hundred eloquent men, if that child *saw something, or heard something.* You cannot *witness* to what you never saw or heard. I want evidence; I do not want talk." Jesus Christ could not make use of any as his witnesses, except as they witnessed concerning what *they saw.* Even he had no choice at this point. The witness to an incident must have *seen* that incident and *heard* what was said.

752. We have brought out many striking points as regards the incidents relating to the Incarnation and Crucifixion which we know on the testimony of women only. As to the events connected with the latter, the *written record* in the Bible depends wholly on the word of the women coupled with John's; no other witnesses are cited. It is more than likely that some unbelievers who witnessed the crucifixion became believers afterwards and testified orally to the events; but these are not cited in the written record.

753. It was a fixed law in the Bible that one witness was not sufficient to establish testimony (Deut 19:15) but, as twice taught in the Gospels also, *"In the mouth of two or three witnesses every word may be established"* (Matt 18:16; see John 8:17). Hence, since John alone witnessed the Crucifixion and the testimony of one is not to be accepted and all the Gospels cite "the women from Galilee" and no others as their other witnesses to these events, we discover that the written record of the events connected with the Lord's Crucifixion rests, in its major part, upon the testimony of women.

754. The Resurrection: We must be ready for yet more surprises as regards the women's testimony to the incidents connected with the Resurrection . . .

TWO DISTINCTIVE EARLY TWENTIETH-CENTURY WOMEN 241

756. To recapitulate, that which we know about an earthquake, of the appearance of an angel, of the rolling away of the great stone, of the "keepers" falling as dead men from fear, of the announcement *"He is risen"*—concerning all this, only the two Marys were witnesses. On that Resurrection morning, two angels were seen by women alone—not by Peter nor by John. The guards felt the earthquake and fell. It is not likely they saw the angels. If by chance they did, they were not fit witnesses. The testimony of women alone is cited here in the Bible record. Providence saw to it that the earthquake did not take place nor the angels descend until the two Marys were brought there to witness and to record the events.

757. The question is, Did Jesus have no higher choice for the women who came with him out of Galilee and accompanied him throughout his three years' ministry—the women who were "last at the cross, and first at the tomb" and on the Resurrection morn—than to let them feed and clothe him? Were they not, all unconsciously to themselves, likewise in a school of training as his witnesses? No, more. Twelve were called for this special work. All failed him when danger was at hand, but one. But he had his chosen witnesses. The Marys were at hand. Did he never think ahead of how this should come to pass when he said so often *"There are first that shall be last, and last first, for many are called, but few chosen."*

758. The twelve who had indeed forsaken much to follow him were not always actuated by the highest motives. Judging from the conversations among themselves which have been recorded, they thought largely of an exalted position to be given them when their Master should come into a kingdom of earthly glory. But the women followed with no other motive than to make themselves of use to Jesus and to his disciples. Could it be possible that the One who was teaching his disciples lessons in humility intended to show in his treatment of those who had humbled themselves and served (while the twelve exalted themselves and discussed which should be the greatest of them) that their practice was consistent with his teaching? The women humbled themselves; Christ exalted them. He gave them visions on the Resurrection morning that no one else had. *He made the witness of women the very meat and marrow of his gospel.*

760. The rabbinical teaching was that the testimony of one hundred women was not sufficient to refute that of one man. But Jesus Christ entrusted to women the part of witnesses (and often the sole witnesses) to the most tremendous facts in his life. He could well take this risk since it was never the divine purpose that testimony to the truths of the gospel should rest wholly, or even principally, upon a human foundation. Those who are his chosen witnesses will always have the convicting power of the Holy

Spirit to enforce the truth of all that is said upon the hearts of those willing to receive it.

DOCUMENT 49

The Bible Status of Women (1926), 21, 22, 176, 249, 379–91
Lee Anna Starr

We have heard much in the past about woman's sphere, and it is a trite saying that "Woman's sphere is home." Woman's God-given sphere is as wide as the earth's circumference, as high as the firmament and as deep as the sea. Talk about a woman getting out of her sphere! She would have to get off the earth in order to do that. Every foot of this globe has been deeded to her as much as to man.

If priority of creation is a proof of superiority, the monkey has advantage over man, for the monkey was on the scene first.

[Jesus'] daily deportment toward the sex was a standing reproof to the spirit of his age. He set at naught every man-imposed restriction on woman. He recognized no double standard: With him there was no such thing as a preferred sex. He stood woman side by side with man and addressed her as a member of the human family. He never singled her out for special instruction. He dealt not with sexes, but with souls. No wonder when he walked the Dolorous Way to Calvary, women followed him and bewailed and lamented him; but Jesus, turning unto them, said, "Daughters of Jerusalem, weep not for me, but weep for yourselves and your children."

Any individual with mind unwarped by prejudice can readily see that the husband is not the spiritual head of his wife. Here is a realm wherein she stands erect—"never in bondage to any man." Her husband has no preferential rights in the kingdom of her Lord. In Christ Jesus "there can be no male and female," for "all are one."

Misinterpretation, mistranslation, and misapplication of Scripture passages concerning woman has wrought incalculable injury to the church of Jesus Christ. It immeasurably retarded the progress of his kingdom. The Interchurch Movement's Survey showed that in the Protestant church of America the ratio of women to men was fifty-nine to forty-one. Almost three-fifths of the membership are women. There are enrolled in the Sabbath schools 15,617,000 young people. In these schools there are 2,000,000 volunteer teachers and officers. It is claimed that 67 percent of these teachers are women. Authorities tell us that 83 percent of all additions to Protestant, churches come from the Sabbath schools, and only 17 percent from other sources. Nor is that all. A recent writer on this subject says: "Sunday schools not only furnish the largest number of additions to the church, but also furnish its most enduring additions. Of the converts brought into the church through customary revival methods, 87 percent fall away in five years, while 40 percent of those brought into the church through educational activity fall away in five years." One has only to stand outside the church at the hour of dismissal of Sabbath school and note how few of the scholars remain to the preaching service, to awaken to the fact that the religious instruction of youth rests very largely in the hands of womanhood. Speaking in general terms, the sermon does not appeal to the young. The scarcity of such in the congregation is a matter that demands serious consideration on the part of all who are interested in the affairs of Christ's kingdom. There are several million enrolled in the young people's societies of the various denominations, and the proportion of females to males is two to one. It is safe to say that four-fifths of the superintendents of junior work are women. It is a rare thing to find a man active in this line.

In tabulating woman's accomplishments in the church of Jesus Christ today, we must not overlook the splendid achievements of Home and Foreign Missionary Societies. It is estimated that, including the wives of missionaries, 40 percent of the working force in the foreign field are women. We must also appraise the services of deaconesses, women evangelists, assistant pastors and church visitors. Our inventory would be incomplete were we to overlook the fact that a number of the smaller denominations have removed the ban against the ordination of women, and in the United States census three hundred of the sex are listed as clergymen.

Now we ask the reader to reckon in his mind what it would mean to the church of Jesus Christ today to dispense with the ministries of woman. To silence her voice in the choirs? To forbid her testimonies in the prayer-meetings? Her teaching in the Sabbath schools? Her superintending junior organizations and conducting young peoples' meetings? Her assisting in evangelistic services? Her functioning in Home and Foreign Missionary Societies? Her serving as Assistant Pastor, deaconess, or church visitor? What would it mean to the church of today to disband the entire working force of women, and send them back to the privacy of domestic life, or divert their energies into other channels?

What it would mean to the church of today, it meant to the church for a period of fifteen hundred years, while woman sat apart in the house of the Lord, her lips sealed, her feet bound, her hands tied, penalized for Eve's transgression.

Some years ago Francis Murphy conducted his temperance campaign in the city of Pittsburgh. The services were held in the Methodist Protestant Church on Fifth Avenue. Afternoon and night the auditorium was thronged. At the height of interest Mr. Murphy invited Miss Frances E. Willard to come to Pittsburgh to assist in the campaign. One afternoon, as she sat on the platform, Mr. Murphy requested her to offer prayer. She was about to do so when the pastor arose and forbade it. No woman could offer audible prayer in a church where he was in charge. It is said that on this occasion Miss Willard bowed her head and wept. Day after day and night after night, for weeks, men, the dregs of society—drunkards and debauchees—were brought into the meetings. No doubt but numbers in that motley throng were fit subjects for segregation. They made their way down the aisle, some of them so much under the influence of liquor as to require assistance. On the table before the pulpit lay the pledge cards. These were presented and signed. Hundreds of these same cards were later displayed in the windows of saloons where they were exchanged for drink.

After the formality of signing, as many of the signees as could be induced to do so were led to the platform to rehearse the story of their downfall. The pastor received them—men in all stages of physical, mental and moral degradation—with extended hand and beaming countenance. Mr. Murphy, himself an ex-saloon-keeper and, as he often stated in his addresses, a pardoned criminal, stood by their side as they related their experiences. These men, at times, seemed to vie with each other in depicting how low they had fallen, and the one who could tell the most lurid tale was the one most lionized. While this was going on, the white-souled Frances Willard sat apart—forbidden to open her lips in prayer—guilty of the one unpardonable sin within the walls of that church—that of being born a woman.

On one occasion a minister entered his church and found a small company of women assembled to discuss some phase of Christian service. The leader requested one of the number to lead in prayer. The minster raised his hand in protest, exclaiming, "Wait!" and hastened from the room. The author was present on another occasion when a professor remarked to his class of young theological students, "A woman sacrifices her modesty when she offers prayer in public."

Not only did the clergy disallow the activities of woman within the church but also disapproved of her public participation in religious affairs outside. A man so pious as the Rev. Samuel Wesley, father of John and Charles Wesley, administered reproof to his wife because during his absence from home she assembled the family servants and a few neighbors and read and commented on God's Word. This attitude of the clergy, during a period of fifteen hundred years, paralyzed the energies of one-half the working force in Christ's kingdom.

It may be pointed out that during the Medieval Age there were not the same opportunities for service on the part of women, even if the clergy had been favorably disposed. There were no Sabbath schools nor young people's societies, nor other lines of Christian service that at the present time especially engage the attention of women. That is true and such would in large measure be the case today if Christian women would lay aside their tasks. If the 67 percent of women teachers would withdraw from the Sabbath schools the system would be disorganized. The same results would follow in young people's societies—two-thirds of the membership being women. If the 40 percent of women missionaries should abandon the foreign field, Mission Boards would be distraught over the situation.

The probabilities are that if the path of Christian womanhood had not been blocked, the forenamed agencies would have been in operation centuries before they were realized. She would not have been, for fifteen hundred years, unmindful of the young.

It is chimerical to affirm that if women vacated their tasks in the church today, they would be replaced by men, and the affairs of the kingdom would function as before, or even better. The thought is fantasy. Right here we confront a stern fact. It is this: *Women never supplanted men in the activities of the church.* They were accepted because men were unavailable. If the latter had responded to the call, women would not have been invested with the right to serve. There was no other resource. Necessity, and not "a willing mind," compelled the prelates to unbar the door.

A like situation confronts the church today regarding the ordination of women to the gospel ministry. The creed of hierarchs on this question is imperiled by the fact that a sufficient number of men are not available to supply the pulpits. In every denomination there is a dearth of ministers, and theological seminaries report a reduction in the number of young men preparing to preach the gospel. In the South and Southwest sections of the United States there are 5,600 vacant pulpits. The following figures are taken from the "Interchurch Survey" and apply to the United States:

"In one denomination 3,388 congregations did not have regular pastoral care. In another there were 994 fewer ministers than in 1914. In the New England section; of one denomination, 35 per cent of the congregations were without regular ministers in 1915. One denomination reports: 2,000 churches pastorless and shepherdless.

"In a denomination having 963 congregations, only 627 have settled pastors. Another reports a net gain in three years of 25,680 members, but only thirty-four ministers.

"Another denomination needs a thousand ministers a year to fill the gaps, but had in 1919 less than 600.

"In 1911 there was a total decrease of 178 theological students as compared with 1910; in 1913 there were 20 percent less than in 1912.

"These losses occurred during a period marked by a large increase in the number of church members and of college students; by extensive evangelistic campaigns, by special religious work in colleges, and by the Student Volunteer Movement.

"In one denomination 1,624 more unordained 'supply preachers' were used in 1918 than in 1898. In another, out of 986 ministers, only 476 gave their full time to ministerial work."

Dr. Frederick Lynch, writing in *The Christian Work*, says: "The English religious press is just now full of letters regarding the serious shortage in candidates for the ministry. The situation seems quite desperate. Since the war the classes in theological seminaries have been only one-half or one-third the size of the classes of pre-war days. In the Anglican communion the problem is already assuming serious condition, as there are hundreds of churches without pastors, and the situation grows more and more alarming."

The various denominations have sent out SOS calls, imploring young men to fill the vacant ranks, but the lack of response is disconcerting. The need is compelling some, even of the stronger denominations, to consider the advisability of ordaining women.

Some writers on this subject attribute the shortage of ministers to inadequate salaries and charge the laity with dereliction in this matter; the author would place the blame elsewhere. It is written in the sacred Scriptures: "And it shall be in the last days, says God, I will pour forth of my Spirit upon all flesh; And your sons and your daughters shall prophesy."

"The powers that be" in the church have answered—our sons shall prophesy—and have barred the doors to daughters. The setting at naught the word of God by their traditions accounts for the present dearth of ministers.

It is an astounding fact that the church of Jesus Christ marches in the rear of every other profession in according full recognition to women—more astounding still that, while down through the centuries the allied forces of evil have offered every inducement to woman to cast her lot among them, the magnates of the church have waved her back and repulsed her efforts to serve the cause of righteousness.

A lecturer of the National Woman's Christian Temperance Union was attending a convention. She was a woman of ability, so much so that her own denomination made her an exception and licensed her to preach the gospel. On this occasion she was invited to occupy the pulpit of a church, the pastor of which was absent. As she entered the vestibule she was confronted by a stern individual and the following conversation ensued:

"Madam, do you believe the Bible?"

"I certainly do," she replied.

"Do you accept it as the inspired word of God?"

"I do," was her answer.

"Then how," said her interrogator, "do you dare to go into that pulpit this morning and preach to this congregation?"

It was about time for the services to begin. Realizing this, she said to her interlocutor: "Sir, there is not time for controversy, but I infer from your remarks that you are opposed to women preaching."

"I most certainly am!" he replied with emphasis.

"So is the devil!" she responded, and passed to the pulpit.

Now that woman uttered a volume of truth in that single sentence. Satan and his entire constituency have, down through the centuries, been averse to woman preaching. They have recognized, as the church has not, her great power for good or for evil. Frances E. Willard believed herself called to the ministry of God's word. In her book, *Woman in the Pulpit*, she gives this testimony. There is pathos in her words:

"Even my dear old mother-church, the Methodist, did not call women to her altars. I was too timid to go without a call; and so it came about that while my unconstrained preference would long ago have led me to the pastorate, I have failed of it, and am perhaps writing out, all the more earnestly for this reason, thoughts long familiar to my mind. Let me, as a loyal daughter of the church urge upon younger women who feel the call, as I once did, to preach the unsearchable riches of Christ, their duty to seek admission to the doors that would hardly close against them now in any theological seminary. Let me pleadingly beseech all Christian people who grieve over the world's great heartache to encourage every true and capable woman, whose heart God has touched, in her wistful purpose of entering upon that blessed gospel ministry through which her strong yet gentle words and work may help to heal that heartache, and to comfort the sinful and sad as one whom his mother comforts."

Man closed the door of the ministry to Frances E. Willard, but God opened to her the world, and she went forth a flaming evangel of truth. Millions waited on her ministry and she tied the white ribbon round the globe.

Anna Howard Shaw sought ordination at the altar of her church, the Methodist Episcopal, and was denied. She applied to the New York Conference of the Methodist Protestant Church and was accepted. She was assigned to a village pastorate and served acceptably for seven years, then stepped outside her narrow bounds to champion a world reform and thrilled two continents with her eloquence.

The Church of England afforded no room for the talent and energy of Catherine Booth, "The Mother of the Salvation Army," so she took her stand by the side of her husband, William Booth, in the work of evangelizing the degraded classes in London. She became a preacher and turned many to righteousness. She was the mother of eight children, seven of whom became preachers. One of these her eldest daughter, Catherine Booth-Clibborn, has a family of five sons and five daughters, and eight of these are preachers. The Salvation Army was organized in 1861 and in the brief period that has elapsed since then has assumed world proportions. Humanly speaking, this would be impossible had the Salvation Army, like the church, failed to recognize the equality of the sexes.

The church had no room for the ministries of Maud Ballington Booth, so she wended her way to jails and penitentiaries, with God's word in her hand, and his love in her heart, and today an army inside prison walls, and thousands who have served their term and been released revere her as "The Little Mother."

Clara Barton found scant encouragement for her God-appointed task within the courts of his sanctuary, so stepped outside and founded the ever alert, ever prepared organization—The American Red Cross—an organization that may be characterized as Christianity in action.

We might extend this list indefinitely. We might add the name of Miss Robart of London, who, in 1839, organized the Young Woman's Christian Association; Elizabeth Fry, whose consecrated efforts tamed "the savages of Newgate prison;" Florence Nightingale, "The Angel of the Crimea," who was in deed and truth, the forerunner of the Red Cross; Anna Wittenmyer, whose great work in the Christian Commission during the Civil War was the means of saving thousands of lives and the restoring of invalid soldiers to health and usefulness. She it was who conceived and established a "Home" for soldiers' orphans. All others are the outgrowth of her initiative. "Mother Stewart," a born leader, who mobilized the womanhood of this country against the drink trade and led them forth in the great crusade of 1873–74; Mattie McClellan Brown, Right Worthy Vice Templar of the International Order of Good Templars, who would gladly have exchanged the platform for the pulpit if the barriers had been removed, but No! ecclesiastics forbade. The International Order of Good Templars saw its opportunity, and this gifted woman laid her eloquence and her fine executive ability on an altar outside the church of Jesus Christ; Katharine Bushnell, who was instrumental in breaking down the system of legalized vice in India, and exposing "the hidden things of darkness" in the opium trade of India and China; Anna Gordon, who presides over a constituency which reaches "from sea to sea and from shore to shore;" Carrie Chapman Catt, whose name appears in almost every published list of the "greatest women of America;" Jane Addams, the Shepherdess of the Hull House Settlement; and a host of others whose names might well be inscribed high on the scroll of the world's benefactors.

The church afforded these women of ten talents no tasks commensurate with their ability, so they lifted their eyes and looked on the fields outside, and lo! they were "white already unto the harvest," and the laborers few. In the need, they read God's call to the larger service. The church lost, but the world gained when they responded: "Here am I; send me." Who can charge them with dereliction?

A new term has been coined by religious writers in these latter days, that of "detached service," meaning Christian and humanitarian effort outside the parameters of the church. The Woman's Christian Temperance Union; Salvation Army; Volunteers of America; Young Women's Christian Association, and American Red Cross all belong in this category.

It is a notable fact that three of the organizations above named were founded by women, and in the establishment of the other two, the wife was an equal participant with her husband. This "detached service" might have been performed within, instead of apart from, the church, if prelates had read aright the Pauline declaration: "There can be no male and female: for you all are one in Christ Jesus."

A bishop said recently: "The brainy women members of our churches are going more and more into club work, and more and more into politics, while they should be devoting themselves to the church." Commenting on this plaint of the bishop, Welthy Housinger says: "This good bishop cannot see that the time has long since passed when the highly trained women, who are leaving our colleges, are willing to take up any work which does not enable them to see the possibility in the future of sharing in the administration of that work. I do know that when a young woman of our church leaves college halls today, she has an intelligent idea of every vocation, from aviation to brokerage; and may enter everyone except the ministry. She may become a policeman or a judge; she may be a mayor or a senator, but she may not be ordained as a minister of the gospel of Christ. So the young women of trained intellect and talent, as they come out to take their share in the world's work, specialize in increasing numbers in law, and not a few have become judges—one is now the Assistant Attorney General of the United States. They specialize in journalism and become editors. They specialize in education and become college presidents. But they may not, in the name of the Father, receive a child into the church nor administer the sacrament to the dying."

If the bishop here spoken of desires to enlist the "brainy women members of the churches," he must advocate for them larger tasks than that of quilting and serving tables. God never entrusted man or woman with ten talents, or even five, and charged the recipient to trade with one, and to hide the others in a napkin. Tasks cannot be assigned the women of today after the measurements of the church at Corinth nineteen hundred years ago. The types of womanhood are different and this difference must be reckoned with. If the authorities of the church persist in pouring new wine into old wineskins, the skins will burst and the wine will be spilled.

Apprehension has been expressed in some quarters that if women are allowed larger scope, the church will become "feminized." We remind these foreboders that for fifteen hundred years the church was masculinized, and while, during that period it built up a powerful hierarchal system, its spiritual life was at lowest ebb. So long as we follow the divine plan, the cause of God will not be disturbed. The divine plan is that the daughters, as well as the sons, "shall prophesy."

The editor of the "Interchurch Survey Volume" (American) sums up the situation in these timely words: "With the development of women's movements, social, philanthropic and political, it may yet develop that the men inside the church will be as much disturbed about the women who are outside the church as the women are today disturbed about the men. City women will undoubtedly soon become a serious problem for the churches. The way must be opened for the fuller participation of women in the control of churches and denominational boards. They must be permitted to minister equally with men."

A third injury resultant on the misconceptions and misapplications of the teachings of the Scriptures concerning woman is race impairment. The degradation of one sex unavoidably effects the degradation of the other also. The race is one, but of two component parts, and to wound the half is to afflict the whole "Whether one member suffers, all the members suffer with it." A writer on this subject says: "There is no man's cause that is not woman's, and no woman's cause that is not man's. The fact is that men and women must rise or sink together."

In closing this discussion, the author desires to pay tribute to the noble men who by voice and pen, in halls of legislation, and in councils of the church, have championed the cause of womankind. Their name is legion and their number has increased with the unfolding of the years. Often in the past the pioneers of this reform were compelled to stand apart and be pelted by their fellowmen; today they are acclaimed as heralds of a renaissance.

Such men have merited the wealth of a mother's love; the full measure of a wife's devotion, and the unstinted gratitude of womankind.

The welfare of the race demands the equalization of the sexes. State and church leaders who ignore the rising tide of public opinion on this question and ruthlessly seat themselves astride the safety valve of progress must arouse to the peril of such adventure or find their place in the rank of discards. Sooner or later the golden rule of Christ will usher in the golden age of humankind.

12

Champions of Full Clergy Rights

Introduction

In her history of women in American Methodism, Jean Miller Schmidt celebrates the fact that "in 1920 women in the Methodist Episcopal Church finally regained the right to be licensed as local preachers that had been taken away by the General Conference of 1880."[1] Certainly the momentum leading to the ratification of the Nineteenth Amendment to the U.S. Constitution that same year deeply affected the attitudes and hopes of women in the life of the church and the actions of the Conference. Having just emerged from the experience of the First World War, women began to sense a new day on the horizon related to women's rights in general. But personal forces led to the changes within Methodism as well. At the same time as Bushnell and Starr were constructing their new narrative about women based on a meticulous study of Scripture, Madeline Southard and Georgia Harkness surfaced as the champions of full clergy rights for women in the political arena of the Methodist Episcopal Church. No two women of the mid-twentieth century affected the defense of women in ministry in the United States more.

M. Madeline Southard (1877–1967), a vanguard evangelist of the Methodist Episcopal Church from Kansas, received her education at Southwestern College and Garrett Biblical Institute.[2] She is most remembered,

---

1. Schmidt, *Grace Sufficient*, 272.
2. On Southard's life and work, see Irons, *Preaching on the Plains* and "From Kansas to the World."

perhaps, for her defense of equal rights for women at the General Confer-
ences of 1920 and 1924, where she served as a lay delegate from her home
State. Kendra Irons identifies three critical events in 1919 that affected
Southard's advocacy role profoundly.

> First, the IAWP with Southard at the helm was founded. Sec-
> ond, her article, "Woman and the Ministry," published in the
> *Methodist Review*, afforded her the opportunity to construct her
> philosophy of ecclesiastical suffrage. Third, Southard completed
> her Master's thesis for a theological degree from Northwestern
> University. Entitled, "Jesus' Attitude toward Woman," Southard
> argued that Jesus treated women with the respect appropriate
> to them as persons, not based upon their relationships to men,
> whether fathers, husbands, sons, or brothers."[3]

Southard, somewhat contrary to her intentions as the founder, served as
president for the International Association of Women Preachers for twenty
years from its founding (except for four years when she was overseas) and as
editor of its newsletter, *The Woman's Pulpit*, from its inception in 1922.[4] The
original purpose of the organization was "to develop the spirit of fellowship
among women who are preaching," but Southard reported in one of the
early issues of *The Woman's Pulpit* that it also sought "to secure equal opportunity for women in the ecclesiastical world."[5] Articles appeared regularly
in this bulletin, including many from Southard's pen, to defend the equal
rights of women in the life of the church.

Southard employed a unique defense of women's ministry and rights.
Irons argues that her egalitarian argument—based on Jesus' actions toward
women that affirmed and supported their fullest possible response to his
invitation to discipleship—represented a departure "from the hermeneutic
used by earlier holiness advocates of women preachers."[6] Complimentary
to the typical defenses based on Galatians 3 and Acts 2, or the Pentecostal
baptism of the Holy Spirit, "Southard focused on the earthly life of Jesus
presented in the Gospels, shifting the analysis not only in terms of persons
of the Trinity, but from doctrine to activity. Faith rather than the work of the
Holy Spirit formed the foundation of Southard's approach."[7] This thread
runs through her various publications.

3. Irons, "From Kansas to the World," 34–35.

4. For an incisive study of the IAWM, see Chaves, "Women that Publish the
Tidings."

5. Cited in Chaves, "Women that Publish the Tidings," 267.

6. Irons, "Madeline Southard," 21.

7. Ibid., 22.

Her *Methodist Review* article on "Women and the Ministry" (Document 50) reminded the reader of the ensuing fortieth anniversary of the 1880 General Conference rejection of the Oliver and Shaw appeal for ordination, highlighting the protracted nature of these efforts for women's equality. She addressed each of the typical arguments that detractors used to oppose the ministry of women, marshaling evidence to the contrary that women possess intellectual and physical capacity, that Scripture authorizes their right to the pastoral office, that the separate spheres concept was obsolete, and that the social gospel and the mandate of evangelism resonated with the consciousness and convictions of women. She argued that women like Frances Willard, who had felt called to the ministry, poured their energies into social reform, noting the way in which ecclesial misogyny inadvertently bifurcated Christianity and social justice through the attrition of capable leaders like her.

The events of 1919 laid the groundwork for her advocacy of women at the 1920 General Conference. Irons's meticulous study of Southard's journals reveals that "Sena Hartzell Wallace wrote Southard encouraging her to draft a memorial petition for the 1920 General Conference asking for ecclesiastical equality."[8] She prepared the petition, submitted it to an editor, and sought endorsements from prominent Methodist leaders (Document 51). She also drafted an open letter to the elected delegates of the Conference (Document 52), providing a wider rationale for the action and encouraging their support. The Conference restored to women the authorization to be licensed as local preachers but offered neither ordination nor Conference membership. The issue of ordination was referred to a commission to report to the next General Conference. Although discouraged, Southard began to plan ahead toward this next opportunity to achieve her larger goal. In no small measure due to her advocacy, "the first highly limited form of ordination for women was approved by the MEC at its 1924 General Conference," notes Schmidt, "[granting] women the right to be local elders."[9] The Conference refused to grant full clergy rights upon the rationalization that "admitting women to the annual conference would introduce the 'peculiar and embarrassing difficulties' of having to guarantee 'to every minister a church and to every self-supporting church a minister.'"[10]

In private reflections on this outcome, unwittingly prophetic, Southard intimated: "it may be that I am thru, that someone else will be raised up to

---

8. Irons, "From Kansas to the World," 35.

9. Schmidt, *Grace Sufficient*, 273–74.

10. Richey, Rowe, and Schmidt, *Methodist Experience in America*, 1:348.

carry on the rest of the way."[11] But Southard did continue on in her pursuit of equal rights for women in the church apart from the political struggle. In 1927 she published her thesis, *The Attitude of Jesus toward Women*, to provide a biblical foundation for women's rights and to challenge the socially constructed view of motherhood that constrained so many women. Concerning this effort, Kristin Du Mez writes:

> For women to claim social power, they needed to conform to the contours of the domestic ideal—an ideal sometimes difficult, if not impossible to attain—and an ideal that Southard increasingly came to believe conflicted with the expansive understanding of Christian womanhood she found in the Scriptures. She sought through her theological writings to divest motherhood of its religious import, a crucial step in her efforts to construct a Christian foundation for women's rights. . . . she argued that a biblical view of womanhood demanded that women not be seen primarily as creatures *of* relationships, but rather as persons *with* relationships. . . . Southard's views on domesticity and motherhood set her apart from the majority of her Protestant contemporaries.[12]

In December 1927 she articulated the foundation of her personal vision and the doctrinal basis of the IAWP in a trenchant article entitled "The Theology of Women Preachers." Her ministry continued several decades beyond that point in time, but she shifted her energies in other directions, willingly relinquishing her role as embattled protagonist to a new generation of women leaders.

"When Georgia Harkness led the movement to secure full ordination rights for women in 1956," Irons claims, "she was walking a path M. Madeline Southard charted some thirty years earlier."[13] In fact, the events of 1924 had bound them together inextricably. Georgia Harkness (1891–1974), noted Methodist theologian, author, and ecumenical leader, completed both her seminary training and her doctoral studies at Boston University.[14] A protégé of Edgar Sheffield Brightman, she immersed herself in the Boston Personalism of Borden Parker Bowne and its primary tenets: the inherent worth of persons, the personal God of love and reason, the moral law of the cosmos, and the social nature of human existence. The central principal of her life—and all her efforts on behalf of women—was the sacred value

11. Quoted in Irons, "From Kansas to the World." 40–41.

12. Du Mez, "Selfishness One Degree Removed," 17–18, 20.

13. Irons, "Madeline Southard," 30.

14. On the life and work of Harkness, see Keller, *Georgia Harkness.*

and worth of every person. Under the provisions of the 1924 action, she was ordained in 1926 as a local deacon in the Methodist Episcopal Church, and subsequently as a local elder in 1939. She served as Professor of Applied Theology—the first woman appointed to teach in a major seminary in the United States—from 1939 to 1950, and then at the Pacific School of Religion, from which she retired in 1960. In 1947 she "was named one of the ten most outstanding Methodists in America."[15]

Her defense of women in ministry began in 1924 with the publication of an article in the Methodist *Christian Advocate*, just on the eve of the General Conference, entitled "The Ministry as a Vocation for Women" (Document 53). "Referring to the church as 'probably our most conservative institution,'" avers Schmidt, "Harkness lamented that the 'wall of prejudice' was too strong for any but the most courageous of women to attempt to enter the ministry."[16] Written in her office at Elmira College, where she was teaching at the time, Harkness identified six arguments typically advanced to exclude women: scriptural prohibition, women's sphere, natural disqualification, professional transiency, institutional interference, and public acrimony. In a terse and tightly articulated counter-argument, she dismantled them one by one. While she argued for ordination, she maintained that the church's failure to affirm women fully as equals before God was a much more grave concern.

Advocates for the full clergy rights of women kept the issue before the General Conferences of both the Northern and Southern churches through the remainder of the 1920s and especially in anticipation of potential church reunification in the 1930s.[17] Harkness continued to play a role in all these developments but also expanded her efforts into the emerging ecumenical scene. "The first major ecumenical event that Harkness, or almost any other woman, ever attended was held at Oxford July 12–27, 1937," writes Rosemary Keller.[18] According to her, "Harkness affirmed the conference report 'that the Church is a supra-national, supra-racial, supra-class fellowship.' But she hastened to remind the delegates 'that the Church is also a supra-sex fellowship.'"[19] An article entitled "Women and the Church" articulated her primary concern in unequivocal language: "It is a paradoxical fact that the Christian gospel has done more than any other agency for the emancipation

15. Engelsman, "Legacy of Georgia Harkness," 340.

16. Schmidt, *Grace Sufficient*, 274.

17. For a discussion of the quest for equal rights for women in the United Methodist Church, see Thompson, *Courageous Past, Bold Future*.

18. Keller, *Georgia Harkness*, 185.

19. Ibid., 188.

of women, yet the church itself is the most impregnable stronghold of male dominance."[20] Martha Scott maintains that Harkness stated her fully developed views on the equality of women in 1939 in an article entitled "What Price Unity," arguing for full clergy rights on the eve of the Conference that united the Methodist Episcopal, Methodist Episcopal South, and Methodist Protestant Churches to form the Methodist Church.[21] She published an expanded version of this essay in *The Christian Advocate* later that year, entitled "Women Ministers" (Document 54), when the efforts of the female advocates proved unsuccessful yet again. She argued that the ordination of women was biblical, practical, and spiritually advisable.

The editors of *The Methodist Experience in America* narrate the sequence of events and actions between 1939 and 1956 that led eventually to full clergy rights for women in The Methodist Church.[22] Both the Methodist union of 1939 and the Evangelical United Brethren union of 1946 represented setbacks for women.[23] A parallel narrative characterizes the historic black Methodist denominations after the Second World War. Keller, in her definitive biography of Harkness, argues that her "most consequential contribution to The Methodist Church came in the lengthy struggle for women's ordination."[24] She championed this cause from the 1944 General Conference until the goal was achieved. When she published her groundbreaking *Toward Understanding the Bible* in 1952, she revealed the foundation upon which she had built her primary argument. "Paul comes nearest to the mind of Christ in Galatians 3:28," she wrote. "The reason is that Jesus treats men and women equally as children of God and persons of supreme worth."[25] Keller notes that "from the 1920s until her death in 1974, Harkness pressed for the opening of equal rights for women . . . and for ordination with full conference membership for women."[26] Even after this goal was achieved she continued to champion this cause. In one of her last books, *Women in Church and Society*, she addressed the evils of discrimination in the life of the church and refined her mature defense for women's rights in a chapter entitled "The Ordination and Ministry of Women" (Document 55). The quest for biblical equality and the ministry of women in the life of the church continues.

20. Harkness, "Women and the Church," 708.
21. See Scott, "Georgia Harkness," 133.
22. Richey, Rowe, and Schmidt, *Methodist Experience in America*, 402–3.
23. See Gorrell, *Woman's Rightful Place*.
24. Keller, *Georgia Harkness*, 279; cf. Keller, "Georgia Harkness."
25. Harkness, *Toward Understanding the Bible*, 26.
26. Keller, "Georgia Harkness," 214.

DOCUMENT 50

"Women and the Ministry" (1919)
M. Madeline Southard

When General Conference meets next spring it will be forty years since Dr. Anna Howard Shaw was refused the privilege of preaching in the Methodist Episcopal Church.

These forty years have wrought many changes, but none more revolutionary than that in the position of women. Since the whole attitude toward woman is now so different, it seems well to reexamine the arguments that have thus far kept her out of the ministry and see if they will stand in the twentieth century. This seems especially important, as the matter will probably be raised again at the coming General Conference.

1. Mental Inferiority. It used to be generally held that women lacked the mental breadth and depth necessary to understand and present the great themes that must be dealt with in the pulpit. When institutions of learning opened their doors only to men this may have seemed true, but since a single generation of liberally educated women have served in the world's work we hear no more of this argument, and the days of the Great War settled the last lingering doubt. Woodrow Wilson in a message to Congress speaks of the women's "instant intelligence quickening every task that they touched; their capacity for organization and cooperation, their aptitude at tasks to which they had never before set their hands." Lloyd George writes especially of their work in administrative offices, states his belief that without their remarkable service Great Britain and the Allies would have failed in the spring of 1918, and thinks "the authors of the war could not have foreseen that one of its effects would be to give woman a commanding position and influence in the public affairs of the world." With such testimony as this on every hand, and with the evidence of administrative ability shown by the great woman's missionary societies, it seems unnecessary to refute an argument founded on the once universal belief in woman's mental inferiority.

2. Physical Disability. As woman was supposed to lack the mental gifts, so she was believed to lack the physical strength for the strain of ministerial life. But now numbers of women have spent many continuous years in the most strenuous kind of preaching, the evangelistic. Deaconesses, in all kinds of weather, have walked innumerable miles and climbed innumerable steps in pastoral visiting. Recently a superintendent from a mountainous region was presenting to a body of seminary students the opportunities of his district. He told of a deaconess who had traveled great distances and

opened up charges that he thought would now support a man pastor. Probably the deaconess would then go farther west and continue her sheltered feminine activity! In view of the difficult tasks accomplished by women for the church, both at home and abroad, in the last half century physical weakness can hardly be held longer as a round for excluding them from the ministry.

3. The Appeal to Scripture. Forty years ago the teaching of the Scriptures was considered an insuperable obstacle to woman's preaching. The Presbyterian General Assembly stated the case for other churches as well as its own when it declared: "Let not the inspired prohibition of the great Apostle be violated. To teach and to exhort or to lead in prayer in public and promiscuous assemblies is clearly forbidden to women in the holy oracles." Great enlightenment has robbed of their force the two paragraphs supposed to prohibit women's preaching. The historical method applied to the first Corinthian Epistle sets Paul's commands to women in the light of the amazing ignorance and immorality of women in notorious Corinth. The abandonment of the proof text method permits a survey of the whole field that makes it almost certain that women preached in the early church. In his Pentecostal sermon Peter declared that sons and daughters, servants and handmaidens should prophesy. Luke records in the book of Acts that four daughters of Philip did prophesy. Paul cautioned the women to wear their head covering when they prayed and prophesied, and Paul defined prophesying as "speaking unto men to edification, exhortation, and comfort!" If that isn't preaching, it is what preaching ought to be.

The fathers were at least consistent in their adherence to Paul's commands, and no woman's voice was permitted to speak or pray in their assemblies, but today, if these prohibitions prove anything, they prove too much. Paul says, "Let your women keep silence in the church." But that would mean that their voices no longer be heard in Epworth League, Christian Endeavor, or the midweek meeting, and that no pulpit be open for their missionary and humanitarian appeals. The Epistle to Timothy says, "I suffer not a woman to teach." A rigorous application of this would work considerable hardship in the public schools, and might make it difficult to properly man our Sunday schools. Yet these two scriptures formed the chief ground of woman's exclusion from the ministry. If modern churches refuse to take them literally in all things else, they can hardly maintain the ancient objection to woman's preaching because of them.

4. Woman's Sphere. There remains one objection to woman in the pulpit, and it is perhaps the only one that still has weight with thoughtful people. It is the plea that woman's preaching is a violation of nature, since she is designed for the life in the home.

It is very true that every genuine woman would find in exalted love and motherhood the most satisfying expression of her womanhood. In an ideal world this would be the lot of all, but this is hardly an ideal world. Frequent wars thin the ranks of men, requiring polygamy if all women fulfill the function of motherhood. A large percentage of the men remaining are morally and physically unfit for fatherhood; enlightened women will not sin against the race by marrying them. So there are of necessity many women who are not mothers and must seek other vocations, while multitudes of women who are mothers are forced into the industrial world to support themselves and their children. This is not a new thing in history. Women have always borne their share of the world's industrial burden. But when denied educational opportunities only menial tasks were open to them. Men did not get excited when women scrubbed their office floors and washed their soiled clothes for a livelihood. It seems to be only when they approach the more desirable and remunerative tasks that lively fears of the disruption of the home are entertained. And perhaps preaching is not essentially inimical to motherhood. Catherine Booth, a great preacher, bore eight children who were infatuated with the ministry. Her eldest daughter, Mrs. Booth-Clibborn, with her sister, organized the Salvation Army in France, preached all her life, and is the mother of ten children, part of whom are preaching now. On the foreign field the church requests the missionary's wife to hire servants so that she may give herself to educational and administrative service, saying it cannot afford to have trained women in these needy fields and not utilize them. Many women in India and China have found motherhood not inconsistent with a real ministry.

This whole argument from nature loses much of its weight when we remember that it is the same time worn word of woman's sphere that so long deprived her of educational opportunity and political justice. It never kept her from the factories nor other hard and ill-paid labor, but for centuries it closed to her the more desirable vocations. Shall the church cling to this argument when in all other fields it has been cast aside as obsolete? In its larger program for the years ahead it is confidently including great numbers of woman workers. Consistency would seem to demand that either, for the sake of the home, the church exclude women from all special lines of its service, or, if it continue to plead with its daughters to do definite religious work, then that it remove all artificial restrictions and let them enter any field their ability may open to them. This would seem almost imperative in view of the new feminine psychology. Girls with the ballot in one hand and a college diploma in the other, with economic independence and strong convictions of justice and democracy, are not to be dealt with as were the women of days gone by. If in the future the church attracts the strongest women to its service, it will have to reckon with the new conditions, for other agencies are offering means of contact with needy humanity. Every profession but the ministry is open to them, and this discrimination against them will not be overlooked by the most thoughtful women.

5. Women and the Social Gospel. The social aspects of the message of Jesus make a strong appeal to the hearts of women. An amazing amount of social reform has been brought about since women have had some part in municipal and educational affairs. The loss on this line that the church has sustained through its resolute closing of the ministry to women is beyond estimate. Many do not know that Frances Willard's real call was to preach. In her book *Woman in the Pulpit* she writes these words: "But even my dear old mother church, the Methodist, did not call women to her altars. I was too timid to go without a call; and so it came about that, while my unconstrained preference would long ago have led me to the pastorate, I have failed of it, and am perhaps writing out all the more earnestly for this reason thoughts long familiar to my mind." A minister reading that said, "Miss Willard did a far greater work than if she had been in the pulpit." But is that true? If she and her coworkers had been able to incorporate as an integral part of church work the reform and humanitarian movements that they so largely originated, who can say how much farther along both the church and social reforms would be today? The church is just now awakening to its loss in allowing certain great social impulses, born of the Christian spirit, to crystallize in secular movements which are indifferent, sometimes hostile, to formulated Christianity. Very much social service fails through lack of spiritual vision, much religious effort fails through lack of practical human contact. It is quite probably that these two aspects of the gospel would not have become so estranged if the mother hearts of women had been given place in the ministry and councils of the church. For the masculine and feminine minds are ever complementary, and only the blended wisdom of the two can give symmetry and wholeness in home and church and state.

6. Woman and Evangelism. The mystical element is very strong in women. Whatever the customs and laws, where there had been free, untrammeled operation of the Holy Spirit women have given gospel messages. When the Pentecostal baptism of the Spirit was still on the early church, women prophesied. Alford declares prophecy to be "the utterance of our conscious intelligence informed by the Holy Spirit." In that revival of pure religion out of which grew the Society of Friends women preached as freely as men. Early Methodism had so much of the power of the Spirit that its women could not be restrained from preaching, Susanna Wesley herself being guilty of expounding Scripture. George Eliot would hardly have given us her portrait of Dinah without an historic basis. In 1791 John Wesley wrote

to a woman preacher that she could not be silent when God commanded her to speak, "Yet, I would have you give as little offense as possible, and therefore I would advise you not to speak at any place where a preacher is speaking at the same time, lest you should draw away his hearers." History gives us the names of a number of these early Methodist women, among them the wife of John Fletcher, who gave the gospel message, but took care not to offend against the prejudice of their day. In the great revival of simple gospel preaching that created the Salvation Army women not only preached but were officially recognized as preachers, and multitudes of earth's wayward sons have been drawn back to God through the tender pleading of these earnest women. The "Battle Hymn of the Republic" was written by a woman preacher, as was that most helpful religious classic, *The Christian's Secret of a Happy Life* [Hannah Whitall Smith]. When God has so clearly given his word through women it is doubtful if any ecclesiasticism is justified in hampering their activity. If women be given unhindered opportunity, the eagerness to bring souls to know God may go far toward bringing that religious awakening which is acknowledged to be the greatest need of the church and world today.

We close with another word from Miss Willard. She urges young women "who feel a call, as I once did, to preach the unsearchable riches of Christ," to seek admission to theological schools. She goes on to say, "And let me pleadingly beseech all Christian people who grieve over the world's great heartache to encourage every true and capable woman whose heart God has touched in her wistful purpose of entering upon that blessed gospel ministry, through which her strong yet gentle words and work may help to heal that heartache and to comfort the sinful and the sad, 'as one whom his mother comforts.'"

DOCUMENT 51

"Memorial to the 1920 General Conference" (1920)
M. Madeline Southard

Whereas, Today the principle of equality of opportunity for women is being recognized in all fields of activity; and

Whereas, This General Conference has gone on record as urging political equality for women by requesting the Delaware House of Representatives to sign the Susan B. Anthony Amendment; therefore be it

Resolved, That the General Conference approve ecclesiastical equality for women, that it remove all restrictions and limitations upon women in the service of the church, and that it instruct the proper committee to make any changes in the Discipline necessary to accomplish this end.

DOCUMENT 52

"A Letter to Delegates Attending the 1920 General Conference" (1920)
M. Madeline Southard

Inasmuch as equality of opportunity is being rapidly granted to women in educational, political, economic and professional life; and

Inasmuch as the church in the service it now asks women to render, practically repudiates every argument hitherto urged against woman's ministry; and

Inasmuch as the woman's missionary societies have amply demonstrated the administrative ability of women, while the service of women in most difficult fields both at home and abroad has clearly revealed their courage, consecration and adaptability; and

Inasmuch as women are now hampered by the restrictions of the church in their service for the Kingdom of Christ; in the foreign field women may expound the Word and lead souls to Christ, but they are not authorized to receive their converts into the church nor administer to them the sacraments; in some instances they must send fifty or a hundred miles to get a man to attend to these matters, perhaps a native preacher whom they themselves have taught—and similar conditions prevail in the home field; and

Inasmuch as many churches now ordain women, and the two most conservative, the Episcopal and the Presbyterian, have now commissions appointed to go into this whole matter in their respective denominations; and

Inasmuch as the church can safeguard herself from undesirable women by making her own requirements; and

Inasmuch as the lack of a modern policy in the church's attitude toward women is driving to humanitarian and other fields some of her most highly gifted and best trained women who would prefer to engage in definitely religious work; and

Inasmuch as there is not now in either home or foreign fields a sufficient number of minsters to break the Bread of Life to the people who are asking for it;

Therefore we, the undersigned, respectfully memorialize the General Conference assembled in Des Moines, Iowa, in May 1920, to carefully consider the whole matter of the status of woman in the Methodist Episcopal Church, to take such action as shall secure for women that equality of opportunity in the church that is rapidly coming to her in other fields, and that shall make it regular for properly trained women to be appointed to preach when the interests of the Kingdom demand it.

DOCUMENT 53

"The Ministry as a Vocation for Women" (1924)
Georgia Harkness

It is generally recognized that church work is a useful avocation for women. Since the church began, our religious leaders have borne witness to the assistance rendered by the faithful Lydias and Dorcases of their flocks. If by chance the Ladies' Aiders sometimes get quarrelsome and require some smoothing of ruffled feathers, they more than atone for their misdeeds when they vote a new coat of paint for the Sunday-school room or a new parlor rug for the parsonage, and what would the Sunday school or the prayer meeting amount to without the women? Well, there probably would not be any.

But while nobody questions the value of the volunteer service rendered by women to the church, there are many who still seem to consider that a special dispensation has been granted to men to fill most of the paid positions within the church. They are willing enough, to be sure, that a woman should be a missionary or a deaconess or a church secretary. But for a woman to preach—impossible!

Not Many Are Called

Now lest some ministerial brother be alarmed for fear a feminine aspirant may be seeking to usurp his legitimate place, let me say at the outset that I do not think many women at present are likely to attempt to enter the ministry. The wall of prejudice is too strong for any except the most courageous. A few remarkably gifted women such as Maude Royden have been able to make a place for themselves in the ministry, but the church which would not choose a mediocre man in preference to a superior woman is one among a thousand.

I do not maintain that this prejudice can be attributed exclusively to the ministers themselves, for most of them are more broadminded than their congregations. There is, however, a deep seated relic of medievalism in the attitude of the church at large which the clergy has not done all it might to eradicate. Such is the shortage of ministers that in many denominations almost any man of good moral character and religious convictions can get a pulpit. But when men are permitted to preach whose education does not extend beyond the eighth grade, and women college trained and sometimes theologically trained, are denied that privilege, something is wrong.

Margaret Slattery tells of an experience wherein she was requested to address a large church audience, not from the pulpit, but from a little oak table down by the register, because as the church officials told her, "No woman's foot has ever stood in this pulpit." It was only when she firmly gave them the option of permitting her to speak from the pulpit or cancelling the engagement that they reluctantly capitulated. This may be an extreme case, but the fact that it can occur at all in this enlightened age affords food for thought.

One does not need to be an ultra-feminist to recognize that such a state of affairs ought not to exist. The church has a task on its hands big enough to demand the consecrated talent of both sexes, and many of us believe that it is neither wise nor Christian deliberately to reject the assistance which trained women would gladly render in its ministry if given an opportunity. When it is announced that in our largest Protestant denomination twenty-seven percent of its ministry have had less than a full high school education and that in this same denomination there has been a net loss of 613 ministers during the past four years, one wonders if it is not time to bring about a change in established traditions.

Why Women Are Excluded

In these days of many investigations, would it not be well to investigate the causes of the exclusion of women from the ministry? The reasons generally given are as follows: 1) that according to Scripture women must "keep silent in the churches," 2) that the ministry would take woman out of her natural sphere, 3) that she is by nature unfitted for success in such work, 4) that she would not be apt to make it a permanent occupation, 5) that increased competition would tend to interfere with the tenure or salaries of men, 6) that the church would lose in public esteem by the general admission of women to its ministry.

The first argument can be disposed of without much controversy. One does not have to be a very profound biblical scholar to recognize the difference between our modern social regime and conditions in wicked, conservative Corinth in the days of Paul, when Christian women must walk warily lest they be confused with the brazen women of the street. A prudent bit of advice to the Corinthian women of the first century ought scarcely to be made a stumbling block to progress in the twentieth. The prayer meeting and the Epworth League and the Sunday school would have a sorry time of it if we were to take Paul's words literally as a permanent injunction!

The second objection has more supporters, for from time immemorial we have heard that "woman's sphere is the home." Undoubtedly it is true that for the majority of women the care of the home is the first duty, and we are not advocating that the preacher's wife exchange places with the preacher (though we may have known cases where such an arrangement would not be disadvantageous!). But in spite of the fact that the "woman's sphere" argument has been urged against every movement for the political and professional advancement of women, an increasing number of intelligent people have come to recognize that woman has also a legitimate sphere outside the home. It is not our purpose here to enter into a discussion of the whole feminist controversy; but if it is granted that woman has a rightful place in business and professional life, there is no more reason why she should be excluded from the ministry than from medicine. Practically every avenue of leadership today is open to woman save in the church, and there she must content herself either with rendering volunteer service or working in a subordinate capacity.

Try and See

To those who fear that we women would not make a success in the ministry, we reply: "Try us and see!" Is there anyone who really believes that a woman with proper training cannot preach as good a sermon as a man? Our voices to be sure may not carry so far, but there are few churches where this would be a serious obstacle and we are not likely very soon to get a chance to preach in those churches. And as for what our voices say, we invite you in all modesty to compare the sermon of the average woman preacher with that of the average man—take the best of each, or the poorest of each, or use any standard you wish so long as it is impartial—and examine the result. We are not afraid to submit to such a comparison. Are you?

But of course preaching is not the only work a minister has to do. A minister must be a pastor, an executive, an educator, a financier—a host of other things. But is there any one of these capacities in which women have not proved their ability? If women are strong enough in physique, intellect and personality to pursue successfully every other profession, why not the ministry? We are not claiming for women any sexual superiority, but it seems a matter of plain common sense that equality of ability ought to bring with it equality of opportunity.

The argument that the ministry ought to be a life job, and that a woman might relinquish it to marry after a few years, is a more tenable objection. But suppose she should! Does this nullify the value of her work in the years before her marriage? And does it interfere with the continuance of her work during the second leisure of middle life after her children have grown to maturity? Furthermore, while most women with professional interests regret the necessity of having to choose between a home and a career while a man can have both, there are many capable women who in full sincerity decide they can render more service to the world by remaining unmarried; and if the church does not offer an opportunity to invest their talents, some other and perhaps less worthy agency will.

Competition

The argument that women might supplant men in the ministry or lower their salaries is not very often publicly advanced by the clergy themselves. However, in the eyes of many people who argue from the general conditions of woman's participation in the industry, this seems an important factor. They seem to anticipate a great influx of women, at whose advance the present occupants of the pulpit must courteously rise and withdraw to give the ladies their pulpit chairs. There is about as much soundness in this argument as in that of the anti-suffragists who feared that if women were given the vote, Congress would be overrun with them and a woman might (*horribile dictu*!) be seated in the Presidential chair! Women will find a place in the ministry only so fast as their ability and training win them a legitimate place, and the demand for ministers is such that if any man is crowded out in the process, it will be because he is unfit for survival.

To those who say that the standing of the church in the eyes of the public would be lowered if women were admitted to its ministry, we reply that if it would, then it is time for public opinion to be remodeled. Does anyone think any the less of the medical profession because women may enter it on an equal footing with men? The public expects and desires men to do its preaching—simply because men always have. The church is probably our most conservative institution. There are many within its fold who, perhaps unconsciously, adopt as the guiding motto of their lives, "Not so, Lord, for I never have." It is obvious that if the church is going to keep abreast of the times and meet the spiritual challenge of the new age it must relinquish some of its conservatism; and whatever our theological convictions may be, it might not be a bad idea to introduce some "modernism" into our conceptions of the function of women in the work of the church.

Ordination Desirable

Some denominations, to be sure, are willing to ordain women, and it is easy to say that if women want to preach they should enter those denominations. But the issue does not lie wholly in ordination. Not many more women are preaching in those denominations where ordination is possible than in those where it is denied. The crux of the matter, to put it boldly, is that women cannot enter a field where they are not welcome. Ordination is desirable, I believe, to put the stamp of the church's approval upon the admission of women to its ministry. But what is needed even more is a general recognition by pulpit and pew of the legitimate place of trained women in this field. Women will never find a welcome in the ministry until the press and our present religious leadership have remolded public sentiment. Ordination is a step in this direction but it is a step—not the final goal.

I am not blind to the fact that some other religious vocations are open to women. In fact, I am in another myself. Every year I have the privilege of directing a good many young women who are thinking seriously of religious or social work as a vocation. But I never advise any of them to prepare for the ministry, though I consider it the highest religious calling. Under present conditions it would be futile for them to think of it, for they might take three years of theological training beyond their college work, only to find themselves superseded by men with high school training or less. If there are men enough in the ministry to do the work and do it well, we are willing to let them. But are there? We wonder if the advancement of the Kingdom is not more important than the maintenance of an ancient prejudice.

DOCUMENT 54

"Women Ministers" (1939)
Georgia Harkness

To the leadership of woman in the church many barriers have been interposed. John Calvin, spiritual forebear of much of American Protestantism, wrote: "It is not permitted to any woman to speak in church, nor to teach, nor to baptize, nor to offer sacrifice: neither to lay claim to the lot of a man or the priestly office....It is plainly evident that this abuse could not become implanted without the barbarous confusion of the whole of Christianity."

Many others within the church have echoed in spirit, if not in diction, the words of Samuel Johnson, "I am very fond of the company of ladies. I like their beauty, I like their delicacy, I like their vivacity—and I like their silence."

Nevertheless, women have not been silent. Women today occupy a significant and growing place in religious leadership. Yet in spite of the emancipating power of the Christian gospel which has opened to women large opportunities in education, medicine, law, politics, and the arts, the church has been reluctant to accept women into leadership on terms of parity with men.

Certainly we women ought not either militantly or plaintively to bewail our fate. Prohibition was not won by Carrie Nation, or woman suffrage by Sylvia Pankhurst. While I do not claim large knowledge of male nature, I am sure that no man likes to be told by a woman that women are abused.

On the other hand, we women must not, either through timidity or indifference, acquiesce in things as they are. Any marked change can come only through the agency of men whose sense of justice and Christian concern for personality are focused on the issue.

To tackle one of the knottiest issues, I wish to speak to the moot problem of ordination. I do not believe ordination to be all-important. I regard it as less important than that women be admitted to the governing bodies and policy making organs of the church. Neither do I believe that large numbers of women are likely to seek ordination. Nevertheless, while ordination is not all important, it is a crucial matter for a principle is at stake.

I believe that ordination on terms of full parity with men should be opened to women for three reasons:

The first is biblical. At the dawn of Hebrew history, Deborah seems to have had full political and religious authority—a situation which has not been duplicated since.

I base my judgment, however, not on the spirit of the Old Testament but of the New. Paul stated it when he wrote: "There is neither Jew nor Greek, there is neither bond nor free, there is neither male nor female; for you are all one in Christ Jesus."

The second reason is practical. The church ought to command the wholehearted allegiance and elicit the best services of all Christians. Every year there are trained, intelligent, and deeply Christian college women who are forced to go into various types of secular social service because they do not find within the church the opportunities open to their brothers.

My third reason is spiritual. The richest and most intimate experiences in the life of the Christian are those which have to do with reception into the membership of the church, with partaking of the sacraments, with marriage, with the baptism of children, with the consolation the minister is called upon to offer when sorrow enters a home.

As long as a person is debarred by reason of sex from acting as the agent of the church in these high moments, no matter what other opportunities are open to her she is debarred from the largest Christian service. A case might easily be made for the contention that women have a special aptitude for entering into the inner lives of persons at these sacred moments.

However, I do not say that women have more or less of tact and understanding for such situations than have men. I say only that where there is equal insight and equal consecration and therefore equal capacity to minister in Christ's name, there ought to be equality of opportunity to do so.

May I at this point become somewhat personal? I trust I can do so without animus, for our church has given me far more recognition than I deserve. A number of years ago I was ordained a local deacon in the Methodist Episcopal Church. I may say, incidentally, that the foundations of the house were not shaken thereby! In April 1939 Bishop McConnell laid his hand upon my head and said, "Take authority," and I became a local elder.

About a dozen fine young men were ordained elders on the same occasion. After our ordination, all of them who had not been previously admitted were received into full connection in the Conference. Because of restrictions in the *Discipline*, I was not, and never could be under the existing legislation.

The large contributions of women in the lay activities of the local church and in the building of Christian homes have long been recognized. They are and ought to be held in high esteem. There is no greater service that a woman can render than to rear up an oncoming Christian generation. Yet it is no disparagement of these great contributions to point out that these are not all that women have to offer.

There are men within the church—even within the Methodist Church—who ask why women are so largely putting their energies into other organizations for women and are neglecting the church.

In a few sentences of the Madras Report lies the primary answer to that question:

"These agencies afford to women large scope for their varied abilities. In the official life of the church, women are offered relatively few opportunities which call forth their full allegiance and command their abilities and energies."

Men will help solve the problem when they realize that a Christian sense of the spiritual equality of all persons, brought to bear upon the facts, is an adequate spur to the removal of limitations. Barriers even now are being broken down through the agency of men and larger opportunities await us all through their united effort.

DOCUMENT 55

"The Ordination and Ministry of Women" (1972)
Georgia Harkness
Source: Harkness, *Women in Church and Society*, 206–12, 215

A Wesleyan criterion of long standing in regard to men in the ministry takes the form of three questions, "Has he gifts? Has he grace? Does he bear fruit?" These queries may well be applied to women also. It is only the woman who is qualified by talent, by training, and by personal Christian vitality and dedication that is under consideration in the entire matter.

There are both theological and practical reasons why women should be ordained and accepted as pastors of churches. I shall deal mainly with the theological factors, for these are basic to any further consideration of the matter whether ecclesiastical or practical. The primary subjects to consider are the nature of the church and what is essential to its ministry, the weight of Scripture and tradition, and the Christian doctrines of creation and redemption.

First, then, what is the church? It is the fellowship of the followers of Christ, to which has been committed the responsibility of service and witness in carrying the gospel of Christ to the world. It is that body of persons of which Christ is the Head. This definition may be sharpened by noting what it is not. The church is a social institution with a ministry of service, but it is not simply a social institution doing various good works which might equally well be done by some other group. It is quite different from a secular club of congenial and respectable people, however much existing church groups may take on this character. The church has a unique mission and message which center in the extension of the life-giving gospel of Christ to the whole of human existence.

The church universal is a very meaningful term which conveys the thought that the church of Christ is intended by God to be universal throughout the world, unrestricted by human barriers of nationality, race, color, economic status, or culture. It is this goal which underlies Christian missions, the ecumenical movement, and the attempt in our time to transcend cultural and racial differences. While regrettably this goal has not yet been achieved in the existing churches, there is general acknowledgment that the church is intended by God to be supra-national, supra-racial, and supra-class in its essential nature. To this must be added that it is also supra-sex.

But what is the ministry, to which women have been occasionally accepted but more often denied? The ministry of the church and of Christ is a very special form of service in which a human figure, whether male or female, endeavors to proclaim the Christian message and lead the people toward greater vitality in the Christian life. It is a high and serious responsibility. The historic functions of the church and of the ministry as its leaders have been the preaching of the Word and the administering of the sacraments. These are, indeed, primary responsibilities of the minister but by no means the only ones. The many duties of a minister or priest include counseling in crises, comforting in sorrow, the encouragement of Christian fellowship, and that wide field of endeavor which used to be called "the cure of souls," instruction in the Christian heritage, a challenge to witness and service in many fields, and, in a quite different but very essential category, the administrative governance of the churches' structure.

These obviously are large tasks which call for dedication and a combination of spiritual vitality, mental acumen, and a love of persons. But are these the sole prerogatives of men? There is not one of them which a woman who is trained, intelligent, and devoted to her sacred calling cannot do. These things are not easy. She cannot do them entirely by her own strength and initiative. Neither can a man. It requires the empowerment of God and the cooperation of the congregation to do them effectively. But women have repeatedly demonstrated their capacity in these fields. Few who have been given "charges"—in the double meaning of charge as such work to do and the place to do it in—have failed in the endeavor. In fact, at the point of sympathetic understanding and counseling, women can feel an empathy with other women and with children better, in most cases, than a man.

Above I used the phrase "her sacred calling." The term, a call to the ministry, is not heard so often today as formerly. This is regrettable. Not everybody ought to be a minister, though every Christian ought to be ministering in whatever field he finds himself. But it is unfortunate to wash out the idea of a special vocation to the Christian ministry. To be sure, a call is not wholly an emotional experience, and it need not be something spectacular and dramatically soul shaking. It requires a careful weighing of one's total situation to determine that to which God is calling, and therefore what one ought to choose as a life commitment. Yet the matter of an inner imperative which pursues one like "the hound of Heaven ought not to be disparaged or taken lightly. Viewed in the total context of one's life, it may well be the Holy Spirit speaking. Women, like men, have felt this call to the ministry and have been willing to overcome great obstacles in order to follow it. There is a parallel here to what Peter said to the Jerusalem church when he returned from the encounter with the Gentile Cornelius, "If then God gave the same gift to them as he gave to us when we believed in the Lord Jesus Christ, who was I that I could withstand God" (Acts 11:17)?

The nature of the church and the nature of its ministry constitute the essential reason why barriers should not be interposed to the ordination of qualified women with an inner sense of vocation. But let us look at some other relevant theological factors.

There is a fresh insistence on the opening of ordination to women which has two main sources. One of these is undoubtedly the twentieth-century discovery of the capabilities of women in many fields, and with it the entrance of women into virtually all the major professions. The fact that the ministry of the church is the most difficult barrier to breach undoubtedly leads some to feel that it must be overcome, even as the denial of the right to vote actuated women a century ago. Nevertheless, there is a difference between women's liberation as this is commonly pursued and the quest for acceptance in the ministry. The one seeks freedom and self-fulfillment in whatever channels one may desire to pursue; the other seeks an opportunity for responsible service in what the seeker regards as her God-given calling. It is not to deny the legitimacy of much of the first to say that the second rests on a deeper and more Christ-centered foundation.

A second foundation of the movement for the ordination of women is a new appreciation of the attitude of Jesus toward women as this is disclosed in a careful reading of the Gospels. To be sure, Jesus said nothing about priesthood, and there were no clerical orders established until a considerable period after his death and resurrection. Yet to Jesus women were persons, as precious to God as were men, persons to be talked with, regarded as friends, healed in body and spirit, treated as important in spite of the prevailing Jewish subordination. Jesus was thus twenty centuries ahead of his times, and in the light of this part of the Scripture record the tradition of woman's inferiority, whether in the church or elsewhere, must be challenged and refocused.

The ordination of concerned and prepared women helps to challenge the present barriers of conservatism in the churches, and perhaps indirectly in other spheres. This would justify it when it is done seriously as a matter of principle, even if no question of expediency were involved. Yet there are important practical reasons today why qualified women should receive ordination and should be appointed to churches. In many areas the churches are understaffed or served by men of meager educational equipment. More than a few are closed for lack of an available minister, and, if the recent trend of male seminary graduates to enter other work than the parish ministry continues, this may increase rather than diminish. At the same time, women with adequate theological preparation and much ability are debarred because of their sex. This ought not to be.

Epilogue

All the Methodist traditions included in this documentary history permitted female preaching and evangelism in the nineteenth century, and some even took steps to secure women's ordination as well. By the close of the twentieth century virtually all these denominations in the United States and Great Britain ordained women and admitted them with equal status to their respective judicatories. As Methodism expanded around the globe, local iterations of these churches often reflected the attitudes and practices they inherited from those responsible for mission and evangelization. In some cases that meant the acceptance of women was assumed and there was no apparent need to develop an apologetic tradition on their behalf, especially in the twentieth century. In other contexts, however, the conservative tendency of the mission community, the contextual dynamics of the groups they evangelized, or some combination of these and other forces fostered resistance to what could be interpreted as the cultural imposition of gender roles from the Western world.

The story of the defense of women in ministry in these contexts—almost all in the non-Western world—cannot be told fully yet. Given the fact that many apologists of women's ministry are still active in this struggle, it is difficult to craft a history of their struggle in these settings. A monumental amount of work needs to be done to gather information, compile documents, and even interview the "living human documents" who are in the process of making history. Garlinda Burton's article on the thirtieth anniversary of women's ordination in the United Methodist Church in Mozambique illustrates how new this is in many parts of the world:

> The anniversary celebration opened with a procession of more than 60 United Methodist women pastors and seminary students, singing original songs "2009 is a year of our hope and strength!" and "Where would we be without women?" in Xitswa (a language indigenous to Southern Mozambique). Young women ushered to the stage the honorees, now-retired clergy-women, the Revs. Amina Isaias and Lea Jatamo, who in 1979

became the first women ordained by any mainstream Christian church in Mozambique. . . . [Isaias] was ordained in 1979, and continued evangelizing, building churches and offering pastoral care during the brutal civil war of the 1980s, "even in places that didn't want me."[1]

The Rev. Isaias retired in 2002, but that was just around the time that Methodist churches in some other regions of the world were beginning to recognize the biblical equality of women in this way. Consider this a challenge, therefore, to those who are anxious to honor this great legacy and do not want to lose it. The story of the defense of women in ministry within the larger narrative of expanding global Methodism must be written. Those who have eyes to see and ears to hear will be able to write it soon if they are diligent to seek for it.

Methodist women in ministry, and all those who have defended them over the past two and a half centuries, stand in that great heritage of the first Methodist woman preacher, Sarah Crosby. Her words are just as applicable today for women in a global parish as when they were written in the eighteenth century to a woman who sought to live out her calling faithfully in the church:

When we know we have our Lord's approbation, we should stand, like the beaten anvil to the stroke; or lie in his hands, as clay in the hands of the potter. . . . Speak and act, as the spirit gives liberty, and utterance; fear not the face of man, but with humble confidence, trust in the Lord.[2]

1. Burton, "Mozambican UMC," 2.
2. Quoted in Chilcote, She Offered Them Christ, 109.

Sequential List of Documents

Alphabetical List of Documents by Author

Bibliography

Alexander, Disney. *A Scriptural View of Female Privileges in the Church of Christ.* Manchester: J. Bradshaw, 1827.

Andrews, William L., ed. *Sisters of the Spirit: Three Black Women's Autobiographies on the Nineteenth Century.* Bloomington: Indiana University Press, 1986.

Angell, Stephen Ward. "The Controversy over Women's Ministry in the African Methodist Episcopal Church during the 1880s: The Case of Sarah Ann Hughes." In *This Far by Faith: Readings in African-American Women's Religious Biography,* edited by Judith Weisenfeld and Richard Newman, 94–109. New York: Routledge, 1996.

Baker, Frank. "John Wesley and Sarah Crosby." *Proceedings of the Wesley Historical Society* 27 (1949) 76–82.

———. "John Wesley's Churchmanship." *London Quarterly and Holborn Review* 185 (1960) 210–15, 269–73.

Baker-Johnson, Sharon. "The Life and Influence of Jessie Penn-Lewis: 'Jesus Christ and Him Crucified.'" *Priscilla Papers* 26.2 (Spring 2012) 23–28.

Batty, Margaret. "Local Preaching in Wesleyanism in the Nineteenth Century." *Wesley Historical Society, North East Branch* 19 (April 1973) 4–8.

Blessing, Carol. "'Oh That the Mantle May Rest on Me!': The Ministry of Mary Tooth." In *Religion, Gender, and Industry: Exploring Church and Methodism in a Local Setting,* edited by Geordan Hammond and Peter S. Forsaith, 156–72. Eugene, OR: Pickwick, 2011.

Booth, Catherine Mumford. *Female Ministry; or, Woman's Right to Preach the Gospel.* London: Morgan & Chase, 1870.

Bourne, Hugh. *Remarks on the Ministry of Women.* Bemersley: Office of the Primitive Methodist Connection, 1808.

Brake, George Thompson. *Policy and Politics in British Methodism, 1932–1982.* London: Edsall, 1984.

Brekus, Catherine A. "Female Evangelism in the Early Methodist Movement, 1784–1845." In *Methodism and the Shaping of American Culture,* edited by Nathan O. Hatch and John H. Wigger, 135–74. Nashville: Kingswood, 2001.

———. "Protestant Female Preaching in the United States." In *Encyclopedia of Women and Religion in North America,* edited by Rosemary Skinner Keller and Rosemary Radford Ruether, 2:965–73. Bloomington: Indiana University Press, 2006.

———. *Strangers & Pilgrims: Female Preaching in America, 1740–1845.* Chapel Hill: University of North Carolina Press, 1998.

Burton, M. Garlinda. "Mozambican UMC Celebrates 30 Years of Ordaining Women." *The Flyer* 41 (January 2010) 1–3.

Bushnell, Katharine C. *God's Word to Women: One Hundred Bible Studies on Woman's Place in the Divine Economy.* North Collins, NY: Munson, 1923.

Cagle, Mary Lee. *Life and Work of Mary Lee Cagle: An Autobiography.* Kansas City: Nazarene 1928.

Calder, Sandy. *The Origins of Primitive Methodism.* Rochester, NY: Boydell, 2016.

Chaves, Mark. *Ordaining Women: Culture and Conflict in Religious Organizations.* Cambridge: Harvard University Press, 1997.

———. "The Women That Publish the Tidings: The International Association of Women Ministers." In *Women and Twentieth-Century Protestantism,* edited by Margaret Lamberts Bendroth and Virginia Lieson Brereton, 257–76. Urbana: University of Illinois Press, 2002.

Chilcote, Paul W. "The Empowerment of Women in Early Methodism" *Catalyst* 11 (1985) 1–3.

———. *John Wesley and the Women Preachers of Early Methodism.* Metuchen, NJ: Scarecrow, 1991.

———. *She Offered Them Christ.* Nashville: Abingdon, 1993.

———. "Women in the Pietist Heritage of Methodism." In *Methodist and Pietist: Retrieving the Evangelical United Brethren Tradition,* edited by J. Steven O'Malley and Jason E. Vickers, 191–214, 227–30. Nashville: Kingswood, 2011.

Clarke, J. B. B., ed. *An Account of the Life of Adam Clarke.* 3 vols. London: T. S. Clarke, 1833.

Cowles, C. S. *A Woman's Place?: Leadership in the Church.* Kansas City: Beacon Hill, 1993.

Crosby, Sarah. *MS Letterbook* (1760–1774). Frank Baker Collection of Wesleyan and British Methodism, Rubenstein Library, Duke University.

Dayton, Donald W., ed. *"The Higher Christian Life": Holiness Tracts Defending the Ministry of Women.* New York: Garland, 1985.

Dickerson, Dennis C. *A Liberated Past: Explorations in AME Church History.* Nashville: AMEC Sunday School Union, 2003.

Dodson, Jualynne. "Nineteenth-Century A.M.E. Preaching Women." In *Women in New Worlds: Historical Perspectives on the Wesleyan Tradition,* edited by Hilah F. Thomas and Rosemary Skinner Keller, 1:276–89. Nashville: Abingdon, 1981.

Douglass-Chin, Richard J. *Preacher Woman Sings the Blues: The Autobiographies of Nineteenth-Century African American Evangelists.* Columbia: University of Missouri Press, 2001.

Du Mez, Kristin Kobes. "The Forgotten Woman's Bible: Katharine Bushnell, Lee Anna Starr, Madeline Southard, and the Construction of a Woman-Centered Protestantism in America, 1870–1930." PhD diss., University of Notre Dame, 2004.

———. "Leaving Eden: Resurrecting the Work of Katharine Bushnell and Lee Anna Starr." In *Breaking Boundaries: Female Biblical Interpreters Who Challenged the Status Quo,* edited by Nancy Calvert-Koyzis and Heather Weir, 144–68. New York: T. & T. Clark, 2010.

———. *A New Gospel for Women: Katharine Bushnell and the Challenge of Christian Feminism.* New York: Oxford University Press, 2015.

————. "Selfishness One Degree Removed: Madeline Southard's Desacralization of Motherhood and a Tradition of Progressive Methodism." *Priscilla Papers* 28.2 (Spring 2014) 17–22.

Eason, Andrew M. *Women in God's Army: Gender and Equality in the Early Salvation Army.* Waterloo, ON: Wilfrid Laurier University Press, 2003.

Elaw, Zilpha. *Memoirs of the Life, Religious Experience, Ministerial Travels and Labours of Mrs. Zilpha Elaw, an American Woman of Colour.* London: T. Dudley and B. Taylor, 1846.

Engelsman, Joan C. "The Legacy of Georgia Harkness." In *Women in New Worlds: Historical Perspectives on the Wesleyan Tradition*, edited by Hilah F. Thomas and Rosemary Skinner Keller, 2:338–58. Nashville: Abingdon, 1982.

Entwisle, Joseph. *Memoir of the Rev. Joseph Entwisle.* Bristol: printed and sold by the author, 1848.

Everhart, Janet S. "Maggie Newton Van Cott: The Methodist Episcopal Church Considers the Question of Women Clergy." In *Women in New Worlds: Historical Perspectives on the Wesleyan Tradition*, edited by Hilah F. Thomas and Rosemary Skinner Keller, 2:300–317. Nashville: Abingdon, 1982.

Fell, Margaret. *Womens Speaking Justified: Proved and Allowed of by the Scriptures.* London, 1666.

Field-Bibb, Jacqueline. *Women Towards Priesthood: Ministerial Politics and Feminist Praxis.* New York: Cambridge University Press, 1991.

Fisher, Annie May. *Woman's Right to Preach: A Sermon Reported as Delivered at Chilton, Texas.* San Antonio: by the author, [1904].

Foote, Julia A. J. *A Brand Plucked from the Fire: An Autobiographical Sketch.* Cleveland: W. F. Schneider, 1879.

Foster, Frances Smith. "Neither Auction Block nor Pedestal: 'The Life and Religious Experience of Jarena Lee, a Coloured Lady.'" In *The Female Autograph*, edited by Domna C. Stanton, 126–51. New York: New York Literary Forum, 1984.

Gifford, Carolyn De Swarte. "American Women and the Bible." In *Feminist Perspectives on Biblical Scholarship*, edited by Adela Yarbro Collins, 13–33. Chico, CA: Scholars, 1985.

————, ed. *The Defense of Women's Rights to Ordination in the Methodist Episcopal Church.* New York: Garland, 1987.

Glen, Robert. "The Writings of John Stamp (1808–1847): A Preliminary Annotated List." Privately circulated, 2016.

Godbey, William B. *Victory.* Ennis, TX: Padgett, 1888.

————. *Woman Preacher.* Atlanta: Way of Life, 1891.

Gorrell, Donald K., ed. *"Woman's Rightful Place": Women in United Methodist History.* Dayton: United Theological Seminary, 1980.

Graham, E. Dorothy. *Chosen by God: A List of the Female Travelling Preachers of Early Primitive Methodism.* London: Wesley Historical Society, 1989.

Grammer, Elizabeth Elkin. *Some Wild Visions: Autobiographies by Female Itinerant Evangelists in Nineteenth-Century America.* New York: Oxford University Press, 2003.

Green, Roger J. *Catherine Booth: A Biography of the Cofounder of the Salvation Army.* Grand Rapids: Baker, 1996.

Griffith, Mary L. "The Position of Women in the Methodist Episcopal Church: A Statement and Appeal to the General Conference." *Daily Christian Advocate* 9.21 (May 25, 1880) 88.

Haddad, Mimi. "An Irrepressible Legacy: Women in Ministry Leadership." *Mutuality* 14 (Winter 2007) 10–12. http://www.cbeinternational.org/sites/default/files/irrepressible_haddad.pdf.

Hamilton, Barry W. *William Baxter Godbey: Itinerant Apostle of the Holiness Movement.* Lewiston, NY: E. Mellen, 2000.

Hardesty, Nancy A. "Holiness Movements." In *Encyclopedia of Women and Religion in North America,* edited by Rosemary Skinner Keller and Rosemary Radford Ruether, 1:424–30. Bloomington: Indiana University Press, 2006.

———. "Minister as Prophet? Or as Mother?: Two Nineteenth-Century Models." In *Women in New Worlds: Historical Perspectives on the Wesleyan Tradition,* edited by Hilah F. Thomas and Rosemary Skinner Keller, 1:88–101. Nashville: Abingdon, 1981.

Hardesty, Nancy, Lucille Sider Dayton, and Donald W. Dayton. "Women in the Holiness Movement: Feminism in the Evangelical Tradition." In *Women of Spirit: Female Leadership in the Jewish and Christian Traditions,* edited by Rosemary Radford Ruether and Eleanor McLaughlin, 225–54. New York: Simon and Schuster, 1979.

Hardwick, Dana. "Man's Prattle, Woman's Word." In *Spirituality and Social Responsibility: Vocational Vision of Women in the United Methodist Church,* edited by Rosemary Skinner Keller, 165–82. Nashville: Abingdon, 1993.

———. *Oh Thou Woman that Bringest Good Tidings.* Kearney, NE: Morris, 1995.

Harkness, Georgia E. "The Ministry as a Vocation for Women." *The Christian Advocate* 99 (April 10, 1924) 454–55.

———. *Toward Understanding the Bible.* New York: Scribner's, 1952.

———. "What Price Unity?: The Place of Women in the Life of United Methodism." *Zion's Herald,* June 7, 1939, 549–50.

———. "Women and the Church." *The Christian Century,* June 2, 1937, 707–8.

———. *Women in Church and Society: A Historical and Theological Inquiry.* Nashville: Abingdon, 1972.

———. "Women Ministers." *The Christian Advocate,* November 2, 1939, 1061.

Hassey, Janette. *No Time for Silence: Evangelical Women in Public Ministry around the Turn of the Century.* Grand Rapids: Academie, 1986.

Haynes, Rosetta Renae. *Radical Spiritual Motherhood: Autobiography and Empowerment in Nineteenth-Century African American Women.* Baton Rouge: Louisiana State University Press, 2010.

Heath, Elaine E. *Naked Faith: The Mystical Theology of Phoebe Palmer.* Eugene, OR: Pickwick, 2009.

Heitzenrater, Richard P. *Wesley and the People Called Methodists.* Nashville: Abingdon, 1995.

Hellier, J. E. "Some Methodist Women Preachers." *Methodist Recorder* Winter 36 (Christmas 1895) 65–69.

Hempton, David. *Methodism and Politics in British Society, 1750–1850.* London: Hutchinson, 1984.

Hogan, Lucy Lind. "Negotiating Personhood, Womanhood, and Spiritual Equality: Phoebe Palmer's Defense of the Preaching of Women." *American Transcendental Quarterly* 14.3 (September 2000) 211–26.

Houchins, Sue E., ed. *Spiritual Narratives*. New York: Oxford University Press, 1988.

Hunter, Fannie McDowell. *Women Preachers*. Dallas: Berachah, 1905.

Ingersol, Robert Stanley. "Burden of Dissent: Mary Lee Cagle and the Southern Holiness Movement." PhD diss., Duke University, 1989.

———. "Holiness Women: Recovering a Tradition." *The Christian Century*, June 29, 1994, 632.

———. "The Ministry of Mary Lee Cagle: A Study in Women's History and Religion." *Wesleyan Theological Journal* 28 (1993) 176–98.

Irons, Kendra Weddle. "From Kansas to the World: M. Madeline Southard, Activist and Pastor." *Methodist History* 43 (2004) 33–44.

———. "M. Madeline Southard (1877–1967) on 'Ecclesial Suffrage.'" *Methodist History* 45 (2006) 16–30.

———. *Preaching on the Plains: Methodist Women Preachers in Kansas, 1920–1956*. Lanham, MD: University Press of America, 2007.

Israel, Adrienne M. *Amanda Berry Smith: From Washerwoman to Evangelist*. Lanham, MD: Scarecrow, 1998.

Jernigan, C. B. *Pioneer Days of the Holiness Movement in the Southwest*. Kansas City: Pentecostal Nazarene, 1919.

Jernigan, Jonnie. *Redeemed Through the Blood; or, The Power of God to Save the Fallen*. Louisville: Pentecostal Herald, 1920.

Keller, Rosemary Skinner. "Creating a Sphere for Women." In *Women in New Worlds: Historical Perspectives on the Wesleyan Tradition*, edited by Hilah F. Thomas and Rosemary Skinner Keller, 1:246–60. Nashville: Abingdon, 1981.

———. *Georgia Harkness: For Such a Time as This*. Nashville: Abingdon, 1992.

———. "Georgia Harkness—Theologian of the People." In *Spirituality and Social Responsibility: Vocational Vision of Women in the United Methodist Church*, edited by Rosemary Skinner Keller, 205–29. Nashville: Abingdon, 1993.

Keller, Rosemary Skinner, et al., eds. *Women in New Worlds: Historical Perspectives on the Wesleyan Tradition*. Nashville: Abingdon, 1982.

Kent, John H. S. *The Age of Disunity*. London: Epworth, 1966.

Kroeger, Catherine Clark. "The Legacy of Katherine Bushnell: A Hermeneutic for Women of Faith." *Priscilla Papers* 9.4 (Fall 1995) 1–5.

Laird, Rebecca. *Ordained Women in the Church of the Nazarene: The First Generation*. Kansas City: Nazarene, 1993.

LaPrade, Candice A. "Pens in the Hand of God: The Spiritual Autobiographies of Jarena Lee, Zilpha Elaw, and Rebecca Cox Jackson." PhD diss., Duke University, 1996.

Lee, Jarena. *The Life and Religious Experience of Jarena Lee, a Coloured Lady*. Philadelphia: Lee, 1836.

———. *The Religious Experience and Journal of Mrs. Jarena Lee*. Philadelphia: Lee, 1849.

Lee, Luther. *Woman's Right to Preach the Gospel: A Sermon Preached at the Ordination of the Rev. Miss Antoinette L. Brown*. Syracuse: by the author, 1853.

Lenton, John H. "Labouring for the Lord: Women Preachers in Wesleyan Methodism 1802–1932; A Revisionist View." In *Beyond the Boundaries: Preaching in the Wesleyan Tradition*, edited by Richard Sykes, 58–86. Oxford: Applied Theology Press, 1998.

———. "Support Groups for Methodist Women Preachers, 1803–1851." In *Religion, Gender, and Industry: Exploring Church and Methodism in a Local Setting*, edited by Geordan Hammond and Peter S. Forsaith, 137–55. Eugene, OR: Pickwick, 2011.

Lindley, Susan Hill. *"You Have Stept Out of Your Place": A History of Women and Religion in America*. Louisville: Westminster John Knox, 1996.

Lloyd, Jennifer. *Women and the Shaping of British Methodism: Persistent Preachers, 1807–1907*. Manchester: Manchester University Press, 2009.

Loveland, Anne C. "Domesticity and Religion in the Antebellum Period: The Career of Phoebe Palmer." In *History of Women in the United States: Historical Articles on Women's Lives and Activities*, edited by Nancy F. Cott, 35–51. Munich: K. G. Saur, 1993.

Mallet, Sarah. "The Journal of Sarah Mallet." In *Biographical Sketches of Holy Women*, edited by Zechariah Taft, 1:79–85. London: Kershaw, 1825.

Marston, Leslie. *From Age to Age a Living Witness: Free Methodism's First Century*. Winona Lake, IN: Light and Life, 1960.

McInelly, Brett C. "Mothers in Christ: Mary Fletcher and the Women of Early Methodism." In *Religion, Gender, and Industry: Exploring Church and Methodism in a Local Setting*, edited by Geordan Hammond and Peter S. Forsaith, 123–36. Eugene, OR: Pickwick, 2011.

McKay, Nellie Y. "Nineteenth-Century Black Women's Spiritual Autobiographies: Religious Faith and Self-Empowerment." In *Interpreting Women's Lives*, edited by Joy W. Barbre, 139–54. Bloomington: Indiana University Press, 1989.

Milburn, Geoffrey. *Primitive Methodism*. Exploring Methodism. Peterborough: Epworth, 2002.

Minutes of the First Conference of the Bible Christians. Alternate title: *Minutes of the First Conference of Preachers in Connexion with William O'Bryan, 1819*. Devon: printed and sold by S. Thorne, 1825.

Minutes of the Methodist Conferences. London: printed at the Conference Office, 1812–.

Minutes of the Methodist Conferences in Ireland, Minutes of the Dublin Conference of 1802. Dublin: Religious and General Book, 1864.

Moore, Henry. *The Life of Mrs. Mary Fletcher*. 6th ed. London: J. Kershaw, 1824.

Murdoch, Norman H. "Female Ministry in the Thought and Work of Catherine Booth." *Church History* 53 (1984) 348–62.

Murphree, J. A. *Bible Readings and Teachings on Important Subjects*. Chicago: Arnold, 1899.

O'Bryan, William. "A Discourse in Vindication of the Gospel Being Published by Females." *The Arminian Magazine (BC)* 2.12 (December 1823) 405–25.

Oden, Thomas C., ed. *Phoebe Palmer: Selected Writings*. Mahwah, NJ: Paulist, 1988.

Oliver, Anna. *The "Test Case" on the Ordination of Women*. New York: W. W. Jennings, 1880.

Palmer, Phoebe. *The Promise of the Father: A Neglected Specialty of the Last Days*. Boston: Henry V. Degen, 1859.

———. *Tongue of Fire on the Daughters of the Lord; or, Questions in Relation to the Duty of the Christian Church in Regard to the Privileges of Her Female Membership*. New York: W. C. Palmer Jr., 1869.

Pawson, John. Autograph Letters and Manuscripts. Methodist Archives and Research Centre, John Rylands Library, University of Manchester.

Pope-Levison, Priscilla. *Turn the Pulpit Loose: Two Centuries of American Women Evangelists*. New York: Palgrave Macmillan, 2004.

Raser, Harold E. "Holding Tightly to 'the Promise of the Father': Phoebe Palmer and the Legacy of the Fletchers of Madeley in Mid-Nineteenth-Century Methodism." In *Religion, Gender, and Industry: Exploring Church and Methodism in a Local Setting*, edited by Geordan Hammond and Peter S. Forsaith, 173–88. Eugene, OR: Pickwick, 2011.

———. *Phoebe Palmer, Her Life and Thought*. Lewiston, NY: E. Mellen, 1987.

Read, John. *Catherine Booth: Laying the Theological Foundations of a Radical Movement*. Eugene, OR: Pickwick, 2000.

Richey, Russell E., Kenneth E. Rowe, and Jean Miller Schmidt, eds. *The Methodist Experience in America*. 2 vols. Nashville: Abingdon, 2000, 2010.

Roberts, B. T. *Ordaining Women*. Rochester, NY: Earnest Christian, 1891.

———. *The Right of Women to Preach the Gospel*. Rochester, NY: by the author, 1872.

Rowe, Kenneth. "The Ordination of Women: Round One; Anna Oliver and the General Conference of 1880." *Methodist History* 12 (1974) 60–72.

Ruether, Rosemary Radford, and Rosemary Skinner Keller, eds. *Women and Religion in America: A Documentary History*. 3 vols. San Francisco: Harper & Row, 1981–86.

Ruether, Rosemary Radford, and Eleanor McLaughlin, eds. *Women of Spirit: Female Leadership in the Jewish and Christian Traditions*. New York: Simon and Schuster, 1979.

Sawyer, Pamela Ballard. "Julia A. J. Foote: Foundational African American Feminist Christian Evangelist of the 1800s." PhD diss., Texas Woman's University, 2011.

Scanzoni, Letha Dawson, and Susan Setta. "Women in Evangelical, Holiness, and Pentecostal Traditions." In *Women and Religion in America*, edited by Rosemary Radford Ruether and Rosemary Skinner Keller, 3:223–65. San Francisco: Harper & Row, 1986.

Schmidt, Jean Miller. *Grace Sufficient: A History of Women in American Methodism, 1760–1939*. Nashville: Abingdon, 1999.

Schneider, Carl J., and Dorothy Schneider. *In Their Own Right: The History of American Clergywomen*. New York: Crossroad, 1997.

Schüssler Fiorenza, Elisabeth. *In Memory of Her: A Feminist Theological Reconstruction of Christian Origins*. New York: Crossroads, 1983.

Scott, Martha L. "Georgia Harkness: Social Activist and/or Mystic." In *Women in New Worlds: Historical Perspectives on the Wesleyan Tradition*, edited by Hilah F. Thomas and Rosemary Skinner Keller, 1:117–40. Nashville: Abingdon, 1981.

Sellew, W. A. *Why Not?: A Plea for the Ordination of Those Women Whom God Has Called to Preach the Gospel*. North Chili, NY: Earnest Christian, 1894; Chicago: Free Methodist, 1914.

Shaw, Anna Howard. "Women in the Ministry." *Chautauquan* 27 (August 1898) 489–96.

Shaw, Thomas. *The Bible Christians, 1815–1907*. London: Epworth, 1965.

Shoemaker, Christopher M. "A Small Work: The Story of Helenor Alter Davisson, Methodism's First Ordained Woman." *Methodist History* 41 (2003) 3–11.

Smith, Amanda. *An Autobiography: The Story of the Lord's Dealings with Mrs. Amanda Smith, the Colored Evangelist*. Chicago: Meyer & Brother, 1893.

Smith, Mitzi J. "'Unbossed and Unbought': Zilpha Elaw and Old Elizabeth and a Political Discourse of Origins." *Black Theology* 9 (2011) 287–311.

Smith, Timothy L. *Called Unto Holiness: The Story of the Nazarenes; The Formative Years*. Kansas City: Nazarene, 1962.

Snyder, Howard A. *Populist Saints: B. T. and Ellen Roberts and the First Free Methodists.* Grand Rapids: Eerdmans, 2006.

Southard, M. Madeline. *The Attitude of Jesus toward Women.* New York: Doran, 1927.

———. "A Letter to Delegates Attending 1920 General Conference, Des Moines, May 5, 1920." Methodist Episcopal Church, General Conference Papers, 1920. United Methodist Archives, Madison, NJ.

———. "Memorial to the 1920 General Conference." *Daily Christian Advocate,* May 11, 1920, 190.

———. "The Theology of Women Preachers." *The Woman's Pulpit* 3.7 (December 1927) 4–5.

———. "Woman and the Ministry." *Methodist Review,* November 1919, 918–23.

Stamp, John. *The Female Advocate; or, The Preaching of Women Clearly Proved.* London: J. Pasco, 1841.

Stanley, Susie C. *Holy Boldness: Women Preachers' Autobiographies and the Sanctified Self.* New York: Palgrave Macmillan, 2006.

Starr, Lee Anna. *The Bible Status of Woman.* New York: Revell, 1926.

———. *The Ministry of Women.* Chicago: Skeen & Aiken, 1900.

Taft, Zechariah. *Biographical Sketches of Holy Women.* 2 vols. London: Kershaw, 1825; Leeds: Cullingworth and Stephens, 1828.

———. *Original Letters, Never Before Published, on Doctrinal, Experimental, and Practical Religion.* Whitby: George Clark, 1821.

———. *The Scripture Doctrine of Women's Preaching: Stated and Examined.* York: R. & J. Richardson, 1820.

———. *Thoughts on Female Preaching, with Extracts from the Writings of Locke, Henry, Martin, etc.* Dover: G. Ledger, 1803.

———. *Thoughts on Women's Preaching.* Leeds: G. Wilson, 1809.

Telford, John, ed. *The Letters of the Rev. John Wesley, M.A.* 8 vols. London: Epworth, 1931.

Thomas, Hilah F., and Rosemary Skinner Keller, eds. *Women in New Worlds: Historical Perspectives on the Wesleyan Tradition.* Nashville: Abingdon, 1981.

Thompson, Patricia A. *Courageous Past, Bold Future: The Journey toward Full Clergy Rights for Women in the United Methodist Church.* Nashville: General Board of Higher Education and Ministry, 2006.

Troxell, Barbara B. "Ordination of Women in the United Methodist Tradition." *Methodist History* 37 (1999) 119–30.

Valenze, Deborah. *Prophetic Sons and Daughters: Female Preaching and Popular Religion in Industrial England.* Princeton: Princeton University Press, 1985.

Walker, Pamela J. "A Chaste and Fervid Eloquence: Catherine Booth and the Ministry of Women in the Salvation Army." In *Women Preachers and Prophets through Two Millennia of Christianity,* edited by Beverly Mayne Kienzle and Pamela J. Walker, 288–302. Berkeley: University of California Press, 1998.

———. "Gender, Radicalism, and Female Preaching in Nineteenth-Century Britain: Catherine Booth's Female Teaching." In *Strangely Familiar: Protofeminist Interpretations of Patriarchal Biblical Texts,* edited by Nancy Calvert-Koyzis and Heather E. Weir, 171–84. Atlanta: Society of Biblical Literature, 2009.

Warren, William F. "The Dual Human Unit: The Relations of Men and Women According to the Sociological Teachings of Holy Scripture." In *Constitutional Law*

Questions Now Pending in the Methodist Episcopal Church. Cincinnati: Carnston and Curts, 1894.

Wayman, Benjamin D. "More Radical than First-Wave Feminism?: The Gospel According to B. T. Roberts." *Free Methodist Historical Society Newsletter* 14.3 (Spring 2014). http://fmcusa.org/historical/files/2014/04/Spring2014_web-1.pdf.

———. *Ordaining Women: New Edition with an Introduction and Notes*. Eugene, OR: Wipf & Stock, 2015.

Welter, Barbara. *Dimity Convictions: The American Woman in the Nineteenth Century*. Athens: Ohio University Press, 1976.

Wesley, Cindy. "Witnessing Women: The Ministry of Women in Early Methodism." In *Courage to Bear Witness*, edited by L. Edward Phillips and Billy Vaughan, 108–23. Eugene, OR: Pickwick, 2009.

Wesley, John. *The Works of John Wesley*, vol. 3: *Sermons III, 71–114*. Edited by Albert C. Outler. Nashville: Abingdon, 1986.

———. *The Works of John Wesley*, vol. 4: *Sermons IV, 115–51*. Edited by Albert C. Outler. Nashville: Abingdon, 1987.

———. *The Works of John Wesley*, vol. 9: *The Methodist Societies*. Edited by Rupert E. Davies. Nashville: Abingdon, 1989.

———. *The Works of John Wesley*, vol. 21: *Journal and Diaries IV (1755–1765)*. Edited by W. Reginald Ward and Richard P. Heitzenrater. Nashville: Abingdon, 1992.

White, Charles E. *The Beauty of Holiness: Phoebe Palmer as Theologian, Revivalist, Feminist, and Humanitarian*. Grand Rapids: Francis Asbury, 1986.

Willard, Frances E. *Woman in the Pulpit*. Chicago: Woman's Temperance, 1889.

Zikmund, Barbara Brown. "The Protestant Women's Ordination Movement." In *Encyclopedia of Women and Religion in North America*, edited by Rosemary Skinner Keller and Rosemary Radford Ruether, 2:940–50. Bloomington: Indiana University Press, 2006.

———. "Winning Ordination for Women in Mainstream Protestant Churches." In *Women and Religion in America*, edited by Rosemary Radford Ruether and Rosemary Skinner Keller, 3:339–83. San Francisco: Harper & Row, 1986.

Zink-Sawyer, Beverly. *From Preachers to Suffragists: Woman's Rights and Religious Conviction in the Lives of Three Nineteenth-Century American Women*. Louisville: Westminster John Knox, 2003.

www.ingramcontent.com/pod-product-compliance
Lightning Source LLC
Chambersburg PA
CBHW032344280326
41935CB00008B/447